The Race
for Security

The Race for Security

Arms and Arms Control in the Reagan Years

Edited by
Robert Travis Scott
Arms Control Association

Lexington Books
D.C. Heath and Company/Lexington, Massachusetts/Toronto

Library of Congress Cataloging-in-Publication Data

The race for security.

Includes index.
1. Nuclear arms control—United States. 2. Nuclear arms control—Soviet Union.
3. United States—National security. 4. Soviet Union—National security. 5. Nuclear weapons.
I. Scott, Robert Travis.
JX1974.7.R33   1987   327.1'74'0973   84-48507
ISBN 0-669-09552-4 (alk. paper)
ISBN 0-669-09553-2 (pbk. : alk. paper)

All of the articles in this book appeared first in *Arms Control Today*, the magazine of the Arms Control Association, and are reprinted by permission.

Published simultaneously in Canada
Printed in the United States of America
Casebound International Standard Book Number: 0-669-09552-4
Paperbound International Standard Book Number: 0-669-09553-2
Library of Congress Catalog Card Number: 84-48507

The paper used in this publication meets the minimum requirements of American National Standard for Information Sciences—Permanence of Paper for Printed Library Materials, ANSI Z39.48-1984.

87 88 89 90 8 7 6 5 4 3 2 1

Contents

Illustrations

Figures

Photographs

Tables

Foreword

Gerard C. Smith
Chairman, Arms Control Association

The current popular wisdom about the Reagan administration's arms and arms control policies is that President Reagan is breathing new life into U.S. defenses and that the United States is stronger and more secure than at any time in its history. Yet history may tell another story. Whereas previous administrations sought constraints, albeit modest ones, on the strategic nuclear competition, President Reagan has begun to disengage the United States from past agreements without replacing them with new accords. Meanwhile, he has launched America's largest peacetime military budget and strategic weapons program. Instead of leading the United States into a period of new-found security, the Reagan administration has created greater uncertainties about the future direction of the arms race and the possibility of nuclear war.

By contrast, the SALT (Strategic Arms Limitation Talks) process set in motion by the Nixon, Ford, and Carter administrations established a framework for regulating and eventually reversing the superpower arms race. That contrast is made vivid if we look back to the preface written by former senator Frank Church for the 1979 book, *Negotiating Security*, which was a predecessor to this volume. Church's optimistic outlook was not unusual for the times:

> If the [Carter] administration is successful in achieving a SALT II Treaty and protocol which merit—and receive—Senate consent to ratification, the way will be open for progress on other initiatives.
>
> Success in SALT II could open the way to an early conclusion of a comprehensive ban on nuclear explosions. SALT II should serve to reassure other nations as to the willingness of the United States and the Soviet Union to continue efforts to control the arms race and should encourage them to join with us in finding the means to reduce further the threat posed by the spread of nuclear weapons. Of course, a successful SALT II could lead to additional qualitative and quantitative controls and, possibly, significant reductions in nuclear weapons as a result of SALT III.
>
> There are also negotiations under way with the Soviet Union and other nations on the limitation of chemical weapons and the control of anti-satellite activities. New undertakings to promote security through restraint may be sought

on a regional basis, in keeping with recommendations made, for example, regarding naval forces in the Indian Ocean or nuclear weapon-free zones in Africa or South Asia.

Today, this optimistic view of arms control has all but disappeared, and the possibility of any new agreement on key issues seems remote. The SALT I Interim Agreement and the SALT II Treaty have been repudiated and present plans for a Star Wars space-based missile defense promise to make a dead letter of the 1972 ABM (antiballistic missile) Treaty. Arms control—which was seen by every administration since that of Eisenhower as a constructive and top priority instrument for strengthening U.S. national security—has ceased to be an integral part of U.S. foreign and military policy. Our hope for a lasting peace has turned into anxiety over the possibility of a new arms race in both offensive and defensive weapon technologies.

Despite the resumption of arms talks, and the possibility of agreements in other, less critical areas, there is little prospect for any agreements in the area of strategic arms control in the foreseeable future.

The major reason for this stalemate is that the Reagan administration is now trying to pursue two contradictory policies: strategic arms control *with* the Soviet Union and strategic "Star Wars" defenses *against* it. If the United States persists in taking this schizophrenic approach, we will not get the arms control agreements that the president says are his highest priority, and the fruitless search for the leakproof "security shield" of his dreams will have been the cause of the failure.

No doubt President Reagan, like the rest of us, is uncomfortable with the dilemma of the nuclear age and is in search of more enduring national and international security. But his zest for an unreal technological solution is taking us in the wrong direction. The race for an exclusively weapons-based security is on, and it is leading us to a more dangerous future.

The Race for Security, like its 1979 predecessor, *Negotiating Security*, is a selection of articles originally published in *Arms Control Today*, the monthly journal of the Arms Control Association. This volume draws on articles that have appeared during the Reagan administration up to January 1986. The book evaluates the security impact of new weapons and offers approaches, old and new, to control them and prevent war. In doing so, it explains the scope of arms control and the efforts necessary to make arms control an effective instrument for national security.

I believe this book will help illuminate the current situation. It offers significant and constructive criticisms of U.S. policies and will serve as an important educational document about the purpose and need for arms control.

Acknowledgments

Robert Travis Scott

The Race for Security is composed of articles originally published from 1981 to January 1986 in *Arms Control Today*, the monthly journal and newsletter of the Arms Control Association. Since its creation in 1972, *ACT* has played a unique role in the U.S. defense debate. Drawing on the work of authors with extensive experience in government and defense policy as well as authors and analysts new to the security studies scene, the periodical has sought to present responsible, constructive commentary and analysis about arms control issues. *ACT* has become a widely recognized voice for arms control and its valuable contribution to national and international security.

The first collection of *ACT* articles to be printed in book form was *Negotiating Security*, edited by former ACA Executive Director William H. Kincade and former *ACT* Editor Jeffrey D. Porro and published in 1979 by The Carnegie Endowment for International Peace. Some years later the Association began considering a second collection of *ACT* articles. As I pulled the pieces together for this book, I saw more than just a random collection of articles on arms control, but rather a digest of commentary about the Reagan administration's nuclear weapons and arms control policies.

Negotiating Security reflected the Association's effort in the 1970s to build a national consensus in support of policies to negotiate international agreements in the security interest of the United States. In contrast, *The Race for Security* reflects the Association's effort in the 1980s to protect the accomplishment of arms control, now placed in jeopardy by the policies of the Reagan administration, and reestablish the modest progress made in previous decades. The book is divided into thematic sections and can be read in whole or in part. The date when each article first appeared in *Arms Control Today* is noted at the end of each piece. Although some of the selections were written several years ago, they remain remarkably relevant. Their insights are as valid today as when they were first committed to print.

I am chiefly indebted to the many fine authors whose contributions appear here, and especially to those who chose to update their work for this book. I regret that, because of space restrictions, we were unable to include some fine articles that have appeared in *Arms Control Today* in the last few years. I am equally indebted to Jeffrey D. Porro, editor of *Arms Control Today* when many of these articles were originally published. Dr. Porro's high standards and lucid editing style are well known and appreciated in arms control circles, and much of the credit for this book should be attributed to him. Many thanks are owed to William H. Kincade, the executive director of the Arms Control Association from 1977 till the end of 1984, who served as a guide and inspiration for *Arms Control Today* and is largely responsible for building the magazine's good reputation.

I have been very fortunate to work directly with a number of highly skilled and knowledgeable people in the preparation of this book and the monthly editions of *Arms Control Today*. Foremost among them is the president of the Arms Control Association, Spurgeon M. Keeny, Jr., whose professional guidance and deep personal interest have brought the highest standards to the journal. Mr. Keeny and several other Association staff members have served as editorial advisors to *Arms Control Today* since early 1985. Those advisors—Jack Mendelsohn, Thomas K. Longstreth, James P. Rubin, and David Halperin—have graciously offered much of their time and expertise to the journal. The advice and contributions of Association board member John B. Rhinelander are also greatly appreciated. Special thanks should be given to Alex Mikulich III, Mark Greenstein, Harry J. Stephan, and Dorinna Suglia,who were instrumental in putting the book through the publication process.

I am grateful to Ambassador Gerard C. Smith, chief negotiator of the SALT I Treaty and chairman of the Arms Control Association, for providing a foreword and offering his endorsement of the book.

My final thanks go to Herbert "Pete" Scoville, Jr., president of the Arms Control Association from 1979 to 1985, who died in July 1985. Dr. Scoville was one of the creators of *Arms Control Today*, and he took a special interest in its content, its funding, and its impact. It was Dr. Scoville who named it *Arms Control Today*, because he liked the acronym *ACT*. His last published article, "Reciprocal National Restraint," appears in chapter 5.

The Arms Control Association is a nonpartisan, nonprofit national membership organization dedicated to promoting public understanding of effective policies and programs in arms control and disarmament. Under a cooperative agreement, the Association participates in a number of joint ventures with The Carnegie Endowment for International Peace. Views expressed in Arms Control Association publications should be understood to be solely those of the authors and should not be attributed to the Association, its board of directors, officers, or staff members, or to organizations that support the Arms Control Association.

Abbreviations

ABM	antiballistic missile
ACDA	Arms Control and Disarmament Agency
ACM	advanced cruise missile
AIRS	advanced inertial reference sphere
ALCM	air-launched cruise missile
AOA	airborne optical adjunct
AOS	airborne optical system
ASAT	antisatellite
ASW	antisubmarine warfare
ATB	advanced technology bomber
ATBM	antitactical ballistic missile
BAMBI	ballistic missile boost intercept
BMD	ballistic missile defense
BWC	Biological Weapons Convention
CBM	confidence-building measure
C³	command, control, and communication
C³I	command, control, communication, and intelligence
CDE	Conference on Disarmament in Europe
CEP	circular error probable
CIA	Central Intelligence Agency
CTB	comprehensive test ban
DDA	designated deployment area
DOD	Department of Defense
ECM	electronic countermeasures
FROD	functionally related observable differences
FY	fiscal year
GAO	General Accounting Office
GLCM	ground-launched cruise missile
IAEA	International Atomic Energy Agency
ICBM	intercontinental ballistic missile
INF	intermediate-range nuclear forces

INFCE	international nuclear fuel cycle evaluation
IRBM	intermediate-range ballistic missile
JCS	Joint Chiefs of Staff
LCC	launch command center
LF	launch facilities
LNO	limited nuclear option
LoADS	low-altitude defense system
LOW	launch on warning
LPAR	large phased-array radar
LTBT	Limited Test Ban Treaty
LUA	launch under attack
MAD	mutual assured destruction
MAO	major attack option
MBFR	mutual and balanced force reduction
MIRV	multiple independently targetable reentry vehicle
MPS	multiple protective shelter
MRBM	medium-range ballistic missile
MRASM	medium-range air-to-surface missile
MRV	multiple reentry vehicle
NATO	North Atlantic Treaty Organization
NCA	National Command Authority
NIE	National Intelligence Estimate
NNPA	Nuclear Nonproliferation Act
NORAD	North American Air/Aerospace Defense Command
NPT	Nonproliferation Treaty
NSC	National Security Council
NSDD	National Security Decision Directive
NSDM	National Security Decision Memorandum
NSS	national seismic stations
NSSM	National Security Study Memorandum
NTM	national technical means
NTPR	Nuclear Targeting Policy Review
NUWEP	Nuclear Weapons Employment Policy
OSI	on-site inspection
PD	Presidential Directive
PNE	peaceful nuclear explosion
PNET	Peaceful Nuclear Explosions Treaty
PRC	People's Republic of China
R&D	research and development
RNO	regional nuclear option
RNR	reciprocal national restraint
SAC	Strategic Air Command
SAINT	satellite inspection technique

SALT	Strategic Arms Limitation Talks
SAM	surface-to-air missile
SAO	selected attack option
SCC	Standing Consultative Commission
SICBM	small intercontinental ballistic missile
SIGINT	signals intelligence
SIOP	Single Integrated Operational Plan
SIPRI	Stockholm International Peace Research Institute
SLBM	submarine-launched ballistic missile
SLCM	sea-launched cruise missile
SNF	small nuclear force
SPAD	space patrol active defense
SRAM	short-range attack missile
SSBN	strategic missile submarine
SSM	surface-to-surface missile
START	Strategic Arms Reduction Talks
STOP	Strategic Talks on Prevention
TASM	tactical air-to-surface missile
TEL	transporter-erector-launcher
TTBT	Threshold Test Ban Treaty
U.N.	United Nations
VLF	very low frequency

1
An Overview

T he Reagan administration's changes in defense policy are nothing less than dramatic. President Reagan has given the nation its largest peacetime military budget and, as Ron Tammen points out in his article, the "largest strategic arms buildup" in the history of the United States. In addition to his nuclear arms program, President Reagan in 1983 announced the Strategic Defense Initiative, quickly dubbed "Star Wars" by the media, to provide the United States with a nationwide missile defense system.

The president has said that he hopes advances in strategic defense technology will render nuclear weapons "impotent and obsolete." Other proponents of SDI foresee a defense system with more modest goals, such as the protection of missile silos and other military assets. In whatever form, the Strategic Defense Initiative represents a significant change in emphasis in U.S. strategic weapons programs. Rather than relying solely on retaliatory nuclear forces to deter nuclear attack, the United States would field defensive systems capable of thwarting an attack in progress. Experts disagree on whether such defense systems are feasible and, even if they are, whether their deployment would lead to a more secure strategic relationship between the superpowers.

Along with these fundamental changes in the U.S. approach to strategic weapons, the administration has also taken a substantially different view of arms control, as is discussed by Spurgeon Keeny, Jr., in "The Uncertain Future of Arms Control." The 1972 Antiballistic Missile Treaty between the United States and the Soviet Union has been placed in jeopardy by the Strategic Defense Initiative. The ABM Treaty and SDI have contradictory purposes: the treaty bans nationwide defense systems and SDI seeks to create them. SDI reflects a new U.S. policy and manner of thinking about the effects of strategic defenses on the arms control process. Administration officials believe that defensive systems will add to stability and security, enhancing the prospects for arms control. Keeny disagrees, arguing that SDI will spur a new arms race in defensive weapons and prevent any hope for reductions in offensive forces.

While the ABM Treaty has been under attack, strategic offensive arms agreements have nearly dissolved. During the 1980 election campaign, Ronald

Reagan repudiated the Strategic Arms Limitation Talks, a process begun in 1969. He called SALT II, which was negotiated by the Nixon, Ford, and Carter administrations, "fatally flawed." Though in 1981 the Reagan administration announced that it would not ratify SALT II, it did pledge to "take no action that would undercut existing agreements as long as the Soviet Union exercises the same restraint." After releasing several reports that accused the Soviet Union of violating its arms control commitments, the administration replaced its "interim restraint" policy with a policy of "proportionate response." "Appropriate and proportionate responses to Soviet non-compliance," Reagan said in 1985, "are called for to ensure our security, to provide incentives to the Soviets to correct their non-compliance, and to make it clear to Moscow that violations of arms control obligations entail real costs." On May 27, 1986, Reagan formally repudiated his political commitment to SALT II and announced that the United States would no longer consider itself obligated to comply with SALT II limits. Nevertheless, House and Senate action could restrain U.S. nuclear weapons programs to keep the United States in *de facto* compliance with key provisions of the agreement. Though SALT II was repudiated, U.S. compliance with its most important limitations could continue.

The Reagan administration's approach to arms control compliance issues, examined by Michael Krepon in "Decontrolling the Arms Race," also has been different from that of earlier administrations. In the 1970s, questions of Soviet treaty compliance were generally addressed and resolved in private consultations between the United States and the Soviet Union. But the Reagan administration has on several occasions made formal public charges of "definite" and "probable" Soviet violations. The Soviet Union has responded with formal charges of U.S. violations. The charges, which for the most part are based on ambiguous treaty provisions and partial or uncertain information, have obscured the overall good Soviet and U.S. compliance records and have been widely exploited by opponents of arms control in and out of government to undermine public confidence in the arms control process.

Events early in his administration made President Reagan conscious of broadly held public views on nuclear weapons issues and of the need for the president to address them. Public concern in the United States and Europe began to grow over the superpower rivalry in nuclear arms and the prospect of nuclear war. A European peace movement rallied against the deployment of new U.S. intermediate-range missiles in NATO countries, and a broadly based grassroots movement for a "freeze" on the production, testing and deployment of U.S. and Soviet nuclear weapons began to spread in the United States. Moreover, Ronald Reagan had quickly gained a reputation as a president who seemed cavalier about the consequences of a continued arms buildup and disdainful of serious arms control negotiations. Indeed, for the first time in over a decade the United States and the Soviet Union were not engaged in negotiations on strategic nuclear weapons. President Reagan's confrontational rhetoric toward the Soviet Union and his reference to the Soviet "evil empire" added to public anxieties. Marshall Shulman's article, "What

Kind of Relationship Do We Want with the Soviet Union?" reviews the current U.S.-Soviet relationship and recommends a constructive U.S. approach.

In this context of controversy and public doubt, the Reagan administration launched new nuclear arms negotiations with the Soviet Union in 1981 and 1982. Although the arms talks in the Reagan years have produced little if any progress on key issues, their mere existence has served to assuage fears, most significantly among the mainstream public in Europe and the United States, and has improved Reagan's image as a man of peace. The first resumed negotiations were the Intermediate-Range Nuclear Force (INF) Talks in the fall of 1981, headed by an ardent opponent of SALT II, Paul Nitze. INF was concerned with intermediate-range nuclear weapons intended for use in the European theater, especially Soviet SS-20 missiles and the new U.S. Pershing II and ground-launched cruise missiles (GLCMs). The Strategic Arms Reduction Talks (START), headed by retired general Edward Rowny, also a leading SALT II opponent, were begun in 1982 to replace the SALT talks. President Reagan's aim in START was "deep reductions" in the nuclear forces of the United States and Soviet Union. In protest against the first deployments of U.S. Pershing IIs and GLCMs in Europe, the Soviet Union left the INF and START negotiations in late 1983. Virtually no progress had been made in either forum.

A new set of negotiations—the Nuclear and Space Arms Talks—opened in Geneva in March 1985. Labeled the "umbrella talks," it brought offensive and defensive strategic and intermediate nuclear force negotiations together under one roof, though still in separate negotiating bodies. In addition to pursuing the former agenda of INF and START, President Reagan aims for the umbrella talks to combine arms control and the Strategic Defense Initiative by calling for deep reductions in nuclear weapons while phasing in space-based defense systems. The prospect for success in Reagan's arms control policy is analyzed by Strobe Talbott in his article. Taken together, the articles in this chapter provide a critical overview of President Reagan's arms and arms control policies.

The Uncertain Future of Arms Control
Spurgeon M. Keeny, Jr.

The resumption of U.S.-Soviet arms control talks in Geneva and the announcement of a summit meeting between President Reagan and General Secretary Gorbachev have generated widespread expectations of renewed progress in arms control. In reality the prospects for arms control have never been bleaker. President Reagan's vision of a defensive shield that will make nuclear weapons "impotent and obsolete" has become not only a barrier to progress but also a threat to the entire structure of arms control developed over the past two decades.

The president's vision, conceived without benefit of serious scientific, military, or diplomatic advice, can no longer be dismissed by critics as misguided political rhetoric or cynically embraced as a potentially valuable bargaining chip. The vision has spawned the Strategic Defense Initiative (SDI), which is rapidly evolving into by far the most ambitious research and development program ever undertaken. Instead of answering questions about the technical feasibility of strategic defense, the SDI threatens to take on a life of its own, leading to eventual deployment as justification for the unprecedented investment in dollars and technological resources. Although the SDI has been widely criticized domestically on technical, strategic, and economic grounds, the fundamental nature of its adverse impact on arms control and the arms race has not been adequately appreciated by a public bemused by hints of breakthroughs in U.S.-Soviet negotiations.

In truth, this new U.S. policy virtually precludes serious progress in the Geneva negotiations. The Soviet Union has taken a firm position that it will not agree to substantial or even modest reductions in its strategic offensive forces as long as the United States is engaged in a massive program with the stated goal of developing a highly effective nationwide defense against ballistic missiles. The Soviet refusal to deal separately with offensive and defensive issues was totally predictable and consistent with elementary military logic. When faced with improved defenses, the military has always sought quantitative or qualitative improvements in its offensive forces to ensure its ability to penetrate those defenses. The ability to retaliate after a preemptive strike has been equated with the ability to deter nuclear war. The surprise at Geneva was not the Soviet reaction but the willingness of the United States to advance such a strategically unsound position.

In the past, when faced with major Soviet strategic defense programs, the United States has consistently acted to ensure its retaliatory capability. In the late 1960s when U.S. officials were concerned that the Soviet Union might be undertaking a nationwide ballistic missile defense, the United States did not abandon or reduce reliance on ballistic missiles but introduced MIRVs (multiple independently targetable reentry vehicles) to increase firepower and assure the ability to penetrate the projected Soviet defense. Similarly, although the Soviet Union for the past thirty years has invested vast sums in its air defense system, the United States has not abandoned long-range strategic bombers. On the contrary, the United States has improved the ability of bombers to penetrate defenses in a series of qualitative improvements involving electronic countermeasures, short-range nuclear missiles designed to suppress defenses, air-launched cruise missiles, the B-1 bomber, and, currently, stealth technology to make aircraft and eventually cruise missiles harder for enemy radars and other sensors to detect. One cannot help but wonder how the U.S. Joint Chiefs of Staff would react if the Soviet Union were to reverse its position in Geneva and call for deep reductions in strategic offensive forces and for the elimination of all constraints on ballistic missile defenses.

In addition to precluding major new strategic agreements in Geneva, the new U.S. strategic defense program poses a direct threat to the ABM Treaty, which is the keystone to the entire framework of existing arms control agreements. The president's vision and the goal of the Strategic Defense Initiative are diametrically opposed to the underlying objective of the ABM Treaty of preventing a nationwide ballistic missile defense. Despite the administration's reassurances that the Strategic Defense Initiative at this stage is only a research program fully consistent with specific treaty obligations, the initiative and the ABM Treaty are by definition on a direct collision course.

Whatever view one takes on the legality of specific activities in the currently defined Strategic Defense Initiative, development and testing that cannot possibly be reconciled with treaty provisions will occur in the not too distant future. The SDI test program so far described by the Defense Department will provide only a few of the answers needed to make a rational decision on deployment and will certainly have to be followed by many more development tests that would be unambiguously in violation of the ABM Treaty. Some critics argue that this breach will in fact result from presently planned tests within three years; the administration asserts that by carefully defining and structuring these tests so that they will conform to treaty provisions the breach can be postponed for at least five years. But regardless of when these tests occur or how successful they may be, the treaty will be breached long before a rational decision could possibly be made on whether to deploy a ballistic missile defense system.

Some critics of the program believe that, if pursued, the initiative will collapse from the weight of unresolved technical problems and mounting costs long before deployment could possibly be undertaken. Others argue that in a few years the momentum of the program will inevitably force a decision to deploy the system. Such a system would in all likelihood not be based on the much-touted exotic technology displayed in the media but on updated versions of present components. The resulting partial defense would have little to do with the president's vision of an invulnerable United States, completely shielded from nuclear attack. But whether the program ultimately collapses or produces some sort of limited defense, the results will very likely be disastrous for the ABM Treaty and for the prospects for future arms control.

The demise of the ABM Treaty and the unratified SALT II agreement, which is already seriously threatened and could not possibly survive the demise of the ABM Treaty, would essentially constitute the destruction of the entire framework of post–World War II arms control efforts. The loss of these restraining agreements would unleash a major acceleration of the strategic offensive and defensive nuclear arms race. Ancillary agreements such as the Outer Space Treaty and the Limited Test Ban Treaty would have little chance of surviving the ensuing military buildup. The terms of these treaties would not only prevent advanced development of such exotic approaches to strategic defense as nuclear-pumped X-ray lasers but would also interfere with the "conventional" nuclear ballistic missile defense systems that the Soviet Union and probably the United States would actually pursue in a serious strategic defense arms race. Finally, the collapse of the U.S.-Soviet arms control relationship would have a profoundly negative effect on efforts to prevent the future proliferation of nuclear weapons to other countries. Both our allies and nonaligned states would inevitably feel compelled to reassess their national interest in obtaining an independent nuclear weapons capability in a world in which the superpowers had abandoned not only all pretense of progress in arms control but also the modest restraints of existing agreements.

The loss of the arms control regime developed over the past twenty-five years would not return the arms control process to square one, but would drive it completely off the board. Burdened then by a legacy of failure and confronted with vastly larger and much more complex offensive and defensive strategic systems, it would be a long and difficult process to discover an acceptable new approach to arms control. The risk of nuclear war would certainly be greatly increased in a world where the course of the arms race and crisis stability would depend solely on the unilateral decisions of two adversarial superpowers whose hostility and suspicion would have been substantially increased by the disintegration of formal undertakings to build restraint and predictability into their strategic relationship.

Tragically, the future of arms control has been made hostage to the pursuit of a technological will-o'-the-wisp that will draw us ever deeper into a fruitless high technology arms race. There is widespread agreement in the scientific community that the possibility of developing a highly effective strategic defense system against a sophisticated and determined adversary such as the Soviet Union is so remote that it should be irrelevant for serious long-range national security planning.

The underlying problem with the president's vision lies in the incredible destructive power of thermonuclear weapons. Each weapon can have more than a million times the yield of a comparable-sized conventional weapon. Since a single thermonuclear warhead can destroy a city and the stockpiles of strategic weapons on each side number around ten thousand, a defensive system must be extremely effective to provide a credible territorial defense. To accomplish this task, a complex network of detectors, assessors, trackers, and exotic kill mechanisms, on earth stations and in outer space, would have to be linked and operated automatically by computers dependent on an unprecedentedly large and complex program that would have to work flawlessly when used for the first time in a hostile environment. This is a staggering technical challenge even under ideal conditions. In the real world, however, such a system would be "fatally flawed" since it would not be operating against a cooperating partner but rather against an adversary determined to foil it. The Soviet Union can draw from a large range of options to defeat the defense at a small fraction of the cost of building and maintaining the defense network.

The offense can attack the vulnerable points of this system. Such an attack could take place at the outset of hostilities or even during peacetime, since a clandestine or even an overt attack on a satellite would be unlikely to trigger an all-out nuclear response. Satellite battle stations will certainly prove to be highly vulnerable and tempting targets. The extreme vulnerability of the prime radars, on which the Safeguard/Sentinel program depended, was a primary reason these early U.S. systems were rejected as serious candidates for a nationwide defense against Soviet attack. Another option for the offense is simply to overwhelm the defense by brute force with more missiles, MIRVs, or decoys designed to simulate real reentry vehicles. Yet another approach is to nullify or diminish the effectiveness of the sensors and the kill mechanisms used by the defense. An example of such techniques would be the use of fast-burn boosters that would prevent or immensely complicate attack against the boost phase of the ballistic missile trajectory by shortening the time of exposure of the potentially vulnerable boosters to attack. Technical ingenuity will produce a host of ideas, such as spinning boosters, shields, and coatings to reduce at relatively low cost the effectiveness of directed energy systems and will thereby increase the cost of defense. Finally, the offense can choose simply to circumvent the ballistic missile defense system with air-breathing systems that fly under the shield. For example, low-flying cruise missiles, using stealth technology to avoid detection and launched from close-in submarines, would constitute an entirely new threat fully as difficult to defend against as ballistic missiles.

Despite the incompatibility of the evolving U.S. strategic position with prospects of progress in arms control, the American public understandably has a strong tendency to give the administration the benefit of the doubt and an opportunity to pursue its new approach. Even if the approach seems incredible, an outsider can never be confident of knowing all the relevant facts. The newspapers are constantly filled with vague reports from unidentified high administration spokesmen that the United States or the Soviet Union has hinted at some new arms control move. There are always authoritative assurances that the president really wants an agreement and sage commentaries on the obvious political advantages to the president of an agreement. In these circumstances, there is a natural reluctance to be seen as undercutting one's own government's negotiating position. A low profile also helps one to avoid the uncomfortable possibility of losing credibility by being seen as a false prophet in the unlikely event that the negotiations should eventually lead to an agreement.

Such restraint, which may have been a sign of wisdom in previous negotiations, is totally inappropriate at this time given the potentially catastrophic consequences of current U.S. policies on the future of arms control. There must be both a strong public defense of existing arms control agreements and a focused attack on those policies that are eroding these agreements and ultimately promise to destroy them. In the latter respect, one can applaud the president and the secretary of state when they call for steps to reverse the erosion of the ABM Treaty. But they must be told clearly that the Strategic Defense Initiative coupled with presidential rhetoric is a far more fundamental and corrosive element of this erosion than the apparently illegal Soviet Krasnoyarsk radar.

Despite the slim prospects for progress, even the most vocal critics of the administration's arms control policy should support the resumption of the Geneva negotiations. The negotiations have had the salutory effect of focusing U.S. and allied attention on the impasse created by the Strategic Defense Initiative. Moreover, even though the negotiations are being exploited more and more by both the United States and the Soviet Union as political theater, the negotiations in themselves do have something of a stabilizing effect on the arms race. True, the administration uses the negotiations to justify additional expenditures for military programs, such as the MX missile, and the Soviet Union uses the negotiations to attempt to weaken the NATO alliance. At the same time, the negotiations even as political theater put pressure on both sides not to abrogate, openly violate, or consensually accelerate the erosion of existing agreements. In the absence of such negotiations, either side could more easily ignore or repudiate the agreements on the grounds that the other side by its actions had effectively destroyed the arms control process.

In this hostile environment, the arms control community should close ranks in emphasizing the critical importance of maintaining the integrity of the arms control process. The principal objective should be to ensure that the United States and the Soviet Union support both the spirit and the word of the ABM Treaty. Both governments should be pressed to reverse the current erosion of the treaty by tightening, not relaxing, their interpretations of its provisions. Where there are gray areas in treaty provisions, such as the definition of treaty terms like *development* or *components,* the United States should take the lead in insisting on as restrictive interpretations as the negotiating and legislative history permit. The United States should not advance self-serving interpretations of these concepts that can only serve to erode the effectiveness of the treaty. If there is serious interest on both sides, problems of definition and disputed provisions can be resolved by supplemental common understandings without recourse to amendments or additional agreements.

A major effort must be made to restrain unilaterally the scope of the Strategic Defense Initiative. Even without the accompanying rhetoric, an undertaking funded at the level of the present U.S. program is entirely inconsistent with the intent of the ABM Treaty. The same can of course be said of the very extensive Soviet ballistic missile defense program, which also undercuts confidence in the long-term Soviet approach. But we can hardly hope to restrain the scope of Soviet activities if we do not ourselves exhibit serious respect for the ABM Treaty and its goals.

A major effort must also be made to ensure that the quantitative and qualitative limits of the unratified SALT II Treaty do not end when the agreement runs out December 31, 1985. In this connection, the president is to be commended for his recent decision, apparently despite contrary recommendations by some senior advisors, to continue adherence at least temporarily to the limits of the unratified SALT II Treaty. The rationale for continued U.S. adherence to the SALT II limits after the scheduled termination at the end of this year is clear and compelling. The question remains: How long will the Soviet Union continue its commitment to the unratified SALT II agreement in the face of an expanding Strategic Defense Initiative?

The erosion of the arms control regime is underway not only as a result of U.S. and Soviet military programs, but also because of the attitudes of the American people, who in the final analysis must be willing to support the continuation of existing as well as any future agreements. Formal charges by the U.S. government of alleged "possible," "probable," "almost certain," as well as "clear" Soviet violations of various "legal" and "political" obligations have seriously eroded public confidence not only in the agreements themselves but also in the entire process of arms control. This unpromising environment for public support is further poisoned by the constant leaks of highly misleading information, charging additional Soviet treaty violations or the intention of breaking out of the treaties. The public can do little to assess independently the validity of such distorted and misleading reports from unidentified sources who are clearly dedicated to the destruction of existing agreements and to the prevention of any future accords.

Compliance issues cannot and should not be ignored. In fact, the arms control community has a special responsibility to face up to such problems and protect the integrity of agreements from all enemies, domestic and foreign. At the same time, a major effort must be made to help the public keep the security implications of alleged violations in proper perspective in relation to the importance and accomplishments of an agreement. Above all, the arms control community should seek and support constructive solutions to genuine problems that have arisen either through misunderstandings or through the misguided efforts of either side to push the limits of its own self-serving interpretation of various treaty provisions.

I have focused on the contribution of the United States to the present arms control impasse. The Soviet Union certainly has earned its share of criticism. The level of Soviet ballistic missile defense research and development is beyond the spirit of the ABM Treaty. The Soviet Krasnoyarsk radar appears to be a clear violation of the ABM Treaty, and other Soviet activities have raised serious questions under this and other agreements. The Soviet position in Geneva, demanding that the United States abandon all research related to the Strategic Defense Initiative while insisting that the Soviet Union can continue similar research, as well as development and testing, is hardly a serious approach to the problem.

Unfortunately, however, it is our own government that has introduced a new crippling concept into the arms control process. In these circumstances, it is clearly more appropriate and more constructive to try to influence the policies of our own government. We do not know what the position of the new Soviet leadership will prove to be. There appear to be strong factions in the Soviet Union interested in containing the arms race and promoting strategic stability for compelling internal economic, political, and military reasons. We can best try to influence the evolution of constructive Soviet behavior by creating U.S. policies that support the existing structure of arms control agreements and are compatible with further arms control progress. While such constructive engagement certainly does not guarantee success, it is a prerequisite to challenging the Soviet Union to a positive response.

Others have suggested that a radical new approach to arms control is necessary to alter the course of events. But when the ship is sinking one must focus on damage control and not speculate on better approaches to transportation. The first order of business is to save the existing structure of arms control. This can only be accomplished by a broadly based campaign of constructive domestic and allied criticism of the military and arms control policies of the Reagan administration. This campaign is the only hope that arms control will indeed have a future.   *(July–August 1985)*

The Reagan Strategic Program
Ronald L. Tammen

On October 2, 1981, President Reagan announced the largest strategic arms buildup in the history of the United States. Though modified by the administration and Congress in subsequent years, this six-year $180 billion program will dominate the defense budget and the strategic debate for a decade.

The president's 1981 message was comprehensive in scope if limited in detail. His five-point plan called for doubling the number of survivable U.S. warheads by 1990 while increasing the flexibility of U.S. strategic forces.

Command and control was singled out for emphasis. Since this area has long been considered the soft spot of the U.S. deterrent, an $18 billion investment was proposed to improve systems ranging from satellite and data processing for nuclear attack warning to the Pave Paws surveillance radars. Additional E-4B airborne command posts were planned, with existing command posts hardened against nuclear effects. A family of new, mobile, survivable, and reliable communications devices would provide redundancy in the event of a first strike against U.S. forces.

The strategic package contained a $63 billion increase in bomber forces, including one hundred B-1Bs and an advanced technology bomber (ATB) to enter the force in the early 1990s. In addition, more than three thousand cruise missiles were planned for deployment on the bomber force.

The sea-based plan called for accelerated development and deployment of the Trident II D-5 SLBM (submarine-launched ballistic missile), which will double the payload of each Trident submarine and permit single warhead hard targeting from SLBMs for the first time.

The $34 billion land-based portion of the deterrent was scheduled for an improvement by substituting silo-based MX missiles for the multiple protective shelter (MPS) basing mode. This interim basing was considered temporary while investigation proceeded on a continuous patrol aircraft, ballistic missile defenses, and new ground-based deception techniques.

Lastly, the buildup contained a strategic defense package for continental air defense, modest civil defense efforts, and continuation of antisatellite and ballistic missile defense research at a cost of $23 billion.

The cost figures for the president's program were given in constant FY (fiscal year) 1982 dollars, which translated into $222 billion in appropriated dollars and included indirect costs as well—thereby inflating the magnitude of the apparent increases.

The Window of Vulnerability

The intellectual underpinning of the president's program rested on the strategic concept called the window of vulnerability. Perhaps no strategic concept in the last twenty years has been manipulated for so many purposes, defined so broadly, or quoted in so many contradictory ways by the highest defense officials of the nation.

The window of vulnerability was once known by the less appealing term "strategic bathtub." Its origin lies in a 1979 reassessment of Soviet strategic programs that found that the Soviets were deploying a higher number of warheads than had been anticipated and that Soviet warhead accuracy was increasing faster than predicted. Using this threat projection, the Pentagon did a year-by-year calculation of the number of U.S. warheads that would survive after a Soviet first strike. Defense officials found that in the 1982–87 time period, there would be a significant dip in the number of surviving U.S. warheads. This was caused by the cancellation of the B-1, the slowdown of the Trident program, and assumptions about the increasing vulnerability of intercontinental ballistic missiles (ICBMs). On the Pentagon graphs, the dip was bathtub shaped. The five-year bathtub took on political significance when renamed the window of vulnerability. Then, depending on who was using the term, it came to mean Soviet strategic dominance, U.S. land-based missile vulnerability, Soviet first-strike intentions, and even Soviet general purpose force superiority. Secretary of Defense Caspar Weinberger defined it as "those two or three rather dangerous years in the middle of the decade . . . during which our current silo-based ICBM force is vulnerable to a Soviet first strike."

The concept of a window of vulnerability was a potent rhetorical device. But it was dispelled in April 1983 by the president's Commission on Strategic Forces, which found that the Triad (the U.S. strategic force structure composed of land- and submarine-based missiles and bombers) complicates the timing, launch, and arrival times of an attack in such a way that a disarming first strike is impossible. This conclusion struck at the heart of the president's rationale for the six-year strategic buildup.

Disarray in Land-based Schemes

The administration's land-based modernization plans were in turmoil from the beginning. Secretary Weinberger, originally a critic of hardened silos for the MX, reversed course and supported that option only to meet with strong resistence from the air force. The chairman of the Joint Chiefs of Staff, Air Force Gen. David Jones said that he "remained to be convinced that [hardened silos] provided survivability." The secretary was forced to retreat and counter with the closely spaced basing scheme or Dense Pack. Congress reacted negatively and canceled Dense Pack in December of 1982.

This impass led to the appointment of the Commission on Strategic Forces. The commission met for three months in early 1983 after which it recommended a reorientation of the president's program with an emphasis on arms control, placing one hundred MX missiles in existing silos and initiating a vigorous research program for a new single-warhead ICBM. While the commission's modernization recommendations have received the most comment, the commission's insistence on pursuing arms control and its recognition of the usefulness of SALT II are infrequently cited.

The commission's recommendations did not end the dispute over land-based ICBMs. Support for the MX continued to erode in Congress primarily because of unease among moderates ⌐ˉboth parties over the vulnerability issue. This process culminated in a dramatic Senate vote in May 1985 to cap the number of deployed missiles at fifty, while allowing for additional testing missiles and a possible future deployment in a more secure basing mode. In confrontation with Sen. Sam Nunn of Georgia, the president decided to agree to the cap rather than lose the vote outright. This will reopen the basing mode question and will invigorate the single-warhead ICBM program.

The Bomber Debate

The president's recommendations for upgrading the bomber fleet have proceeded on schedule, unlike the debate over ICBM basing, although not without periods of friction with the Congress.

Arguments for the B-1B revolved around filling a bomber "gap"—a hazy period when the B-52 fleet would no longer effectively penetrate Soviet air defenses and the ATB had not yet reached deployment. "We need the B-1 early to fill the gap and to bring along the other [ATB] capability," argued the commander of the U.S.A.F. Aeronautical Systems Division.

Defining this gap caused problems for Pentagon witnesses before Congress. Secretary Weinberger opened the issue with the statement that the B-1B would not be able to penetrate Soviet airspace after 1990 "unless somebody wants to direct suicide missions." With an initial operating capability of the first squadron planned for 1986, it did not take long before congressional critics were asking if a $28 billion program was cost effective over a four-year life. A quick correction by the Secretary placed the penetration date off "well into the 1990s."

Caution in accepting the B-1B penetration argument was suggested by former Strategic Air Command (SAC) Comr. Gen. Richard H. Ellis, who warned Congress that the B-1B "would have questionable capability" in the early 1990s in part since dependence on electronic countermeasures (ECMs) "is a weak crutch." Former Under Secretary of Defense William J. Perry concurred in stating that "I would not want to ever suggest that the confidence of the success of a weapon system should rest entirely on ECM. We may be dangerously close to leaning on that lead almost exclusively."

Pentagon estimates of the availability of the ATB also showed flexibility. Secretary Weinberger's original statements indicated that the first ATB aircraft would come off the production line in 1989, with an operational capability in 1990 or 1991. But that date soon was stretched out beyond the early 1990s.

The effect of postponing the penetration date of the B-1B and stretching out the ATB initial operational capability was to weaken the arguments of the B-1B opponents. They responded by enacting legislation each year to ensure that the ATB and stealth cruise missile programs could not be delayed or starved of funding.

Will One Hundred Aircraft Be Enough?

The last annual purchase of B-1B aircraft will be made in the FY 1986 budget with forty-eight planes. Will this then cap the one hundred aircraft program and close down the production line? According to the air force and the Pentagon hierarchy, the answer is yes. Nonetheless, Rockwell International and its allies have plans to extend the production schedule, and given their success in keeping the B-1B program alive after its cancellation in 1977, the possibility should not be foreclosed.

Rockwell's approach is based on several propositions. First, company officials argue that the cost of the last B-1B will be one-half to one-third the cost of the first ATB. Second, they point out that there would be a loss of highly skilled workers. Third, they cite the ability of the B-1B to use stealth technology. And last, they state that the B-1B can be used for conventional bomb-carrying purposes.

If the ATB falters or increases dramatically in price, then Rockwell's arguments may carry the day.

SDI and the Buildup

The most dramatic and important change in the 1981 strategic program has been the initiation of the Strategic Defense Initiative (SDI). Announced in March 1983 by President Reagan, SDI's purpose is to make "obsolete the balance of terror" and to "render nuclear weapons impotent and obsolete." This broad mandate has given rise to friction between two factions of SDI supporters—those who believe in longer-term, countrywide, space-based defenses and those who argue for near-term, point, and area defense systems.

A five-year $24 billion energetic research and technology program is designed to answer basic questions about the feasibility of SDI. Testing of components may allow early decisions to advance one technology over another. Whatever the outcome of these tests, SDI raises profound questions of strategy and arms control that will influence U.S. strategic programs for the foreseeable future.

Among the most fundamental issues that must be addressed are the integration of SDI with arms control; assurances of positive cost exchange ratios; imperviousness to countermeasures; technology sharing with the Soviet Union; and of great importance, the impact of SDI on the European allies.

None of these issues was considered in 1981 when the strategic buildup was announced. Yet each will inevitably change the composition of that program.

The Financial Legacy

The Reagan administration's strategic buildup and its general increase in defense funding will influence defense spending for a decade. To understand the financial implications of the 1981 program, it must be understood that the Congress appropriates funds for defense that may actually be spent several years later. When the Congress gives the Pentagon $100 million for air force missiles, only $11 million is spent the first year, with $33 million the next and $36 million in the third year.

This means that a budget high in weapons procurement or research and development content is front-end loaded with appropriations that will spend out in later years. These unspent appropriations are building up dramatically. When President Reagan assumed office the Pentagon had $92 billion in unexpended backlog. Today it has $280 billion. This backlog will be spent in succeeding years regardless of efforts by Congress to cut back on current appropriations. That is the legacy of the Reagan administration's strategic program. The next president will inherit a substantial backlog, most of which must be spent because of contracts already signed. The defense budget in this respect is like a supertanker at sea that takes some time to gain momentum and cannot be stopped abruptly.

Looking Back and Ahead

The major components of the Reagan strategic plan have gone forward. Several of these were inherited from the Carter administration including the emphasis on cruise missiles, ATB, upgrading the B-52s, improving command control and communications, and of course, the MX. To that degree the 1981 plan was neither new nor revolutionary. Judging the success of this program depends on its perceived interaction with arms control negotiations, on questions about the pace of the program, and on the loss of public confidence in defense spending. A successful arms control treaty would dispel many concerns. Failure at Geneva will open the door to financial and strategic controversies. *(December 1981, updated May 1985)*

The Second Reagan Term: Arms or Arms Control?
Strobe Talbott

Strobe Talbott delivered this speech at the annual meeting of the Arms Control Association in 1984.

My cautious optimism about the second Reagan term was based on a couple of assumptions and predictions. First, I took seriously the president's seriousness about arms control in the sense that I was convinced that the softening of his rhetoric toward the Soviet Union and his repeated protestations of eagerness to see arms control revived were more than just election-year filmflam. Second, I had a sense that what might be called the correlation of forces within the administration was shifting in favor of the more moderate, traditionalist elements. The president seemed, in a number of ways, to be migrating toward the center, joining the ranks of the moderates in his own administration, and the other camp, the hard-core anti–arms control faction, seemed to be on the defensive and even in the doldrums. Some of its leading members were talking about getting out of government, going into more lucrative lines of work, opening restaurants—that kind of thing.

President Reagan is, for all his stubbornness and strong views, essentially a pragmatist; his inclination is to get along with others, and that notably and relevantly includes getting along with the Congress. He learned more in his on-the-job education about the politics of arms control than about the technological and doctrinal aspects of the subject, and the politics of arms control are simple enough: Public opinion and the Congress will not support an administration's rearmament programs unless they see an energetic, good-faith effort to conduct diplomacy that complements defense in the enhancement of national security. There was talk about major changes in personnel and procedure, and possibly new initiatives, right after the election.

Yet a third reason why I had some optimism had to do with the Soviet Union. While the signals being emitted by Moscow were anything but lucid and anything but consistent, there seemed to be some intriguing indications that the leadership there was interested in resuming the negotiating process that it broke off [in December, 1983] when Ambassador Karpov went home from Geneva for the holidays and made it clear that it was going to be a very long recess indeed, and not a very festive one. Certainly the Soviets ought to be interested in arms control. They have massive problems within their own country and within their empire that cry out for both attention and resources, and those problems will arguably be easier to cope with in an international climate of reduced tension.

Also, while the Soviets may have tipped the balance in the military competition further in their favor by their new deployments of the last couple years, the prospects for the competition down the road are not all that good for them, given the array of new generations of high-tech U.S. weaponry looming on the horizon. To put that same proposition more favorably, the long-term bargaining relationship, as opposed to the short-term military relationship, may favor the United States and therefore constitute an inducement for the Soviets to bargain seriously, sooner rather than later.

So for all those reasons, I expected that fairly soon after the election we would see the things begin to happen.

And Now the Bad News

But now for the less-than-glad tidings. There are other straws in other winds blowing in less favorable directions. I have three major concerns about the future, three dents in my optimism: one has to do with the people and process on the U.S. side; another has to do with Star Wars; and the third has to do with compliance and interim restraints.

So far, my sense is that the president has yet to be fully convinced that there is something deeply wrong with the way his administration has been conducting arms control policy. By "something wrong," I do not just mean that the system produces proposals with which kibitzers like myself and like the editors of *Arms Control Today* find fault. Rather, I am referring to the seemingly endless discord between fundamentally incompatible approaches to U.S. strategy and interests; I am talking about the degree to which a knockdown, drag-out battle between State and Defense (or the two Richards, or however you want to characterize the contending factions) has become not only impacted, but institutionalized. Never mind what one thinks of the product, the process is a crazy way to do business, a helluva way to run a railroad. Yet people who have been in to see the president and who have tried to persuade him of this have found him almost oblivious to the problem, rather snappish in denying that it exists.

This is partly because the Soviets have inadvertently encouraged the United States to stand pat—or perhaps I should say encouraged those in the administration who *want* to stand pat—by playing the heavies the way they have. With villains like the Soviets, it is easy enough for Ronald Reagan to play the hero simply by saying over and over again how much he wants to negotiate, never mind the substance of his negotiating position.

As for that substance, there is the problem of President Reagan's well-known and, among his supporters, pretty well conceded disengagement from the nitty-gritty of arms control. Let me add one more example to many already on the record, and I pick this one because it comes from the second presidential debate, which is one of my favorite moments in contemporary political history. During that debate, President Reagan tried to refute the charge that he did not understand nuclear diplomacy by explaining his original START (Strategic Arms Reduction Talks) proposal. He was obviously well prepared for that explanation, in the sense that he had had some talking points written up for him and he had memorized a little soliloquy. Which makes it all the more amazing that he still got it wrong. He made a big point of explaining how SLBMs were to be limited as part of Phase II of START, while in his speech at Eureka College in May 1982, he had made a big point of explaining how all ballistic missiles—SLBMs and ICBMs—would be in Phase I, and it was bombers and cruise missiles that would be in Phase II.

I guess I should not dwell on this too pedantically or unkindly, but I think it does illustrate that the problem persists of the president's being, at least figuratively, out-at-the-ranch where the substance of arms control is concerned.

Another factor is that the president's public posture, his own speeches, and the background music of policy all seem to be playing pretty well, and this president has had a tendency to feel that pronouncements *are* policy, that public applause constitutes the success of policy. His landslide reelection has tended to bolster the arguments of those who come to him and say, "Mr. President, if it ain't broke, don't fix it."

I should say, however, that there is also some evidence that some key people in the administration, notably including the national security advisor and the secretary of state, are acutely aware that the system is broken and does need fixing. What still remains to be seen is whether they are willing and able to bring the president around to that view.

What Has Changed

Those [in the administration] who have been so successful in the past in blocking progress, both preemptively and after the fact, are still very much in place, and the system that has allowed them to work their will does not seem—yet, at least—to have been changed. The National Security Council staff has become a giant bakery for half-a-loaf compromises between the competing factions and viewpoints, and these compromises, rather than the fights that lead to them, are what the president sees. The pattern in the past has been that the NSC, and the interagency process, takes the Pentagon thesis and the State Department antithesis and grinds out a synthesis that actually pleases no one and certainly does not offer the basis of meaningful business with the Soviets.

There has been some evidence that the pattern has continued since the election on a variety of issues. It has continued over the question of what sort of new initiatives the United States might make. The State Department has a quite imaginative, realistic, and even promising package of plans that would set up the possibility of trade-offs among different areas—intermediate-range weapons, strategic weapons and space weapons, offense and defense. But the Pentagon has fought vigorously, sometimes bitterly, and often successfully against these ideas both in their discrete parts and in their aggregate. That fight is not over. Nor are the fights over Star Wars and interim restraints, the two other issues I wanted to raise here.

Star Wars

A word about Star Wars. I agree with the warning that the Strategic Defense Initiative poses a very grave danger: that is the danger of a simultaneous, mutually exacerbating pair of new arms races, one in offensive weaponry and the other in defensive systems. One—but by no means the most serious—consequence would be the total collapse of arms control.

One of the big issues facing the administration is whether strategic defenses as a whole—as a concept and as a package of programs—are negotiable, or should they be provided with their own comprehensive protective shield against the giveaway tendencies of the arms controllers?

There is no question that the Strategic Defense Initiative scares the living daylights out of the Soviets. The Soviets might be willing to make significant concessions in their offensive weaponry in exchange for severe constraints on defense. But there is a view in the administration and elsewhere that anything that so clearly scares the Soviets is something we should have, that U.S. technological superiority constitutes a permanent, potentially decisive advantage over the Soviets, and that these high-tech systems—be they MIRVs fifteen years ago or cruise missiles last year or Star Wars next year—should indeed be protected against arms control, not traded away in arms control. Are they, in other words, bargaining chips, or are they family jewels?

And if Star Wars is to be negotiated, how is it negotiable? Star Wars in all its glory has a kind of all or nothing quality to it. How do you break it down to constituent parts that can be traded away one by one?

Those issues have not been resolved in the administration—not by a long shot. And I, for one, am not terribly optimistic about how it will be resolved, or even whether it will be resolved.

The optimistic view of President Reagan is that he has, somewhat belatedly, been bitten by the bug of traditional statesmanship and wants, in his second term, to leave a legacy of improved U.S.-Soviet relations in the form of a new agreement. As I indicated earlier, I am inclined to that view myself.

Arms Control or BMD

But I can also imagine that President Reagan might be equally tempted by the notion that the legacy he has an opportunity to leave is *not* another one of these agreements, which are always so controversial in the public arena and esoteric in their technicalities and legalisms, and in many ways disappointing in their impact on the arms race. Rather, he may feel that he has an opportunity to leave a legacy of breathtaking simplicity and revolutionary importance: a defense that defends, the end of mutual assured distruction (MAD), the defanging of the nuclear monster—that whole wonderful vision he conjured up in his March 1983 speech announcing Star Wars.

One thing that has to be kept in mind about Ronald Reagan is that he not only gives good speeches, he *believes* his speeches. That is one reason why they are so good. I feel an acute sense of suspense about what he will say when he delivers his next speech on Star Wars. It could be even more important than his first one.

Let me add one other thought about Star Wars. Having now heard a number of administration officials speak privately on the subject, I am developing a suspicion that they regard the Strategic Defense Initiative in its more grandiose, controversial, budget-busting, and utopian form—which is to say, in the form that President Reagan seems to have cottoned onto the idea—as a smoke screen or stalking horse for ballistic missile defense (BMD): that is, for point or hard-site defense around military targets rather than for comprehensive defense of the civilian population.

My sneaking suspicion is that they are hoping the public and the Congress will get worked up into a frenzy over the controversy about whether the nation should have a leakproof defensive umbrella over the entire United States, and that in the end, inevitably perhaps, we will decide as a nation, no, we should not and cannot have such a thing. But meanwhile, the idea of extensive ballistic missile defense will have come to seem so much more modest and reasonable and realistic by comparison that there will be a ready-made, willy-nilly foundation of public and congressional acceptance for it.

Even among opponents of BMD, acceptance of the thing will seem like a small price to pay for blocking SDI. Anyway, we will see. And one of the things we will see is what happens when the president finally figures out that many of his advisers are quietly planning for a fundamentally different sort of strategic defense than the pie-in-the-sky dream he laid out back in March 1983.

Interim Restraints

Finally, there is the question of interim restraints—the artificial life support system that is keeping SALT I and SALT II alive while the superpowers stagger around in search of something better. The Congress has mandated a recommendation from the administration early next year on whether to continue informal compliance with SALT. There is, as one would expect, sharp division within the administration over what to recommend, with the arms control opponents urging no and the moderates urging yes. The way in which the administration answers that question—should the United States continue to comply with the agreements of the past—may depend in some measure on how it answers another, very familiar one: Have the Soviets themselves complied with those agreements?

The hardliners in the administration and on Capitol Hill are seeking a guilty verdict on the issue of Soviet cheating, not least of all because such a verdict will provide them with ammunition to use against the moderates in the fight over interim restraints next year—and possibly in subsequent fights over whether to ratify any agreement [U.S. negotiators] may eventually, against the odds, achieve.

I am already feeling a bit Scrooge-like in all the cautionary and downright discouraging observations I have made. But lest I spoil Christmas altogether, let me end by reiterating that I remain an optimist and that I still think there are favorable trends. It is just that there are less favorable countertrends—and a certain worrisome persistence of the status quo, with all its inertia and obstructionism—and that too must be kept in mind.

They must be kept in mind by those of us who observe from the outside, but more important, they must be kept in mind, and eventually coped with, by those who seek to make and change policy on the inside. My optimism hinges on the hope that those who fit that description will sooner rather than later include the president himself.   *(December 1984)*

Decontrolling the Arms Race: The United States and the Soviet Union Fumble the Compliance Issues
Michael Krepon

The nuclear arms competition between the United States and the Soviet Union is entering a new stage. Washington and Moscow are not simply intensifying their weapons buildups, they are also moving to deregulate existing controls on the competition.

To be sure, arms control still has a prominent place in the official pronouncements of both capitals. Reagan administration officials point to the decline in the number of nuclear warheads and in the amount of megatonnage since the 1960s, while the Kremlin lends its support to a nuclear freeze. Both sides champion deep reductions in nuclear forces and offer visions of a nuclear free world. But their actions convey an entirely different agenda.

"Modernization" programs proceed at a brisk pace. Over the next decade, the United States and the Soviet Union plan to deploy the MX, Midgetman, Trident I and II, Pershing II, SS-20, SS-21, SS-22, SS-23, SS-24, SS-25, SS-N-20, and SS-N-23 missiles, air-, ground-, and sea-launched cruise missiles, Trident and Typhoon submarines, B-1, stealth, Blackjack and Bear H bombers, and assorted tactical nuclear weapons. These forces will provide further additions to the size and capabilities of superpower inventories, now estimated to total over forty thousand in number.

Many of these new weapon systems reflect the firm commitment by defense establishments in both nations to place opposing nuclear forces at risk. Nuclear war-fighting capabilities have become a central requirement for "effective" deterrence and "favorable" outcomes in the event deterrence fails, notwithstanding official rhetoric about there being no winners in a nuclear war.

In contrast to the evolution of strategic doctrine and nuclear forces, arms control negotiations remain stagnant. Progress to foreclose future avenues of competition in satellite warfare and nuclear weapon testing has been stymied by the Reagan administation's refusal to resume negotiations in these areas, dormant since 1979. Future progress in negotiations will be mortgaged to developments in the interim, including repeated U.S. tests of an advanced antisatellite weapon and the generation of new nuclear weapons requirements for space warfare.

Those areas in which nuclear arms control negotiations were resumed after 1979 are now either deadlocked or suspended. The fears and rigidities of both Washington and Moscow have been mutually reinforcing, producing the current impasse. In the Strategic Arms Reduction Talks, the Reagan team promised a far better deal than in SALT II but on terms that no Soviet leader could accept. Congressional interventions subsequently moderated these proposals but not before the Kremlin's position hardened. Meanwhile, in the INF (intermediate-range nuclear forces) talks, the Kremlin's insistence that no new missiles be deployed by NATO only reinforced the Reagan administration's objective of responding to Soviet missile capabilities in kind. The result was predictable: instead of being a forum for negotiated settlement, the talks became a test of wills over new NATO deployments.

With failed negotiations, prospective improvements in nuclear capabilities, and strained superpower relations, the fabric of previously agreed limits on the nuclear competition has begun to unravel. Both Washington and Moscow have now publicly accused each other, with varying degrees of certitude, of violating or circumventing several arms control agreements. In so doing, the prospect of ironing out these disputes quietly through established diplomatic channels has become more remote, at least in the near term. The slide toward deregulation continues.

Compliance questions are bound to arise even during periods of détente, because no arms control agreement can regulate every eventuality and because there will always be those who wish to pursue activities that are not expressly forbidden. In the current political environment the impulse to hedge bets at the expense of arms control agreements is far greater, and the checks against doing so are weakened. The SALT I Interim Agreement expired six years ago. The SALT II Treaty was never ratified; its provisions are set to expire within two years. These limitations are in place through informal and highly conditional statements by U.S. and Soviet officials. With current negotiations deadlocked, who within the councils of government in either Washington or Moscow would argue against a colleague's proposal because it would undermine current agreements or make new pacts more difficult to reach? In the past, duly ratified arms control agreements have not fared well during periods of increased international tension. There is no reason to expect that unratified and expired agreements will fare any better in the 1980s, unless the current state of U.S.-Soviet relations improves.

President Reagan set the stage for SALT deregulation at his first press conference when he characterized his negotiating partners as "liars and cheats." His first secretary of state, Alexander Haig, declared that "We consider SALT II to be dead. We have so informed the Soviet Union and they have accepted and understood that." His secretary of defense, Caspar Weinberger, declared that U.S. defense programs were in conformity with SALT I and II restraints as a matter of coincidence rather than design, and the president's White House counselor, Edwin Meese III, stated that the Reagan administration had no moral or legal commitment to abide by expired or unratified SALT agreements. When legal experts at the State Department and Arms Control and Disarmament Agency challenged this assertion, the White House issued a defense of Mr. Meese's position, calling it "entirely accurate."

The Reagan administration gave substance to these public pronouncements by championing several military initiatives that could not be pursued within the confines of the SALT agreements. The ill-conceived Dense Pack deployment scheme for the MX would have required digging holes for new missiles, an activity prohibited by the SALT I and II agreements. Administration officials explained that the excavations would be allowed because they were for new "hardened capsules" rather than silos and would be completed after the expiration of SALT II, in any event. Later, the president agreed to press ahead with a second new intercontinental ballistic missile—the Midgetman—to complement the MX. Again, its deployment would be permitted because it would begin after the terms of the SALT II agreement—which permitted only one new ICBM—were to expire. The president has also endorsed a "Star Wars" defense against nuclear attack that cannot be tested in space or deployed without violating the ABM Treaty. New phased-array radars are under construction for permitted purposes, but they can eventually have ABM applications.

While the Reagan administration's military initiatives suggest prospective compliance problems, Soviet military activities are of immediate concern. Flight testing is proceeding on two new land-based missiles instead of the one new type permitted by the SALT II agreement. The Kremlin insists that one of its two new missiles is a permitted variant of an older missile. Arguments will persist over whether the missile in question can be shoehorned into a profile permitted by SALT II, especially as the Soviets encrypt virtually all of the data generated by its flight tests—another practice inconsistent with the agreement. A large, phased-array radar is under construction in Siberia which the Kremlin states is for tracking objects in space but which appears far more suited as an early warning radar. The former is allowed in this location under the ABM Treaty; the latter is not.

Concern over Soviet compliance with the SALT agreements has been magnified by evidence that Soviet troops and Soviet-equipped Vietnamese forces have used "yellow rain" in Afghanistan and Southeast Asia. The Reagan administration contends this constitutes repeated violations of the Geneva Protocol and the Biological Weapons Convention (BWC). Questions about Soviet compliance with the BWC have also been raised by an accident at a suspected biological weapons facility in Sverdlovsk in 1979.

In the past, the United States has ratified arms control agreements, like the Biological Weapons Convention, which had no verification or compliance provisions. The reason for doing so seemed straightforward: the United States had no military interest in these weapons. For nuclear arms control agreements, U.S. presidents from Kennedy to Carter demanded different verification standards. The treaties in question had to be "adequately verifiable." This meant that the United States had to be in a position to "identify attempted evasion if it occurs on a large enough scale to pose a significant risk," and to do so "in time to mount a sufficient response." These were the instructions of President Richard Nixon to the SALT I delegation; similar guidelines were used to draft and defend the Limited Test Ban and SALT II treaties.

Compliance questions were also handled in a remarkably similar fashion in congressional ratification debates. Previous administrations argued that the Kremlin bureaucracy, having become associated with an agreement, would not then turn around to undermine it. Moreover, U.S. detection capabilities presented a formidable deterrent to violations. Finally, the United States could always abrogate the treaty in question if violations were detected.

Clearly, this approach to compliance issues is no longer valid, if indeed it ever was. It does not account for the ambiguities that inevitably arise over the nature of agreed limitations, or the habitual efforts of some within defense establishments to take advantage of those ambiguities when conceivable advantages could result. These instances call for a response other than treaty abrogation.

As in the past, U.S. presidents will have to argue persuasively that treaty compliance can be verified. In the future, administrations will also have to present coherent strategies for securing the viability of agreements when compliance questions arise. The available evidence does not suggest that the United States is dealing with a committed treaty violator. The United States is, however, dealing with an extraordinarily difficult negotiating partner that is looking for advantage where it can prudently be gained, even within the confines of negotiated agreements. In response, the United States needs an effective compliance strategy for the same reasons agreements are sought in the first place: to assure the public that the nation's security is being advanced and to foreclose destructive avenues of competition that cannot work to either side's advantage.

An effective compliance strategy begins with a question: Is the maintenance of the arms control agreement still in the national security interest of the United States? The answer to this question will then guide subsequent actions. If it is in the nation's interest to maintain the viability of the agreement, a two-track approach is required.

First, the United States should work exhaustively through diplomatic channels to clear up ambiguities in the agreements, "fence in" problems when they occur, and work out agreed understandings to prevent those agreements from being undermined.

Second, if diplomatic solutions fail to be satisfactory or if offsetting military actions are required, the United States should adopt proportional countermeasures within treaty constraints to send the appropriate political and military messages to Moscow. For example, in response to the construction of the new Soviet radar, the United States can accelerate programs to improve the penetration capability of U.S. nuclear forces, or construct a new space-tracking radar of its own, depending on which course of action appears the most effective at least cost. These countermeasures are allowed under the terms of the ABM Treaty and can effectively offset whatever advantage may accrue from Soviet pressing at the margins. While these countermeasures are underway, the object of diplomacy is to maintain the viability of the ABM Treaty by working out agreed limitations on new radar construction, since the ABM Treaty can be undermined by the proliferation of powerful modern radars, even for permitted purposes. Each compliance question will require different U.S. responses; all should reflect the two-track approach suggested here, combining adroit military countermeasures with patient diplomatic efforts.

A significant segment of the Congress and the American public will continue to take a lively interest in compliance questions, fueled by periodic news leaks asserting Soviet violations. Some of these charges will be entirely groundless; others will be cause for concern. All will strike a resonant chord in a large segment of the American public that does not expect the Soviets to live up to their treaty obligations. Administrations have a responsibility to inform the public and their elected representatives on compliance questions, but they also must weigh this responsibility against the need for confidentiality in negotiations, particularly delicate negotiations to iron out compliance problems.

As a general rule, it makes sense for an administration to issue periodic reports on compliance questions that have been satisfactorily resolved, and to avoid negative conclusions in ongoing disputes since publicizing grievances is likely to make their satisfactory resolution more remote in private exchanges. But at what point should an administration "go public" when its concerns have not been satisfied? The answer will depend on the particulars in each case. There are three key questions that relate to the timing of public disclosure: Is the activity in question militarily significant? Are there humanitarian reasons for early disclosure? Are there treaty provisions for handling compliance questions in private? Where consultative provisions exist and when there is no urgent need to act quickly, it makes sense to exhaust diplomatic remedies before concluding in public that violations have occurred. On the other hand, public expressions of concern are quite appropriate when the United States receives no satisfactory explanation for possible violations of agreements without compliance mechanisms, or when the United States needs to act quickly for security or humanitarian reasons.

The avenues of public diplomacy chosen are critical, however, because maladroit public initiatives can easily make appropriate solutions more difficult to achieve. For multilateral agreements like the Geneva Protocol and the Biological Weapons Convention which have no provisions for handling compliance questions in private, the focus of U.S. government activity should usually be to establish compliance procedures and to disseminate information on questionable practices. Where there is evidence of noncompliance in such cases, the United States cannot generate international political pressures solely by diplomatic demarches. We must build a case and present it to other treaty signatories.

An entirely different approach is needed for bilateral agreements, like the SALT agreements, which have established channels for ironing out compliance issues. Here, the Standing Consultative Commission (SCC) worked reasonably well during the Nixon, Ford, and Carter administrations. During this period, both nations recognized that this forum was being used to iron out potential problems rather than to prosecute cases of noncompliance. Problem areas could also be ironed out because both nations believed that it was in their separate as well as mutual interests to maintain the viability of the SALT I accords. However, compliance questions often require patient diplomacy. Take, for example, the case of the surface-to-air missile (SAM) radar tests "in an ABM mode." In 1973 and 1974, the U.S. intelligence community noticed that a Soviet SA-5 radar had been used to track strategic ballistic missiles during flight. This appeared to be inconsistent with Article VI of the ABM Treaty, which prohibited each side from testing SAM radars "in an ABM mode." The picture was clouded, however, because there was no common agreement on what constituted tests in an ABM mode and because the United States maintained that tests for range safety and instrumentation were permitted.

In this case, the Nixon, Ford, and Carter administrations all could have asserted that the Soviets violated Article VI of the ABM Treaty. None chose to do so. At first, wishing to protect intelligence sources and methods, the United States did not raise this issue at the SCC. When the Ford administration did raise the subject of the Soviet SA-5 radar, the practice stopped. It then required approximately two years of quiet diplomacy during the Carter administration for the two SCC delegations to work out a common agreement governing these practices.

The Reagan administration has adopted an entirely different approach to compliance diplomacy, with markedly inferior results. In part this is due to the downturn in U.S.-Soviet relations and to Soviet practices that are clearly worrisome. Domestic factors have also played a significant role. This administration's compliance diplomacy has been muddled and ineffective because it has not decided whether it wants to uphold the nuclear arms control agreements the Soviets are allegedly violating. Indecision has bred confusion. Press reports indicate that the Reagan administration initially declined to discuss SALT II compliance questions at the

SCC, then asked for a special session to discuss urgent concerns in the summer of 1983, and then was unable to agree on negotiating instructions to the U.S. delegation when the SCC convened in the fall.

Unlike his predecessors, President Reagan acted quickly when SALT compliance questions were not resolved to the satisfaction of his advisers. On the basis of the guidelines presented here, the administration's report of Soviet violations and "probable" violations seems premature and ill-advised in all cases but one— the use of yellow rain. Here, the evidence is far from conclusive in a laboratory sense, but it is suggestive enough to warrant official, public concern, given the lack of private channels for handling chemical weapons compliance questions and the continuing, although diminished, reports of toxic weapons attacks.

In contrast to the yellow rain case, SALT compliance questions are perfectly suited to private consultations in the SCC. The Reagan administration short-circuited this process with its public report on Soviet noncompliance. For example, on the serious problem of the new Soviet radar in Siberia, the administration reportedly concluded that a violation had "almost certainly" taken place after a single, inconclusive session of the SCC. In this instance, public officials who are prepared to wait stoically for ten years while a new weapon system is deployed apparently found the pace and prospects of diplomatic progress intolerable after several weeks of effort.

With the premature release of SALT "violations," President Reagan has temporarily placated irreconcilables in the Senate, but he has made it extraordinarily difficult for the U.S. delegation of the SCC to make headway on outstanding compliance problems. The U.S. delegation, led by Gen. Richard Ellis, is quite capable of ironing out these issues. However, the Kremlin may conclude that there is little incentive to be forthcoming if such exchanges are unlikely to change the Reagan administration's conclusions. Thus, in operational terms, the practical effect of the Reagan team's compliance strategy is to close off diplomatic solutions, while the approach pursued during the Nixon, Ford, and Carter administrations kept them open.

Whatever satisfaction skeptics about arms control may gain from the report on Soviet noncompliance and from the possible end of business-as-usual at the SCC must be weighed against the broader implications of the Reagan administration's approach to compliance diplomacy. A report, after all, is no substitute for an effective strategy either to secure Soviet compliance with arms control agreements or to improve U.S. security. New agreements are built on those that have preceded them. If this scaffolding falls down, how can it be reconstructed, and what will take its place? The key to arresting the slide toward arms decontrol is an ability to iron out compliance questions that undermine current agreements and work against ratification of new ones. Success can only come with improved U.S.-Soviet relations and more effective leadership in both Washington and Moscow.   *(March–April 1984)*

What Kind of Relationship Do We Want with the Soviet Union?
Marshall D. Shulman

Marshall D. Shulman delivered the following speech at the annual membership meeting of the Arms Control Association on December 13, 1985.

The Soviet Union is entering upon a new historical stage in its development. When this fact sinks into our consciousness it will require us to reexamine our own thinking about the kind of relationship the United States wants with the Soviet Union, first because many of the assumptions that have guided our thinking in the past may be inadequate guides for the future, and second, because U.S. actions may in some degree influence the direction of the changes now beginning to take place in the Soviet Union. The central factor in this relationship requiring reexamination is the management of the nuclear military competition between the two countries. The time has come for the United States to open a new debate on whether its own security interests require that this competition be managed in a more rational way than is now the case.

The long-heralded generational change in the top leadership of the Soviet Union has now taken place. Before a leadership change comes about, it is always very difficult to predict what its character will be. There are usually few advance indicators of what the Soviet political leaders will do when they take the top job; although perhaps there are a few more indicators this time than has been the case in the past. But what has become apparent on the basis of his eight months in office is that the new Soviet leader is very different from what we have been accustomed to. He is a remarkable man, extremely able, intelligent, energetic, educated, tough-minded, and self-confident.

There has been a dramatic change in tone in the Soviet Union. Those who have traveled there have noticed that over the past ten years the immobilism at the top had bred an atmosphere of pessimism, of cynicism, of brooding about the deepening economic problems, the corruption, the bribery in everyday life. People had begun to question whether a system so organized can compete effectively in the world. But very quickly after the new leadership took office, a change in tone began to be felt through all strata of the society, a new hope, a sense of expectation, perhaps even too much expectation. Mikhail Gorbachev is reported to have said, "They think I'm a miracle worker." And indeed it has often been the case in the Soviet past that the time of greatest danger is when hopes are raised that are slow to be fulfilled. It is true that a few of the more world-weary types tend to say, "Well, there is only talk and no action, the system will grind him down." But among most people there is a strongly positive expectation, buoyant and even a touch arrogant. They say, "Come back in a year and see what we will have done." Even outside the Establishment, people who are nonpolitical, who live in the interstices of the society, are touched by his style. They sit before their television sets and applaud his speeches. They say, "He doesn't talk party language." And when he says as he did in one of his speeches, "You don't have to take rudeness from the people in the stores, they are there to serve you not you to serve them," they shake their heads in wonderment and say, "He is really talking to me."

Now, what has Gorbachev done? First of all he has consolidated his position more quickly than anyone could have foreseen. He has made numerous personnel changes, he has made the Politburo his own, he has his own prime minister, his own foreign minister, his own head of Gosplan, he has made a number of other ministerial changes and changed about 30 percent of the regional party secretaries. By the time of the Party Congress in February, he will have his own Central Committee. But he has moved cautiously, like a shrewd chess player, always planning several steps ahead. He has made it clear that he is not going to repeat the mistakes of Nikita Khrushchev. He has avoided alienating significant power groups among the bureaucracies. In his first stage to now, he has moved on the problem of work discipline, continuing the efforts begun by former General Secretary Uri Andropov. He has addressed the problems of absenteeism, alcoholism, and corruption.

In anticipation of the next stage Gorbachev has been preparing for the Party Congress at the end of February. He has supervised the preparation of a revised Party Program that is remarkable in dropping some of the cant of the 1961 Party Program; he has prepared new party statutes. He has had the twelfth five-year plan redrafted, setting fourth extremely ambitious goals for productivity and for the modernization of industrial technology. The expectation is that after the congress he will begin to address some structural problems; will reduce the power of the ministries and give greater autonomy to the enterprises; will try to put in place a more realistical price system than the Soviets have had; and will take the central planning organizations out of the retail business of supervising every detail of every plan and set them to the task of defining the objectives and the priorities for the economy as a whole. Gorbachev has made it abundantly clear that he is a revolutionary (he uses the word frequently), but he is a revolutionary not in a Marxist-Leninist sense but in technology. The crucial point that he addresses time and again is that the key to the future must be for the Soviet Union to apply modern technology to Soviet industry.

The party Congress may be one of the important events of the decade. It involves plans to the year 2000. They are bold and ambitious and they are truly revolutionary in their implications.

Now some cautions are in order. Economic reform does not mean liberalization. It may indeed mean a tightening of discipline and of controls at least in the short run. Gorbachev is not necessarily the consumer's friend. The changes he is proposing are in the interest of building up industrial technology and not in the first instance greatly improving the lot of the consumers.

Can he do it? No one can say at this point whether he will succeed in what he has set out to do. The obstacles are obviously formidable. He faces serious limitations in the available hard currency, and this is likely to get worse as oil prices go down. Resistance from some quarters is probable but is difficult to judge. There is of course enormous inertia and bureaucratism of the kind that has to be seen to be believed. Soviet society is basically conservative and resistant to change. But Gorbachev has enormous advantages on his side. He came along at the right time in the political situation. He follows a long period of immobility that had created a restiveness, a readiness for a strong leader. There is in the Soviet culture a more comfortable feeling with a structured society built around a strong and competent leader, bolstered by a fear of disorder and anarchy.

So, if Gorbachev succeeds even in part, the Soviet Union will be entering upon a period of profound changes, some conscious, intended to encourage initiative and innovation, and perhaps over the longer run some that may be the unintended consequences of his actions. The present period is likely to be as different from the Brezhnev period as the Brezhnev period was from the Stalin period. Certainly some important characteristics of the system will persist and others may be different in ways that are difficult to foretell. And that is what the conservatives in the Soviet Union are worried about. They have the traditional view of the defenders of orthodoxy everywhere that if you change one brick in the edifice the whole structure of the party's authority will be weakened. So Gorbachev must move cautiously. But the weight of his authority, shrewdly exercised, is likely to result in the realization of at least some of the changes he has projected.

Although Gorbachev has made it clear that the modernization of the Soviet economy is his first priority, it is evident that his program has important implications for Soviet foreign policy. The significant indicator was the last paragraph in that fascinating interview he gave to *Time* magazine (September 1985):

> I would like to end by just saying a few words that are important in understanding what we have been talking about all along. I don't remember who, but somebody said that foreign policy is the continuation of domestic policy. If that is so, then I ask you to ponder one thing: if we in the Soviet Union are setting ourselves such truly grandiose plans in the domestic sphere, then what are the external conditions that we need to be able to fulfill those domestic plans? I leave the answer to that question to you.

The central question for Soviet foreign policy has traditionally concerned its relations with the United States. This has been its central preoccupation, a major determinant of the tone of Soviet foreign policy in successive periods. It affects inputs into its planning on military expenditures and on prospects for foreign trade. This had been the hallmark of the foreign policy of Andrei Gromyko. His removal as foreign minister has introduced a period of much greater flexibility in foreign policy. It has opened the question of whether Soviet foreign policy should be less U.S.-centered than it has been. That question has not yet been answered. The Soviet leadership still appears to be asking itself, and debating, what kind of relations with the United States are possible. By its decision to accept a summit meeting with the United States after prolonged debate and before it was really ready for such a meeting, the Soviet leadership appeared to be saying that the question was worth testing. It has a clear preference for improved relations with the United States, if that is possible, as the condition most favorable for carrying forward its domestic economic program. But if that proves not possible, the Soviet Union has indicated that it is prepared to accept a relationship of continued or increased tension with the United States for as long as may be necessary. And there are many in the Soviet Union who think that is the more probable course of events.

The most interesting aspect of the summit was the tactical decision of Gorbachev to accept a qualified positive tone despite the failure of the summit to make any progress on what the Soviet Union regarded as its central issue, the competition in nuclear weapons. Instead of parting on a note of harsh denunciation for this failure, seeking to put the onus on the United States as the obstacle to an arms control agreement, Gorbachev chose to emphasize the positive value of the civil dialogue that had been established, and to express optimism about the beginning of a process that is to be continued in subsequent meetings, while treating the unreconciled differences on arms control frankly but more in sorrow than in anger. Although the experience of personal contact between the two leaders is a positive factor that may have effects difficult to measure or to forecast, it is clear that the present state of the relationship between the two countries is transient and unstable.

If the differences between the United States and the Soviet Union on the management of the nuclear military competition are not bridged in the coming months, events will strain and sooner or later snap the thin lifeline of tentative communication that has been established, notwithstanding the progress that has been made and may continue to be made on secondary issues. Both countries have in various stages of development new ballistic missiles, new cruise missiles, new intercontinental bombers, new submarines. As these come into deployment they will be sources of tension. Within the foreseeable future the United States is likely to be engaged in debates with the Soviet Union about the development and testing of elements of the SDI program and whether these do or do not violate the ABM Treaty. U.S. and Soviet lawyers will argue whether these tests involve components or subcomponents of weapons systems designed for use in space. This will be another source of tension. In February, at the Party Congress, the Soviet Union will be giving some indication of the scale of its military plans for the coming period. And this too is likely to be a source of tension, particularly if they make the same mistake that U.S. policymakers do of believing that a military buildup is likely to make an adversary more prone to negotiate.

The present ambiguous relationship cannot be prolonged. The military competition will continue to intensify within the limits of the resource and budgetary constraints on both sides. Some weapons systems will go forward even if additional appropriations are limited. Whether public opinion in the United States and in Western Europe will remain quiescent is problematical. The Soviet Union will face a choice. Already defensive about having come away from Geneva empty-handed, the Soviet leadership will find it increasingly difficult to maintain its optimism about the value of a civil dialogue with the United States in the absence of progress on arms control. As hopes dim for progress on arms control, and this means in the first instance on the space defense issue, there will be a growing inclination to reaffirm the conclusion expressed by Andropov a month before his death, that the United States is not prepared to negotiate seriously on this central issue.

The Soviets may see both external and internal advantages in putting the onus on the United States for the continued tension and rising military competition. They can hope to mobilize public pressures on the United States from Europe which have been blunted by the present acquiescent line they chose to adopt. Domestically, the characterization of the United States as threatening is not only congenial to the conservatives and the ideologists, but it can be a means of mobilizing support for economic reforms, for sacrifices, for higher military spending. Some Soviet propaganda regarding the United States has been, with a brief lull during the summit, extremely harsh and may become more so.

Some in the United States may believe that it is good from the U.S. point of view that rising Soviet military expenditures would have the effect of slowing down or stopping Soviet efforts at economic reforms. But it is worth bearing in mind that if the Gorbachev program is impelled by a spirit of mobilization against the United States as a menacing threat, it means that any hope that the United States may have of an easement of Soviet repressive practices toward human rights is going to be reduced; any hope for a greater degree of autonomy for Eastern Europe is going to be reduced; and any hope for moderation and a degree of collaboration in regard to regional conflicts will also be reduced. There will be costs to the United States in greater strains in its alliance relations with Western Europe, with Japan, and perhaps even with China, which has come to see greater risks and costs in unbridled military competition than they formerly saw in the threat of Soviet imperalism. There will be adverse effects wthin U.S. society in the further militarization of the economy and adverse effects on national security as the military competition passes beyond the point of any control.

Faced with the absence of progress in the arms control negotiations, the Soviet Union will have choices to make with what kind of military programs and at what level to respond. Because the Soviets do not want to be seen as weak or as yielding to pressure, they will respond at some higher level unless they are wiser and more self-confident than U.S. policymakers are. In any case, even a modest increase in their military programs will have its costs for them, given the already large proportion of their gross national product going into military expenditures. It will mean some impairment of the realization of their primary goal of modernizing industrial technology. This is not just to be understood in aggregate terms of how many rubles go into the defense sector as against into the civilian sector, but it is more importantly seen in qualitative terms because the new military systems involve high technology, computers, electronics, scientists, laboratories, alloys—all the things that are most needed for the Soviet Union to bring its industrial technology up to world standards.

Is it foreordained that things will go this way, or is there an alternative before us? I think there is indeed a moment of opportunity for an alternative course before us at the present time. The incentives are very strong for the Soviet Union to negotiate seriously about arms control. In fact, I think we have seen a serious intent on their part since the early 1970s. During the period of the SALT II negotiations it was evident, although not widely appreciated by the American people, that the list of major concessions by the Soviet Union was considerably longer than that of the United States, indicating that they had begun to see a self-interest in trying to moderate the military competition, and this is even more true in the present period. This was illustrated by the rapidity with which the Soviets came forth with new initiatives in the eight weeks before the summit, unprecedented in Soviet history, in contrast to their usual pattern of reacting to U.S. proposals. Granted that their proposals were made with negotiations in mind, and not everything was to be taken at face value. But with all due allowance for the bargaining room built into their positions to have something to trade with, there was a dramatic eagerness manifested in the Soviet proposals.

The immediate problem before us is the management of nuclear weapons and that means how to deal with the main obstacle to arms control, the Strategic Defense Initiative. We all know that there are different sources of support for the SDI in the United States. There are some who seek to use it to encourage the Soviet Union to negotiate about their offensive systems; there are some who seek to achieve military superiority in space; there are some who are simply seeking an escape from the dilemmas of mutual deterrence; and there are also some, including some of my colleagues at my own university, who are salivating for some of the research funds offered.

There are possibilities for seeking some common ground on the SDI issue that should be explored. Part of the problem we face with the SDI is the way it was launched. It was initiated in a way that inevitably aroused suspicions about U.S. intent, clouded as it has been by contradictory statements as to its forms and purposes. The Soviet concern with the SDI centers on the boost-phase aspect of the program. Soviet propaganda about SDI has not made clear their real concerns. What clearly worries them most is not just a question of whether it will work or not. A Soviet concern is that the priority emphasis in the SDI program on research on directed-energy weapons in space, whether or not it succeeds in creating a defense system in orbit over the Soviet Union, will lead to space weapons capable of offensive use and a new stage of military competition in space. This is a challenging problem for them because it relies less on new science than on engineering and technology, in which the United States has considerable advantages. Because a Soviet lag in following the U.S. lead into this new area of military competition would take time and considerable effort to overcome, the Soviets feel that they cannot afford to wait and see what comes of it and then react. They have to anticipate the possible consequences of the new U.S. programs. What this means is that if the United States proceeds with the SDI program as presently projected, the Soviet reactions will not be delayed until the United States decides whether or not to deploy a space defense system, but will begin now.

There are, however, a number of possible ways by which the United States could meet the Soviet concerns, if the United States finds it in its interest to do so, and still enable the president to remain faithful to his deep commitment to a stronger defense component in U.S. strategic forces. There are some indications that at least some in the Soviet Union are prepared to think of going beyond the suggestion advanced by Gorbachev that development and testing of space-based defense be prohibited and that work on it be limited to fundamental research laboratories. If the Soviets learned one thing from the summit it was that the president is deeply committed on this point and that he has shown no sign of changing his mind. The following examples illustrate the range of other possible ways around the impasse. The United States can seek clarifying agreements with the Soviet Union regarding possible ambiguities in the ABM Treaty about the kinds of tests permitted under the treaty. The United States can seek agreement to lengthen the period of warning notice under the treaty, to allay Soviet fears of a breakout on short notice, while negotiations toward reductions in offensive weapons are going forward. It may be possible to find grounds for agreement on permitting ground-based ABM systems that would emphasize the terminal rather than the boost phase. A hardpoint defense may or may not have some utility; it would be expensive, and it would require monitoring against its development into an area defense, but if as a practical political matter the United States remains committed to some form of antimissile defense, this form of it would at least not be destabilizing.

If there proves to be significant thinking on both sides about how to work around this impasse on the SDI so as to open the way to reductions in offensive weapons, then the question presents itself: how to initiate the process? The Soviets are hesitant to take the initiative in the postsummit situation. They are already defensive about the summit outcome. They do not want to appear to be the supplicants, to appear to be leading from weakness. They are also concerned about proposing concessions without any assurance that the United States is ready to discuss them seriously, lest the United States simply pocket whatever they offer and give nothing in return. And it does not appear likely that the United States will take the initiative either, given the inhibitions within the government created by the depth of the president's commitment to the SDI program.

Might it not be possible to deal with this hesitancy on both sides by encouraging a strategic dialogue in some form between the two countries? Such a dialogue could give us a fresh start in introducing a serious discussion on what kind of mix might be possible between offensive and defensive systems in a period of transition. The delegations at Geneva are not a promising vehicle for such a strategic dialogue, given their composition and their propensity for striking propagandistic postures. But if there is a serious interest in such a strategic dialogue, it might be carried forward more effectively by unpublicized discussions between defense scientists and military professionals of the two sides. Or, if the will exists, more imaginative use could be made of the Standing Consultative Commission for this purpose, or of back channels of communication through trusted intermediaries. If such exchanges are productive, they could open the way to a reconciliation of the apparently irreversible commitment of the U.S. government to some form of strategic defense with the earlier efforts of the two countries to stabilize and moderate the deterrent balance.

The way was opened, during the presummit jockeying, for negotiations leading toward 50 percent reductions in offensive missiles, provided that the SDI obstacle can be resolved, and that gaps can be closed between the subceilings on various systems proposed by each side, which should be possible. There are indications at least in some Soviet circles of a growing appreciation that their highly MIRVed heavy missiles may not be worth the cost of the apprehensions they have aroused and the stimulation they have given to new U.S. weapons programs, and this appreciation may be reinforced by the realization of the increasing vulnerability of these systems. This suggests the possibility that the Soviet Union might be prepared to go further than the formal proposals they advanced before the summit toward more substantial reductions in their heavy missiles and/or the number of warheads with which they are armed. A Soviet movement in this direction, which would help to meet U.S. security concerns, would be more likely if the United States were prepared to accept further limitations on bombers than were offered in its presummit proposals, and were willing to negotiate compensating limitations on the MX and Trident II missile systems, both of which were stimulated by the Soviets' building of the heavy missiles.

It will also be necessary for U.S. policymakers to clarify their thinking about whether the United States would like to encourage or discourage movement toward the acceptance of mobile land-based missiles, and how the nation comes to rest on the trade-offs between the stability they offer through increased survivability of land-based systems as against the problems they create for verification. This would also require genuine acceptance within the government of the desirability of moving toward smaller, mobile, single-warhead land-based missiles.

The way would also be open, once common ground had been reached on the SDI set of issues, toward closing the gap on the theater nuclear weapons problem. This is more a political than a military problem, and its solution should be made easier if, as may be the case, there is some appreciation on the Soviet side that their widespread deployment of the SS-20s has cost them much more than the missiles were worth.

Once we can work our way through the minefields of the immediate and pressing aspects of the nuclear military competition, it would become possible to think more productively about the U.S. interest in encouraging a longer-term evolution in the relationship. It is relevant in this connection to return to the question of the prospects for longer-term changes in Soviet society and the Soviet system resulting from the Gorbachev program. At best the question can be answered only speculatively, since so many uncertain variables are involved; for that matter, we cannot even foretell how U.S. society will develop over the coming decades.

While U.S. capacity to influence the course of Soviet developments is limited, the United States does have at least marginal effects on them, and its leaders need to give some thought to what kind of effects they would like to have. This requires a longer-term perspective than we are used to; we are generally not very good at seeing beyond today's crisis. It also requires that U.S. policymakers make up their minds about whether the United States would like to see Gorbachev's reforms work and improve the Soviet economy, which could either make the Soviet Union a more formidable adversary or a better neighbor, or whether what the United States really wants is to see the Soviet system as it is now collapse.

In any case, U.S. policymakers have to proceed without illusions. They have to accept the fact that this is fundamentally a competitive relationship, that the Soviet Union still has residual commitments to a view of history that is at variance with and in conflict with that of the United States, and that there are aspects of the Soviet system of control that are repugnant to American values. But U.S. policymakers have to ask themselves how to manage that competition more rationally so that it is less likely to lead to war and to high and destructive tensions. They also have to be more conscious than they have been about how U.S. actions help to shape the tone and direction of changes in Soviet behavior.

The United States needs to make it clear, as Gorbachev faces his options for the future, that if he sees a Soviet self-interest in moving toward some greater restraint and responsibility in Soviet behavior in the world, and in continuing the trend of recent years toward a foreign policy based more upon pragmatic nation-state interests rather than upon a revolutionary ideology, that the United States is prepared to respond in the interest of a less dangerous and more productive relationship.

Clearly the Soviets will also have some choices to make. They will have to have learned the lesson that their exploitation of areas of political upheaval in the Third World cannot help but affect their relations with the United States. They will have to have learned that such egregious violations of international norms as they have committed and are committing in Afghanistan continue to prejudice their acceptance in the community of nations. They will have to have learned that the total intolerance of any expression of variant views by their own citizens, administered by the arbitrary actions of political police (an organization that tends to take on a life of its own, as such organizations do wherever regimes place their reliance upon control of the population by political police), not only prejudices the acceptance of the Soviet Union as a modern great power, but deprives the country of the full creativity of its own people. But it should also be clear that the condition most favorable to modifications of Soviet behavior in these respects is a nonthreatening environment. This is a lesson that the United States has not fully absorbed.

Finally, what are the obstacles to a move in these directions? Why is it that organizations like the Arms Control Association have not been more effective in gaining political support for a more rational way of advancing U.S. security and of managing the nation's competitive relations with the Soviet Union? Clearly, the political trends in the United States are currently adverse. The United States is still in the midst of a conservative swing in its domestic politics that has been linked to a resurgence of nationalism in foreign policy. The voices of opposition to these trends are strangely subdued and are relatively ineffective. An excess of political caution has muted the voices of those from whom alternative approaches might have been expected. The fear of being thought soft on Communism and weak on defense is still a powerful inhibition in U.S. political life.

Has not the time come to discard these sterile stereotypes from the past? What is at issue is not the "hard-soft bugaboo," but to see with greater clarity what the interests of the United States really are, without illusions about the depth of the competition with the Soviet Union, or about the directions in which present U.S. policies are leading. Has not the time come for the United States to awaken from its period of sleepwalking toward a situation that will endanger its own security interests, will intensify strains in its alliance relationships, and will push the Soviets toward a more intransigent and bellicose entrenchment in the bunkered mentality of the past?

A civil dialogue has begun, and for that we can be thankful. But the time has come to put some content into that dialogue. That content should come from some fresh thinking about how U.S. interests are affected by the potentially profound changes that may be taking place in the Soviet Union, and how the United States can, in some degree, influence the direction of those changes. *(November –December 1985)*

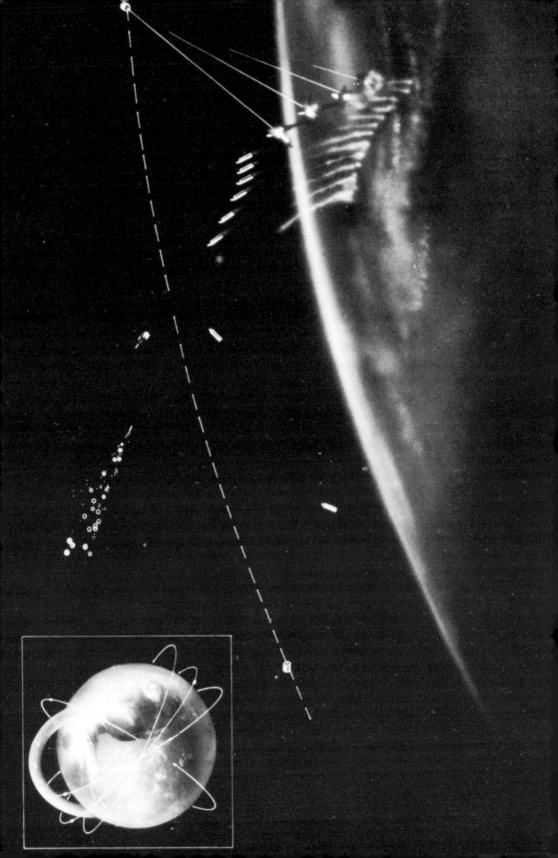

2

Star Wars and the Race in Space

On March 23, 1983, President Reagan went on national television to deliver a speech in support of his defense budget request then before Congress. He addressed the Soviet threat and his administration's effort "to rebuild America's defenses and strengthen the peace." He then proposed a dramatic alternative that came as a surprise to almost everyone, including most of his security advisors:

> Let me share with you a vision of the future which offers hope. It is that we embark on a program to counter the awesome Soviet missile threat with measures that are defensive. . . . What if free people could live secure in the knowledge that their security did not rest upon the threat of instant U.S. retaliation to deter a Soviet attack, that we could intercept and destroy strategic ballistic missiles before they reached our own soil or that of our allies?
>
> . . . I call upon the scientific community in our country, those who gave us nuclear weapons, to turn their great talents now to the cause of mankind and world peace, to give us the means of rendering these nuclear weapons impotent and obsolete.

Overnight, the president's proposal initiated the most fundamental defense controversy in the post-war period. Labeled "Star Wars," the program was criticized as technically infeasible, costly, and destabilizing. But the president pushed ahead, signing several directives to restructure previous U.S. missile defense efforts and initiating two study groups, the Fletcher and Hoffman panels, to identify the technological requirements and the strategic implications of his goal. The Strategic Defense Initiative Organization was established within the Department of Defense and Lt. General James Abrahamson was appointed as director. In the fiscal year 1986 budget request, Star Wars was a six-year, $33 billion program. Though difficult to forecast, estimates for the actual deployment of a nationwide antiballistic missile system run in the neighborhood of $1 trillion. In testimony before the House Armed Services Committee in November 1983, Richard DeLauer, under secretary of research, development, and engineering for the Department of Defense, said, "Every single one of [the nine different SDI research areas] is equivalent to or greater than the Manhattan project."

Despite these formidable obstacles, the president has sold the program on the basis that it will defend America from nuclear war. The president's argument is that strategic defenses will finally make disarmament a real possibility, a view expressed by Secretary of State George Shultz:

> The pace of technological advance now opens possibilities for new ways of strategic thinking—never an easy process. The vehemence of some of the criticism of the President's Strategic Defense Initiative (SDI) seems to come less from the argument over technological feasibility—which future research will answer one way or another in an objective manner—than from the passionate defense of orthodox doctrine in the face of changing strategic realities. We are proceeding with SDI research because we see a positive and, indeed, revolutionary potential: defensive measures may become available that could render obsolete the threat of an offensive first strike. A new strategic equilibrium based on defensive technologies and sharply reduced offensive deployments is likely to be the most stable and secure arrangement of all.
>
> Our concept can be described as follows: during the next ten years, the U.S. objective is a radical reduction in the power of existing and planned offensive nuclear arms, as well as the stabilization of the relationship between offensive and defensive nuclear arms, whether on earth or in space. We are even now looking forward to a period of transition to a more stable world, with greatly reduced levels of nuclear arms and an enhanced ability to deter war based upon an increasing contribution of nonnuclear defenses against offensive nuclear arms. This period of transition could lead to the eventual elimination of all nuclear arms, both offensive and defensive. A world free of nuclear arms is an ultimate objective to which we, the Soviet Union, and all other nations can agree.

Soviet leaders see the ultimate objective of Star Wars as something quite different from total disarmament. They argue that President Reagan's program is designed to give the United States strategic superiority and will only result in a destabilizing arms race in both offensive and defensive weapons. They believe that the Strategic Defense Initiative completely contradicts the 1972 Antiballistic Missile Treaty in both letter and spirit. In the Nuclear Arms and Space Talks, the Soviets have linked reductions in offensive nuclear weapons to restraint on development of strategic defenses. The Reagan administration remains committed to the pursuit of strategic defense, and SDI is clearly the fundamental barrier to progress at the Geneva talks.

The articles in this chapter investigate the technical and political dimensions of the Strategic Defense Initiative, with a special emphasis on its implications for arms control. Since technological developments for antisatellite (ASAT) weapons overlap antimissile technology, an article concerning ASATs is included. As a whole, the section evaluates what Reagan calls "an effort which holds the promise of changing the course of human history" and attempts to determine whether that change in course would be for better or worse.

The Case for Arms Control and the Strategic Defense Initiative

George A. Keyworth II

Arms control, if it is to produce lasting benefits, must achieve three goals. It must reduce the risk of nuclear war, it must reduce the levels of arms, and it must lessen the consequences of war. The modern history of arms control has focused almost entirely on the first of those goals—reducing the risk of war strictly through deterrence—and allowed the other two factors to grow to unacceptably large proportions. Not surprisingly, the people of the world are no longer willing to accept assurances that the risk of war is so low that the other factors can be overlooked.

The first condition of any arms control step we contemplate should be that it increases stability, and I agree with those who assert that stability is less a matter of numbers of weapons than of balance of forces. For that reason the movements to freeze the current numbers of nuclear weapons or to seek modest reductions in stockpiles that already number in the tens of thousands of warheads have little bearing on any of those three elements of arms control. At best such schemes are a kind of "phantom arms control" that enables people to feel that they have achieved something when conditions are in fact unchanged.

On the other hand, I *disagree* with those who claim that the mutual buildups of weapons by the United States and the Soviet Union—and the posture of mutual assured destruction—over the past two decades have produced acceptable stability that can be taken for granted into the future. Working against that stability is the inevitable march of technology, technology that has, over the past decade, steadily eroded both nations' ability to protect their nuclear forces against a preemptive strike. Although the United States still has an ample margin of protection because of its ability to retaliate using submarines that can remain hidden at sea, the nation can no longer rely on the survivability of either its land-based missiles or its aircraft. The Soviets have built such a huge arsenal of land-based ICBMs, and they have so improved their technology that virtually all the U.S. fixed-base weapons systems are at high risk in the event of a Soviet preemptive attack. And with the Soviets now concentrating massive resources on antisubmarine warfare, U.S. policymakers have to face the possibility that some day submarines too may become vulnerable.

This possibility of preemptive attack—whether as an outright bolt-from-the-blue first strike or as a disabling blow at an early stage of escalating conventional hostilities—has been the single most destabilizing factor in the arms race. At worst it has caused each side to proliferate in order to retain a survivable retaliatory force.

At best it has allowed neither side to back down one inch. The preemptive option dominates defense planning and public anxiety for good reason, because it increasingly confers the perception of an advantage on the side that strikes first. Obviously, stability demands that there be an unmistakable *dis*advantage for the aggressor, yet we are moving steadily in the wrong direction.

How, then, can we change our course? How can we reestablish the more stable situation that existed two decades ago when the retaliatory consequences to the aggressor clearly outweighed any first-strike advantage? Our first step would have to ensure that a preemptive strike would fail resoundingly.

Strategic defense can be the vital catalyst toward that goal. Few of its critics any longer deny that it might be possible for the United States to develop a highly effective antiballistic missile defense. Taking advantage of technologies simply not available during the earlier ABM debates of the late 1960s, the United States now can project the means to destroy Soviet ICBMs during their boost phases, thereby largely negating two of the attributes that make ICBMs such potent offensive weapons: their ability to proliferate by merely MIRVing and their ability to decoy. Boost-phase defenses would attack the ICBMs at their most vulnerable time, and then would be augmented by additional defense layers that would come into play later in the ICBM flight path—to catch those that are not destroyed by the earlier defenses.

These would not necessarily be "leakproof" defenses, especially during early transition phases. But they do not have to be. In its initial implementation, strategic defenses have only to negate the first strike option to achieve a great leap in stability. After all, a first strike, or a preemptive strike, is an all-or-nothing military gamble. It cannot partly succeed, because a first strike virtually guarantees unacceptable retribution upon the attacker unless it essentially removes the other side's ability to retaliate. No military planner would seriously contemplate a first strike unless he had very high confidence that his opponent would be crippled by it—that is, unable to retaliate.

Why is this defense against ICBMs, as opposed to defenses against other offensive weapons, so important? The reason is that the Soviets have chosen, over the past twenty years, to emphasize land-based ICBMs as their weapons of choice. ICBMs constitute 75 percent of the Soviet strategic force, a force that has six times the payload capacity of the U.S. ICBM fleet. In spite of that margin the Soviets have steadfastly insisted, in arms negotiations, that their six- or eight-to-one advantage in prompt hard-target killers must be maintained. Why? While the United States structures its nuclear weapons as a retaliatory deterrent, their strategy is to maintain a preemptive strike option to curtail any possible reprisal on the part of the United States in case of war. That difference in the way nuclear weapons are perceived is the primary reason the two countries have made so little progress in achieving meaningful arms reductions over decades of trying. It is also one of the most frightening aspects of the strategic mismatch, because the Soviet bias toward preemption can cause rapid and terrible escalation in the event of hostilities.

But an antiballistic defense could, in short order, drastically devalue those ICBMs as *preemptive* weapons. The Soviets are justly concerned about this new direction in U.S. defense, because it forces them to make serious changes in their fundamental weapons systems and strategies.

There are three critical questions about how the Soviets will respond, either now or a few years from now when U.S. research programs have made even clearer that SDI will work.

1. Will the Soviets find technical means to overcome U.S. defenses?

Critics initially suggested many ways by which the ABM defense might be thwarted, but none of them, when looked at seriously, is practical. Spinning a booster to spread the destructive power of a laser beam does not work when a laser attacks with a short pulse rather than with heat. Coating the booster to reflect laser light has the same fault. Armoring the booster against a beam pulse adds so much weight to the booster that it drastically reduces the payload capacity. In effect, it de-MIRVs the Soviet Strategic Rocket Force. A fast-burn booster would still have to pass through a vulnerable phase as it exits the lower atmosphere. And trying to saturate the defense system, while that would have worked against the terminal defenses proposed in the late 1960s, becomes prohibitively expensive against a sustainable boost-phase defense that knocks out whole ICBMs. For the sake of argument, even an 80 percent effective boost-phase defense would require an enormous—and enormously expensive—increase in the Soviets' fleet. They would have to increase their booster fleet by a factor of five just to achieve the same number of warheads passing through merely the first layer of the defense. But in addition to that problem they still would have no assurance of *which* warheads would get through—which means no assurance of which targets could be attacked. The Soviets' traditional preemptive strategy would simply be incompatible with such a boost-phase dominated defense.

2. Will the Soviets view the U.S. action as so threatening that they might consider taking preemptive steps before the U.S. system can be implemented?

While the Soviets hardly welcome the United States' ABM plans, which can force them to write off their massive investment in ICBMs, they know that nothing will happen suddenly to threaten them. In any case, the Soviets themselves are actively pursuing (though pretending they are not) their own ABM defenses and in all likelihood will be phasing them in during the same general time that the United States could be. There would be no time during this gradual shift from virtually all offensive weapons to a mix of offensive and defensive when either side would be without powerful means to retaliate against a preemptive attack by the other.

3. Will the Soviets conclude that their margin in ICBMs is becoming meaningless and agree, at last, to serious negotiations to reduce ICBMs?

When they look seriously at the loss of utility of their ICBMs as a preemptive force, the Soviets will have no choice but to admit that the age of the ICBM as *the* dominant weapon is passing. They, and the United States, will no doubt begin to replace ICBMs with other weapons, but in so doing the United States will be phasing out the most feared and most destabilizing of the nuclear weapons. This is the key issue and, to my mind, the strongest reason the United States has to pursue the strategic defense initiative. With the ICBM tarnished and with the need to look to other options to preserve national security, both the Soviets and the United States will have a mutual basis on which to negotiate reductions in ICBM forces. If ICBMs serve only to retaliate in case the other side does attack first, then both sides can consider truly massive reductions in ICBM warheads. Ten or twenty nuclear weapons are virtually all the retaliatory deterrent that any country needs—and those are the levels of weapons that arms controls ought to be aiming for. *(April 1985)*

The Real Relationship between Star Wars and Arms Control
McGeorge Bundy

In the two years since President Reagan's Star Wars speech of March 23, 1983, there has been a gradual clarification of the issues his initiative presents. Some false hopes have been largely cleared away and quite different objectives have been put forward. But illusions persist, and we are still in the early stages of the kind of analysis the subject needs. In particular, there remains great confusion as to the real relation between Star Wars and the pursuit of the limitation of nuclear armaments. Let me briefly describe the present realities as I understand them.

First, almost no one except the president himself and the self-styled "true believer," Caspar Weinberger, continues to hold out the hope that any remotely achievable defense can make nuclear weapons "impotent and obsolete." The Pentagon continues to insist on the indispensability of a large and varied set of new strategic nuclear systems, as do Soviet commanders. The number of strategic warheads on both sides is rapidly rising. What is perhaps still more serious, new and sweeping strategic doctrines on the U.S. side require U.S. military leaders to "prevail" in a series of nuclear battles fought under totally unpredictable conditions. These doctrines are creating entirely understandable pressure from responsible military planners for still larger and more varied forces designed not to be impotent and obsolete but to be highly survivable and usable. A cynic could be forgiven for supposing that Star Wars is merely a protective political shield for the deployment of such weapons as MX.

Second, it is now entirely clear that unless and until there is a drastic modification in the current positions of Moscow or Washington or both, the Star Wars program will block any prospect of new arms control agreements. Administration spokesmen tell us that Star Wars has brought the Soviet Union back to Geneva.

They may well be partly right, although the more powerful force is probably the Kremlin's belated recognition that its walkout at the end of 1983 was a severe self-inflicted wound in the battle for European opinion. But what administration spokesmen neglect is the self-evident reality that the Soviet purpose in Geneva is to attack Star Wars, not to negotiate any agreement that makes its objective legitimate.

On the U.S. side, initial hopes, in which I shared, that Mr. Reagan's genuine desire for a good agreement would lead him to modify his commitment to Star Wars have been disappointed. The administration has now made it entirely clear that Star Wars will not be used in any way as a bargaining chip. The administration's objective remains the achievement by negotiation of dramatic reductions in offensive weapons, and especially in Soviet heavy land-based missiles, but not by bargaining on Star Wars. No one inside the government and no outside supporter of Star Wars has yet explained how it is possible to hope that the Soviet Union will agree to dramatic reductions in its most prized weapons at a time when the existence of the Star Wars program is bound to be seen in Moscow as imposing a requirement for the most energetic reinforcement of all forms of Soviet nuclear capabilities—offensive, defensive, and counterdefensive.

Third, the increasing implausibility of Mr. Reagan's sunny hopes is producing from administration spokesmen an increasingly honest explanation that the deeper motive for the Star Wars program is fear, and in particular a continuing fear of the possibility of a Soviet first strike. Like the Committee on the Present Danger, from which so many of them came, these people simply do not accept the conclusion of the Scowcroft Commission that no strategic window of vulnerability exists at present. Sweeping assertions of the danger of a Soviet preemptive strike are increasingly the order of the day. The multiple uncertainties and hazards in any such attack are regularly ignored. Star Wars is defended by such advocates as Edward Teller on the ground that it will increase Soviet uncertainties, but honest analysis of the existing strategic balance, and of any remotely in prospect for the next generation, continues to demonstrate that the risk of self-destruction in any first strike is already overwhelming and will so remain. The nuclear age has been full of false hope and unreal fear, but it is hard to find another instance in which the former has been so flagrantly used as a political shield for the latter.

Fourth, recently there has been important signs of a more reasonable line of argument from the administration. In January the White House issued a pamphlet in which it was expressly stated that the Star Wars program would not move beyond research unless and until the defensive systems under analysis could be shown to meet a double requirement of survivability and cost-effectiveness. On February 20, Paul Nitze developed this line of argument more fully in an important speech in Philadelphia. The acceptance of these requirements, in particular that of cost-effectiveness, in itself gives the lie to the notion that there is any prospect of a defense that would truly make nuclear weapons impotent, because no ordinary question of cost-effectiveness would govern a decision to buy such a system.

I believe that critics of the Star Wars program should enthusiastically accept these tests of survivability and cost-effectiveness, and should focus their efforts on the ways and means of ensuring that the tests are applied by dispassionate and fair-minded analysts, and not by people who have already decided in favor of space-based defenses. In matters of such gravity, the advocate must not be the judge. The weight of independent technical judgment has been and still is that space-based defenses cannot meet either the test of survivability or that of cost-effectiveness. If that judgment is not overturned, the administration now recognizes that there should be no such deployment. Conversely, if that judgment is credibly reversed on the basis of further research, then the case for a Star Wars program becomes entirely different, although I believe that the program should also be required to meet a third and different test: that of contributing to the stability of mutual deterrence. This is the test that was so tragically neglected in the cardinal case of MIRV.

Fifth, we should note that, largely under pressure from Prime Minister Margaret Thatcher, the administration has now emphatically committed itself to a prolonged research phase in which it has promised to respect the provisions of the ABM Treaty. Here again it is important that the judgment as to what is lawful research and what is a trespass against the treaty should be made not by advocates but by uncommitted and dispassionate authorities. To put it bluntly, it would be a grave error to entrust this judgment to any self-confessed true believer. Whether the period in which the entire program will be confined to research is three years or ten—and Mr. Nitze's speech leaves doubt on the point—it is vital that U.S. respect for the treaty be maintained in a way that is credible beyond the circle of the zealous friends of Star Wars.

Sixth, no one can or should oppose a sensibly designed program of research in this field. The administration is right when it insists that there must be adequate insurance against a possible Soviet breakout, but this requirement can be met with research at a budgetary level far below the one the administration now projects.

Finally, the friends of arms control will do well to focus intense and continuing effort on the prevention of any premature weaponization of space. Unless and until the tests of survivability, cost-effectiveness, and contribution to stability can be persuasively met, the case for going slowly in space is overwhelming. The complex interface between missile defense and antisatellite capabilities is such that those of us who believe in the limitation of the arms race should strenuously insist on restraint, unilateral if necessary and bilateral if possible, in the development of all forms of space weapons. Congress should extend and reinforce the current moratorium on ASAT testing, and Soviet interest in the ways and means of protecting space from the nuclear arms race makes that question the one promising area for serious exploration in Geneva. *(April 1985)*

Reviving the ABM Debate
Albert Carnesale

The following article was written for the April 1981 issue of Arms Control Today, *two years before President Reagan announced the Strategic Defense Initiative. Dr. Carnesale pointed to developments in technology and strategy that he predicted would propel antiballistic missile issues to center stage in future arms control debates. This prescient analysis is still very relevant today.*

The 1972 Treaty on the Limitation of Antiballistic Missile Systems was perceived widely as the obituary for the United States' domestic debate over whether to deploy an ABM system. In light of the stringency of the treaty limitations on the development, testing, and deployment of ABM systems, termination of the debate was an understandable expectation.

The ABM Treaty

Embodied as the basic principle of the ABM Treaty is the undertaking by the Soviet Union and by the United States "not to deploy ABM systems for the defense of the territory of its country and not to provide a base for such a defense." An ABM system is defined as "a system to counter strategic ballistic missiles or their elements in flight trajectory, currently consisting of . . . ABM interceptor missiles, . . . ABM launchers, . . . and . . . ABM radars."

Under the treaty (as modified by a 1974 protocol), each side is permitted one geographically, quantitatively, and qualitatively constrained ABM deployment— either at its national capital or at an ICBM deployment area. Technological innovation is inhibited by provisions banning the development, testing, and deployment of "ABM systems or components which are sea-based, air-based, space-based, or mobile land-based" and of "ABM interceptor missiles for the delivery by each interceptor missile of more than one independently guided warhead." Moreover, the agreement provides that if exotic new "ABM systems based on other physical principles and including components capable of substituting for ABM interceptor missiles, ABM launchers, or ABM radars are created in the future," their deployment would be prohibited unless specific limitations were agreed upon through consultation and amendment of the treaty.

The ABM Treaty is of unlimited duration. The two sides are to review the agreement at five-year intervals, but the treaty remains in force unless one or both of the parties takes positive action to terminate it. (Either party may withdraw upon six months notice "if it decides that extraordinary events related to the subject matter of this Treaty have jeopardized its supreme interest.")

The World Has Changed

The world has not remained as it was when the treaty was ratified on October 3, 1972. While the vital signs of the ABM debate have been obscured for almost a decade, it appears that the patient is about to be revived (either by resuscitation or by resurrection). Even the jargon has been transformed: the term antiballistic missile (ABM) system is now less fashionable than ballistic missile defense (BMD), though the two are used interchangeably to describe systems for defense against ballistic missiles.

Most fundamental are the changes in the political and military setting. A central characteristic of the American political scene at the time of SALT I was disenchantment with the war in Vietnam and an attendant hostility toward all things military, including ballistic missile defense. Ending the war, establishing an opening to China, achieving détente in relations with the Soviet Union, and limiting nuclear weapons were high priority goals for the United States. Now America has emerged from its post-Vietnam era, the "China card" is firmly in hand, détente is viewed as a disappointment (at best), the SALT II agreements have been rejected, and the Soviets are seen as adventurous and expansionist.

The balance of offensive strategic forces, which a decade ago tipped in favor of the United States, now is roughly level; indeed, in the view of some this balance now tips in favor of the Soviet Union. At the conclusion of SALT I the Soviets had not yet tested a MIRVed missile: now MIRVs of high yield and high accuracy are characteristic of the Soviet missile force. The numerical balance of defensive strategic weapons—BMD and air defenses—remains much as it was a decade ago; that is, decidedly in favor of the Soviet Union. The Galosh ABM system, with its number of launchers for interceptor missiles reduced from sixty-four to thirty-two, remains deployed around Moscow. Meanwhile a U.S. ABM system at Grand Forks, North Dakota, has gone through the full cycle of having been constructed, operated, and dismantled. In the field of air defense, the Soviets continue to modernize their massive network of surface-to-air missile (SAM) systems, while the United States has for all practical purposes completed the phasing out of its SAM deployments.

The Basic Questions

While the environment in which BMD-related decisions are made has been altered considerably over the past decade, the important underlying issues have changed hardly at all. The key questions remain these:

For what missions (if any) are BMD deployments needed?

Would BMD deployments based upon the technologies currently available provide adequate protection against projected threats?

What would be the effects of BMD deployments upon the strategic balance and upon strategic stability?

What would be the effects of BMD deployments upon the United States' relations with its allies?

What would be the effects of BMD deployments upon the proliferation of nuclear weapons?

What would be the effects of BMD development, testing, and deployments upon the prospects for arms control?

It is useful to examine each of these issues, and to identify those considerations that have changed since SALT I and those that have not.

For What Missions (If Any) Are BMD Deployments Needed?

At the time of Salt I several BMD missions were under consideration by the United States: a "thick" area defense for protection of the population and economic base against even a massive Soviet attack; a "thin" area defense to protect against a potential Chinese threat or against accidental or unauthorized launches from any source; and a localized defense of B-52 bases and Minuteman silos. The thick defense notion was abandoned because it could not be accomplished with the BMD technologies then (or now) available; the thin defense against a yet-to-emerge Chinese threat was unable to attract popular support; and the survivability at that time of the bombers and ICBMs was unquestioned.

Estimates differed widely on the length of time over which the salutory survivability condition could be expected to persist, and ABM supporters came to focus primarily on the ICBM defense mission.

Today ICBM defense is the only BMD mission to receive serious attention. Most analysts agree that by the mid-1980s the Soviets could have the capability to destroy in a first strike more than 90 percent of the Minuteman force, and there is little relief in sight. Some form of shell-game deployment scheme for the MX missile might come into being in the early 1990s, but few would bet on it. Moreover, some analysts argue that even that system might not be able to achieve acceptable levels of ICBM survivability without BMD.

Would BMD Deployments Based upon the Technologies Currently Available Provide Adequate Protection against Projected Threats?

Critics of BMD argued a decade ago that a BMD deployment would be inadequately reliable, excessively vulnerable, and cost-ineffective. They cited the inherent sophistication of BMD technology, the complexity of the integrated system, the inability (because of the Limited Test Ban Treaty) to test either the nuclear kill mechanism relied upon to neutralize incoming reentry vehicles or the effects of nuclear detonations upon radar performance, the infeasibility of a full-scale test under operational conditions, and the potential vulnerability of the system to countermeasures such as saturation decoys, chaff, electronic jamming, radar blackout, and maneuvering reentry vehicles. The BMD proponents countered that deployment of a system (namely, Safeguard) based on then current technology, despite its (in their view exaggerated) imperfections, would increase the cost (in deliverable offensive warheads, and, therefore, in rubles) to the Soviets of an attack against U.S. land-based strategic forces and would vastly complicate Soviet calculations of the effectiveness of such an attack.

The basic arguments of BMD opponents and proponents have changed little in the intervening decade. BMD technology has improved, but the current and projected threats are more formidable than before.

What Would Be the Effects of BMD Deployments upon the Strategic Balance and upon Strategic Stability?

BMD affects the operational utility of strategic offensive forces. To be useful in a retaliatory role, the forces should be capable of surviving an attack and subsequently penetrating to designated targets in the homeland of the adversary. The survivability of one's ICBMs and to a small extent one's heavy bombers could be enhanced by one's deployment of a defense against ballistic missile attack, but deployment of BMD by the adversary would degrade the penetrability of all of one's offensive weapons—ICBMs and SLBMs directly, and bombers and cruise missiles indirectly (by affecting adversely the execution of precursor ballistic missile attacks upon the air defenses).

The tension between survivability and penetrability is at its worst with area defenses, for such defenses degrade penetration to all retaliatory targets, counterforce and countervalue. The tension is at a minimum when defenses are limited geographically and qualitatively to localized protection of ICBMs, for then penetration to countervalue retaliatory targets such as cities is unimpaired. Indeed, BMD deployments that enhance the prelaunch survivability of offensive strategic forces without degrading their ability to penetrate to countervalue targets would, in principle, enhance strategic stability.

What Would Be the Effects of BMD Deployments upon the United States' Relations with Its Allies?

How a U.S. BMD would affect relations between the United States and its allies has been and continues to be unclear. The anti-BMD argument is that U.S. defense would be viewed by U.S. allies as an attempt to make their homelands, rather than the United States, the targets of choice. The pro-BMD line is that reduced U.S. vulnerability would be attractive to the allies because it would increase U.S. willingness to risk escalation of a war that might start elsewhere (for example, in Europe.)

The effect on U.S. allies of Soviet BMD deployments is more easily seen. The missile forces of the United Kingdom and France now can penetrate with high confidence to virtually any target in the Soviet Union. If the Soviets were to deploy BMD at levels significantly higher than those now permitted by the ABM Treaty, the British and French independent deterrent forces could be neutralized.

What Would Be the Effects of BMD Deployments upon the
Proliferation of Nuclear Weapons?

Any direct connection between perturbations in the magnitude or structure of the massive strategic arsenals of the superpowers and the acquisition of nuclear weapons by additional countries remains elusive. BMD opponents maintain that U.S. and/or Soviet BMD deployments would be viewed as further steps in the arms race and, therefore, would undermine the Nonproliferation Treaty. They note that in Article VI of the treaty each of the parties—including the United States and the Soviet Union—"undertakes to pursue negotiations in good faith on effective measures relating to cessation of the nuclear arms race at an early date . . ." They hold that the nonproliferation cause is more likely to suffer than to benefit if the ABM treaty—the principal accomplishment (for better or worse) of more than a decade of SALT—were to be scrapped. Moreover, they maintain, BMD deployments would signal the superpowers' intention to monopolize not only the ability to attack with nuclear weapons, but also to remain invulnerable to such an attack—a signal that is likely to be counterproductive. The proponents of BMD argue that BMD deployments by the superpowers would reduce incentives for proliferation by reducing the felt need for independent deterrent forces and by rendering small offensive arsenals useless against the heavily defended nations.

What Would Be the Effects of BMD Development, Testing,
and Deployments upon the Prospects for Arms Control?

BMD-related activities consistent with the provisions of the ABM Treaty are unlikely to affect the prospects for further arms control, but there can be no doubt that abrogation of the treaty would be a devastating blow to arms control—one from which it would not soon recover. The fuzzy areas are those that involve attempts (whether or not successful) to modify the treaty.

A fundamental arms control objective of the United States is to achieve meaningful constraints on Soviet arms. Such constraints are not available gratis. The price to be paid by the United States for constraints upon the Soviet threat is the acceptance of constraints upon U.S. forces. The benefit to the United States potentially to be derived by relaxing or eliminating the current constraints on BMD is the deployment of defenses that would enhance the survivability of U.S. ICBMs.

The potential cost to the United States is the deployment by the Soviet Union of BMD systems that could threaten the ability of U.S. strategic offensive forces— ICBMs, SLBMs, heavy bombers, and cruise missiles—to penetrate to (at least some of) their targets. In the end, the overall U.S. assessment of any proposed arms control accord—including a modified ABM Treaty—should be based primarily on a weighing in the balance of these benefits and costs.

In this light it is interesting, if not remarkable, that absent from the extensive public debates in the United States over arms control and BMD has been any sustained consideration of the implications for U.S. security of Soviet BMD deployments and programs. Rather, the debates have focused almost exclusively on the pros and cons of U.S. BMD.

The near-term U.S. interest in BMD deployment is confined to systems for defense of ICBMs. To deploy such defenses at a meaningful level would require modification of or abrogation of the ABM Treaty. In either of these events, the Soviets too would be free to deploy BMD. Only in the case of modification of the treaty would Soviet BMD be subject to mutually agreed constraints, and the revised constraints would be less stringent than those currently in effect.

The Choice

Choices must be made among realistic alternatives. A world in which the United States has strategically important BMD deployments, while the Soviet Union does not, is attractive to Americans, but in all likelihood it is unattainable. Similarly, a world in which the Soviet Union has important BMD deployments, while the United States does not, would be unacceptable to Americans. In the real world, either both nations will have significant BMD deployments, or neither nation will have them.

The ABM Treaty, with its severe constraints on ballistic missile defense, represents a joint U.S.-Soviet selection of a world in which neither side has a meaningful defense. To move from this non-BMD world to one is which both sides have extensive BMD deployments would be to gamble for high stakes; one possible outcome could be enhanced strategic stability, but another could be disastrous instability. The burden of proof rests on those who would have the United States make the move.   *(April 1981)*

Star Wars versus the ABM Treaty: Which Path Offers More Security?
Edward M. Kennedy

A time-honored adage cautions that those who cannot remember the past are condemned to repeat it. The Reagan administration and its "Star Wars" plan for defense against strategic missiles could bear out this warning on a scale never before imagined in both cost and strategic consequences.

Fifteen years ago, the Nixon administration eked out a one-vote victory in the Senate to maintain $1 billion in funding for the Safeguard antiballistic missile (ABM) system. The concern of the Senate was clearly demonstrated in this cliffhanger vote: many senators believed that an ABM system was too expensive, that it probably would not work anyway, and that its very presence would exacerbate tensions in a crisis. As President Eisenhower's science advisor, Dr. Herbert York, observed, "History is littered with Maginot Lines."

In 1972, a Democratic Senate consented to the ratification of the Antiballistic Missile Treaty—negotiated by a Republican administration with the Soviet Union— and agreed that the United States would not undertake "to deploy ABM systems for a defense of the territory of its country." So effective and beneficial has been the ABM Treaty that on two occasions both the United States and the Soviet Union have reviewed and reaffirmed its value as being in their continuing mutual interest. So manifestly ineffective are ABM systems that the United States has not even maintained the ABM fortifications allowed it by the treaty.

Today, however, the issue of ballistic missile defense is prominent once again, and the ABM Treaty is in serious jeopardy. The United States and the Soviet Union are careening down a path that could lead to the end of the treaty. As outlined in his Star Wars speech and in the Strategic Defense Initiative (SDI), President Reagan is working to commit the United States to developing an elaborate defense against ballistic missiles. For its part, the Soviet Union is pursuing programs that constitute an even more imminent threat to the treaty.

At the moment, the debate about the president's Strategic Defense Initiative is focused on the same questions that were debated in 1969. Will the system work as advertised? Will the system be prohibitively expensive? A statement I made then is as relevant today to President Reagan's vision of Star Wars ballistic missile defense as it was fifteen years ago to the Safeguard system: "It is the single most complex undertaking man has yet set for himself in his time on Earth—but if experience with previous national defense projects teaches any lesson it will be years late in completion and may never work at all."

While the question of SDI's effectiveness and cost are of paramount importance, there are more basic questions that have so far been ignored. We have now lived for twelve years with a treaty that bans the development, testing, and deployment of a nationwide ABM system. Will President Reagan's Strategic Defense Initiative violate the ABM Treaty? Has the treaty served U.S. national security interests in the past, and will it do so in the future? These are the questions that mandate national attention. It is time to have a thorough and thoughtful national debate on whether the ABM Treaty does or does not have continuing value to U.S. national security.

Would not it be ideal if we could escape from the madness of mutual assured destruction and actually construct a defensive shield that would protect Americans from the ravages of nuclear attack? Would not it be wonderful if we really could end the balance of terror called deterrence so that our children could go to sleep at night with some sense of security that, if their city or town were attacked, they would be defended and could wake up the next morning?

While this argument is understandably appealing, it is also illusory. It offers the lure of a perfect defense, of a sanitized battlefield filled with new technologies operating in outer space, hundreds of miles from vulnerable populations. This argument is, in fact, an invitation to scrap deterrence and assume instead a defensive posture that has all the security of a leaky umbrella in a rainstorm. It ignores at least three points, any of which alone would be reason enough to stick with the ABM Treaty.

First, strategic defense is only desirable if the system is 100 percent effective. If the United States were able to build a 95 percent effective ABM system and if the Soviets were to launch a nuclear attack on the United States in which 5,000 of their 8,000 missile warheads were released, 250 warheads would still penetrate U.S. defenses and reach the U.S. population, easily annihilating the nation. With an unimaginable success rate of 99 percent, this hypothetical attack would result in 50 warheads falling on the nation.

In fact, the very technologies that have so stimulated President Reagan's optimism over the SDI—the X-ray and excimer lasers—can be rendered ineffective by relatively simple and cheap countermeasures. The deployment of a missile defense system will inevitably lead to the development of countermeasures followed by counter-countermeasures, and so forth. One such countermeasure would be simply to multiply the number of missiles, or the number of warheads and decoys, to overwhelm the ballistic missile defense system with sheer numbers. Components of the defense system, particularly weapons based on space platforms, will also be vulnerable to direct attack by many types of Soviet weapons.

Second, a nationwide defense system can never really be tested. Although components of the system can be tested separately under controlled conditions, the system as a whole cannot be tested short of an actual nuclear war. The people of the United States will take little comfort in an untested defense system, particularly a system as complex as that contemplated in the Star Wars defense.

Third, even the proponents of an elaborate antiballistic missile defense system concede that it cannot prevent strategic bombers, cruise missiles, or depressed-trajectory (low-flying) ballistic missiles from reaching their targets in a nuclear war. Even proponents of such a system recognize these shortcomings and have recommended more traditional air defense weapons to combat these threats.

It is, in short, a cruel and fatal illusion to contend that the Strategic Defense Initiative can ever be foolproof. As the Congressional Office of Technology Assessment recently concluded, SDI technology is "so remote that it should not serve as the basis of public expectation or national policy."

In light of the U.S. inability to produce a foolproof defense system, the Soviets can only conclude that a U.S. decision to go forward with such a system is actually intended to defend against a ragged retaliatory attack by the Soviet Union *after* a first strike by the United States. Indeed, recent congressional testimony indicates that, because of technological obstacles, the Reagan administration is changing the goals of the SDI from protection of people to defense of land-based missile silos. Ironically, rather than being part of a purely defensive strategy, the development of an elaborate ABM system can only be seen by the other side as being an *offensive* move.

The problem is that such a defense would not only protect U.S. ICBMs from a Soviet first strike, it would theoretically give the United States a nuclear war-fighting capability. Such a partial missile defense is likely to stir the phantom of nuclear superiority and in the process intensify the arms race in offensive weapons. That strategic defense makes sense only as a measure for achieving a first-strike capability against the Soviet Union is one of the most destabilizing, dangerous aspects of the entire undertaking.

The great virtue claimed by the Reagan administration for its Strategic Defense Initiative—that it would protect people and permit the United States to abolish offensive nuclear weapons—is a hollow promise. SDI's true function is coming to light: to build a defense to protect missiles, not people, and in the process to abandon the ABM Treaty.

Compliance with the ABM Treaty

The layered defense against ballistic missiles envisioned by President Reagan in the SDI is, in my view, plainly inconsistent with the ABM Treaty. The administration's plans to develop missile defenses and their components will either require a withdrawal from the treaty or result in a violation of it very soon.

Although the precise nature of the system that would be deployed under the SDI program is as yet undetermined, it is likely to include use of lasers and other directed-energy weapons to attack missiles and reentry vehicles. Such directed energy weapons are expected to be deployed in space, but might also be land-based or deployed aboard airborne platforms.

However, Article V of the ABM Treaty commits each nation not to "develop, test or deploy ABM systems or components which are sea-based, air-based, space-based or mobile land-based." Under the interpretation of the term "development" offered by the United States, the prohibition takes effect at the point that ABM systems or components enter the field-testing or engineering development phase. In other words, if the SDI's research and development program proceeds on schedule, then before the end of the 1980s it will have to be decided whether to risk abrogation of the ABM Treaty.

The Reagan administration has tried to assure Congress that the research associated with the SDI can be conducted within the terms of the ABM Treaty and that development is a long way off. But development and testing could undermine U.S. compliance with the treaty before the end of a second Reagan term. Indeed, the 1984–88 Defense Guidance submitted by Secretary of Defense Weinberger states that the United States plans to initiate "the prototype development of space-based weapons systems . . . so that we will be prepared to deploy fully developed and operationally ready systems." The Fletcher Panel, which was appointed by President Reagan to examine the technological feasibility of the SDI, recommended that demonstrations of key components of a missile defense system be conducted by the end of the decade. In January 1984, following the Fletcher Panel's recommendations, the president signed National Security Decision Directive (NSDD) No. 119, which directs the SDI program manager to conduct four major demonstrations of critical missile defense technologies before 1990. Such testing will violate the ABM treaty.

Immediate Threats to the ABM Treaty

While there can be no dispute that the administration's proposed Strategic Defense Initiative and corresponding programs inside the Soviet Union pose the most serious long-term threats to the treaty, current developments in both countries already place the treaty in serious jeopardy. Of particular concern is the development of advanced air defenses that may have ballistic missile defense capabilities. In addition, there is the recent exchange of charges and countercharges of treaty violations. Taken together, these trends suggest that the superpowers are approaching a point—Star Wars aside—where they must either reaffirm their commitment to the treaty and take concrete steps to renew it, or risk its abrogation.

The compliance issue has become particularly disconcerting since the recent discovery of a large phased-array radar near Krasnoyarsk in the vicinity of Soviet ICBM fields in central Siberia. A report from the Reagan administration issued in January 1984 stated that this radar is "almost certainly" a violation of the treaty's prohibition against deploying early warning radars except if they are located on the periphery of the national territory and oriented outward. This provision was meant to prevent either nation from deploying early warning radars that could be expanded for use in a nationwide missile defense network.

Ultimately, the Soviet Union must address this charge directly if the integrity of the ABM Treaty is to be preserved. To date, instead of providing countervailing evidence, halting construction of the radar, or even dismantling it, the Soviets have issued a countercharge that the U.S. Pave Paws early-warning radar network is being upgraded to perform a ballistic missile defense (BMD) role. Although two new Pave Paws facilities (to be constructed in Texas and Georgia) can provide warning for significant portions of the continental United States, they are in keeping with the treaty's requirements as to location of deployment, and they therefore do not raise a serious compliance question.

There is further evidence that the Soviets intend to push the ABM Treaty to its limits. Of immediate concern is the issue of whether the Soviet Union is redesigning its widely deployed, surface-to-air antiaircraft missiles (SAMs) to give them an ABM capability, and thereby quickly place the United States at a strategic disadvantage. The treaty prohibits both nations from testing non-ABM missiles in "an ABM mode"—against a target having a flight trajectory characteristic of a strategic ballistic missile. At the time the treaty was negotiated, the major U.S. concern was Soviet antiaircraft missiles. Today, the Soviet Union may be equally concerned about the U.S. development of the Patriot missile—an antiaircraft system that is sufficiently flexible to allow modification to an ABM capability. To deal with that concern, the Senate Armed Services Committee recently expressed its intention to limit the Patriot program to defend against short-range missiles consistent with the U.S. Army's stated goals for the missile.

Despite the administration's professed intention to pursue the SDI within the terms of the ABM Treaty, its current plans to demonstrate new space-based technology will violate the treaty. It will be difficult to ensure Soviet compliance with the treaty if the United States continues with programs that signal its willingness to ignore and eventually abrogate it. The Reagan administration may feel that such an overtly negative act as abrogation would be impolitic, so it may be using the SDI as a means to force the Soviet Union into withdrawing from the treaty first. The treaty provides the right for either nation to withdraw if it decides that new developments relating to the subject matter of the treaty jeopardize its supreme national interests.

How to Save the ABM Treaty

The question, therefore, arises, what can be done to save the ABM Treaty from being cast aside?

Congress must do everything in its power to prevent the administration from slipping through the backdoor into de facto abrogation of the treaty. The Senate Armed Services Committee has begun that process by directing the Reagan administration to conduct the SDI in strict compliance with the terms of the ABM Treaty during fiscal year 1985. Protecting the treaty will require not only prohibiting the funding of any weapons research or development that could violate it, but also applying congressional pressure on the administration to strengthen its commitment to the treaty. For an administration that views arms control as a trap, generating such pressure will require stimulating greater public awareness of the national security risks at stake if the United States withdraws from the ABM Treaty. The National Campaign to Save the ABM Treaty, recently launched by Ambassador Gerard Smith, the chief negotiator of the treaty, will serve this purpose very well.

In addition, we should not shy away from the idea of renegotiating certain provisions in the treaty to eliminate ambiguities that may encourage both nations to violate the spirit of the treaty. For example, the nature of ABM testing and the types of radars permitted under the treaty could be clarified. Serious proposals for change should come as no surprise to the Soviet Union since such proposals have already been discussed in the United States defense community for several years. Negotiating such changes would provide evidence for both sides that a permanent treaty can in fact be modified to take account of changing circumstances. The result would be a significant boon to the arms control process.

Rather than opening up the entire treaty for revisions, it might be more advisable to work within the confines of the Standing Consultative Commission (SCC) to secure supplemental "agreed statements" or "common understandings" to deal with treaty ambiguities. This process would not require renegotiation of treaty provisions, only clarification of existing restrictions.

Finally, the key to containing offensive strategic developments lies not in defensive technology, but in the successful negotiation of reductions in nuclear weapons. President Reagan and Secretary Weinberger have attempted to sell the Strategic Defense Initiative with the argument that it will eliminate the need for offensive nuclear weapons. Given that a leakproof defense is technologically impossible, nothing could be further from the truth. An arms race in defensive technology can *only* succeed in stimulating the offensive arms race as each side seeks to deploy countermeasures and greater numbers of offensive weapons to overwhelm any defense. The best way to reduce the threat posed by offensive weapons is to have an immediate, mutual, and verifiable nuclear freeze followed by major weapons reductions.

Conclusion

The ABM Treaty represents a joint recognition that effective nationwide defense against nuclear weapons is technologically impossible and that a partial defense would be strategically destabilizing. These principles are as valid today as they were when the treaty was ratified in 1972. The treaty is as much in the mutual interest of the United States and the Soviet Union today as it was in 1972. As President Reagan's own Commission on Strategic Forces has warned about the SDI, "The strategic implications of ballistic missile defense and the criticality of the ABM Treaty to further arms control agreements dictate extreme caution in proceeding to engineering development in this sensitive area."

For either country to abandon the ABM Treaty would be tantamount to wholesale rejection of arms control itself. Without the ABM Treaty, our world will instantly become more dangerous and more threatening, less stable and less secure. *(July–August 1984)*

How to Save the ABM Treaty
John B. Rhinelander

John B. Rhinelander, the legal adviser to the SALT I delegation, presented the follow-ing statement when he appeared before the House Foreign Affairs Subcommittee on Arms Control, International Security and Science on April 24, 1985. He testified on the Strategic Defense Initiative and antisatellite systems and their impact on the 1972 Anti-ballistic Missile Treaty. His statement, excerpted here, includes a concise appraisal of the compliance questions raised by U.S. and Soviet ABM programs. Mr. Rhinelander also critiques the administration's new SDI report and offers specific recommendations for enhancing the ABM Treaty in light of advancements in defense technology. The views expressed here are his own.

Mr. Rhinelander is a co-author with Thomas K. Longstreth and John B. Pike of the Report on the Impact of U.S. and Soviet Missile Defense Programs on the ABM Treaty *(Washington, D.C.: The Campaign to Save the ABM Treaty, 1985), re-ferred to as the "Impact Report" in this article.*

The president and members of his administration have given two entirely dif-ferent versions of SDI. The president originally suggested that SDI could be a perfect "astrodome" defense that would make nuclear weapons impotent and ob-solete. It would be a "people" defense that would fundamentally change the offense-dominated, mutual deterrence relationship. Secretary Weinberger has in-dicated that SDI would equally shield U.S. allies. During his 1984 campaign, the president stated the United States would be prepared to share SDI technology with the Soviets as both moved toward a defense-dominated relationship. The president's wish to make nuclear weapons impotent and obsolete clearly struck a responsive chord in many who are fearful of nuclear war and hope that nuclear weapons will one day be abolished. His vision has been viewed by most, however, as totally unachievable.

Others in the administration, including Lt. Gen. James Abrahamson, the direc-tor of the SDI Organization, have suggested that SDI would enhance the deter-rence relationship with the Soviet Union but would not replace it. SDI, in this view, would provide a "thin" defense for people and a more capable defense of ICBM silos.

No one in the administration suggests that SDI would be effective against bombers or cruise missiles. Further, SDI does not presently include programs de-signed for and limited to "hardsite" defense.

Paul Nitze, in his now famous Philadelphia speech of February 20, 1985, repeated the four-sentence Strategic Concept that he authored in December and that the president accepted in January as the basis for his negotiating position in Geneva, and then provided the most sophisticated and subtle SDI posture. In brief, Paul Nitze's concept is three-phased: deep cuts in offense and stabilization of the offense-defense relationship during a period of at least ten years while SDI is explored; a transition period including phased deployment of SDI-type defenses; and, finally, achievement of the ultimate goal of a nuclear-free world at some time in the future. His Philadelphia speech added two fundamental caveats: for SDI to be feasible, it must be survivable and cost-effective at the margin over countermeasures, and he added that transition from offense to defense could be "tricky."

In my judgment, SDI will never be able to satisfy Paul Nitze's criteria. Whether or not elements of SDI will ever be feasible in purely technical terms, it seems highly unlikely that a deployed system could ever be survivable and even less likely that any nationwide ABM system could be cost-effective at the margin. Moreover, if SDI were pursued, it would be destablizing and would heighten the paradox that *defensive* weapons have the capability to be used offensively as part of a first-strike strategy. *Offensive* weapons at present are in fact defensive.

One obvious Soviet response to SDI will be to proliferate offensive systems and to take other measures to be able to overwhelm any level of U.S. and allied defenses. This was the U.S. response with MIRVs in the late 1960s and early 1970s to the initial Soviet ABM efforts. It would be a U.S. response now if the Soviets had announced SDI as their goal. It also reflects current U.S. policy.

The U.S. Air Force is pursuing systems designed to ensure that U.S. strategic weapons can overwhelm any Soviet ABM or air defenses whatever their levels or sophistication. There is every reason to believe the United States will maintain its current penetration capability, and that the Soviets will do likewise.

In my view, the choice is between arms control and a quest for defensive systems such as SDI. It cannot be both. SDI will be fundamentally inconsistent with the ABM Treaty in a few years. If the ABM Treaty is repudiated, it is doubtful there will be any effective limitations on offensive nuclear arms. Other important agreements, such as the Nonproliferation Treaty, will also be threatened by an unrestrained U.S.-Soviet nuclear weapons competition.

The ABM Treaty—The Need to Enhance It

The ABM Treaty does not limit "research." Under Article V(1), neither the United States nor the Soviet Union may "develop" or "test" space-based, air-based, sea-based, or mobile land-based ABM systems and components, whether utilizing "current" or new technologies such as kinetic or directed energy. None of the key terms in Article V is the subject of agreed interpretation with the Soviets. The United States has been following a unilateral statement on the dividing line between permitted "research" and prohibited "development" and "testing" since 1972.

Article III restricts *deployment* of fixed, land-based ABM systems or components to "current" components as defined in Article II and (as amended by the 1974 ABM Protocol) to one site in the United States and one site in the Soviet Union. ABM systems are defined in terms of countering strategic ballistic missiles. The negotiating history made clear that "adjuncts," such as a telescope used in conjunction with a permitted ABM radar, may be deployed as part of an Article III system. Article IV limits the development and testing of "current" and new technologies for fixed, land-based ABM systems and components to agreed test ranges. Pursuant to Agreed Statement D, Article III must be amended before fixed, land-based ABM systems based on new technologies (such as lasers), which substitute for "current" ABM components, are deployed.

Article VI(a) prohibits the "upgrade" of non-ABM systems, such as surface-to-air missiles (SAMs), antitactical ballistic missiles (ATBMs) and antisatellite (ASAT) systems, by either giving them the "capabilities to counter strategic ballistic missiles" in flight trajectory or by "test[ing] them in an ABM mode." Article VI(b) limits large phased-array radars (LPARs) for early warning of strategic ballistic missiles to locations along the "periphery of its national territory" and "oriented outward."

Article IX prohibits deployment or transfer of ABM components or technology to third countries. Article X prohibits circumvention of the treaty by other international agreements.

Current interpretation issues arise because there have been inadequate attempts in the Standing Consultative Commission (SCC) or elsewhere to define key terms, including *develop, test, component, adjunct, capabilities, substitute for, early warning,* or even *strategic ballistic missiles.* For the purposes of the ABM Treaty, seven Agreed Statements and five Common Understandings were reached during SALT I. The Common Understandings, which were culled from the negotiating record before the treaty was submitted to the Senate, need to be reviewed, updated, and formally adopted. The only terms subsequently defined in the SCC—ABM test ranges and *test them in an ABM mode*—were the subject of a 1978 agreed statement, which is still classified. Recent efforts to expand the definition of *test them in an ABM mode* have not been completed.

This absence of agreement on specific terms leads to difficult issues of interpretation as SDI is construed in the context of the ABM Treaty, which was written in terms of 1960s technology. I am not aware that the responsible legal officers in Defense, State, and ACDA (Arms Control and Disarmament Agency) have prepared a comprehensive interagency analysis of SDI and the ABM Treaty. Certainly no such document has been released in unclassified form. The SDI Report describes a compliance process within the Department of Defense (DOD) with final decisions made by the under secretary of defense for Research and Engineering with advice from the DOD general counsel. The absence of a comprehensive legal analysis and compliance review chaired by the State Department or ACDA casts doubt on the persuasiveness of the administration's position that SDI and other U.S. programs strictly comply with the ABM Treaty.

Administration spokesmen claim that SDI is a "research" program that is entirely consistent with the ABM Treaty. This is only partially accurate—it is true for the moment but not so beginning in 1988.

The SDI program as presently conceived cannot be carried out consistently with the ABM Treaty starting in 1988 when certain tests are scheduled to begin. Further, boost phase and post-boost phase intercepts, which are central to the SDI concept, are fundamentally inconsistent with the purpose and letter of the ABM Treaty, including Article I(2) (which prohibits a "base" for a nationwide ABM system).

Based on our analysis, SDI currently involves four distinct time periods:

First, research and early development between 1985 and 1987;

Second, continued research and development, but also field testing of components and integrated systems, from 1988 until 1993 (some of which might be done jointly with U.S. allies) and possible deployment of ATBMs in Europe during this period;

Third, a possible deployment decision in 1993 with some ABM components deployed for defense of the United States from 1994 through 1997; and

Fourth, final deployment from 1998 through 2005.

Based on our analysis, the first period (1985–87), which largely coincides with President Reagan's term in office, will be consistent with the ABM Treaty. There is, however, one test scheduled for 1988 on the Airborne Optical System (AOS), which is also referred to as the Airborne Optical Adjunct (AOA), that appears inconsistent with Article V(1).

The second period (1988–93), which is covered in part by DOD's current five-year plan, would require either Soviet agreement to amend the ABM Treaty or abrogation of the treaty by the United States. The amendments would have to include: Article V to delete the ban on developing and testing and might have to include Article VI(a) to permit deployment of ATBMs with capabilities to counter strategic ballistic missiles: Article IX to permit deployment of such ATBMs outside the United States and transfer of ABM technology for joint development by some Allies; and Article I(2) to delete the ban on a base for a nationwide ABM system.

This second period is critical. Whether the ABM Treaty were to be amended cooperatively with the Soviets or abrogated unilaterally, it probably could not be put back together again even if a later decision were made not to deploy SDI. The barrier against advanced development and testing is fundamental to a stable regime, as is the need to avoid deployment of ATBMs capable of countering strategic ballistic missiles. The barriers in Article V will, and in Articles I(2), and IX might, have to be breached in the 1988–93 period if SDI proceeds as planned.

If a decision to deploy were made in 1993, the third and fourth periods (1994–2005) would require scrapping the entire ABM Treaty as presently written unless deployment were limited to a fixed land-based "hardpoint defense." Fundamentally, there is no place for the ABM Treaty if the United States seeks a defense-dominated relationship or even U.S. defense superiority.

I cannot conceive of the Soviets' agreeing to amend Article I(2), V, VI (a), and IX to permit SDI to proceed consistent with a then-truncated ABM Treaty. In addition, no one has even suggested a conceptual approach to the offensive-defensive relationship and the role of any ABM Treaty during a "transition" period to defense-domination.

Since the beginning of the SALT process in 1967, the United States has recognized that limitations on strategic offensive and defensive systems are interrelated. Limitations on strategic defensive systems have been, and in our judgment remain, a precondition to limitations on offensive systems. No technological or other developments have changed this basic relationship. Whether or not SDI continues as presently conceived through the early 1990s—research leading to development and testing of space-based components, both of which are inconsistent with the ABM Treaty—SDI is not, in our judgment, in the best interests of U.S. national security policy.

Deep reductions of U.S. and Soviet offensive nuclear systems, combined with some reshaping of those systems over time, should remain a basic objective of U.S. security and arms control policies. SDI will make this objective unachievable in a few years if SDI is not sharply curtailed. Further, SDI could destabilize both U.S.-Soviet and U.S.-alliance relationships before then.

There is a fundamental difference between an SDI policy limited to research, which is the current declaratory policy of the administration, and a massive research and development program funded by Congress that builds momentum toward the capability to begin to break out of the treaty in 1988–93. This latter policy lies behind the current fiscal year's request for $3.7 billion in SDI funds and additional funds in DOE's budget.

The SDI time schedule will present an implicit ultimatum to the Soviets by 1988: either agree to amend Article I(2), V, VI(2) and IX of the ABM Treaty to allow SDI to continue to develop and test ABM components in 1989–93, to allow joint SDI research and development programs with U.S. allies, and to allow deployment of ATBMs capable of countering strategic ballistic missiles in Europe; or the United States will abrogate the treaty. SDI also contains an implicit threat by the United States to abrogate the treaty in its entirety, if the Soviets do not agree to scrap it, in the mid-1990s if the United States decides to deploy an SDI defense.

SDI was probably an important factor in bringing the Soviets back to the negotiating table in Geneva on March 12, but the Soviets were certain to have returned anyway. The Soviet strategy that focused on the 1983 INF (intermediate-range nuclear forces) deployment decisions had backfired on them. They would have returned after the president's reelection to appeal to European public opinion.

The Soviets undoubtedly understand the Hobson's choice that faces them. Their propaganda, and apparently their negotiating strategy at Geneva, is focused entirely on opposing SDI. Further, there is no reason to believe that Soviet policy in this respect will change. What the Soviets do not know is whether the administration or the Congress, acting together or separately, will curtail SDI if over the next year or two the Soviets agree to mutually acceptable deep cuts on offensive nuclear systems. Perhaps only President Reagan knows the answer to this question. This, and the question of how an overarching agreement in principle might be negotiated, are the keys to Geneva.

In the meantime, the Soviets will undoubtedly react with programs of their own. In sum, SDI as declaratory policy might under the best of circumstances help achieve a treaty of indefinite duration on comprehensive limitations and reductions on offensive strategic systems—a priority U.S. objective since the SALT negotiations began in 1969. The quid pro quo would be a severe curtailment of SDI as currently envisaged for later years. On the other hand, SDI as an action policy annually funded by Congress at levels presently favored within DOD would lead to an increasingly destabilizing relationship with the Soviet Union over the next four years, including a certain stalemate at Geneva.

U.S. alliance relationships are likely to deteriorate sharply over the next four years unless SDI is both clarified and limited to a prudent level of research before and after 1988. The United Kingdom, France, Germany, and Canada, which publicly support SDI to the extent limited to research, are not the only allies that will be fundamentally affected by the future shape of the program.

The sixty-day letters delivered to the U.S. allies on March 26, which invite them to join in the SDI efforts, should trigger an early and searching review of SDI and its consistency with the ABM Treaty. Cooperative efforts on research would not be inconsistent with the treaty, but cooperative development or testing of ABM components would be. The suggestion by a DOD official that the allies of the United States would "not be excluded" from production contracts to develop weapons appears to be directly contrary to Articles V, IX and X of the ABM Treaty. Further, any sharing with the allies would be inconsistent with the administration's efforts to tighten controls on the export from the United States of highly sensitive technology.

Assuming that the best were to occur and that the United States and the Soviet Union reaffirm the ABM Treaty, the treaty must be enhanced through numerous agreed statements and common understandings. Because the ABM Treaty was written primarily in terms of 1960s technology—that is, fixed land-based ABM systems and fixed land-based early warning radars—there is an enormous and complex task for the defense space working group in Geneva.

The goal should be to achieve specific, mutual, and verifiable interpretations relevant to emerging technology under the definitional (Article II) and each substantive article (Articles I(2), III, IV, V, VI and IX) of the treaty. If such an effort is not undertaken or is not successful, the ABM Treaty will wither away even if not formally amended or abrogated. Technological changes will not sit still. This is a fundamental point that all those who support arms control must understand.

With one exception, enhancements of the ABM Treaty can be entirely consistent with the ABM Treaty as amended by the 1974 ABM Protocol. However, if an ASAT agreement is reached prohibiting, inter alia, development and testing of ASATs, then consideration should be given to an additional protocol to the ABM Treaty. The purpose would be to prohibit the currently legal development and testing of fixed, ground-based, exoatmospheric ABM systems and components. The reasons are simple. Much ASAT and ABM technology is dual capable. Tests of ASAT systems provide some ABM applicability. Tests of fixed, land-based, exoatmospheric ABM systems provide ASAT capabilities.

We believe that both ABMs and ASATs must be tightly constrained for either to be effectively limited over time. Therefore, we support a separate ASAT Treaty.

Impact Report

The current, or third, edition of the Impact Report analyzes U.S. and Soviet programs and the impact of both on the ABM Treaty. The credit should largely go to Tom Longstreth and John Pike, the coauthors of the first two editions and still the principal authors of the third. Their research made possible the analysis contained in the third edition. We want to stress, however, that our Impact Report was written before the administration's unclassified SDI Report was released.

Without covering the entire Impact Report, I will briefly describe its basic scope, coverage, and recommendations.

First, our Impact Report summarizes the ABM Treaty and analyzes the most important areas of ambiguities. These ambiguities reflect a failure on the part of both the United States and the Soviet Union to use the Standing Consultative Commission (SCC) to seek, let alone agree upon, specific agreed interpretations over the past twelve years so that the treaty will remain current and relevant as new technology is pursued. The major challenges include:

1. The term ABM *component* must be defined in terms of prohibited emerging technology for space-, air-, sea- and land-mobile ABM systems. Prohibited components limited by Article V must be distinguished from permitted subcomponents, "adjuncts," and non-ABM technology. Conclusive presumptions may have to be agreed upon by the U.S. and Soviets to prohibit certain types of space-based, air-based, etc., kinetic, and directed energy systems or components because of the dual uses of basic technologies.

2. The distinction between permitted "research" and prohibited "develop" and "test" must be defined for purposes of Article V. The United States currently relies on the unilateral U.S. statement prepared for the congressional record in 1972 after reviews of the U.S. SALT delegation reporting cables. (The statement in part reads, "The prohibitions on development contained in the ABM Treaty would start at that part of the development process where field testing is initiated on either a

prototype or breadboard model. . . . Engineering development would clearly be prohibited.") The Soviets have never publicly commented on it. Further, the Russian text of Article V uses a verb (*sozdavat*) that is best translated as "create" for the English word "develop." The Russian word apparently can mean simply putting pen to paper and suggests an earlier prohibition in the R&D (research and development) cycle than the 1972 unilateral U.S. interpretation. However, the Soviets have never publicly stated a proposed verifiable standard. *A verifiable cutoff point of prohibited "develop" and "test" must be defined in conjunction with ABM "components."* This is critical not only for U.S. research efforts, and any joint research with U.S. allies, but also for gaining clear limits applicable to future Soviet efforts. Specific limitations applicable to the United States must be equally applicable to the Soviets.

3. Limits on "non-ABM" dual-capable systems and components limited by Article VI(a) must be defined for surface-to-air missiles, antitactical ballistic missiles, and antisatellite systems both in terms of "capabilities to counter strategic ballistic missiles" and "testing in an ABM mode." The dual use prohibitions, which would affect all three U.S. military services, will be extremely difficult to achieve because basic systems have tactical and theater as well as potential strategic roles. A practical definition of *capabilities to counter* is fundamentally necessary.

4. Effective constraints on large phased-array radars and on space-based sensors with ABM capabilities must be reached. The dual capable problems of LPARs on earth will soon be duplicated by space-based sensors. The differentiation problem will become more difficult.

The full list is daunting, as is the challenge of negotiating and drafting. All interpretations must be specific and verifiable. The prohibitions must be clear and mutual. The failure to define key terms and concepts will lead to an ever escalating series of charges and countercharges of noncompliance by both sides.

Second, our Impact Report discusses the various program elements that make up the SDI and summarizes those raising treaty issues. This aspect of the Impact Report, together with the administration's SDI Report, should provide Congress with initial information to consider in reviewing the present funding request for SDI and to consider appropriate limitations and conditions on funds that are appropriated for FY 1986 and later fiscal years.

Third, our Impact Report reviews various Soviet programs including their research efforts. Our information on Soviet programs is not complete. Our general conclusion, nevertheless, is that the Soviets have maintained a large research program, but are significantly behind the United States in the high-tech approach to ballistic missile defense. The Soviets have a low-tech capability, both in their current ABM system around Moscow and in their ABM components being tested or deployed, which could be deployed long before any U.S. Star Wars system. Current Soviet ABM technology that is deployed and being deployed does not appear to be as advanced as that of the U.S. Safeguard site at Grand Forks, North Dakota, which was shut down in 1976.

Fourth, our Impact Report reviews compliance by both the United States and the Soviet Union. I will summarize some of the major issues.

The U.S. Pave Paws large phased-array radars (LPARs designed for early warning of SLBMs and for space tracking) that are under construction in Georgia and Texas raise compliance issues under Article VI(b) of the ABM Treaty. While pointed outwards, they could have some ABM battle management capability, and they provide coverage of significant parts of the continental United States. The orientations of the sites have apparently been modified, reducing this concern, but the 240-degree coverage of the two active faces at each site raises the legal and factual issues of whether they are oriented "outward." More precise factual information is necessary for a judgment as to whether those sites are consistent with the treaty.

The U.S. early warning LPARs under construction in Greenland and the United Kingdom as replacements for mechanical-scan-type radars at those sites raise compliance issues based solely on a question of treaty interpretation. In my judgment, the better interpretation of the treaty, which grandfathered these two sites, is that Article VI(b) permits the United States to "upgrade" the radars with phased-array technology. (But this is a very close question because Agreed Statement F prohibits the deployment of phased-array radars except for listed purposes.)

The U.S. SDI programs will clearly be inconsistent with Article V if research leads to development and testing of space-based components in 1988 and in later years. Even now, a declared intent to pursue programs that will be prohibited by the ABM Treaty raises a fundamental issue. The analogy to an anticipatory breach of contract may be apt.

The Soviet large phased-array radar under construction near Krasnoyarsk raises an immediate compliance problem. From its location, and the orientation and elevation of its one active face, it clearly appears to be for ballistic missile early warning rather than for space tracking. Its construction is therefore inconsistent with Article VI(b). However, the Krasnoyarsk radar does not appear to be well sited or suited for a battle management radar and should not, in our judgment, be considered an ABM radar prohibited by Article III.

The new Soviet SAM and ATBM systems clearly have more capability to counter strategic ballistic missiles than did comparable Soviet SAM systems in 1972. The Article VI(a) issues are whether the new systems have the "capability to counter" strategic ballistic missiles or whether they have been "tested in an ABM mode." SAMs and ATBMs that can counter short-range ballistic missiles but do not have the capability to counter strategic ballistic missiles (and that which also have not been "tested in an ABM mode") are permitted under the treaty. If Soviet defensive systems are developed to counter medium- or intermediate-range ballistic missiles, such as the Pershing II, the distinction between the permitted and prohibited will become meaningless. These are among the most important near-term interpretation and compliance issues under the treaty.

The administration may be as divided on the SAM/ATBM issue as the Nixon administration was in 1972 when concern over Soviet SAMs was countered with a desire not to impinge on the U.S. SAM-D (now Patriot) system. An allegation of Soviet violations relating to its new SA-12, which has been tested against a short-range, tactical ballistic missile (the SS-12), would implicitly brand proposed U.S. ATBM efforts under consideration for deployment in Western Europe as contrary to the treaty. The administration has apparently not yet made up its mind on this fundamental question, but cannot have it both ways under Article VI(a). In our view, both current Soviet and proposed U.S. programs raise Article VI(a) compliance questions.

In brief and in summary, our Impact Report reviews U.S. and Soviet programs that raise compliance issues. Colorable legal justifications can be made by each side for its programs, but there are reasons for concern with activities of both sides. Each tends to interpret the ABM Treaty strictly with respect to programs of the other, but permissibly for its own programs. Present actions of each, coupled with a failure to enhance the ABM Treaty, will serve to undermine the treaty.

Fifth, our Impact Report suggests various substantive approaches, that could be considered by the United States and the Soviet Union to enhance those provisions of the ABM Treaty that need the most immediate attention. We have offered various approaches to "reverse the erosion of the ABM Treaty," which is a declared objective of the administration. The list is illustrative and not exhaustive, but we hope it will generate further discussions.

Sixth, our Impact Report notes the critical lack of early interagency review in the United States for U.S. programs. In some ways, the problem is similar to the notorious compartmentation in the Soviet Union. To the best of our knowledge, there has not been a full review of SDI by attorneys in the General Counsel's Office of ACDA or in the Office of the Legal Adviser at State.

U.S.-Allied Cooperation on SDI R&D

Since the ABM Treaty does not constrain research, it is our opinion that cooperative efforts limited to research would not be inconsistent with the treaty. Nevertheless, the Soviets are certain to object strongly to any joint research by the United States and its allies for political reasons, and the Soviets may rely on a broad definition of *create* in the Russian text of Article V, and Agreed Statement G to Article IX, which prohibits the transfer by the United States of technical descriptions or blueprints, to buttress their case.

When Articles V, IX and X are read together, along with Agreed Statement G, the treaty prohibits cooperative efforts involving any transfers or assistance from the United States to its allies at the point that research on ABM components moves to advanced development or testing. This would specifically preclude the United States from providing technical descriptions and blueprints for advanced development of any type of ABM component. The treaty would also prohibit any joint engineering development or joint production of ABM components, even in cases where the United States may legally pursue development and testing of programs such as components of a fixed, land-based ABM system.

The United States provided sixty-day letters to its allies on March 26 inviting them to indicate whether they were interested in joint research efforts, but there is no public indication that this U.S. offer made clear that cooperative efforts would conflict with the ABM Treaty if they moved beyond the research phase.

The Administration's SDI Report

The administration's unclassified SDI Report due March 15, made available on April 18, provides a comprehensive overview of SDI, but only a brief review in the nine-page Appendix B of the administration's analysis of the relationship of SDI to the ABM Treaty. I will simply summarize my conclusions.

First, Appendix B of the administration's SDI report in general accurately describes what is prohibited and permitted under the ABM Treaty. Appendix B admits that "development and deployment, given a decision to proceed, would almost certainly require modifications to the ABM Treaty." This key sentence is tentative when a frank admission is warranted. Further, no date is suggested.

Second, Appendix B indicates that DOD has restructured various program elements to provide colorable arguments of compliance in all cases. Many experiments are described as laboratory experiments, or if outside then in a fixed, land-based mode. Many are characterized as below the power or size of a weapon system, or otherwise do not represent an ABM component. Others are described as subcomponents, adjuncts, or parts of anti-ASAT systems.

Third, if the administration's policy is in fact to prevent the "erosion of the ABM Treaty," then Appendix B demonstrates what should not be done as a matter of U.S. national policy. Rather than seeking to exploit admittedly gray areas in the treaty, the administration should be trying to clarify them.

The basic legal position of the administration's SDI Report is that none of the "elements," "subsystems," or "experiments" of space-based projects, that may be "demonstrated" through the early 1990s should be construed to be prohibited from advanced development or testing of "ABM components." This position is factually suspect and legally questionable. If this represents the administration's basic approach to preventing erosion of the ABM Treaty, it makes a mockery of treaty compliance.

All should recognize that there are legitimate areas of ambiguity given the failure of the United States and the Soviet Union to seek specific agreed interpretations. The SDI Report itself is a good road map of those gaps in the treaty that should be closed rather than exploited.

If Congress were to decide that projects to be funded in FY 1986 should be limited to those that are now, and if carried through to fruition will be, strictly consistent with the ABM Treaty, Congress would have to specify the conditions.

There is no basis for believing that Congress and DOD would necessarily interpret general statutory or report language linked to compliance with the ABM Treaty in the same way.

More fundamental than Appendix B, the administration's SDI Report does not attempt to address the transition problems from offense to defense domination. Discussion and broad agreement between the executive branch and Congress, between the United States and its allies, and with the Soviets on how this could be accomplished should precede the kind of R&D program set forth in the SDI budget request.

Conclusion

Funding for SDI in FY 1986 and thereafter should be curtailed to levels consistent with a prudent hedge against Soviet breakout. This could be in the $1.5 billion range for FY 1986. This would deny funding to the "demonstration projects" while permitting approximately 30 percent real growth for the research projects. It would limit funding to particular projects that strictly comply with the ABM Treaty. This is the legal test the Soviets are held to by the administration in U.S. compliance reports. Congress should hold the administration to the legal standard of strict compliance on SDI at this juncture.

In Geneva, the U.S. should reaffirm the ABM Treaty, as presently written, as one fundamental to a long-term, stable relationship with the Soviets. The focus should be on enhancing the ABM Treaty through specific mutual, and verifiable agreed interpretations.

The basic challenge of Geneva and at a summit should be to achieve a Vladivostok-type approach coupling deep cuts on offensive systems spanning INF and START with an enhanced ABM Treaty (including an ASAT Treaty). Years of detailed, hard bargaining will be necessary after such an umbrella agreement in principle is reached in order to produce agreement in detail.

In the final analysis, SDI raises the question of whether U.S. security would be enhanced in a world without arms control. In my judgment, the answers are obvious:

> The United States cannot pursue SDI to the advanced development and test phases and expect to achieve reductions on offensive nuclear systems.

> Without comprehensive limits on U.S. and Soviet offensive and defensive strategic systems, the survivability of the multilateral post–World War II arms control regimes is dubious, and new agreements such as a comprehensive test ban will not be achievable.

> Without effective arms control agreements, the threat of continued proliferation and actual use of nuclear weapons in unstable areas of the world will increase.

In my own view of the future, there will never be a world without nuclear weapons as long as there is civilization on this earth. There will never be a perfect defense against nuclear weapons. The challenge, basically political, is to restrain technological changes and enhance the stability of deployed weapons over time at reduced levels.

Whether there should ever be a role for defensive systems against ballistic missiles and other types of offensive delivery systems is unclear. The central questions are not technological, since applied research will inevitably prove out the feasibility of some new systems in laboratory and controlled test settings. The more important questions relate to the interaction between defensive systems, countermeasures on offensive weapons systems, and the basic stability of the balance. To date, analyses suggest that between adversarial states such as the United States and the Soviet Union, *defensive* systems deployed by one will be viewed in terms of their *offensive* capabilities by the other. In essence, the basic issues have not changed since the searching ABM debates of the 1960s that led to the ABM Treaty in 1972. The current fallacy is the belief that Star Wars technology might change the underlying fundamentals. It cannot.

Arms control in the nuclear age cannot assure either peace or security. The demise of arms control will, however, raise the threat of instability, increased proliferation, and possible use of the types of weapons that have not been used in war since 1945. The ABM Treaty should be preserved and enhanced as part of a comprehensive process of stabilizing the basic deterrent relationship.   *(May 1985)*

The Reagan Strategic Defense Initiative: A Technical and Strategic Appraisal

Sidney D. Drell
Philip J. Farley
David Holloway

A special report on The Reagan Strategic Defense Initiative: A Technical, Political, and Arms Control Assessment *was published in 1984 by the Center for International Security and Arms Control at Stanford University. Authors Sidney D. Drell, Philip J. Farley, and David Holloway combine their knowledge and experience in politics, arms control, Soviet studies, and physics and engineering, providing a thorough and lucid analysis of U.S. and Soviet antiballistic missile programs and their strategic, political, and arms control impact.*

The book includes chapters on "The ABM Treaty and the U.S.-Soviet Strategic Relationship," "Soviet Perspectives on the ABM Treaty," "The Strategic Defense Initiative and

Its Implications for the U.S.-Soviet Strategic Relationship," and the effect of SDI programs on U.S. allies and other countries. The study concludes that the best prospect for enhancing stability and security will come under negotiated ABM limitations. It draws seven conclusions and makes seven recommendations, including specific actions that can be taken to preserve the ABM Treaty while maintaining a useful research program on strategic defense technologies.

The following article was adapted from the portion of the book concerning the technical feasibility of the Strategic Defense Initiative.

In his address to the nation on March 23, 1983, President Reagan announced, "I call upon the scientific community in our country, those who gave us nuclear weapons, to turn their great talents now to the cause of mankind and world peace, to give us the means of rendering these nuclear weapons impotent and obsolete."

The vision expressed by the president appeals to powerful natural and moral sentiments. Indefinite reliance on the threat of retaliation by means of weapons of immense destructive power and conceivably apocalyptic effects is a forbidding prospect. Easing the balance of terror and lessening and if possible removing the threat of nuclear war have been preoccupations of responsible leaders since 1945. The impulse to look to our weapons and armed forces to *defend* us rather than to threaten others is a natural one—and has precedent in the history of antiballistic missile development and negotiations over the past two decades.

Thus serious pursuit of ABM is not a new idea in the strategic arms race. Acceptance in 1972 of the ABM Treaty and of strictly limited deployments of ABM systems in the Soviet Union and the United States did not reflect any lack of awareness on either side of strategic defense and the arguments for it. Rather, it was a pragmatic conclusion. Whatever the abstract desirability of ABM defenses, in the early 1970s each of the superpowers, in sum, judged nationwide deployment of ABM to be futile, destabilizing, and costly.

It would be *futile*, because in a competition between defensive systems and offensive missiles with nuclear warheads, an offense would win, especially against populations and urban areas.

It would be *destabilizing*, because the arms race would be accelerated as both sides developed and deployed not only competing ABM systems, but also offsetting systems to overpower, evade, or attack and disable the opposing ABM system. Furthermore, each side would fear the purpose or the capability of the other's ABMs (especially against a weakened retaliatory strike), and in a crisis these fears could bring mounting pressures for striking first. What strategic theorists refer to as arms race instability and crisis instability could both result.

It would be *costly*, because both ABM development and deployment, and the buildup, modernization, and diversification of offsetting offensive forces, must be purchased. And the offensive countermeasures to maintain the reciprocal deterrent threat of intolerable retaliatory damage appeared not only capable of overwhelming the defense, but also easier and less costly.

More than a decade later, the president has challenged the nation to reexamine these earlier judgments. Have the technological advances and strategic developments of the past decade, or those now in prospect, made it practical for us to realize his vision of a virtually leakproof defense that renders nuclear weapons impotent and obsolete? How would any potential change in technical and systems feasibility affect stability and costs?

The New Frontier

Up to the present, the dominance of offense over defense has been based on technical considerations. In recent years the technology pertinent to this problem has advanced significantly. Great strides have been made in the ability to produce, focus, and aim laser and particle beams of increasingly high power. These new "bullets" of directed energy travel at or near the velocity of light and have led to revolutionary new ideas for defense against ballistic missiles. There has also been a revolutionary expansion in our ability to gather, process, and transmit vast quantities of data efficiently and promptly. This makes it possible to provide high-quality intelligence from distant parts of the earth and space in order to assess and discriminate among the properties of attacks very promptly. The technical advances in the ability to manage a defense and to attack distant targets very quickly have removed a number of shortcomings from previous defense concepts.

The major technical fact that has not changed with time is the overwhelming destructive power of nuclear weapons. "Rendering nuclear weapons impotent and obsolete" by defending one's vital national interests—people, industries, cities—against a massive nuclear attack still requires a defense that is almost perfect. Technical assessments of ABM *concepts* cannot escape this awesome *systems* requirement. If but 1 percent of the approximately eight thousand nuclear warheads on the current Soviet force of land-based and sea-based ballistic missiles succeeded in penetrating a defensive shield and landed on urban targets in the United States, the result would be one of the greatest disasters in all history!

Many components form a defense system against ballistic missiles, and all are crucial to its effective operation. These include: the sensors providing early warning of an attack; the communication links for conveying that information to analysis centers for interpretation, to the command centers with authority to make decisions as to the appropriate national response, and to the military forces to implement the decisions; the sensors of the ABM that acquire, discriminate, track, point, fire, and assess the effectiveness of the attack; and, finally, the interceptors or directed-energy sources that make the kill.

The systems for managing the battle and for delivering destructive energy concentrations with precision must be operational at the initiation of an attack and must remain effective throughout. This means being on station, yet being able to survive direct attack. The ability to satisfy these two requirements simultaneously is a major operational challenge. Even if the very ambitious research and development program recently proposed by the administration attains all of its major goals, great operational barriers will still remain.

The Layered Defense

The concept of a "defense in depth" has developed because no single technology alone is adequate to provide an impenetrable defensive shield, or antiballistic Maginot line. This is composed of four layers. The first layer attacks the rising missiles during their boost phase while their engines are burning. Typically, this phase lasts three minutes for modern intercontinental ballistic missiles (ICBMs) powered by rockets that burn solid fuel, and up to five minutes for liquid-fuel boosters. During this time the missile rises above the atmosphere to heights of two to three hundred kilometers.

The second (and perhaps third) layer of the defense attacks the warheads, or reentry vehicles, as well as the post-boost vehicle (which is the small bus that aims and dispenses the individual MIRVs) during their midcourse trajectories lasting about twenty to twenty-five minutes (for ICBMs).

The final or terminal layer of the defense attacks the reentry vehicles during the last minute or two of their flight as they reenter the atmosphere, which strips away the lighter decoys accompanying them in midflight. A three-layer system, each of whose layers is 90 percent effective, would allow only eight out of an attacking force of eight thousand reentry vehicles to arrive on target and, if achievable, would be an effective though less than perfect defense.

Boost-Phase Intercept

The possibility of boost-phase intercept is the principal new element in considering ABM technologies. It also has the highest potential payoff for two reasons: success achieved in the initial layer reduces the size of the attacking forces to be engaged by each subsequent layer; if a missile is destroyed when it is relatively vulnerable during the boost phase, all of its warheads and decoys are destroyed with it.

In the midcourse phase, the defense has more time to perform its functions of acquiring and discriminating warheads from decoys, attacking its targets and confirming their destruction. But midcourse interception must also cope with many more objects because a single large booster is capable of deploying tens of warheads and many hundreds of decoys. Thus the two defensive layers for boost-phase and for midcourse intercept face very different technological challenges. An effective boost-phase layer that greatly reduces the number of objects that subsequent layers must analyze, attack, and destroy is crucial to overall effectiveness of a defensive system.

In order to illustrate the general problems for boost-phase intercept, we consider two types of systems, one with interceptors based in space and the other with interceptors based on ground and ready to "pop-up" on receipt of a warning of an enemy attack. A hybrid concept with mixed ground and space basing is also discussed. All defensive systems rely on space-based sensors for early warning, command, control, and communications (C^3), and overall battle management. The combination of tactics and technology to ensure the survival of the space-based components of a defense against direct enemy attack has yet to be developed.

Space-based Chemical Lasers. One of the most widely discussed systems for boost-phase intercept is a constellation of high-energy lasers based on platforms orbiting the earth in space. Well-focused laser beams have the attractive feature of traveling vast distances at the speed of light in space above the atmosphere. The disadvantages of space-based lasers are that they are complex and expensive, and vulnerable to attack, and many effective countermeasures are available to the attacker. Generally, their beams are degraded by scattering and absorption by the atmosphere, so they must function above it. Furthermore, each platform of any space-based system will be "on station" over the launch area of Soviet ICBMs only a small percentage of time as it circles the globe in a low earth orbit. That is, each platform will have a large "absentee ratio." Therefore, it will be inherently inefficient, having to be replicated many times over if the defense is to provide continual protection against ICBM launches.

The effective coverage of a laser system depends on the ability to power and focus the beam like a flashlight. The range at which it can kill a missile will increase with the power of the laser and with the quality of the optical system. However, even with perfect optics the beam will spread and become more diffuse as it propagates over long distances because of the wave nature of light (that is, due to diffraction). The kill range also depends on the structure of the target ICBM—how much energy per unit area has to be deposited in order to damage the missile by melting through the relatively thin skin of the booster. The harder the missile, the shorter is the effective range of the laser; or at a given distance, the longer the laser must fix its beam on the booster to damage it seriously.

In addition to specific countermeasures, such as hardening the missile against the destructive effects of laser beams, a defense system with components predeployed in space faces generic difficulties. Foremost among these is that space-based components are likely to be vulnerable to direct enemy attack. Among the simplest direct threats are small and relatively cheap space mines with conventional explosives, which could be deployed even during the early stages of building up to a full space-based defensive layer. They could be launched into orbits and detonated by ground radio command to damage the large, delicate, and highly vulnerable optical parts. The presence of such space mines would not be covert. They could "shadow" a satellite in a manner similar to that used by ships on the high seas. Of course, the Soviets could also put nuclear bombs in orbit, which would have an enormous damage range.

Ground-based laser beams pose another direct threat to the sensitive optical sensors of such a system. The space-based defenses would have to be prepared to "blink" if so attacked in order to avoid damage, particularly if the incident radiation comes in short, intense pulses.

Not all laser platforms would have to be attacked and put out of action, just a sizable fraction of that small percentage that are on station over the ICBM launch areas during boost phase. The offense can then be confident that a significant fraction of his attack will penetrate the first layer of the defense.

There are additional problems that can be created for such a defensive system. Precursor nuclear bursts at high altitudes can precede an attack and disrupt defensive operations, particularly sensors and communication links. There is no spare time available for replacing or reconstituting these components because the entire system must perform within the first few minutes in order to destroy an ICBM during boost phase. The defensive system can also be diverted by false targets consisting of bright rockets and other hot sources simulating the missile exhaust.

Space-based systems are much more delicate and expensive than the individual ICBMs against which they are deployed. Therefore, the task of protecting them is inherently more difficult than that of hardening the ICBMs against them. The history of military technological innovation suggests that the Soviet Union, faced with a prospective U.S. defense system undergoing development and testing, would simply increase its arsenal of offensive missiles and warheads in order to maintain its deterrent. At $5–$10 million apiece, the Soviets could buy a lot of warheads before equaling the 1981 DOD estimate of $500 billion for a space-based laser defense.

In the final analysis, a very extensive and expensive constellation of chemical lasers predeployed in space appears to offer no credible prospect of forming an effective defensive layer against a large-scale attack at the current high levels of the threat.

Pop-up Systems: Ground-based X-ray Lasers. In an effort to avoid most of the problems just described, the defense may choose not to predeploy in space, but to "pop up" from the ground when alerted to an attack. The weapon components of the defensive system could be mounted on missiles that can be launched very rapidly upon receipt of information of an enemy attack. A chemical laser system would be much too massive for this kind of rapid launch.

One such system being considered consists of X-ray lasers driven by nuclear explosives. By itself, a nuclear explosion releases a very large amount of energy that is not focused but that emerges in all directions. However, if a sufficiently large fraction of the energy from the nuclear explosion can be used to drive one or more lasers, and thus be focused into very highly collimated beams, it can destroy an object at very large distances by hitting it with a strong shockwave—a so-called impulsive kill. The kill mechanism in this case is caused by a very short intense pulse of incident energy, in contrast to the continuous thermal heating by the chemical laser. This technology is still very immature.

The major practical problem with a pop-up system of this type is the difficult and important operational issue of whether it can be deployed rapidly enough to attempt a boost-phase intercept. A pop-up system has only a few minutes to be boosted to a high enough altitude above the atmosphere to initiate an attack. In practice, an X-ray laser can only operate at altitudes above one hundred kilometers, because at lower altitudes much of the X-ray energy is absorbed. Thus a defensive X-ray laser would have to be launched literally within seconds of an initial enemy attack.

Furthermore, such a pop-up system would have to be based far offshore from continental U.S. soil and near to Soviet territory. Otherwise, because of the curvature of the earth, it would be impossible for the X-ray system to "see" the booster above the horizon before the end of its burn. This defensive concept also requires that the command and control chain must operate almost instantaneously over great distances—and do so in a heavily disturbed nuclear environment created by the first explosions of the X-ray lasers. (The nuclear disturbed environment would also affect the ability of the sensors to acquire, track, discriminate, and assess target damage.)

Evidently, such a system would have to be almost entirely automated for quick response. This poses serious policy problems because the firing process must include authorized release of nuclear weapons, as well as decisions about whether and how to respond, depending on the intensity and tactics of the attack. For example, since an X-ray laser can fire only once, destroying itself in the act, should it be launched against a single attacking ICBM, or only against a suitably large barrage?

In addition to these formidable operation requirements, there are two technically available countermeasures by the offense that can deny any possibility of a pop-up X-ray laser defense. The first countermeasure is simply to redesign the offense with new high-thrust "hot" missiles that complete their burn at altitudes below the top of the atmosphere. Unclassified studies presented to the Fletcher Panel calculate that such a rapid burn, lasting only about one minute, would require the missile's payload to be reduced by only 10–15 percent.

A second countermeasure is to alter the trajectory of the launch, depressing it so as to complete its burn below one hundred kilometers. Because the lower atmosphere is opaque to the X-ray beams, missiles of high thrust can complete their boost before they can be attacked.

Hybrid System for Boost-Phase Intercept. Other technologies and systems concepts have been proposed in an effort to escape the drawbacks of space-based and pop-up systems. One such concept that has been widely discussed is a system of ground-based lasers whose beams are aimed up to a small number of large relay mirrors in geosynchronous orbits 36,000 kilometers above the earth's surface. These high-altitude relay mirrors direct the beams to various mission mirrors orbiting earth at lower altitudes, which in turn redirect the beams onto their targets.

This hybrid system avoids three of the problems of a space-based laser defense: (1) fewer of its parts have to be protected from direct attack in space; (2) its ground-based lasers do not have to be replicated many times over in order to compensate for the large absentee ratio for lasers circulating in low earth orbits; and (3) it is not necessary to shuttle large amounts of fuel into orbit. It also avoids the very severe problem of time constraint for boost-phase intercept that is encountered by pop-up systems.

However, it faces several severe and unavoidable technical and operational challenges. First, the large focusing mirrors, which are high value and crucial modes of the system, remain vulnerable in space. Also, the directed light beams must travel very great distances—36,000 kilometers up and 36,000 back—from the relay mirrors in geosynchronous orbit. Therefore, large optics and short wavelengths are necessary to reduce the diffraction and keep the energy focused on such a long path from laser to target.

The hybrid system must rely on "active optics" in order to compensate for the effects of atmospheric turbulence, which cause scattering and defocusing of the directed light beams in a manner similar to which distant stars are seen to twinkle. Active optics means the following: a weak laser beam shines to the ground from space, and its beam spread is analyzed as a measure of local atmospheric effects. This atmospheric distortion is then compensated for by use of deformable focusing mirrors for transmitting a strong beam from the ground-based laser. This technology, though still immature, has been progressing rapidly and in principle can achieve the goal of transmitting highly focused beams through the atmosphere.

In addition to atmospheric compensation there is the problem of weather, particularly cloud cover, which can absorb the laser energy. Ground-based lasers would have to be deployed at widely distributed sites or on mountaintops above the clouds in order to have a high probability that an adequate number are free of cloud cover.

However, in the final analysis, even assuming that the formidable technical goals are achieved, there still remains the operational problem of the vulnerability of the few large relay and mission mirrors in space. They and the large ground-based laser stations are reminiscent of the large phased-array radars that proved to be the Achilles' heel of early generation ABM systems. It has yet to be specified or understood how the small number of large and delicate space mirrors and ground-based installations can be protected with confidence.

Other Concepts for Boost-Phase Intercept. Somewhat more exotic directed-energy weapons include high-power microwaves and particle beam systems. These are very immature technologies, much less advanced than laser beams. High-power microwaves are in a very early stage in which the basic physics is still being studied. It is too early to offer even educated guesses about the potential effectiveness of microwave systems, particularly against countermeasures. Particle beam weapons suffer from many of the same problems as laser stations. They would require large space platforms and would be fragile to attack and more expensive than their targets—the ICBMs.

Another possibility for a boost-phase defensive layer is material interceptors, such as small missiles or pellet screens, launched from a constellation of space-based battle stations. Destruction of the target is achieved by the kinetic energy impinging on the booster when it encounters a high-velocity interceptor or a cloud of matter in the form of debris or pellets. Such "high frontier" proposals are advanced as potentially being ready for deployment sooner than the more exotic directed-energy beams. However, such schemes have been generally judged ineffective for boost-phase intercept on grounds of time constraints and countermeasures.

This view was expressed in response to questioning by Dr. Robert Cooper, director of the U.S. Defense Advanced Research Projects Agency, during his testimony to the Senate Armed Services Committee on May 2, 1983. He indicated that such high frontier concepts do not provide a cost-effective potential for ballistic missile defense and could be countered at relatively low cost by the offense. Finally, these large space platforms share the vulnerability of all extensive space-based systems to direct enemy attack.

Midcourse Intercept and Battle Management

The concept of a defense in depth envisages one or two layers operating during the midcourse phase, which lasts twenty to twenty-five minutes, following the completion of the booster burn and prior to reentry of the warheads into the atmosphere. Although the time constraints are less severe, there are other factors that increase the difficulties of midcourse interception. The post-boost vehicles, and especially the warheads released by the bus, are generally more difficult to destroy than the boosters because they are much smaller and more difficult to track. Also, the bus can be designed to be harder and to release the reentry vehicles very rapidly. The warheads are built to withstand extreme stresses due to deceleration and intense heat from atmospheric friction as they slam back into the top of the atmosphere. In addition to the numerous warheads, each missile may dispense hundreds of light decoys that follow the same paths in the absence of friction above the atmosphere as do the warheads.

While it is true that the technological capacity to analyze and transmit data has increased greatly in recent years, so has the size and sophistication of offensive weapons—as well as its ability to confuse the defense. The offense can, for example, use antisimulation measures to confuse the sensors and stress, if not saturate, the data-handling capacity of the defense. Antisimulation is the technique of making real warheads look like decoys. One antisimulation method is to enclose the warheads in balloons with several thin metal-coated layers so that all the balloons have the same appearance, whether or not there is a warhead inside.

Additional difficulties can be created by precursor detonations of nuclear weapons. The infrared radiation from the air heated by high-altitude nuclear explosions creates a severe background—known as red-out—that hinders the ability of the ABM sensors to "see" the warhead.

No viable concept has yet been demonstrated or devised for a highly effective midcourse defense against a massive threat of many thousands of warheads, plus many times more decoys. The critical needs include not only a battle management software that far exceeds anything in complexity and difficulty accomplished so far, but also the ability to protect all the critical space-based components against enemy attack, whether from space mines, debris clouds, direct-ascent antisatellite weapons, or directed energy weapons on ground or in space. The entire system—including intelligence, communications, and surveillance satellites and the optical and directed high-energy components, whether on ground, in low earth orbit, or at synchronous altitude—must survive and operate in a hostile environment for many minutes or hours in order to engage the threat.

As described in Defense Department documents, the different layers of a defensive system would operate semiautonomously with their own sensors and data processing, as well as with weapons and rules of engagement. As part of the overall task of battle management—monitoring, allocating the available defensive systems, assessing the results of the attack, and refiring if necessary—data would also be passed to successive layers in the defense. Input data from the sensors must be organized and filtered to see which objects can be discarded and which are candidates for further analysis—leading to tracking, attacking, and damage assessment. An effective boost-phase intercept that clears away close to 90 percent of the threat is thus very important in making the battle management and data-handling problems more tractable.

Terminal Defense

The terminal layer of the defense takes advantage of the atmosphere, which slows down and strips away the lighter decoys accompanying the warheads in free space. The requirements for a terminal defense of hardened military targets, such as missile silos and command posts, are much simpler and more readily achievable than for a strategic nationwide defense. If the target is small and hardened to withstand very high levels of overpressure, interception of the incoming warhead can be made successfully much nearer the target. In addition, the goal of such a hard-site defense is not to destroy all incoming warheads, but only enough of them to cause the attacker to expend more of his force than he destroys.

Improved technologies in recent years have enhanced the prospects for a cost-effective hard-site defense that operates without prior layers of the defense. Important advances include interceptors that achieve much higher accelerations and sensors that can distinguish warheads from decoys at higher altitudes. Until recently, ABM weapon technologies for terminal defense have depended on nuclear blasts to knock out attacking warheads. Special nuclear weapons were designed to destroy nuclear weapons. Improvements in weapon accuracy have now raised the possibility of nonnuclear kill.

Whether a hard-site defense of a missile silo will, in reality, exact an "entry price" of two or three or as many as six or seven attacking warheads per hardened target is sensitive to many quantitative assumptions. The point to emphasize, however, is that hard-site defense, whatever its potential and genuine merits, is very different from the goal of a nationwide defense designed to render nuclear weapons "impotent and obsolete." As such, it should be debated on its own merits.

Standing alone, a terminal defense offers no prospect of defending the nation against a massive attack. This conclusion was reached during the ABM debates of 1969–70, and the new technologies have added little to alter it. If, however, a terminal defense operates behind effective boost-phase and midcourse defensive layers that remove all but a few percent of the attacking warheads, the conclusion may be different. With improved sensors and interceptors, the defense may engage the incoming warheads at higher altitudes and contribute to limiting damage to the targets being defended. A terminal defense may thus limit damage as the final tier of a partially effective defense in depth.

Overlap with Other Forms of Strategic Defense

The 1972 ABM Treaty attempted to deal with the problem of advances in surface-to-air missiles, or SAM upgrades. Efforts to defend against aircraft and cruise missiles have led to modern generations of air defenses having improved radars, computers, and high-acceleration interceptors with growing potential to defend against short-range missiles. Intermediate-range ballistic missiles on one-thousand-to-two-thousand-mile trajectories generally fly at lower speeds than longer-range strategic missiles. This increases the time available for the defense to attack them in the terminal phase. Work is underway in both the Soviet Union and the United States to exploit this possibility of theater, nonstrategic ABMs. Ways of updating the ABM Treaty to take account of this new form of the SAM upgrade problem will have to be addressed in future reviews of the treaty.

ASAT Technology and Defense versus Defense

Satellites are simpler targets to attack than missiles because they are softer, fewer, predictable both in their position and time, easier to discriminate, not easily replaced, and have communication and control links from earth that can be attacked. There is no doubt about the technological feasibility of antisatellite (ASAT) systems that will be effective against satellites in low earth orbit in the near future. Extending ASAT effectiveness to geosynchronous orbit altitudes and higher will be a technical challenge, but it presents no fundamental problems.

The significance of ASAT for strategic defense lies in the threat it poses to ABM space platforms, in particular to the warning, acquisition, and battle management sensors. On the other hand, the significance of the Strategic Defense Initiative for ASAT is that it will spur technical developments that inevitably will be threatening to the critical communication and early warning satellite links on which a ballistic missile defense must rely. This presents an unavoidable dilemma: ASAT threatens ABM, but ABM developments contribute to ASAT.

More generally, ABM deployments on each side will pose threats to the other's defensive systems, and in particular to the space-based components. This introduces the prospect of defense as an adjunct of a first strike. For example, a pop-up X-ray laser system launched as part of an attack can contribute to the overall advantage of a first strike by contributing to the suppression of both the defense and the retaliatory strike.

Conclusions

There have been major technological advances in recent years, but we do not now know how to build an effective nationwide strategic defense against ballistic missiles. This is true whether the goal is to transcend deterrence with a nearly leakproof defense or to enhance it with an effective but partial defense. It is true against the current Soviet threat—and there is no present prospect of achieving such a defense against an unlimited offensive threat that can overwhelm, evade, or directly attack the defense. Many years, if not decades, of research are required before we can begin to proceed from imaginative concepts and crude ideas and estimates to educated guesses. If the system is to meet the president's stated goal of rendering nuclear weapons "impotent and obsolete," it must not only work to almost 100 percent perfection, directing an enormous task of battle management in very short times, but it must do this the very first time that it is used. No realistic shakedown tests are conceivable, especially in the nuclear environment the system will encounter in a real engagement.

The overall conclusion stated in the Stanford Report is as follows:

Our analysis raises grave doubts, on technical and strategic grounds, that substantial acceleration or expansion of ABM research and development is warranted or prudent. Deliberation and restraint are imperative not simply because of the enormous costs of the proposed near-term SDI research and technology program, but because the strict limitation of ABM deployments is one of the few points of real agreement reached in the U.S.-Soviet dialogue about nuclear war and arms control. It has practical consequences of great importance for the effectiveness of the U.S. deterrent, for such fragile strategic stability as has been achieved, and for the prospects of avoiding nuclear war.

If defensive systems are to contribute to a safer and more stable strategic relationship between the United States and the Soviet Union, they will have to be embedded in a strict arms control regime that limits offensive systems. Technology alone will not solve the political problem of managing the strategic relationship with the Soviet Union. *(July–August 1984)*

Is There an ABM Gap? A Comparison of U.S. and Soviet ABM Programs
John B. Pike

Public assessments of the U.S.-Soviet strategic balance are too frequently colored by perceptions of a present or impending "gap" in U.S. capabilities. The "gap" is a standard argument in favor of an increased U.S. effort on some type of weapons system. In retrospect, the "gaps" of the past have had a perverse reality. There was indeed a bomber gap, and also a very real missile gap, though both were over-whelmingly in the United States' favor.

Thus it is not surprising to hear reports of an "ABM gap." The 1984 edition of *Soviet Military Power*, the U.S. Defense Department's foremost analysis of the Soviet military, includes an eleven-page description of Soviet strategic defense activities, in contrast to the five pages allotted this topic in the 1983 edition. The status of the Soviet antiballistic missile program is of legitimate concern for U.S. strategic planners. One rationale for the U.S. ABM program is to provide a hedge against Soviet breakout from the ABM Treaty, and to deter such a breakout by maintaining a technological edge.

ABM systems may conveniently be divided into four generations, each succeeding generation having greater technological sophistication. ABM programs are now at varying stages of maturity in both countries. The United States has essentially abandoned the first- and second-generation systems, is in the process of perfecting the third generation, and is making some progress on the fourth generation. In contrast, the Soviets are only just now making the transition from the first to the second generation, and face very real obstacles to further immediate progress.

There is indeed an "ABM gap." But like previous gaps, the ABM gap is in the United States' favor. The United States continues to enjoy a significant lead over the Soviets in this field. This lead has been maintained for over a decade by a prudent program of research, funded at a generally constant level. The state of the Soviet ABM program does not offer any basis for the drastic acceleration of the U.S. ABM program of the sort proposed by the Reagan administration.

First- and Second-Generation ABM Systems

First-generation ABMs, such as the U.S. Nike Zeus and the Soviet Griffon and Galosh systems, use a variety of mechanically steered radars to guide a long-range rocket interceptor armed with a high-yield nuclear warhead. This system is designed to destroy or disable an attacking warhead as it falls to earth. These ABM systems can be readily defeated by relatively simple countermeasures, and are ineffective against attacks of any significant size or sophistication.

The first Soviet ABM was the Griffon, which was paraded in Red Square in 1963. A highly modified version of the Griffon, the Gammon, was subsequently deployed as an air-defense missile. The ABM-1 Galosh missile was paraded in Red Square in 1964 and characterized as an ABM interceptor. In the late 1960s construction started on eight launch sites for this system in the vicinity of Moscow, with four of these sites actually becoming operational. In the late 1970s two of these sites were deactivated in anticipation of subsequent upgrades. Each site has sixteen launchers with associated radars and battle-management computers.

Second-generation ABMs utilize more capable phased-array radars and a two-layer antimissile system. Phased-array radars have no moving parts; the tracking elements are rotated electronically rather than mechanically, allowing greatly improved tracking and targeting over their predecessors. The two-layer missile system employs long-range rockets for interceptions outside the atmosphere, and high-acceleration short-range rockets against incoming targets during reentry.

The second-generation U.S. ABM was a system begun in 1968 called Sentinel, which evolved from the Nike-X. In 1969, President Nixon announced a similar but more modest program, Safeguard, to replace Sentinel. Under the Safeguard system, a long-range Spartan rocket was designed to use high-yield nuclear warheads to destroy incoming reentry vehicles beyond the atmosphere. It was teamed up with the short-range Sprint rocket for lower interception.

The radars of these systems were very expensive and highly vulnerable to direct attack. They were also subject to blinding by the explosions of the long-range interceptors' warheads. More importantly, the cost of the defense was greater than the cost of the offensive buildup needed to overcome it.

The decision to deploy Safeguard was very controversial. There were many reasons for this, including the marginal effectiveness and vulnerability of the system. Although a single Safeguard site was put into operation near Grand Forks, North Dakota, in 1975, it was deactivated after only a few months.

Immediately following the signing of the ABM Treaty, U.S. missile defense research focused on improving techniques for defending ICBM silos. The Site Defense Program developed a rapidly deployable radar and interceptor system for this mission, although congressional restrictions limited the program to component development and precluded prototype testing. Site Defense formed the basis for the Low Altitude Defense System (LoADS), which was considered in the early 1980s for defense of the MX missile.

Since the mid-1970s the Soviets have been developing a more advanced second-generation follow-on to the Galosh system. This new system, the ABM-X-3, will probably become operational around Moscow during the mid-1980s. Five new launcher sites are under construction, and two Galosh sites are being converted for the new system.

The ABM-X-3 will incorporate several improvements over the Galosh, including phased-array radars and two types of interceptor missiles. The interceptors will be deployed in underground silos to reduce their vulnerability to direct attack. Nonetheless, the ABM-X-3 is the technological equivalent to the U.S. Sentinel/Safeguard ABM, and will clearly share the major limitations and vulnerabilities of that system.

Soviet Air Defense and ABM

The Soviet Union maintains the world's largest force of air defense surface-to-air missiles (SAMs). The Soviets' ten thousand launchers include a variety of SAMs and have been continually upgraded over the years. The technology required to intercept high-performance aircraft is not unlike that required to intercept ballistic missiles. This has led to concerns in the United States that Soviet SAMs could form the base for a ballistic missile defense system.

However, the missile-defense capabilities of the Soviet air defense forces are sometimes exaggerated. Most of the Soviet SAMs, such as the SA-1, SA-2, and SA-3, are armed with conventional high-explosive warheads and lack the performance required for the ABM mission. The SA-5, SA-10, and SA-12 have some ABM potential, but this potential is rather limited. Moreover, the Soviets have not demonstrated overwhelming proficiency in air defense technology. Actual combat experience has indicated the need to fire between fifty and one hundred SAMs to down a single airplane.

The task of intercepting a missile warhead is in many respects considerably more demanding than the task of intercepting an airplane. The radar cross section of a missile warhead is typically several orders of magnitude less than that of an airplane. The warhead will also be accompanied by dozens or hundreds of decoys and fragments of the booster rocket, whereas the airplane travels alone. The radars that are normally deployed with SAMs are clearly inadequate to deal with these demands and would have to be supplemented with more sophisticated systems.

The SA-5 Gammon was originally developed in the early 1960s. But the Soviets were apparently unimpressed with its ABM potential. The missile has a comparatively modest acceleration rate and relies on its small wings for maneuverability. Both characteristics reduce its ABM potential. Furthermore, the mechanically steered radars used by the SA-5 are vulnerable to saturation by decoys.

The SA-10 is a new Soviet SAM that is roughly equivalent to the American Patriot, an antiaircraft missile that is credited with a limited tactical ABM potential. When the SA-10 system was first noticed, U.S. intelligence analysts were concerned about its ABM potential. More recently, this system has been regarded as primarily a counter to very low altitude targets such as cruise missiles.

The SA-X-12 antitactical ballistic missile (ATBM) system is the most recent addition to the Soviets' air defense arsenal, achieving operational status in mid-1984.

Both the missile and its associated phased-array radars are transported on large tracked vehicles. The SA-12 is designed to intercept both aircraft and tactical or theater ballistic missiles. If the SA-12 were to be deployed in conjunction with a more capable radar, it could approach the performance requirements for interception of longer-range missiles. But the limited acceleration and maneuverability of the SA-12 (compared to that of an ABM interceptor such as the U.S. Sprint) would make such a defense very vulnerable to countermeasures such as heavy penetration decoys and even simple manuevering decoys.

Third-Generation ABM Systems

Third-generation ABMs are multiple-layer systems based on technology that has been under active development in the United States for over a decade. These technologies will receive increased attention under President Reagan's Strategic Defense Initiative. There is no direct evidence of Soviet work in this area, and indeed such systems require technologies that are probably beyond the state of the art in the Soviet Union today.

The key components of effective third-generation ABM systems are highly capable battle-management computers and extremely sensitive and discriminating sensor systems. At present, the United States holds a major lead in both of these areas. The United States is using fourth-generation computers to design hardware and software for advanced fifth-generation computers capable of executing in excess of 100 million instructions per second. The Soviets are still struggling with third-generation computers.

In the place of radars, third-generation systems substitute mobile air-based and space-based infrared sensors, such as the Airborne Optical System. Nonnuclear "hit-to-kill" kinetic-energy interceptors, such as the Homing Overlay Experiment, can intercept targets both in and above the atmosphere. The mobile sensor platforms of these systems are much less vulnerable to direct attack than are fixed radars, and kinetic energy weapons avoid the self-blinding effects of their nuclear predecessors.

Infrared heat-seeking sensors offer major improvements over radars for interception of missiles and warheads in boost-phase and midcourse flight. This is a field where the United States holds a significant lead over the Soviet Union. To date, the Soviets have not demonstrated a mastery of this challenging technology. Whereas the United States has routinely used infrared sensors on early-warning satellites in high-altitude geostationary orbits, the Soviets have failed in their one attempt, in 1975, to emulate this technique. Furthermore, the Soviet infrared-guided antisatellite system has failed in all six of its tests.

Fourth-Generation Directed-Energy Systems

Fourth-generation ABMs are multilayered systems that include directed-energy weapons such as lasers or particle beam weapons. The principal attraction of these systems is their potential for intercepting missiles during their boost phase, when they are relatively vulnerable and before they can deploy multiple warheads and decoys. These systems have stimulated considerable discussion in recent years and will receive considerable emphasis in President Reagan's Strategic Defense Initiative. Although both the United States and the Soviet Union have active programs for the development of some of the techniques required for such systems, both countries are many years, if not decades, away from perfecting them.

The Soviets have placed considerable emphasis on their directed-energy program, which is generally regarded as being at approximately the same level of development as the U.S. program. The Soviet level of effort has clearly been much greater than that in the United States, employing several times as many technical personnel. The parity of results illustrates the much lower per capita productivity of Soviet science.

The Soviets have made a number of original contributions in directed-energy research. But it is significant that many Soviet breakthroughs are in areas of basic, or theoretical, science, where the Soviets are admittedly strong. The transition from theoretical principle to working weapon continues to be a major Soviet weakness. It is also significant that the areas of Soviet breakthroughs are those, such as particle beams, that show the least promise for near-term deployment.

The Soviets could possibly conduct an integrated on-orbit test of a space-based laser in the later part of this decade. The initial prototype will certainly have marginal capabilities, but the actual military significance of such a demonstration is questionable. The laser itself is the least challenging element of an integrated weapons system. The pointing and tracking sensors and the battle-management command and control systems are the most critical elements of an effective space weapon system, and these are areas of known Soviet deficiency.

Conclusions

Despite the Soviets' strenuous efforts, their ABM systems under development and in deployment typically lag behind their U.S. counterparts by at least a decade. The Soviets will undoubtedly continue their efforts to improve their ABM capabilities through research on more advanced third- and fourth-generation ABM technologies. But the United States enjoys a clear lead over the Soviets in many of the scientific and technical fields that are crucial for progress on such systems. Although the Soviets have a significant directed-energy program, both countries are far from fielding effective weapons of this sort.

Soviet design and procurement practices differ greatly from those in the United States and often give the appearance of a lead that does not exist. Given the limitations of the Soviet scientific and engineering community, the Soviets must invest several times the number of personnel and amount of facilities as the United States to achieve the same results. Developmental experiments that can be conducted in the laboratory or using computer simulation in the United States require actual field testing in the Soviet Union. Moreover, the Soviets tend to field militarily ineffective systems in order to gain operational and training experience. Whereas the low operating and personnel costs to the Soviet military make this viable, high costs discourage this practice in the United States.

Regional nuclear threats provide the Soviet Union with added incentives for a limited ABM capability. The nuclear forces of China, and one day perhaps Pakistan, give Soviet leaders reason to believe that ABM forces deployed around their capital may at some time prove useful. Fortunately, the United States does not face similar incentives for a small ABM system.

The Soviets have generally maintained a good record of compliance with the ABM Treaty, indicative of a strong degree of commitment to this regime. Since the early 1970s, occasional Soviet activities have raised questions regarding their strict compliance with the terms of the ABM Treaty. All of these issues were discussed in the Standing Consultative Commission (SCC), a joint U.S.-Soviet forum for discussion and implementation of SALT I, and resolved to the satisfaction of both parties.

Despite the satisfactory resolution of these issues, the dynamic pace of the Soviet program continues to create instances where questions arise concerning compliance with the treaty. The most troubling of these is the new radar at Abalakova, which is very difficult to reconcile with U.S. interpretations of the treaty. This issue is presently under discussion in the SCC. Several other matters have received publicity but have not been raised in the SCC.

These incidents do not constitute compelling evidence of a concerted effort on the part of the Soviets to break out of the ABM Treaty in the near future. In fact, the Soviets do not have strong incentives to terminate the ABM Treaty. The systems that are available to them now and for the foreseeable future have only limited capabilities and marginal effectiveness. These would not seem to offer the prospect of a cost-effective investment for the defense of hardened military targets, and they hold virtually no promise for the defense of urban-industrial targets.

The United States has maintained an active program for the development of penetration aids, and this program was reaffirmed in President Reagan's National Security Decision Directive 91 of August 1983. At present, U.S. strategic missiles, and in particular submarine-launched ballistic missiles, carry an extensive complement of penetration aids that would severely stress any prospective Soviet ABM system. Soviet deployment of a significant ABM capability would require several years at a minimum. This would be more than enough time to add any additional penetration aids needed to overcome the Soviet defense.

But larger political considerations might prompt the Soviets to disregard these objections and to proceed with deployment. If the United States was perceived as making major strides toward perfecting third- or fourth-generation ABM systems that the Soviets were unable to match, the Soviets might feel impelled actually to deploy a less-effective second-generation system. Such a Soviet system could be operational many years before the more advanced U.S. system, and could rectify, though temporarily, the perceived imbalance in capabilities. *(July–August 1984)*

Déjà Vu: The Antisatellite Debate in Historical Context
Paul B. Stares

In retrospect, 1983 may well be considered the year in which the United States irrevocably committed itself to a new military course in space. For more than twenty-five years, space has been used primarily for "passive" military purposes such as reconnaissance, early warning, communication, navigation, and weather forecasting. However, recent events point to the beginning of a new trend in the militarization of space: President Reagan's "Star Wars" speech in March 1983 advocated the development of a space-based defense system against ballistic missiles; two study groups created to investigate the feasibility of space-based ballistic missile defenses (BMD) recommended further research and development; the United States has shown little interest in a Soviet draft treaty banning space weapons; and the United States is preparing for the first in-space test of a U.S. antisatellite (ASAT) system that has been in development since 1977. The purpose here is to challenge the official rationale for the recent change in U.S. policy by putting the whole debate in its historical context.

We Have Been Here Before

The recent wave of books, articles, radio, and TV shows about this subject have all rightly emphasized the novelty of these developments. Yet for those familar with the "space debates" of the late 1950s and early 1960s, there must be a strong sense of déjà vu. The current debate about the wisdom of developing ASAT and space-based BMD systems reflects with uncanny similarity the arguments that were used during this earlier period. In the immediate years following the launch of *Sputnik* in 1957, the likelihood of an arms race in space appeared to be very high. Fear of Soviet domination and attack in or from space created strong pressures for the United States to field a variety of space weapons to counter the apparent threat.

Despite this pressure, successive U.S. administrations believed that it was not in the best interests of the United States to militarize space in this fashion. This restraint, however, did come with an insurance policy of allowing some research and development and, after 1963, the *limited* deployment of antisatellite weapons in case Soviet actions dictated a rapid U.S. response. The Soviet threat in space never materialized, although the Soviets did begin to test a co-orbital satellite interceptor in 1968. This program's record of intermittent testing and numerous failures suggests that this was not a high-priority concern for the Soviet Union.

The possibility that this low level of activity was in response to U.S. developments should not be discounted. By 1978, both countries had agreed to discuss antisatellite weapon limitations and were arguably close to an agreement when the negotiations fell victim to the post-Afghanistan freeze on arms control. Unfortunately, even these bare historical facts have been largely forgotten or conveniently overlooked to justify the current U.S. position.

Putting the Record Straight

The existence of an earlier U.S. ASAT program is rarely, if ever, officially acknowledged. In fact, the United States first began thinking about antisatellite weapons before there were any satellites to disable. Some of the earliest studies in the early 1950s of the military utility of artificial satellites included discussions of the countermeasures that could be used if satellites became a hostile threat to the United States. It was not until the crisis caused by *Sputnik*, however, that this early interest was translated into serious research and development proposals for ASAT and other space weapons. As noted earlier, the fear of Soviet surprise attack in space caused an overnight scramble by the military services to propose an expansion of the national space program beyond the planned "passive" military satellites. Their stated rationale, which is being repeated today in almost identical lanaguage, was that the United States needed to "take the high ground" to "control space" and prevent Soviet "domination." As a result, each of the services prepared its own ASAT research projects—some of which were eventually tested—in the expectation that the United States would develop such a capability.

For example, on October 19, 1959, the United States became the first country—contrary to most people's perception—to conduct an antisatellite test. Under the code name *Bold Orion*, a missile was launched from a B-47 aircraft, and it successfully intercepted the *Explorer VI* satellite as it passed over Cape Canaveral. The army also proposed using its Nike Zeus antiballistic missile in the ASAT role, as did the navy with Polaris launchers. Space-based ballistic missile defense systems such as projects BAMBI (ballistic missile boost intercept) and SPAD (space patrol active defense), which are readily acknowledged to be the antecedents of today's high frontier concept, were also proposed at this time.

With the exception of a satellite inspection (SAINT) program, the Eisenhower administration did not support any of these proposals beyond preliminary research. Apart from President Eisenhower's more altruistic desire to prevent an arms race in space, he and his advisors recognized that this could seriously undermine U.S. military goals in space. Their reasoning was clear: due to the closed nature of Soviet society and the finite operational life of U-2 aircraft overflights of the Soviet Union, the time would come when the United States would have to depend on military satellites for strategic reconnaissance. Because the Soviet Union was less dependent on space systems, it was not likely to be deterred from attacking U.S. satellites by the threat of reciprocal action. As satellites could not be adequately defended, the United States encouraged the principle and legitimacy of "peaceful" (that is, nonaggressive) military activities in space. Thus, the development of antisatellite or other space weapons would not only have undermined the U.S. public position, but also would possibly have encouraged the Soviet Union to take direct action against U.S. satellites. This viewpoint was also encouraged by the enormous financial costs and technological problems from which many of these proposals suffered.

By the early 1960s, the specter of a Soviet threat in space had increased. Soviet diplomatic opposition to U.S. reconnaissance satellites and veiled references to nuclear bombardment from orbit were often linked to the continuing success of the Soviet space program in achieving a series of spectacular "firsts" in space. The Kennedy administration, in the face of bitter opposition from the services—particularly the Air Force—endorsed its predecessors' guidelines for the "peaceful" exploitation of space. Moreover, President Kennedy showed great statesmanship in negotiating with the Soviets and in gaining domestic support for the 1963 Limited Test Ban Treaty and United Nations Resolution 1884. The test ban prohibited testing, and the U.N. resolution prohibited deployment of nuclear weapons in space. The latter became the basis for the 1967 Outer Space Treaty.

As a precautionary measure, President Kennedy also authorized in great secrecy the development of two antisatellite weapons systems in case the Soviet Union did deploy orbital bombs. The first, known as Program 505 (Mudflap in its early stages), consisted of a modified Nike Zeus ABM missile. This was deployed on Kwajalein Atoll in the Pacific and tested on at least eight occasions between May 1963 and 1967 when it was decommissioned. The second known as Program 437, consisted of modified Thor intermediate-range ballistic missiles and was deployed in the Pacific at Johnston Island. Sixteen tests were conducted between May 1964 and 1970, although the system remained nominally operational until 1975. Both systems had a nuclear warhead, which meant that they would only have been used in extreme emergencies. Their fixed site and limited range (160 miles for the Nike Zeus and 700 miles for the Thor missile) meant they would only have been able to attack low-altitude targets as they passed overhead.

Although a replacement was considered for the Thor system, especially after the Soviet Union began testing its own antisatellite system in 1968, no new program was commissioned. The cessation of Soviet ASAT testing after 1971 and the general climate of détente in the early 1970s lowered interest in this issue. Moreover, as a series of study groups examining this question during the Ford and Nixon administrations recognized, the United States was still more dependent on satellites than was the Soviet Union, despite the increase in the Soviet military use of space. They concluded that the presence of a U.S. ASAT system would not enhance the survivability of U.S. space assets.

By 1976, the attitude of the Ford administration had begun to change. The sudden resumption of Soviet ASAT testing in February of that year created new pressures for the United States to field its own system. In the last days of the Ford administration, the decision was taken to develop a U.S. ASAT program. The ostensible rationale was that the United States needed to counter the indirect threat posed by Soviet satellites, particularly ocean reconnaissance satellites, to U.S. naval and ground forces in wartime. The core reason appears to have been a visceral feeling that the United States could not allow the Soviet Union an unchallenged ASAT capability.

The incoming Carter administration kept the program but made its eventual deployment conditional on the progress reached toward an antisatellite arms control agreement. In other words, the program became a bargaining chip. Three rounds of talks were held: in Helsinki from June 8 to 16, 1978; in Bern from January 23 to February 19, 1979; and finally in Vienna from April 23 to June 17, 1979. Although the United States hoped that a comprehensive agreement could be reached that would prohibit antisatellite weapons altogether, progress seems only to have been made toward defining a "no hostile act" agreement with additional "rules of the road" for operations in space. The most significant obstacles to an agreement were reported to have been Soviet insistence that the U.S. space shuttle be included in the agreement and that "third party" satellites be excluded. Both conditions were unacceptable to the United States. Unfortunately, as noted earlier, the rupture in East–West relations after the Soviet invasion of Afghanistan prevented all further progress.

Breaking with the Past

Under the Reagan administration, the U.S. ASAT program has progressed to the testing phase without any indication that arms control has been considered as a viable alternative. In fact, just as the bargaining chip strategy appears to be working—witness the recent Soviet proposals—the United States has shunned the opportunity to negotiate from a position of strength. So what has changed to justify this policy? The answer, unfortunately, is very little. The U.S. ASAT will not counter the Soviet system but will encourage further Soviet development of ASAT technology, making the problem worse, not better. Moreover, the long-term costs in financial and operational terms make the whole enterprise prohibitively expensive. Even the argument that the United States needs an ASAT system to negate Soviet satellites ignores the range of other countermeasures available to the United States. In short, the long-term costs will more than outweigh the putative benefits of an ASAT capability. The path of restraint that previous presidents have shown to be more desirable is still open to this administration—but for how long?   *(December 1983)*

3
Strategic Nuclear Weapons and Strategy

T he Reagan administration came to office in 1981 with a pledge to strengthen an alleged weakness in U.S. military forces, particularly strategic nuclear weapons. President Reagan supported the continued development and deployment of the MX intercontinental ballistic missile (given the name Peacekeeper), though he proposed that only one hundred MX missiles be deployed in fixed silos, as opposed to the two hundred MXs in an elaborate multiple-shelter system proposed by the Carter administration. President Reagan also restarted the B-1 bomber program, which had been canceled in the Carter administration, and continued the development and deployment of other existing strategic weapons programs, including the "stealth" advanced technology bomber, air-, ground-, and sea-launched cruise missiles, and the Trident II missile and submarine program.

In his first term, President Reagan gathered together a bipartisan panel of experts to advise the administration and Congress on nuclear weapons policy. The panel, headed by retired Lt. Gen. Brent Scowcroft and hence called the Scowcroft Commission, was generally supportive of Reagan administration policies and weapons programs, though with a few significant distinctions. The panel concluded that although the Soviet ability to launch a successful first strike against U.S. strategic weapons was a grave concern, it did not present the immediate danger claimed by President Reagan and other administration officials. The U.S. retaliatory force was still effective and was not, the Commission implied, facing an imminent threat through a "window of vulnerability," as Reagan had often stated. In two reports, the panel advocated the deployment of the MX missile and proposed that the United States study the possibility of deploying a single-warhead missile in a mobile basing system, a weapon that would be less vulnerable than fixed silo-based ICBMs. This Midgetman missile soon became a priority program. Finally, the panel's recommendations, particularly in its second report, strongly urged that serious arms control negotiations complement the U.S. strategic arms modernization programs and warned that "the strategic implications of ballistic missile defense and the criticality of the ABM Treaty to further arms control agreements dictate extreme caution in proceeding to engineering development in this sensitive area."

The Scowcroft Commission's arms control recommendations were especially relevant because the existing restraints on U.S. and Soviet strategic arms as embodied by the SALT agreements were under attack by members of the administration. Administration opponents of SALT II finally had their way when, on May 27, 1986, President Reagan formally repudiated SALT II and announced the U.S. intention to exceed its limits in the fall of 1986. Jack Mendelsohn demonstrates in his article, "Saving SALT," that U.S. security will be jeopardized if the United States abandons the SALT framework without replacing it with new controls. Although the Reagan administration has been critical of the SALT process, it has remained in adherence with the strategic arms limits of the SALT I and II agreements for years. The SALT process, in fact, has had a much greater effect on U.S. and Soviet strategic weapons programs during the Reagan years than any new arms control proposals initiated by the Reagan administration. In their discussions of strategic weapons, the authors in this chapter have taken into consideration the implications these weapons have for arms control and the SALT agreements.

Saving SALT
Jack Mendelsohn

On June 10, following a flurry of conflicting press reports and broad hints to the contrary from inside the administration, President Reagan announced that the United States would continue to abide by the terms of the expired SALT I and unratified SALT II agreements. To this end, the president stated that the United States will deactivate and dismantle an existing Poseidon strategic missile submarine (SSBN) when the seventh U.S. Trident submarine starts sea trials in the fall.

The June 10 announcement served the president well. It kept the United States in compliance with a key SALT II quantitative limit on MIRVed missiles. It eased the administration past a potentially serious crisis in relations with Congress and the Western allies. It retained the framework required for any hope of progress in the continuing arms control discussions in Geneva, and it improved the chances for and atmosphere surrounding an eventual summit meeting with Soviet General Secretary Mikhail Gorbachev.

But the president's announcement also served to put arms control "on notice." In effect, the president decided that, for the balance of his term, U.S. policy regarding SALT will be determined on a case-by-case basis and will be subject to four contingent factors:

1. A show of "comparable restraint" by the Soviet Union. Presumably this means that the Soviet Union must demonstrate its commitment to arms control by staying within the applicable SALT limits.

2. The "active pursuit" by the Soviet Union of arms reduction agreements. Presumably this means that the Soviet Union must take some initiative in the strategic offensive weapons talks in Geneva.

3. Actions by the Soviet Union to "correct" noncompliance. Presumably this means that the Soviet Union will be pressed to rectify alleged SALT violations that are "reversible," such as telemetry encryption and SS-16 deployments.

4. An "appropriate and proportionate" U.S. programmatic response to "irreversible" noncompliance. Presumably this means that the administration will use "irreversible" Soviet SALT violations, such as the SS-X-25 missile, to justify requests to Congress for new or augmented strategic programs.

Clearly, the June 10 announcement left unresolved the fundamental issue of whether or not the United States would continue to abide by the limits of SALT I and II pending negotiation of a formal follow-on agreement. It also transformed what could have been a major policy decision into a miniseries of potential crisis points. And it left arms control hostage to each new Trident boat, to the MX missile and B-1 bomber programs, to progress in Geneva, and to Soviet good behavior. In sum, the president's announcement amounted to little more than a declaration that the United States will comply with the provisions of SALT for now but stands ready to reverse this policy at any time.

A Policy for Strategic Leverage?

By adopting this policy of "reversible compliance" and by establishing a set of criteria by which to judge Soviet behavior, the administration evidently hopes to obtain leverage over the Soviet Union and force it to accept the U.S. approach to arms control. Failing this, the administration will, in its own estimate, have made the case for sustaining a defense buildup and, possibly, for abandoning arms control.

The fatal flaws in the administration's new policy are obvious. In the first instance, in light of the vigorous Soviet strategic development and deployment program, the U.S. threat to breach the quantitative limits of SALT is unlikely to be translated into meaningful strategic leverage. According to recently leaked intelligence information, by the end of the decade the Soviet Union may deploy up to 200 SS-25 ICBMs in a road-mobile version and up to 350 new, ten-warhead SS-24 ICBMs in silos and as a rail-mobile system. Without the quantitative constraints of SALT the Soviets would be free to deploy both these new ICBMs without any compensating reductions in their existing ICBM forces. However, under SALT limits the Soviets would have to deactivate a MIRVed ICBM such as the SS-17, SS-18, or SS-19 for each SS-24 and a single-warhead SS-11 or SS-13 for each new SS-25. In addition, without the SALT II limit on warhead loadings, the Soviet Union would be capable of rapidly increasing the number of warheads on its 308 SS-18 heavy missiles from ten to fourteen. This move alone would result in an increase, within three years, of 1,200 hard-target kill warheads in the Soviet ICBM force.

In contrast, the United States currently plans to deploy the MX missile in existing Minuteman III silos. Unless additional silos are built—a time-consuming and expensive process—MX will displace some portion of the current U.S. ICBM force. Although the number of U.S. ICBM warheads will grow somewhat, the number of launchers and aim points will not. This "SALT-free" combination of Soviet and U.S. deployments will inevitably result in a sharp increase in the numbers and capability of the Soviet ICBM forces vis-à-vis those of the United States and place U.S. fixed, land-based forces at even greater risk. This would, of course, be the very outcome the United States has sought to avoid over the past decade, and it would exacerbate the fatal flaw of previous arms control agreements that the administration has pledged to rectify.

Without SALT, the Soviet Union could also improve its relative position as regards sea-borne systems. The 1986–89 Trident production schedule calls for the United States to deploy three SSBNs after the USS *Alaska*. But recent reports indicate that the Soviet Union has at least eight new SSBNs under construction and, with a current average production rate of three SSBNs per year, could launch at least twelve SSBNs during the same period. Even though the new U.S. Tridents have more launchers per boat and more MIRVs per missile, without the SALT requirement to retire older SSBNs as new ones come on line, the Soviet Union could add almost three times as many SLBM (submarine-launched ballistic missile) tubes and twice as many SLBM reentry vehicles as the United States by the end of the decade.

The one area in which the United States possesses a more active, larger-scale program than the Soviet Union is air-launched cruise missiles (ALCMs) and heavy bombers. Even here, however, totally unconstrained Soviet deployments of the new Bear-H cruise missile carrier and Blackjack heavy bomber—current intelligence projections reportedly predict some 140 Bear-Hs and 30 Blackjacks within the next three to four years—would more than double the existing Soviet heavy bomber force. In addition, abandoning SALT II would allow the Soviet Union to upgrade Backfire bombers by arming them with long-range cruise missiles and affording them true intercontinental attack capabilities.

These estimates of Soviet force developments are quite conservative. According to stories leaked at about the time of the president's SALT announcement and confirmed by subsequent unclassified testimony, the new CIA National Intelligence Estimate on Soviet strategic forces predicts even larger increases over the next decade. According to these reports, the Soviet Union could add between seven thousand and twelve thousand warheads to its arsenal by the mid-1990s. The more accurate these estimates, the less credible is the notion that the United States can exert leverage over the Soviet Union by threatening to breach the quantitative limits of SALT II or by abandoning the current policy of mutual restraint.

Negotiating Leverage?

The administration's policy of reversible compliance is also unlikely to generate any leverage over the Soviet Union at the negotiating table. Neither a U.S. commitment to abide by SALT nor a U.S. threat to abandon it will impel the Soviet Union to pursue actively arms reduction agreements. The current stalemate in Geneva is not over strategic arms reductions: both sides favor a significant decrease in current inventories. The real impasse stems from disagreement over the role of strategic defenses and the effort to reverse the current offense-dominated, deterrence-based relationship. Unless and until that issue is resolved, it is unlikely that the Soviet Union will be prepared to reduce its strategic offensive forces. As a matter of fact, if the United States plans to reverse the present offense-dominated relationship and deploy strategic defenses, it would make more sense to maintain the SALT limits than to allow the Soviet Union to deploy additional offensive weapons as a countermeasure.

Nor is the administration's policy of "contingent" arms control likely to garner much support from the NATO allies. Without exception, the NATO allies have a genuine interest in preserving the current SALT framework. National Security Advisor Robert McFarlane, in his June 10 press backgrounder, grudgingly alluded to this when he admitted that "however flawed European thinking might be upon the real value of arms control . . . [sentiment in its favor] is real." The U.S. threat to abandon SALT, combined with the current hard-sell on Star Wars and the ongoing INF (intermediate-range nuclear forces) deployments, only highlights for Europeans the fragility of the administration's commitment to arms control and puts political pressure on those governments with domestic constituencies that are sensitive to this issue. The result is likely to be a growing uneasiness within the alliance over the direction of U.S. policy, a malaise that will play directly into the Soviet Union's upcoming campaign to improve relations with Western Europe.

In short, the political arguments for maintaining SALT are as compelling as the strategic ones. The administration will have difficulty reconciling a dramatic— and potentially unverifiable—increase in Soviet strategic forces with its stated goal of overall reductions and an eventual transition to a nuclear-free world. It will also have difficulty explaining how a growth in offensive weaponry on both sides will improve the chances for deploying even a moderately effective ballistic missile defense. And lastly, any effort to exercise leverage over the Soviet Union by threatening to abandon the quantitative limits of SALT unless progress is registered in the arms reduction negotiations would seriously undermine the credibility of the administration's entire approach to arms control.

Leverage on Congress?

McFarlane, in the background briefing cited earlier, noted that "The President's judgment is that you do better with [adherence to SALT] in terms of getting your [military] programs through Congress." On this issue, the president's judgment is sound: Congress is probably the only area where the administration can exert leverage by invoking its policy of reversible compliance. As a matter of fact, it seems likely that the primary utility of this policy will be to justify requests to Congress for budgetary support of the administration's defense programs.

As part of his June 10 decision, President Reagan directed the Secretary of Defense to submit by November 15 a report identifying and outlining actions the United States could take "as a proportionate response" to alleged Soviet violations. No doubt Secretary Weinberger, who has been one of the most vociferous opponents of extending the SALT limits, will use the report to call for full funding of the MX missile, the Strategic Defense Initiative, and other programs that have been constrained by Congress. And no doubt the administration will make a strong case for these programs both as a price for continued adherence to SALT and as a response to Soviet noncompliance. But it remains to be seen whether the administration, using arms control as a carrot and compliance issues as a stick, will be able to win Congress to its side in all the coming budgetary battles.

Compliance Politics

In a tacit acknowledgment of its severely limited strategic and political leverage, the administration has also made U.S. adherence to SALT contingent on Soviet actions to "correct" noncompliance. To support its accusations of Soviet bad faith, the administration has sent three reports to Congress and leaked vast amounts of information about alleged Soviet violations. The end result of this campaign has been to obscure totally the issues that are at stake and to make it almost impossible to distinguish genuine compliance problems from those that are debatable, marginal, or nonsubstantive.

The most serious of the alleged Soviet violations put forward by the administration involve (1) the testing of two new ICBMs when only one is allowed under SALT II, and (2) the encryption of missile flight-test data. In the first case, the administration claims that the throwweight, or payload capacity, of the SS-25 missile is greater than that of its predecessor, the SS-13, by more than the five percent that is permitted by the modernization provisions of SALT II. If correct, this means that the Soviet Union has tested and deployed a second new ICBM in addition to the SS-24. But the data on the SS-13 and the SS-25, as well as the precise definition of throwweight, are unclear and subject to varying interpretation. Some published reports indicate that the available data could support the conclusion that the Soviet Union is in fact in compliance. In any event, the SS-25 argument appears to be only marginally significant from a security point of view since the SS-25 is a mobile, single-warhead missile—a type that the United States has concluded is desirable for strategic stability.

The encryption issue is equally complicated and even more open to interpretation. The Soviet Union has argued that encryption is permitted by the SALT II Treaty (in Article XV, Second Common Understanding) so long as the overall ability to verify the agreement remains unimpeded. The United States, on the other hand, maintains that any encryption that "impedes" verification is banned (in the same Article XV). The dispute, which hinges on the meaning of the word *impede*, can be traced to a failure in the treaty to establish precisely how and when encryption impedes verification.

The administration has unwittingly adopted contradictory positions on these two compliance issues. Even though the Soviet Union is reported to have extensively encrypted recent flight-test data, the United States has nonetheless succeeded in collecting a great deal of intelligence on these new systems. As a result, any claim that Soviet encryption has impeded verification would appear to be undercut by the detailed charges the United States has leveled concerning the throwweight comparison between the SS-13 and SS-25, for which precise data is certainly required to make a sound judgment.

Ironically, an ill-considered response to alleged Soviet violations could impair the ability of the United States to employ the national technical means of verification used to monitor compliance. The United States is capable of picking up such fine-grain intelligence through an array of redundant capabilities that provide alternate means of monitoring Soviet activities. If the United States allows SALT to collapse, the Soviet Union will be under no obligation to allow these alternate collection systems to operate unimpeded. Though the Soviets are unlikely to interfere directly with U.S. reconnaissance satellites at this time, they could easily adopt a number of camouflage, concealment, masking, and deception techniques that are now prohibited by SALT. Such a move, together with large-scale data encryption, would vastly complicate U.S. intelligence-gathering efforts. Here again, because continued adherence to SALT and preservation of its verification provisions largely favor the United States, the bargaining leverage of the United States vis-à-vis the Soviet Union is limited.

Prognosis for SALT

The short-term prognosis for this new era of reversible compliance and contingent arms control is fairly clear:

1. The administration will continue to stress the Soviet threat. News of the high projections for Soviet strategic forces in the most recent National Intelligence Estimate was leaked at just about the time of the June 10 decision, and an unclassified version of the study was released in late June. We can expect more administration reports on impressive military improvements and destabilizing strategic deployments by the Soviet Union over the next months. But threat projections can cut two ways: they can encourage Congress to fund strategic programs, or they can also strengthen the case for retaining the limits of SALT, which require the Soviet Union to deploy new systems in place of, rather than in addition to, existing ones.

2. The administration will continue to uncover and publicize evidence of alleged Soviet noncompliance. Reports are already circulating about new Soviet heavy ICBMs and SLBMs (both banned by SALT II), as are claims that the Soviet Union

is violating the overall quantitative limits of SALT II on delivery vehicles (by adding Bear-H bombers without compensating reductions). This barrage of accusations is likely in the short run to blur even further the distinction between political issues and strategic concerns, and in the long run to risk restricting the administration's ability to devise and conclude any sensible agreement with the Soviet Union.

3. The administration will continue to press its case for counting the SS-25 as a second new ICBM. The president has already indicated that the SS-25 is an "irreversible" act of noncompliance and that the United States reserves the right to respond "in a proportionate manner at the appropriate time." In this regard, his June 10 announcement noted that "the Midgetman small ICBM program is particularly relevant." At some point, the administration will announce its intention to test and deploy a second ICBM in addition to the MX. The Soviet Union, of course, has never admitted that the SS-25 is anything but an ICBM modernization program permitted under SALT. Passing Midgetman off as a response to the SS-25 is thus certain to become a contentious issue between the sides. One danger is that, in announcing its breach of the ICBM modernization provision, the United States could provide the Soviet Union with the pretext to abandon or seek to modify other ICBM modernization constraints, such as the ban on new heavy ICBMs.

4. The administration will present a big bill to Congress to fund new or planned systems currently constrained by the defense budget. In addition to seeking full funding for Midgetman, MX, SDI, and Poseidon submarine conversion, the administration may also request funds according to reports, for additional Minuteman III Mark 12-A warheads and for an increase in the size of the B-1 bomber force.

5. The administration will continue to flog the Soviet Union over lack of progress in Geneva. But this tactic may also cut two ways: the Soviet position on limiting strategic offensive weapons is likely to evolve over the next few months as the Soviets repeat their offer to reduce delivery vehicles by 25 percent or more and to establish a limit on what the Soviet Union calls "nuclear charges." The U.S. position on SDI will then reemerge even more clearly as the real sticking point in the Geneva negotiations, and abandoning the quantitative limits of SALT for lack of Soviet "active pursuit" will be increasingly difficult to justify.

Exit Arms Control?

In some ways, not much has changed. According to the administration, the Soviet Union is still threatening strategic breakout, still violating its treaty commitments, and still stonewalling in Geneva. Nevertheless, the president has decided to save SALT for the time being, provided appropriate and proportionate responses can be devised by the Defense Department and supported by the Congress.

But in other ways, a great deal has changed. The president's decision to continue to abide by SALT on a case-by-case and contingent basis—the policy of reversible compliance discussed earlier—means that the United States has entered the era of roller-coaster arms control, with the administration teetering on the brink of abandoning SALT each time a new strategic system rolls down the ways or out of the plant, each time a new Soviet threat is unveiled, or each time an alleged act of Soviet bad faith is detected. The president's decision also means that the Defense Department is authorized to explore programmatic options deliberately designed to erode the framework of SALT. And the president's decision to link adherence to SALT with alleged Soviet noncompliance means that the United States might sacrifice crucial quantitative limits in order to respond to marginally significant violations of qualitative restrictions.

Perhaps the president will come to realize that the strategic and political arguments for retaining the informal arms control arrangements of the past six years are compelling and that the costs of abandoning them are enormous. Perhaps he will also come to realize that U.S. leverage over the Soviet Union is quite limited and, in most cases, nonexistent. And perhaps he will sufficiently moderate his earlier vision of the "evil empire" to use his meeting with Soviet General Secretary Gorbachev to begin the process of resolving the standoff between the sides. Until we know the answers to these questions, it is too early to say "Exit arms control." More likely, arms control will be on center stage for the indefinite future.   *(June 1985)*

The Reagan Nuclear Strategy
Robert C. Gray

The nuclear policy of the Reagan administration has received an extraordinary amount of attention in the press for a number of reasons including the five-year strategic modernization program, the continuing attempts to find an acceptable basing mode for the MX missile, and the slow pace of arms control negotiations. But the most important cause of public interest in the Reagan nuclear strategy is also the root cause of the upsurge in antinuclear activism in Europe and the United States—the incautious rhetoric about nuclear war of the president, former Secretary of State Alexander Haig, Secretary of Defense Caspar Weinberger, and some lower-ranking officials at the National Security Council and the Department of Defense.

Secretary of State Haig's casual reference to the use of nuclear weapons in Europe inflamed sentiment there. President Reagan declared that "on balance the Soviet Union does have a definite margin of superiority." Secretary of Defense Weinberger has repeatedly referred to *"restoring* the deterrence that has kept the peace since World War II," suggesting that at the moment, the Soviets are not deterred. And lower-ranking officials such as Richard Pipes of the NSC (National Security Council) staff and T.K. Jones, deputy under secretary of defense for Strategic and

Theater Nuclear Forces, have clearly suggested that nuclear war is winnable if the United States adopts the correct policies.

The administration's national security policies richly deserve much of the criticism they have received. Ronald Reagan's instincts toward the Soviet Union have been excessively confrontational. It is indefensible that the administration took sixteen months to make a strategic arms control proposal. And there are indeed people in responsible positions who hold extremist views on nuclear policy.

If one looks carefully at the evolution of strategic nuclear policy, however, there are good reasons for believing that the press has overstated the novelty of the Reagan administration's policies. Before dealing with this argument, however, it is necessary to clarify the terms of debate over strategic nuclear policy.

Shifting Terms of Debate: Three Schools of Thought

One source of confusion in discussing strategic nuclear policy today is that the terms of reference have shifted to the right in recent years. When Secretary of Defense James Schlesinger announced the move toward limited nuclear options in the mid-1970s, the ensuing debate was between advocates of assured destruction and those who believed that deterrence would best be preserved by increasing the flexibility and selectivity of nuclear plans (and, hence, the credibility of using nuclear weapons). Almost a decade later many observers still talk as if the debate were unchanged—assured destruction versus war-fighting deterrence, with the latter being viewed as an extreme position.

What has happened in the past decade, however, is that American strategy, force planning, and employment policy have all moved in the direction of a war-fighting deterrent posture. Indeed, war-fighting deterrence has become the new conventional wisdom, evolving from the Nixon and Ford administrations through that of President Carter and to that of President Reagan. The new extremist position is the notion of *war winning,* an idea associated most prominently with the writings of Colin Gray.

The question that should be asked about nuclear strategy under President Reagan is not whether it is a war-fighting one. Like that of previous administrations, it certainly is. The key question is how far toward a war-winning strategy the Reagan planners will carry us. Brief characterizations of each of these schools of thought will serve to highlight the differences between them.

Assured Destruction. Assured destruction is based on the premise that deterrence is maintained by having the capability to inflict unacceptable levels of damage on the cities and industry of the adversary in response to a first strike. Capabilities for damage limitation, whether by offensive means (highly accurate missiles) or defensive ones (ABMs or civil defense) are viewed as fruitless endeavors at best and destabilizing developments at worst. Forces are needed for the second-strike mission. Thus counterforce weapons such as the MX missile are viewed as undermining stability and the mutual hostage relationship.

Employment policy (how nuclear weapons would be used if deterrence fails) poses problems for advocates of assured destruction. No one would want a president to respond to a limited attack by actually destroying Soviet cities, so most advocates of assured destruction accept the need for some modest capability for flexible response in the event of a deterrence failure. For this and other reasons, the United States has probably never pursued a pure policy of assured destruction. In the 1960s, when assured destruction was emphasized by Secretary of Defense Robert McNamara, the United States nonetheless acquired forces with characteristics well in excess of those required for assured destruction. Military assets have been targeted in U.S. nuclear war plans at least since the 1950s.

Still, advocates of assured destruction seek to keep the focus of U.S. strategy on the mutual hostage relationship. They would certainly oppose using flexible response or war-fighting criteria for force planning. And they oppose increasing the number of options to a point at which nuclear war becomes more "thinkable."

War-fighting Deterrence. This strategy has evolved from the Schlesinger initiatives of 1974–75 through the countervailing strategy and Presidential Directive 59 of the Carter administration. It preserves assured destruction (by way of secure reserve forces) as the ultimate deterrent but focuses on what would happen in response to an attack on U.S. allies or a limited nuclear attack on the United States. In explaining Presidential Directive 59 in his speech at the Naval War College in August of 1980, Secretary of Defense Harold Brown acknowledged the war-fighting dimensions of U.S. policy: "In our analysis and planning, we are necessarily giving greater attention to how a nuclear war would actually be fought by both sides if deterrence fails. There is no contradiction between this focus on how a war would be fought and what its results would be, and our purpose of ensuring continued peace through mutual deterrence. Indeed, this focus helps us achieve deterrence and peace, by ensuring that our ability to retaliate is fully credible."

In his final *Annual Report* (for fiscal year 1982), Secretary Brown devoted considerable attention to explaining the countervailing strategy. The "essence" of the strategy was "to convince the Soviets that they will be successfully opposed at any level of aggression they choose, and that no plausible outcome at any level of conflict could represent 'success' for them by any reasonable definition of success." Brown was unusually explicit about the "force employment" elements of the countervailing strategy. The five major areas were as follows:

1. flexibility ("A continuum of options, ranging from use of a small number of . . . weapons . . . to employment of large portions of our nuclear forces")

2. escalation control (making possible "negotiated termination of the fighting")

3. survivability and endurance (of both nuclear forces and communications, command, control, and intelligence—C³I)

4. targeting objectives ("four general categories")
   a. strategic nuclear forces
   b. other military forces
   c. leadership and control targets
   d. industrial and economic base
5. reserve forces (maintenance of nuclear forces and related C^3I "both during and after a protracted conflict")

Thus, the United States was to continue (as under Schlesinger) a policy of flexible options coupled with assured destruction forces. Greater emphasis, however, was now being placed on measures necessary to make nuclear forces and C^3I assets "endure" during a "protracted conflict."

What made war-fighting deterrence possible, its supporters argued, were advances in weapons technology, particularly increases in the accuracy of delivery systems. What made it seem necessary were the growth of the Soviet arsenal, growing doubts about Soviet concepts of nuclear war, and changing views of what best deterred the Soviets. In view of evidence that some elements in the Soviet Union saw victory in a nuclear war as a possibility, the Carter administration devised policies designed to persuade the Soviet leadership that those elements were wrong.

The key decisionmakers of the Carter administration did not believe that nuclear war was winnable nor were they optimistic that limited nuclear war was possible. As Harold Brown put it, he was "not at all persuaded that what started as a demonstration, or even a tightly controlled use of the strategic forces for larger purposes, could be kept from escalating to a full-scale thermonuclear exchange." He believed, however, that because of "uncertainties on this score . . . it should be in everyone's interest to . . . halt the exchange before it reached catastrophic proportions." In sum, it is possible—as with the Carter administration's countervailing strategy—to adopt a war-fighting deterrent strategy and to plan the forces necessary to support that strategy without believing that nuclear war is winnable or even that it is likely that the use of nuclear weapons can be kept limited.

War Winning. The third school of thought is based on the notion that, in the words of Colin Gray and Keith Payne, "victory is possible." Several propositions are involved. First, a nuclear war can occur. Second, it can be won in some meaningful sense. And third, for the United States to prevail, it must have strategic superiority. Deterrence is one object of war winning, but in contrast with assured destruction and even war fighting, deterrence is to be achieved by the threat to use nuclear weapons to "defeat" the Soviet Union (while activating measures to protect the United States) in the event of a deterrence failure.

One key requirement of a war-winning strategy is a theory of victory. Perhaps the most detailed elaboration of a concept of victory has been set forth by Colin Gray, who argues that the United States needs a strategy in the sense of specific political objectives to be achieved in war. Gray recommends that the United States "seek to impose such military stalemate and defeat as is needed to persuade disaffected Warsaw Pact allies and ethnic minorities inside the Soviet Union that they can assert their own values in very active political ways."

But, of course, the breakup of the Soviet Union as a national state would only get us halfway to victory. The other half involves damage limitation to ensure the survival of enough of the United States to enable it to continue as a national state. Colin Gray has observed that "a combination of counterforce offensive targeting, civil defense, and ballistic missile and air defense should hold U.S. casualties down to a level compatible with national survival and recovery." And although he is understandably uncertain over the actual number that would survive, he suggests that an offensive-defensive strategy "should reduce U.S. casualties to approximately 20 million, which should render U.S. strategic threats more credible."

The Colin Gray view is, to say the least, open to question. By viewing nuclear war as an instrument of political strategy for destabilizing the Soviet regime (or as an instrument of any other such strategy designed to "win"), advocates of war winning discard the dominant view of the past thirty-eight years that nuclear war is *qualitatively* different from previous forms of warfare. Instead, they seem to be suggesting that it is only quantitatively different, but that with the correct posture, we can adjust. One need not embrace the totality of the assured destruction position in order to believe that any substantial use of nuclear weapons is likely to transform social and political reality so completely that it becomes misleading to invoke lessons from military campaigns of the past.

The war-winning position assumes that it would be possible to achieve and maintain the "strategic superiority" it views as necessary for a strategy of defeating the Soviet Union. But to do so would seem to necessitate extensive preparations on a scale that would require the perpetual mobilization of the American public for nuclear war. There is no reason to believe that the American public would support the adoption of a "victory" strategy that involved both expansion of offensive forces and the creation of substantial (and very expensive) defensive capabilities that would serve as constant reminders that nuclear weapons might actually be exploded on U.S. territory. The advocates of war winning overestimate what the domestic political traffic seems likely to bear in the way of preparing for nuclear war.

Finally, advocates of war winning probably underestimate the impact on prewar deterrence of the course of action they advocate. Whether or not the Soviet political leadership currently believes in the possibility of "winning" a nuclear war, the Soviets would be highly motivated to develop their own "theory of victory" if the United States adopted one. If both sides come to be equipped with theories of victory, significant war-fighting plans and capabilities, and substantial defensive measures, the probability of nuclear war's occurring would almost certainly increase.

Strategic Nuclear Policy under President Reagan

Assessing the strategic nuclear policy of the Reagan administration is no simple task, for there is no extensive description analogous to the detailed exposition in

Secretary Brown's final *Annual Report*. The most interesting material about strategic nuclear policy has come in the form of leaks to the press from a classified document, the *Defense Guidance*. In a *New York Times* article of May 30, 1982, Richard Halloran reported that this document set a requirement for U.S. forces to have the capability to "render ineffective the total Soviet (and Soviet-allied) military and political power structure." So as to prepare for "a protracted conflict period and afterward," emphasis was to be placed on C³I. Halloran wrote that the views of the Reagan military planners "on the possibility of protracted nuclear war differ from those of the Carter administration's military thinkers." As indicated earlier, however, Harold Brown referred explicitly to "a protracted conflict." Without knowing the details of the plans under Brown *and* seeing the Weinberger *Defense Guidance,* it is impossible to assess the validity of Halloran's assertion.

Secretary Weinberger's response to the leak of the *Defense Guidance* came in a speech at the Army War College on June 3. He defined the capability for a protracted response as essential for deterrence and declared that the notion that "nuclear war is winnable . . .has no place in our strategy." In an August letter to some seventy newspaper and magazine editors, Weinberger denied that the administration was "seeking to acquire a nuclear 'war-fighting' capability." The latter statement was singularly inept, inasmuch as the war-fighting trend in U.S. policy has been evident for almost a decade and was explicitly referred to in the statement by Secretary Brown quoted earlier.

In an attempt to repair the cumulative damage of the diverse casual statements and leaks of the first two years, Secretary Weinberger submitted a prepared statement, "United States Nuclear Deterrence Policy," to the Senate Foreign Relations Committee on December 14, 1982. More professional than the August letter to the editors, the statement was nonetheless quite defensive. It reiterated the basis of deterrence, traced the evolution of policy with long quotations from McNamara, Schlesinger, and Brown, and summarized the Reagan strategic modernization program. The text set forth the case for a war-fighting deterrent such as the countervailing strategy (without using that name). There was no mention of "protracted war" or "prevailing." It was a document designed to reassure the Senate Foreign Relations Committee that the ship of strategy had been put right.

Even this document designed to reassure raises more questions than it answers, however. It states that because we must think about the failure of deterrence, "we must plan for flexibility in our forces and in our response options so that there is a possibility of *re-establishing deterrence at the lowest possible level of violence, and avoiding further escalation."* (Emphasis added.) The *Defense Guidance,* on the other hand, allegedly states "that should deterrence fail and strategic nuclear war with the U.S.S.R. occur, *the United States must prevail and be able to force the Soviet Union to seek earliest termination of hostilities on terms favorable to the United States."* (Emphasis added.) The obvious difference in emphasis in these two passages is that the first, designed for public presentation, portrays the goal of a U.S. response as re-establishing deterrence at the lowest possible rung on the escalation ladder, with no reference to prevailing. The second passage, presumably not designed for public release, emphasizes prevailing, with no reference to containing escalation. The problem facing the Reagan administration is that, with the leak of a document that it feels it cannot responsibly discuss, it persists in making statements sufficiently at variance with that document as to raise questions about differences between its public statements and its actual policies.

It is possible, of course, that there is no contradiction between these two statements. One could argue that deterrence could not be re-established without "prevailing." And one could include in the seeking of the "earliest termination of hostilities on terms favorable to the United States" the subgoal of "re-establishing deterrence at the lowest possible level of violence." What the Reagan administration should do is to formulate a public statement of some length and sophistication describing its concept of deterrence. Until that is done very little will be clear, and the possibilities for questioning the "real" policies of the administration will be manifold.

War Fighting versus War Winning: The Emerging Debate?

On the limited evidence available, strategic nuclear policy in the Reagan administration seems to be an extension of the countervailing strategy it inherited from its predecessor. The nuclear force and C³I improvements outlined in the strategic modernization program are consonant with a war-fighting deterrent policy.

To be sure, some efforts have been made that would please advocates of the war-winning school of thought. Spending on civil defense (in the form of crisis relocation plans) is up. Air defense is being upgraded. Research and development on ballistic missile defense have been increased.

If one were to believe the more alarmist interpretations of the goal of "prevailing," one might suspect that a theory of victory was not far behind. And Colin Gray and others who believe nuclear war is winnable are associated with the administration. Despite these developments, however, by far the most likely outcome is that the Reagan administration will implement a war-fighting deterrent strategy. More money will be spent than would have been by the Carter administration, but the nuclear strategy may not be that different. Nuclear planning is highly incremental in nature. The labels describing policy change much more frequently than the actual war plans. It may even be that, within certain limits, nuclear planning has dynamics of its own. Jimmy Carter entered office wanting to eliminate nuclear weapons from the earth and ended up signing Presidential Directive 59. Even if Ronald Reagan entered office wanting to implement the war winners' every thought, budgetary limits, the moderating advice of some of the uniformed military who question spending large sums of money on such a remote contingency as protracted war, and the awesome responsibility of nuclear decision making might well pull him back somewhere near a war-fighting deterrent (not a war-winning) nuclear strategy.

I could of course be wrong. If that is so—if the Reagan administration were to adopt a war-winning position—the consequences could be grave. The Soviets might well perceive U.S. policy the way some Americans have viewed Soviet nuclear policy. It is the seeming congruence between aspects of Soviet declaratory policy, force size and characteristics, and employment policy that has motivated U.S. decisionmakers to formulate a war-fighting strategy. If the Soviets perceived a similarly threatening congruence between a U.S. war-winning declaratory policy, forces with a first-strike capability, extensive defensive measures, and a supporting employment policy, then it is difficult to believe that the United States would be in a more secure position in the world.

A more preferable outcome would be to convince the Soviets that there is no possibility of meaningful victory in nuclear war *and* that the United States will pursue arms control where possible and arms modernization where necessary. Implementation of a war-fighting countervailing strategy without a willingness to engage in serious arms control/reduction negotiations would be dangerous. Adoption of a war-winning strategy, *or* operationalization of a war-fighting countervailing strategy in such a way that it *appears* to the Soviets as a war-winning one, will almost certainly fail to bring about negotiated arms reductions and may well increase the risk of nuclear war.

It is inconceivable that the Reagan administration would move policy back to assured destruction. All the key Reagan national security decisionmakers would oppose it. Moreover, developments during the last decade have institutionalized a declaratory policy that promises to deny victory to the Soviets, an employment policy that is decidedly war fighting, and an acquisition strategy that key decisionmakers believe has made such a policy possible.

In the near term, the strategic debate may be between defenders of a war-fighting deterrence/countervailing strategy and advocates of a war-winning one. "War winners" will argue that advances in ballistic missile defense technology, and improvements in the United States' hard-target kill capability make their strategy increasingly realizable. Those committed to assured destruction may have to join forces temporarily with defenders of war-fighting deterrence to prevent the greater danger: the victory of those who would convert the illusion of winnable nuclear wars into national policy.   *(March 1983)*

Final Report of the President's Commission on Strategic Forces

The President's Commission on Strategic Forces, led by Lt. Gen. Brent Scowcroft, U.S.A.F. (Ret.), submitted its final report to President Reagan on March 21, 1984.

Excerpts from the report, which emphasizes arms control as a critical element of strategic stability, are reprinted here. These excerpts appeared in the May 1984 edition of Arms Control Today.

Dear Mr. President:

In its report to you on April 11, 1983, your Commission on Strategic Forces recommended in integrated strategic program which you subsequently endorsed. Its principal elements are a limited deployment of the MX missile, development of a small, single-warhead intercontinental ballistic missile (ICBM), and an arms control structure which emphasizes the enhancement of strategic stability. The commission believes that each of these elements is essential if the utility of the program is to be realized.

After the commission made its report, you asked that it participate in discussions on revisions of your START [strategic arms reduction talks] proposals for presentation at the October 1983 negotiating session with the Soviets. Much of that dialogue was not public because of considerations of the confidentiality of negotiations. It is clear that continued progress of both the MX and small missile crucially depends on the course of arms control negotiations. Therefore, while continuing to emphasize all of its recommendations, the commission believes it is important to focus, in this final report to you, on the arms control aspects of its earlier recommendations.

Arms Control

The arms control recommendations of the commission received the least detailed consideration in the early debate on the commission's proposals. Those recommendations were based on our fundamental belief that arms control should focus less upon aggregate numbers and more on overall strategic stability. This proposition was illustrated in the report through the example of the negative effect of arms control counting rules on stability.

The disappointing history of U.S.-Soviet arms control negotiations thus far may raise the question of why we should try to pursue formal arms control measures at all. Why should we not rely on the natural rationality and prudence of the two superpowers and the restraints of arms costs to keep the strategic competition within bounds? This question is especially pertinent now, in light of the many expectations for arms control which we have held in the past. Because of these many disappointments in arms control, it is important to keep our expectations within bounds by understanding what arms control cannot, as well as what it can, do.

Arms control cannot end the threat of nuclear war. While the likelihood of nuclear war can be reduced, the threat will remain with us. We cannot "disinvent" nuclear weapons. Imagining otherwise presents us with the paradox of the unattainable best being the enemy of the attainable good.

By itself, arms control is unlikely to reduce the casualties and damage should a nuclear war occur. Only a small number of nuclear weapons are required to inflict unbelievable damage on civilian populations. Attempting to reduce the arsenals on each side to "safe" numbers would risk instabilities which could themselves enhance the likelihood of nuclear conflict. Stability at a higher level is preferable to instability at a lower level.

Nuclear arms control will not enable us to make either deep or early cuts in defense budgets. At best, it can slow the pace of budget growth. Strategic nuclear forces have typically cost less than 15 percent of the total defense budget. Extending arms control to nonnuclear forces could potentially have a favorable impact on the defense budget, but the problems involved in nuclear arms control are simple compared to those in controlling conventional forces. Thus, while some reductions can perhaps be made, great economies should not be expected. Indeed, a reduction in nuclear forces could create a need for a substantial increase in the strength and therefore the cost of conventional forces.

While arms control cannot attain such illusory objectives, it can, nonetheless, make a substantial contribution to U.S. security. A nuclear conflict would be so devastating that we must, while protecting our freedoms and vital interests, leave no avenue unexplored which might reduce the chances that such a conflict would occur. The central purpose of our arms control efforts should therefore be to enhance U.S. security by increasing strategic stability. Increasing strategic stability reduces the possibility that a nuclear conflict between the two sides, one that neither wants, will occur. Given the stakes involved, this is of great importance.

There are other objectives arms control can achieve. Through arms control it may sometimes be possible to avoid some expenditures on weapon systems which otherwise would be deployed. A prime example is the Antiballistic Missile (ABM) Treaty of 1972. It allowed both sides to avoid heavy expenditures on systems which, at that stage of technology, would have been of only marginal effectiveness.

The very fact of arms control negotiations also has utility. The discussions which take place have, over the years, expanded the understanding of both sides about the strategic concepts, the priorities, the hopes, and the fears of the other. While, on occasion, this dialogue can be trying, it may reduce the element of surprise and enhance the understanding of certain military programs or actions which otherwise could be dangerously misinterpreted.

Finally, arms control should be pursued because the peoples of the world expect it of their leaders. That is a reason of special importance in a democracy. But while it is a mandate for the pursuit of arms control, it imposes a duty on those leaders not to permit exaggerated expectations of the results that any arms control process can bring. Even after the disappointments of previous years, many still hold inflated notions of the contributions which arms control can make. Failures to fulfill those expectations are too frequently ascribed to the ineptness or obstructionism of the negotiators rather than to the great difficulty—given the ideological gulf and the asymmetry in force structures—of finding specific areas of common interest.

Some, of course, view arms control essentially as a trap for democratic societies, a device manipulated by Soviet leaders to lure the West away from essential military development and deployment programs. While such a danger cannot be ignored, careful definition and pursuit of realistic arms control measures should be adequate to prevent its occurrence.

We can not foresee an end to U.S.-Soviet competition, out of which recurrent crises will arise. What we can and must do, through a combination of arms control and weapons programs, is reduce the chances that such crises will result in nuclear war.

Dealing with Force Asymmetries

The first goal of nuclear arms control efforts should be to ensure that the nature of the forces on each side does not provide a military incentive to strike first with nuclear weapons in a crisis. If possible an agreement should create a military disincentive to a first strike (i.e., the force balance for an attacker should be worse after an attack than before). Such a mutual balance of forces, if it can be achieved at all, will come only after extended and sustained effort over many years. There are no easy shortcuts or quick solutions. With crisis stability as a goal, however, each step successfully negotiated has immediate effect in improving the character of the strategic balance.

Reducing the Risk of Accidental War

Other devices which can enhance stability are a collection of measures intended to reduce the likelihood of accidental war. For example, these measures might include: bilateral exchange of information about steps which could be misconstrued as indications of an attack (e.g., maneuvers), dialogue between U.S. and Soviet defense officials, and agreements to improve the reliability and survivability of missile warning systems. A variety of such measures, designed to improve communication and predictability, would contribute to stability by improving mutual understanding and reducing surprise and misinterpretation. While less dramatic than agreements relating directly to the central nuclear balance, they nonetheless can make a very valuable contribution to arms control objectives.

Verification and Compliance

Two major and unresolved problems of arms control are the twin issues of verification and compliance. The arms control process can be sustained over time only if compliance with agreements is satisfactory and verification is adequate to determine compliance and deter noncompliance. Otherwise, the restraints of arms control agreements may appear to be one-sided and indispensable public support will evaporate. Because our society is open and the Soviet society is closed, verification is more essential and more difficult for us to achieve than for the Soviets. We must be able to determine, through a process in which each side has confidence, that arms control commitments are being fairly observed. As both sides increasingly turn to strategic systems which rely on concealment and mobility for survival, the problems of verification become more complex and new verification techniques may be required. The essential test of an effective verification system is that it will detect with a high degree of confidence any set of violations which would have a significant impact on the strategic balance. The commission believes that goal remains within our reach.

Compliance consists of verification and a procedure for consultation and explanation of questionable events or procedures, plus a resulting determination as to whether the observed act or condition is in fact a violation. In the event of noncompliance, the first step is to take action on any violation which significantly affects the strategic balance. The second step is to decide what to do about other activities or conditions which constitute violations of agreements but which have only marginal or inconsequential military significance.

Decisions regarding minor violations can be very difficult. Even though they may not have significant military impact, such violations erode the confidence of the American people and government in the agreements themselves. In addition, failure to take action may encourage the Soviets to believe that they can act with impunity. There may not always be available, however, effective responses proportionate to the violations themselves. The proper course of action is to maintain a system of communication for review and correction of such incidents.

The Role of Strategic Defense

Ballistic missile defense is a critical aspect of the strategic balance and therefore is central to arms control. One of the most successful arms control agreements is the Antiballistic Missile Treaty of 1972. That fact should not be allowed to obscure the possibility that technological developments at some point could make it in the interests of both sides to amend the current treaty. In considering this issue, it is important to distinguish between defensive systems designed to enhance the survivability of offensive systems and those designed to put a shield over wide areas, or all, of the United States or the Soviet Union. However, no move in the direction of the deployment of active defense should be made without the most careful consideration of the possible strategic and arms control implications.

The commission was requested to review the administration's proposals for research on strategic defense. In the commission's view, research permitted by the ABM Treaty is important in order to ascertain the realistic possiblities which technology might offer, as well as to guard against the possibility of an ABM breakout by the other side. But the strategic implications of ballistic missile defense and the criticality of the ABM Treaty to further arms control agreements dictate extreme caution in proceeding to engineering development in this sensitive area.   *(May 1984)*

Tilting toward War Fighting: The Scowcroft Commission and the Future of Deterrence

Leon V. Sigal

This commentary, which appeared in the September 1983 edition of Arms Control Today, *addresses the first report of the President's Commission on Strategic Forces (the Scowcroft Commission), released in April 1983.*

Since the late 1970s, the debate between strategists who want to maintain the doctrine of stable deterrence and those who advocate a shift to nuclear war fighting has intensified. The outcome of this debate will help determine the number and character of the United States' nuclear forces, as well as nuclear targeting and operations. Most important, it could increase or decrease the likelihood of nuclear war. At issue is the priority that should be given to stabilizing the nuclear balance. Despite changing weapons technology, stability continues to take three distinct but related forms at the nuclear level: strategic stability, crisis stability, and arms race stability.

Stability

When both sides are assured that each has a secure second-strike capability—enough invulnerable nuclear warheads to threaten unacceptable damage to the other side even after suffering a first strike—strategic stability, or mutual deterrence, exists.

Even if both sides are confident of a second-strike capability, one side or the other may worry that a sizable portion of its nuclear forces may be vulnerable to attack. During an intense crisis or conventional conflict in which the use of nuclear weapons seems imminent, one side might be tempted to launch a preemptive strike. Knowing that, so might its antagonist. If either side finds itself in such a predicament, both sides are less secure for fear of surprise attack. When neither side has reason to contemplate or fear preemption, crisis stability exists.

Each side may continue to test and deploy new weapons under conditions of strategic and crisis stability. Arms race stability prevails when neither side is concerned that its opponent may be trying to build weapons that would endanger either strategic or crisis stability.

Strategic stability deters either side from undertaking premeditated nuclear war. Crisis stability greatly reduces the chances of preemptive nuclear war or of escalation through miscalculation, through reciprocal fear of surprise attack. Arms race stability minimizes the incentives for preventive war.

War Fighters versus Stable Balancers

What distinguishes stable balancers from nuclear war fighters is not a willingness to engage in nuclear war deliberately or to seek options short of all-out nuclear attack on enemy populations. Both schools accept the need to prepare for nuclear war, should it occur, and to have weapons, force postures, and targeting plans capable of avoiding attacks on cities in that event. Where the rival schools part company is in the war fighters' readiness to jeopardize stability in hopes of somehow making the threat of nuclear retaliation more certain of execution.

Nuclear war fighters argue that nuclear weapons, like all previous advances in military technology, are usable and, indeed, likely to be used; that limited nuclear war is possible and winnable; and that a Soviet attack on Western Europe is deterred only by the certainty that the United States will use nuclear weapons, which is assured only by having nuclear options for every conceivable contingency.

Stable balancers disagree, believing that nuclear weapons mark a distinct breakpoint in the historical evolution of warfare and in the current continuum of military capability; that first use of nuclear weapons will lead to reciprocal escalation, eventually spiraling into general war; and that a Soviet attack on the allies in Europe is best prevented by stout conventional deterrence, which inevitably carries with it some risk of escalating to the nuclear level.

Nuclear war fighters propose to add to existing capabilities and options for waging limited nuclear war with the Soviet Union. Stable balancers are skeptical of these efforts. They recognize that nuclear weapons are so destructive, most Soviet military targets so collocated with population centers, and both sides' command-and-control so fragile that nuclear war will be almost impossible to control in practice. They also reject the war fighters' notions of "protracted" nuclear war, if that means more than a matter of hours, or of "prevailing" in any meaningful sense of the word.

For some thirty years after Hiroshima and Nagasaki, the doctrine of stable deterrence remained in precarious ascendancy in the strategic community. Stable balancers have set the terms of the public debate. They have imposed some limits on the acquisition of weapons with particularly perverse implications for stability, most notably ballistic missile defenses. But they have not kept the war fighters in check. Stable balancers could not prevent the Air Force from devising targeting plans at odds with stable deterrence, nor could they block the procurement of many more nuclear weapons with far greater accuracy than is desirable for stability.

With the accession of Ronald Reagan, war fighters have gained access to the inner circles, even positions of prominence, in the government. But have they triumphed? Without intimate knowledge of current plans and operating practices for nuclear weapons—knowledge to which few civilians in or out of the government are privy—it is impossible to give a definitive answer. Nevertheless, enough information has seeped into the public domain to provide the basis for at least a tentative assessment.

The attempt to redirect the U.S. strategic force posture according to war-fighting doctrines has run headlong into a wall of hard realities. One is that in spite of all the loose talk about protracted nuclear war, nobody really has the foggiest idea how to wage one. To be sure, most strategists favor making the U.S. nuclear forces and C³—command, control, and communications—more capable of riding out nuclear attack. But that is as much a cardinal principle of stable deterrence as of war-fighting doctrines. No one, however, can have much confidence in the United States' ability to ensure survivability for very long under conditions of nuclear war, let alone to protect populations. For that reason, if no other, any such war, once underway, has little prospect of being limited, short of mutual exhaustion.

A second hard reality limiting nuclear war fighters' success is that fulfilling even minimal requirements for war fighting puts very great demands on capabilities. Waging and limiting protracted nuclear war would require that leaders, weapons, and C³ must survive for more than a few hours or else must be readily reconstituted; intelligence assets must remain intact to conduct postattack damage assessments and permit retargeting of surviving weapons; economic and population centers must be spared. Furthermore, belligerents must keep in communication—not just in contact, but in a political position to negotiate based on compatible conceptions of the course of the conflict and its possible resolution, and based on some capacity to make and carry out decisions and control their forces.

A third hard reality is that these demands are far in excess of what the American people seem ready to tolerate, either fiscally or practically. Public resistance to various MX basing schemes provided a rerun of the ABM controversy of a decade or so ago. The strategic force buildup and loose talk from administration officials about nuclear war have provoked a sharp upsurge in antinuclear protest and an equally precipitous drop in public support for accelerated defense spending. This sentiment has been amply reflected in congressional floor debate, though not in action.

These three realities have instilled some caution into senior defense officials, who appear to be returning to doctrinal orthodoxy, at least in their public rhetoric, by talking in terms of stable deterrence. Whereas the *Defense Guidance* for fiscal year 1984–88 called for nuclear capabilities that "must prevail even under the condition of a prolonged war" and can "render ineffective the total Soviet (and Soviet-allied) military and political power structure," the most recent posture statement of the secretary of defense speaks only of "flexibility"—of ensuring that U.S. nuclear forces "should be capable of being used on a very limited basis as well as more massively."

The Scowcroft Commission and the Great Debate

If nuclear war fighters have yet to achieve total victory in the battle over policy, how much ground have they gained? The report of the President's Commission on Strategic Forces, commonly called the Scowcroft Commission, holds part of the answer. It bears close scrutiny because it marks the boundaries of currently acceptable doctrine.

The report was a political product—a last-ditch attempt to devise both a marketable rationale and a presentable package for the MX. As benefits any attempt to compromise, the commission has fashioned a doctrinal position of remarkable ambiguity. No wonder it has been hailed in some quarters as a reaffirmation of the new doctrinal orthodoxy and in others as a veritable counterreformation.

Stable balancers, for instance, were heartened to have the commission restore the concept of stability to its former meaning and place in nuclear strategy and arms control. Even before 1981, the Reaganauts were demeaning "stability" as a first step toward displacing it entirely from the criteria for force planning and for negotiation: any weapons the United States had or was planning to build, administration officials called stabilizing and moved to protect at the negotiating table; any weapons the Soviet Union had or was planning to build, they called destabilizing and constructed proposals for drastic reductions. The Soviets predictably argued the obverse.

By contrast, the commission's definition of stability was more forthright. It combined elements of strategic and crisis stability: "the condition which exists when no strategic power believes it can significantly improve its situation by attacking first in a crisis or when it does not feel compelled to launch its strategic weapons in order to avoid losing them." The commission held stability up both as the criterion for sizing and posturing U.S. forces and as the measure of arms control.

The commission also dismissed the public case that Reagan defense officials had been making for the MX. That case was predicated on strategic instability, that the increasing vulnerability of U.S. land-based missiles might tempt the Soviet Union to launch a premeditated attack on them. As a rationale for MX, the "window of vulnerability" was too easy to see through; the commission shattered it. Assessing different components of the U.S. strategic forces "collectively and not in isolation," the commission concluded "that whereas it is highly desirable that a component of the strategic forces be survivable when it is viewed separately, it makes a major contribution to deterrence even if its survivability depends in substantial measure on the existence of one or the other components of the force." By this logic, the commission could recommend basing MX in existing Minuteman silos, where it was unlikely to survive attack.

While the commission rightly rejected the connection between ICBM vulnerability and strategic instability, it thereby ignored the real problem that ICBM vulnerability poses for crisis instability. That vulnerability still gives both sides some incentive to preempt, once nuclear war seems imminent. Putting MX with its ten warheads into existing vulnerable silos only makes matters worse, giving the Soviets more of an incentive to preempt. It in turn adds to the U.S. incentive—and ability—to preempt in advance of Soviet preemption, and so on in a vicious circle. The commission did nothing to alleviate this reciprocal fear of surprise attack in a crisis. Instead, it tried to turn it into an argument for deploying MX—saying that the resulting instability will "encourage the Soviets to move in a stabilizing direction." The commission was silent about what happens if the Soviets do not accept such "encouragement." It also conveniently ignored existing hard-target kill capability in Minuteman IIIs, as well as Pershing II missiles in Europe and the D-5 missiles to be installed in Trident submarines in the next decade.

The MX as a Bargaining Chip?

The administration's rejection of the bargaining chip argument thus won commission endorsement. The report says nothing about putting all two hundred MX missiles on the bargaining table. Instead, only the second tranche of one hundred MXs is to be available, according to commission member John Deutsch, to be swapped for cuts in Soviet SS-18s and SS-19s. The initial tranche of one hundred MXs is to remain in place for the duration, a sword of Damocles hanging over the Soviets to compel them to reconfigure their strategic force structure. The commission's use of the ABM analogy here is also misplaced. "The ABM Treaty of 1972," the report says, "came about only because the United States maintained an ongoing ABM program and indeed made a decision to make a limited deployment." Yet that decision carried the Senate with only the barest majority, a sure sign to the Soviets of the lack of enthusiasm for the program. Moreover, the United States offered to trade away all of the ABMs, something the administration is not prepared to do with MX.

The commission's rejection of the bargaining chip argument, a point that its defenders have tried to obscure, also seems antithetical to a key recommendation on which some stable balancers have pinned great hopes: development of a single-warhead mobile missile—Midgetman—and encouragement of Soviet movement in the same direction. Midgetman only makes sense with a drastic reduction in the number of accurate multiple independently targetable reentry vehicle (MIRV) missiles in the Soviet inventory. Otherwise, it can be defeated by barraging the areas where it would roam. Such a drastic reduction may be achievable, but only with considerable difficulty and time, and with a U.S. quid pro quo. This would mean an equally drastic cut in accurate U.S. MIRVs, most notably, MX and D-5. If the United States is refusing to put all of its MXs on the table, then presumably the Soviet Union will insist on retaining at least a comparable number of accurate warheads of its own—one-thousand-plus counters to Minuteman III. The higher number of Soviet MIRVs drives up the number of Midgetman missiles required to be based in a mobile configuration, which will be extremely expensive to build and operate. Given the expense, it will be hard to justify arming them with just one warhead—and even harder to get the Soviets to go the single-warhead route. Without a willingness to trade away all of MX, the numbers do not add up.

Instead of aggravating crisis instability by recommending the deployment of one hundred MXs in vulnerable silos, the commission could have shown the way by putting all two hundred MXs on the bargaining table and proceeding directly to development of a single-warhead mobile ICBM without passing through this dangerous and expensive transition. The Soviets may be preparing an option to go this route themselves with recent test firings of what they call a modernized version of the single-warhead SS-13, possibly deployable in a mobile-basing mode.

The commission also lends support to the war fighters' cause by resting its case for MX on the requirements of extended deterrence under conditions of mutual vulnerability. While discounting the possibility of a Soviet threat against the United States or its allies of "limited use of nuclear weapons against military targets" because such use would be "likely to result in a nuclear war," the report nonetheless insists that the threat of nuclear blackmail remains. "In order to deter such Soviet threats," it argues, "we must be able to put at risk those types of Soviet targets—including hardened ones such as military command bunkers and facilities, missile silos, nuclear weapons and other storage, and the rest—which the Soviet leaders have given every indication by their actions they value most, and which constitute their tools of control and power."

This claim begs the question of how much more of a capability the United States needs for such purposes. After all, much of the present strategic force is so targeted. Adding one thousand MX warheads to the existing Minuteman III force, which has at least some prompt capability against hardened targets, plus Pershing II, with D-5 yet to come, creates a formidable force indeed—one far in excess of what is necessary to deter "limited use of nuclear weapons against military targets" by some capability to do likewise. Prudent Soviet planners could conclude that the United States has something more in mind, with all the consequences that this conclusion would have for crisis instability. Moreover, the commission never elucidates just how the addition of that much capability "for controlled prompt limited attack on hard targets" would deter limited Soviet threats.

A Hunting License for ABM?

The commission recommendations give war fighters a hostage, if not a hunting license, for their pursuit of a defense against ballistic missiles, the most destabilizing of potential developments. The commission's assessment may at first seem reassuring to stable balancers: "Applications of current technology offer no real promise of being able to defend the United States against massive nuclear attack in this century." Yet the very next sentence gives nuclear war fighters their opening:

"An easier task is to provide ABM defense for fixed hardened targets such as ICBM silos." Once MX is emplaced in vulnerable Minuteman silos, it will be hostage to the war fighters' desire for ABM. In the meantime, the commission is content to remain silent on preserving the stabilizing effects of the ABM Treaty.

On arms control, the commission left ambiguities for war-fighters to exploit as well. The commission accepted the stable balancers' belief that stability is to be advanced only by reducing the ratio of warheads to launchers. Yet the commission blunts the point by emphasizing limits on warheads and by recommending that "over the long run" agreements "be couched, not in terms of launchers, but in terms of equal levels of warheads of roughly equivalent yield." War fighters have taken the reference to "equivalent yield" as endorsement of megatonnage as a unit of account in START. If the administration insists on equal megatonnage, or its functional equivalent, sharp cuts in Soviet MIRVed ICBMs, then it will be a long run indeed before agreement is reached.

In the meantime, the pernicious effects on the policies of the United States's partner in nuclear adversity, the Soviet Union, may be incalculable. Soviet leaders are unlikely to be taken in by a change in public rhetoric. Their reactions are apt to be guided more by what the United States does than by what the United States says it is doing—more by procurements and force posture than by declaratory policy. The hardware that the United States is now buying could drive the Soviets farther in a direction in which they were already heading—toward preparing for preemption in nuclear crisis and perhaps launch on warning.

The commission's tortured reasoning seems straightforward enough once it is recalled that, despite obvious bipartisanship and ostensible doctrinal diversity, its membership had one thing in common from its formation: everyone favored deploying MX. A few, including its chairman, were also concerned with breaking the deadlock in the strategic arena that threatens to hold up both arms control and force modernization. Consensus may be laudable in a field rife with ideological division, but if it comes at the expense of clarity, that concensus can leave too much room for interpretation. And consensus, if it is to embrace both proponents of doctrinal change and defenders of doctrinal orthodoxy, is bound to favor those who want something new. For perspicacious warfighters in the bureaucracy looking for cues to action, the Scowcroft Commission's report has much to offer.

War fighters argue that their victory is inevitable because technological change, especially improved accuracy and increased yield, is forcing strategic doctrine to be rewritten. Yet this need not be so. New technology only limits the range of possible doctrines; it does not dictate choices among them. Moreover, doctrine can be used to guide and control technological innovation rather than to rationalize it. This is why the Scowcroft Commission's report is so distressing. By lending credence to the war fighters' resurgence, it gives new indication that the United States has yet to come to grips with the implications of mutual vulnerability in the nuclear age. *(September 1983)*

Counterforce Targeting: How New? How Viable?
Desmond Ball

U.S. strategic nuclear policy can usefully be divided into several different facets, of which the most important are declaratory policy and action or employment policy. Declaratory policy is that set of public pronouncements made by the president, the secretary of defense, or sometimes other senior administration officials regarding the requirements of deterrence, targeting policy, and strategic doctrine. Action policy, on the other hand, comprises the actual war-fighting strategy that the United States would adopt in a nuclear exchange; the designation of the forces to be used, the targets to be hit, and the allocation of the forces to those targets; and the rate at which the exchange is to proceed. It is the policy laid down in various presidential memoranda, spelled out in the Nuclear Weapons Employment Policy (NUWEP) issued by the secretary of defense and given effect in the Single Integrated Operational Plan (SIOP).

In the past decade, the most important of the various documents designed to provide national guidance for U.S. strategic nuclear employment policy have been National Security Decision Memorandum (NSDM) 242, signed by President Nixon on January 17, 1974; the Nuclear Weapons Employment Policy signed by Secretary of Defense James Schlesinger on April 4, 1974, and subsequently designated NUWEP-1; Presidential Directive (PD) 59 signed by President Carter on July 25, 1980; a second NUWEP, sometimes referred to as NUWEP-2 and sometimes as NUWEP-80, issued by Secretary of Defense Harold Brown in October 1980; National Security Decision Directive (NSDD) 13, signed by President Reagan in October 1981; and a new NUWEP, designated NUWEP-82, issued by Secretary of Defense Caspar Weinberger in July 1982. These documents are highly classified, and only very infrequently have responsible officials chosen to publicly discuss any details of this aspect of U.S. strategic nuclear policy.

Most of the public discussion of action or employment policy is therefore based on extrapolations from the declaratory level. In the mid- and late 1960s, for example, when the Department of Defense annual reports stressed the requirements for assured destruction, there was a widespread concomitant assumption that the U.S. strategic nuclear forces were targeted principally on Soviet urban-industrial centers. However, extrapolations of this sort have invariably been quite wide of the actuality, since the periods when declaratory policy has coincided with the realities of targeting practice have been few and far between. Declaratory policy has generally moved in cycles, with the emphasis sometimes on counter-city targeting, massive retaliation, and assured destruction, on the one hand, and sometimes on counterforce, damage limitation, limited and selective options, and escalation control on the other hand. By comparison, action policy has been remarkably resilient. U.S. war plans have *always* contained a wide range of target categories, including Soviet military capabilities, political and military command, control, and communication (C^3) systems, and economic and industrial centers. The principal changes in the plans since the late 1940s and early 1950s have been, first, an enormous increase in the number of potential target installations, from about seventy in 1949 to about forty thousand some three decades later; and, second, the division of these targets into an increasingly large array of "packages" of varying sizes and characteristics, providing the National Command Authority (NCA) with "customized" options for an extremely wide range of possible contingencies. These two developments have been due only very marginally to changes in U.S. basic national security policy. Far more important determinants have been, first, the growth of the U.S. strategic nuclear forces (from fifty atomic bombs in May 1948 when the Joint Chiefs of Staff approved the "Halfmoon" Joint Emergency War Plan, to the more than ten thousand bombs and missile reentry vehicles in the SIOP forces today); and, second, the increasingly detailed intelligence regarding potential target installations in the Soviet Union that was derived from overflights of U-2 spy aircraft in 1956–60 and then, since August 1960s, from surveillance satellites. The designation of more than forty thousand target installations in the current SIOP not only allows great scope for choice but, given that there are only ten thousand weapons available for SIOP employment, actually requires such choice.

From this perspective, there was little new in either President Carter's PD 59 of July 1980 or President Reagan's NSDD-13 of October 1981. Indeed, there is a direct historical lineage between PD 59 and a series of studies set in train soon after President Nixon took office in January 1969. These studies led directly (if rather fitfully) to National Security Study Memorandum (NSSM) 169, approved by President Nixon in late 1973, and then, in turn, to NSDM-242 of January 17, 1974.

NSDM-242 contained three principal policy components. The one that engaged the most public debate was the re-emphasis on the targeting of a wide range of Soviet military forces and installations, from hardened command and control facilities and ICBM silos to airfields and Army camps. The second element of NSDM-242 was the requirement for "escalation control," whereby the NCA should be provided with the ability to execute its selected options in a deliberate and controlled fashion throughout the progress of a strategic nuclear exchange. And, third, NSDM-242 introduced the notion of "withholds" or "nontargets," that is, things that would be preserved from destruction. Some of these, such as "population per se," have now been exempted absolutely from targeting; others, such as the centers of political leadership and control are exempted only for the purposes of intra-war deterrence and intra-war bargaining, and strategic reserve forces are to be maintained to allow their eventual destruction if necessary.

NSDM-242 also authorized the secretary of defense to promulgate the Policy Guidance for the Employment of Nuclear Weapons and the associated Nuclear

Weapons Employment Policy (NUWEP), signed by Secretary Schlesinger on April 4, 1974. The NUWEP was developed through close military and civilian cooperation, and sets out the planning assumptions, attack options, targeting objectives, and the damage levels needed to satisfy the political guidance. (For example, NUWEP-1 contained the requirement that the U.S. strategic nuclear forces must in all circumstances be able to destroy 70 percent of the Soviet industry that would be needed to achieve economic recovery after a nuclear war). The concepts and objectives set out in NSDM-242 and NUWEP-1 provided the framework for the development of new strategic nuclear war plans. The first Single Integrated Operational Plan (SIOP) prepared under the new guidance was SIOP-5, which was formally approved in December 1975 and took effect on January 1, 1976.

There was some apprehension within the Pentagon in early 1977 that the administration of President Carter and Secretary Brown might move to reverse the developments of the previous several years, but it proved unfounded. On August 24, 1977, President Carter issued PD 18, entitled *U.S. National Strategy*, which explicitly reaffirmed the continued use of NSDM-242 and NUWEP-1 in "the absence of further guidance for structuring the U.S. strategic posture." This further guidance was provided by a Nuclear Targeting Policy Review (NTPR), an interagency study directed by Leon Sloss in the Pentagon. Various supporting studies were undertaken throughout the defense establishment during 1978, on such subjects as Soviet views on nuclear war fighting, the possibility of exploiting Soviet fears of China, and problems of termination of nuclear war. Phase one of the NTPR was completed in December 1978, and formed the basis of a new presidential directive drafted in early 1979. Although the National Security Council (NSC) staff pressed for the formal acceptance of this draft there was opposition from the State Department and from some elements within the Pentagon, and it was shelved for more than fifteen months—until it was retrieved just prior to the Democratic Convention, revised and updated, and formally signed by President Carter on July 25 as PD 59.

The guidance issued by the Reagan administration does not differ significantly from that of the Carter administration except with respect to the increased attention accorded to policy for a protracted nuclear war and the requirements for ensuring the endurance of U.S. strategic command, control, communications and real-time intelligence (C^3I) systems over a prolonged period. For planning purposes, this period is defined in the guidance as being from two to six months.

The current SIOP includes more than forty thousand potential target installations, as compared to about twenty-five thousand in 1974 when NUWEP-1 was promulgated and the development of SIOP-5 initiated. These targets are divided into four principal groups, each of which in turn contains a wide range of target types. The principal groups are (1) the Soviet nuclear forces, (2) the general purpose forces, (3) the Soviet military and political leadership centers, and (4) the Soviet economic and industrial base. Examples of targets within each category were given by the Defense Department to the Senate Armed Services Committee in March 1980:

1. Soviet nuclear forces:

    ICBMs and IRBMs, together with their launch facilities (LFs) and launch command centers (LCCs)
    Nuclear weapons storage sites
    Airfields supporting nuclear-capable aircraft
    Strategic missile submarine (SSBN) bases

2. Conventional military forces:

    Casernes
    Supply depots
    Marshaling points
    Conventional air fields
    Ammunition storage facilities
    Tank and vehicle storage yards

3. Military and political leadership:

    Command posts
    Key communications facilities

4. Economic and industrial targets:

    a. War-supporting industry

        Ammunition factories
        Tank and armored personnel carrier factories
        Petroleum refineries
        Railway yards and repair facilities

    h   Industry that contributes to economic recovery

        Coal
        Basic steel
        Basic aluminum
        Cement
        Electric power

The SIOP is further divided into four general categories of options available for the employment of nuclear weapons: (1) major attack options (MAOs), (2) selected attack options (SAOs), (3) limited nuclear options (LNOs, which are "designed to permit the selective destruction of fixed enemy military or industrial targets"), and (4) regional nuclear options (RNOs, which are "intended, for example, to destroy the leading elements of an attacking enemy force"). Within each of these classes of options are a wide range of further options, including so-called withholds, four general categories of which have been publicly identified: (1) population centers; (2) national command and control centers (exempted from attack at least in the initial phases of a nuclear exchange so as to enhance the prospects of escalation control); (3) particular countries targeted in the SIOP (so that attacks on the Soviet Union would not necessarily involve simultaneous attacks on Eastern Europe, China, Cuba, Vietnam, or other countries included in the SIOP); and (4) "allied and neutral territory." Special categories of targets have also been delineated for preemptive attacks against the Soviet Union and for launch-on-warning (LOW) or launch-under-attack (LUA) scenarios in the event of unequivocal warning of a Soviet attack.

While the general structure and contents of the SIOP will be essentially maintained, there are some five particularly noteworthy aspects of the recent developments in targeting policy which warrant consideration. The first, and the one that featured most prominently in journalistic discussion of PD 59, was the directive that relatively less emphasis be accorded the destruction of the Soviet economic and industrial base and that greater attention "be directed toward improving the effectiveness of our attacks against military targets." It should be noted, however, that military targets already account for more than half the forty thousand target installations in the SIOP (as compared to some fifteen thousand economic-industrial targets) and that the destruction of these has always been a prime objective. (For example, attack options I and II in the 1962 SIOP were aimed at "the destruction or neutralization of [Soviet] strategic nuclear delivery forces" and "[conventional] military forces and military resources in being" respectively; the successful execution of attack option II would have reduced the "Soviet-Satellite residual ground forces" to seven Soviet and ten Satellite divisions and neutralized the Eastern bloc air forces as effective combat elements).

A second noteworthy aspect of the recent developments, and one of greater novelty, is the appreciation that the choice of targets is as much an exercise in deterrence as the execution of the plans is in war fighting. As one White House official stated in late 1977, at the outset of NTPR: "In the past nuclear targeting has been done by military planners who have basically emphasized the efficient destruction of targets. But targeting should not be done in a political vacuum. Some targets are of greater psychological importance to Moscow than others, and we should begin thinking of how to use our strategic forces to play on these concerns."

Hence, there have been some changes to the targeting guidance so as to exploit potential Soviet fears, such as threatening the Soviet food supply and making a target of Soviet troops and military facilities in the Far East ("kicking the door in") so that the Soviet Union would be more vulnerable to attack from China; and some consideration has been given to the adaptation of targeting to the dismemberment and regionalization of the Soviet Union, enhancing the prospects for regional insurrection during and after a nuclear exchange.

The most important consequence of this notion of targeting what the Soviets fear most, however, is the attention now being devoted to the targeting of the Soviet assets for political control—the Soviet state and its instruments of domestic and external coercion. This includes key Communist party and governmental buildings, military headquarters, command centers, KGB offices and border posts, communications facilities, and so forth. Again, U.S. war plans have always included some installations of this sort. For example, some two thousand of the more than forty thousand potential targets designated in the current SIOP are leadership and control targets; however, it would not be unreasonable to expect that by the time SIOP-6 is authorized these targets would account for as much as 20 percent of the Soviet target base—perhaps some ten thousand out of a likely total of fifty thousand designated target installations.

A third point, emphasized by Secretary Brown in a message to the defense ministers of the NATO countries on August 10, 1980, is that greater attention has been accorded planning for the use of very limited and selective options in order to "improve the contribution of our strategic nuclear forces to deterrence across the full spectrum of threats with which we must all be concerned." Various packages of selected attack options (SAOs), limited nuclear options (LNOs), and regional nuclear options (RNOs) are being prepared for use not just in nuclear situations but also in what hitherto would have been purely conventional situations. According to testimony of the commander of the Strategic Air Command (SAC), Gen. R.H. Ellis, before the Senate Armed Services Committee in March 1980, "Deterrence can no longer be neatly divided into subgroups, such as conventional and nuclear. It must be viewed as an interrelated, single entity. SAC is developing new options which provide the National Command Authorites with additional flexibility to respond to future conflicts is a timely and controlled manner."

As an example of the use of RNOs and LNOs, General Ellis suggested that "combat missions could be launched from Andersen [Air Force Base in Guam] to the Middle East" in response to Soviet conventional military activity in that region. As an example of an SAO, Ellis said plans for nuclear strikes against Soviet military facilities near Iran, including military bases and airfields inside the Soviet Union, have been prepared so as "significantly [to] degrade Soviet capabilities to project military power in the Middle East–Persian Gulf region for a period of at least 30 days."

A fourth point is that PD 59 and NSDD-13 emphasize that the preplanned target packages in the SIOP must be supplemented by the ability to find new targets and destroy them during the course of a nuclear exchange. While Soviet strategic nuclear installations and economic and industrial facilities would remain essentually fixed during wartime, there would be much movement of Soviet conventional military forces (including second-echelon formations), and much of the Soviet political and military leadership would presumably be relocated. PD 59 and NSDD-13 require the development of new reconnaissance satellites and signals intelligence (SIGINT) systems to provide the real-time intelligence capabilities necessary to effect this rapid retargeting.

The fifth noteworthy aspect of the recent developments in targeting policy is the recognition that the current U.S. command, control, and communications system is inadequate to support any policy of extended nuclear war fighting.

In this respect, PD 59 and NSDD-13 should be considered together with Presidential Directives 53 and 58 and a wide range of other measures intended to improve the survivability and the endurance of the U.S. C³ system. PD 53, entitled National Security Telecommunications Policy and signed by President Carter on November 15, 1979, proclaimed that "it is essential to the security of the U.S. to have telecommunications facilities adequate to satisfy the needs of the nation during and after any national emergency, . . . to provide continuity of essential functions of government, and to reconstitute the political, economic and social structure of the nation." Its principal goal is described as ensuring "connectivity between the National Command Authority and strategic and other appropriate forces to support flexible execution of retaliatory strikes during and after an enemy nuclear attack." PD 58, signed by President Carter on June 30, 1980, is concerned with the maintenance of "continuity of government." It directs the Department of Defense and other agencies to improve the capacity of selected parts of the government, from the president on down, to withstand a nuclear attack. The measures under consideration include plans for evacuating military and civilian leaders from Washington in time of crisis; the construction of new hardened shelters for key personnel; data-processing equipment and communication systems; and the improvement of early warning systems.

All of these various developments are intended not just to improve the U.S. capability actually to fight a nuclear war, in a tightly controlled fashion, but in so doing also to enhance the U.S. deterrent posture. But to be of value to deterrence these moves must be credible and be perceived as such by both the Soviet and U.S. national command authorities. However, is it really possible to conduct a strategic nuclear exchange, no matter how controlled, without significant civilian casualties? How realistic, both as a strategic policy and as a targeting objective, is the notion of targeting the Soviet political and military leaderships and their control apparatus? Is it really possible to design a C³ system that can operate in a nuclear environment in such a way and for a sufficient length of time to support the current U.S. strategic policy of escalation control? And, in any case, is the Soviet Union likely to cooperate in U.S. efforts to control a nuclear exchange?

With respect to the first question, there seems little doubt that even granted the precision with which intercontinental strategic nuclear delivery vehicles can now be targeted, the collateral casualties that would accompany any limited counterforce exchange would still be very high. A comprehensive counterforce attack against the United States would involve strikes against about one thousand ICBM silos, two submarine support bases (Bremerton and Charleston), and forty-six SAC bomber bases. Whereas the ICBM silos are generally located in relatively unpopulated areas, the two SSBN bases and many of the bomber bases are quite near major cities. Depending on the assumptions made about the scale and character of the Soviet strikes, U.S. fatalities from such a comprehensive counterforce attack range from 2 to 20 million, with 14 million perhaps the most reasonable. In the case of a comprehensive U.S. counterforce attack against the Soviet Union, the targets would include nearly fourteen hundred ICBM silos, three SSBN bases (Severomorsk near Murmansk, Petropavlovsk on the Kamchatka Peninsula, and Vladivostok, the major Soviet city in the Far East), thirty-two major air bases, and perhaps also the IRBM and medium-range ballistic missile (MRBM) bases. Many of these are located in some of the most densely populated areas in the Soviet Union. Twenty-two of the thirty-two major air bases, some three-quarters of the IRBM and MRBM sites, and more than half the twenty-six Soviet ICBM fields are located west of the Ural Mountains. Fatalities from a U.S. counter-ICBM attack alone would range from 3.7 to 27.7 million, depending principally on the level of fallout protection assumed; a full counterforce attack against bomber bases and submarine support facilities as well as ICBM silos would obviously kill many more than this. Four of the ICBM fields (Kozelsk, Teykovo, Kostroma, and Yedrovo) are located sufficiently close to Moscow and are spread around in such a way that the national capital would receive extensive fallout regardless of the prevailing wind direction. Given casualties of this magnitude, and the particular Soviet difficulty of distinguishing a comprehensive counterforce attack from a more general military-cum-urban-industrial attack, the notion of limiting a nuclear exchange to supposedly surgical counterforce operations appears rather incredible.

Second, there would seem to be many problems with the concept of counter-political control targeting. One is that political control assets comprise, potentially at least, an extremely large target set. Political control in the Soviet Union emanates from the Kremlin in Moscow outward through the capitals of each of the republics and down through those of the oblasts and the krays. Targeting the CPSU head-quarters and other governmental and administrative buildings in each of these, as well as military headquarters and command posts and KGB centers throughout the Soviet Union could require many thousands of weapons.

There is also the problem that the locations of many political control assets are not known. This is a tacit admission in the following statement by Secretary Brown in his FY 1981 posture statement: "Hardened command posts have been constructed near Moscow and other cities. For the some 100,000 people we define as the Soviet leadership, there are hardened underground shelters near places of work, and at relocation sites outside the cities. The relatively few leadership shelters we have identified would be vulnerable to direct attack." Even where facilities have been identified, it would be difficult (if not impossible) to know exactly which elements of the leadership had dispersed to which facilities. Moreover, the destruction of the political control facilities does not necessarily mean the destruction of the political control personnel. KGB officers are less likely to be in KGB buildings than dispersed among the population they are tasked with monitoring and controlling.

Indeed, this points to a larger problem. Many of the political and military leadership centers are located in or near major urban areas, particularly Moscow and the republic capitals. Attacks on these would be virtually indistinguishable from counter-city attacks. Escalation control would be difficult to pursue following such attacks.

In fact, such attacks would probably mean the end of escalation control. As Colin Gray has pointed out: "Once executed, a very large strike against the Soviet political and administrative leadership would mean that the U.S. had 'done its worst.' If the Soviet Government, in the sense of a National Command Authority, were still able to function, it is likely that it would judge that it had little, if anything, left to fear."

Finally, a counter-political control strike would make it impossible for the Soviets to negotiate war termination.

The third question pertains to the vulnerability of the strategic command, control, and communication infrastructure. Despite the fact that the United States has spent some U.S. $25 billion on strategic C^3 over the past decade, much of it on means of enhancing the survivability of particularly critical C^3 systems, it remains the case that the C^3 infrastructure is more vulnerable and has less endurance than the strategic forces it is intended to support. Strategic C^3 systems are vulnerable to all the threats to which the forces could be subject plus a variety of additional ones. The strategic forces gain protection through hardening, proliferation, mobility, and camouflage. Many C^3 systems, such as radar sites, very low frequency (VLF) antennae, and satellite sensor systems are necessarily relatively "soft"; some C^3 elements, such as the National Command Authorities, cannot be proliferated; major command posts, satellite ground stations and communication nodes are generally fixed; and radar sites and communication stations are extremely difficult to camouflage because of their electronic emissions. C^3 systems are generally more vulnerable to the blast effects of nuclear weapons than are the strategic forces and have various peculiar vulnerabilities as well: susceptibility to electromagnetic pulse, electronic jamming, deception, and so forth.

The vulnerabilities of such critical elements of the strategic C^3 architecture as the National Command Authorities themselves; the airborne C^3 systems that are relied upon for continuity of command and control in a nuclear environment; the satellite systems used for communications, early warning, photographic reconnaissance, and signals intelligence; the "hot line" that would be required for communication and negotiation between the adversary leaderships; and the communication systems for ballistic missile submarines, which at least in the U.S. case carry half the warheads of the strategic nuclear forces—these impose quiet, debilitating physical constraints on the situations in which escalation might be controlled, the time period over which control might be maintained, and the proportion of the SIOP forces that could be employed in a controlled fashion. The boundary of control in any militarily significant exchange (as compared to demonstration strikes) is unlikely to lie beyond either a few days or a few tens of detonations!

The fourth problem with respect to the practicality of the concepts embodied in PD 59 and NSDD-13 is that control and limitation require that all the participants in the conflict be willing and have the capability to exercise restraints—in weapons, in targets, and in political objectives. It is most problematical as to whether the Soviets would "play the game." Despite some improvements in the capabilities for control, Soviet doctrine still seems to be that in the event of a nuclear exchange the Soviet forces would be used massively and simultaneously against a range of targets: nuclear forces, other military forces, the military-industrial base, and, almost certainly, the U.S. and NATO military, political, and administrative control centers.

Finally, the recent developments in targeting policy have some important implications for arms control. So long as declaratory policy emphasized concepts such as assured destruction or sufficiency, it was possible to develop firm criteria for determining the size and characteristics of the U.S. strategic nuclear forces. War-fighting concepts, on the other hand, are essentially open-ended in terms of force requirements. To cover all the Soviet political control assets and the wider range of military targets as required by the new targeting guidance will in turn require a large increase in the SIOP forces, as will the requirement for strategic reserves both to cover Soviet second-echelon forces and to provide intra-war deterrence against escalation to urban-industrial attacks. On April 9, 1979, General Ellis wrote to Secretary Brown to the effect that U.S. strategic force levels were inadequate to support the policy of countervailing targeting—at least without the deployment of "sufficient numbers" of air-launched cruise missiles (ALCMs), Trident SLBMs, and MX ICBMs. Moreover increased expenditures on strategic C^3 systems and real-time surveillance capabilities are also required. To be effective, then, the recent targeting developments are likely to come into conflict with arms control objectives.

The Carter administration began with great enthusiasm for arms control. It was not to last. Much of the opposition to the original draft of PD 59 that was prepared in early 1979 was based on arms control arguments—in particular, Secretary of State Vance believed that formal approval of the "new" doctrine would endanger the prospects for SALT II. President Carter's endorsement of PD 59 on August 14, 1979, however, signaled the death knell of the arms control stance of his administration; according to that directive, arms control was to be pursued only insofar as it served broader U.S. national security interests. In an environment of increasing Soviet military capabilities and increasing Soviet willingness to use those capabilities, the technological momentum that produced greater counterforce potential and more sophisticated C^3 systems proved irresistable. Under the Reagan administration there is little attempt at resistance; instead, the concepts that are embodied in NSDM-242, the NUWEP, and PD 59 have been pursued to even further extremes. From this perspective the fact that many of these concepts have inherently insoluble problems is not merely unfortunate; given the propensity of many members of the Reagan administration to accept the possiblity of limited nuclear war it is also extremely dangerous.   *(February 1981, updated May 1985)*

Cruise Missiles: The Arms Control Challenge
Thomas K. Longstreth

Cruise missiles—pilotless vehicles that fly in the atmosphere, propelled by jet engines— have been in the U.S. arsenal for many years. The first versions, however, were very large, very inaccurate (the Snark missed targets by a thousand miles), and very unreliable. A number of technological innovations that came to fruition in the early 1970s have made cruise missiles much more attractive weapons: efficient turbofan engines, miniaturized computers, smaller warheads, less radar-reflecting airframes, and the terrain-contour-matching guidance system. Cruise missiles are now seen as very survivable, versatile, resistant to detection, accurate, and cheap. While the United States has a lead in cruise missile technology, the Soviets are not standing still. Thousands of nuclear and nonnuclear-tipped cruise missiles will be introduced into U.S. and Soviet ground, naval, and air forces over the next decade. This article examines the record of arms control in dealing with cruise missiles and offers some suggestions for future progress.

Background

Though U.S.-Soviet arms control negotiations have attempted to grapple with the subject of cruise missiles since 1974, there has been little progress toward meaningful limitations. The first significant U.S. cruise missile proposal tabled at the Vladivostok SALT negotiations in January 1976 included restrictions on both air-launched cruise missiles (ALCMs) and sea-launched (SLCMs). Each strategic bomber that carried twelve to twenty ALCMs was to be counted against the limits placed on MIRVed ICBMs and SLBMs (1,320 missiles). Individual ALCMs were not to be counted. SLCMs launched from submarines would be limited to a range of 372 miles (600 kilometers), though there would, again, be no limits on numbers. SLCMs launched from surface ships could have ranges of over 2,000 miles, but would be limited to a total of 250 missiles deployed on no more than twenty-five ships. The Soviet proposal, tabled the same month, would have also counted ALCM-carrying bombers against the 1,320 MIRV subceiling, but the ALCM range would have been limited to 1,000 miles. All other cruise missiles, ground- and sea-launched, would have been limited to a range of 372 miles.

The two proposals seemed to form the basis for a compromise, but progress was first slowed by other outstanding issues, including verifiability, and then stopped when the 1976 U.S. presidential elections intervened. In the face of Ronald Reagan's conservative primary challenge, President Ford believed that he could not appear willing to make a deal with the Soviets.

Cruise missiles were taken up again in the SALT negotiations conducted by the Carter administration between 1977 and 1979. After much hard bargaining, the SALT II Treaty introduced innovative counting rules and verification measures that alleviated at least some problems associated with cruise missiles. Like the 1976 Vladivostok proposals, SALT II counted strategic bombers armed with long-range ALCMs (over 372-mile range) against the limits placed on MIRVed ICBMs and SLBMs. Further, all ALCM-carrying bombers had to be fitted with functionally related observable differences (FRODs) that distinguished them from bombers that did not carry ALCMs. While these provisions made the inclusion of ALCMs in

SALT II possible, they did not resolve the problem of what to do about SLCMs and ground-launched cruise missiles (GLCMs).

Restrictions on SLCMs, and GLCMs were contained in the Protocol to the SALT II Treaty. The protocol banned deployment of cruise missiles with ranges in excess of 372 miles on ground- and sea-based launchers. The protocol had no real effect on the U.S. cruise missile program, however, since it allowed the continued testing and development of SLCMs and GLCMs. Moreover, it was scheduled to expire at the end of 1981, well before any SLCM or GLCM deployments were planned. The Soviet Union did not then have any cruise missiles with a range of more than 372 miles, so it was unaffected by the SALT II Treaty or protocol restrictions. But SALT II was never ratified, and its limits on cruise missiles have been in limbo.

When the Reagan administration came to office it embraced the cruise missile with even more enthusiasm than did its predecessors. The planned ALCM buy was increased to 4,350, almost 1,000 more than what President Carter had planned to acquire. The total was reduced slightly after the administration's decision to stop production of the first generation ALCM and proceed with the second generation "Stealth" ALCM (sometimes called the advanced cruise missile or ACM). The buy of SLCMs was also increased to more than 4,000, (including about 750 nuclear versions) and plans were drawn up to put SLCMs on most naval surface vessels and submarines. Battleships were even pulled out of mothballs to serve as giant SLCM launch platforms. The NATO plan, first agreed to during the Carter administration, to put at least 464 GLCMs in Europe was reaffirmed. Tactical applications for conventional cruise missiles, like the medium-range air-to-surface missile (MRASM) continued to be studied. In all, it has been estimated that the United States may eventually build more than 30,000 cruise missiles at a procurement cost of over $60 billion.

As arms control experts have warned for years, cruise missiles present unprecedented difficulties both for intelligence in general and for verification of arms agreements in particular. Cruise missiles are much smaller than ballistic missiles and can be launched from a variety of platforms. Their launchers and support facilities are less easily monitored by satellites and other national technical means. Testing and development of cruise missiles are also easier to hide. Moreover, cruise missiles of identical size and external appearance can have different ranges, missions, and warheads. Because they are relatively inexpensive, cruise missiles can be purchased in large quantities.

In addition, there has been great reluctance on the U.S. side to limit cruise missile deployment. Negotiators have spurred on development, sometimes against Pentagon resistance, because they saw cruise missiles as a potential bargaining chip. Civilian defense planners have pushed cruise missiles as a less expensive alternative to other new weapons systems, such as manned bombers. The military has been reluctant to accept limits on a technology in which it had a significant lead.

The net result has been that both the U.S. and Soviet cruise missile programs have gone forward. While some U.S. defense planners argue this serves U.S.

interests, there is growing evidence it may harm U.S. security in the long term. It now appears that the Soviet Union, unable to slow the U.S. through arms control, has begun a program of its own to develop modern, sophisticated air-, sea-, and ground-launched cruise missiles.

Large numbers of sophisticated, long-range ALCMs carried on Soviet bombers will, for the first time, make the Soviet bomber fleet a major threat to U.S. security. There can be no question that all Backfires armed with such weapons would have to be considered capable of intercontinental missions. To protect its security, the United States will have to invest billions of dollars even beyond the Reagan modernization program in extensive continental air defenses. This is an area in which, historically, the United States has made little investment because the Soviet bomber threat was not a serious one.

A modern long-range Soviet SLCM could create severe headaches for U.S. strategic planners too. The Soviet Union already has extensive operational experience with antiship SLCMs. These weapons are completely integrated into Soviet naval forces. Long-range nuclear SLCMs spread among hundreds of Soviet surface vessels and submarines presently equipped with only crude antiship versions will complicate U.S. strategic defense requirements.

Present U.S. antisubmarine warfare (ASW) capabilities against the Soviet ballistic missile submarine force (SSBN) are such that those submarines tend to stay in protected waters near the Soviet Union in order to preserve their survivability. This extends the warning time available to the United States in the event of a Soviet SLBM attack. But a large number of Soviet hunter-killer submarines armed with land-attack SLCMs would make the U.S. ASW effort much more difficult. Even if only a few Soviet cruise missile submarines (each of which could carry upwards of twenty-five SLCMs) manage to penetrate within close proximity of the U.S. coastline, there are many important military targets they could attack, with little or no warning time.

An Arms Control Regime

If future arms control agreements are to have any meaning, restrictions on all types of cruise missiles will be necessary. Although ongoing U.S. and Soviet deployments have complicated this task, it is not insoluable.

Future restrictions on cruise missiles must build, to the extent possible, on previously agreed-to definitions and counting rules. SALT II provides a good framework for monitoring and limiting ALCM deployment. Such a regime counts weapons that are most easily counted (bombers) and forces each side to trade off ballistic missiles for greater cruise missile deployments. These ALCM launcher counting rules should be extended to any future START agreement.

SALT II, of course, did not settle all of the problems asociated with ALCMs equipped with nonnuclear warheads. If future problems are to be avoided, an attempt should be made to preserve the distinctions between launchers of conventional and nuclear, strategic and tactical ALCMs. Alternatively, changing the dimensions of a nonnuclear ALCM to make it observably different from the ALCM could be considered.

Of all the variants of cruise missiles now entering the inventory or in the testing phase, experts are generally in agreement that none has complicated arms control efforts as much as the SLCM. SLCMs pose all the verification problems common to cruise missiles, and then some. First, long-range nuclear SLCMs are being deployed on traditionally nonstrategic vessels (major surface combatants and attack submarines). Second, nuclear SLCMs are being placed alongside nonnuclear SLCMs, from which they are virtually indistinguishable. Third, ships and submarines can hold a large number of SLCMs. A single, Spruance-class destroyer could hold upward of 120 in vertical launchers. Fourth, stored in torpedo rooms of submarines and launched from torpedo tubes, SLCMs will be impossible to detect and count even with verification procedures far more intrusive than those that exist today.

Despite the complications SLCMs present for arms control, the introduction of some SLCM types deployed in significant numbers is unavoidable. While the easiest arms control solution would have been simply to ban SLCMs of all types and ranges, this is simply not feasible. SLCMs have become increasingly attractive to defense planners because of their versatility, their lethality, and their cost. The constituency for SLCMs within the Department of Defense, the Congress, and elsewhere has grown considerably in the last few years, particularly after their effectiveness was so graphically demonstrated in the Falklands war.

Nevertheless, certain projected roles and missions for SLCMs should be viewed skeptically. This is especially true of the nuclear land-attack version. Approximately 750 nuclear SLCMs are to be used as part of a "strategic reserve" force of nuclear weapons to supplement the SLBM force. They would be used to attack whatever targets remained in the Soviet Union after execution of the Single Integrated Operational Plan (SIOP). Thus, attack submarines armed with SLCMs would become part of the U.S. strategic nuclear forces. This strategy is questionable on a number of grounds.

First, it is essentially a means for the Navy to circumvent the SALT SSBN limits in order to proliferate submarine-based launch platforms. The Soviets can be expected to follow with a similar program. Second, it makes little sense to put nuclear SLCMs on attack submarines, whose primary function in war is to seek out and destroy enemy ships. Giving an attack submarine a strategic reserve mission means it must hide from enemy ships, not seek them out and expose itself to the ASW threat. If more survivable forces at sea are desired, then a higher percentage of SSBNs could be put on patrol at no cost to the attack submarine mission.

Third, there are technical shortcomings with a SLCM-oriented strategic reserve force. The SLCM's usefulness in a protracted nuclear conflict is dependent on its retargeting capability, which is quite limited. Even if the missiles themselves can be made more effectively retargetable, they will still retain the same deficiencies as all submarine-based forces—the limited ability of commanders to communicate with them during a nuclear war.

Finally, placing strategic nuclear weapons aboard attack submarines compounds the already significant problem military commanders will face in war: assessing the situation in order to respond in a manner that keeps the escalation graduated and controlled. The control of escalation will be all but impossible if the distinction between strategic and conventional forces is blurred. If the Soviet Union should attack U.S. submarines or surface ships armed with nuclear SLCMs, is the United States to respond as if this were an attack on its strategic nuclear forces? Military commanders will certainly be tempted to view such an assault as a significant notch up the escalatory ladder.

How then might SLCMs be incorporated into an arms agreement? One possible solution is to ban all land-attack SLCMs. This could be accomplished by prohibiting SLCMs with ranges in excess of the longest antiship version (the U.S. tactical air-to-surface missile's range is 250–500 miles, the longest Soviet antiship SLCM has a range of about 300 miles). Theoretically, range limits on new cruise missiles are verifiable, even though cruise missile range is difficult to define and estimate precisely. Flight test telemetry can be monitored and, along with other observed missile characteristics, can be used to determine range on the basis of the fuel consumption rate and estimated fuel capacity. However, such a ban would be extremely difficult to negotiate today since both the United States and the Soviet Union have already tested and begun deploying long-range SLCMs.

It is, however, an option that should not be closed out completely. The Soviet START proposal includes restrictions on SLCMs with ranges above 372 miles. While such a proposal may not be acceptable in its present form (it would preclude deployment of any planned U.S. SLCMs) negotiators could explore what the Soviets are willing to give up to prevent deployment of longer-range U.S. SLCMs. Trading off U.S. SLCMs for Soviet Backfire bombers, as was proposed in Vladivostok in 1976, is one possible approach.

If it is not possible to ban land-attack SLCMs, their deployment might be constrained in other ways to reduce counting and verification problems. SLCMs could be prohibited from deployment aboard attack submarines, which are probably the most difficult platform from which to count them. Submarines are also the most survivable platform though, so such a limitation might remove any rationale for deployment of nuclear land-attack SLCMs.

Another method would be to include ships and submarines that carry long-range SLCMs as designated strategic systems under a SALT I–type limit (no more than X number of launchers on X number of ships and submarines). There is a precedent for this in the U.S. Vladivostok proposal of 1976. Certain types of launchers for SLCMs (armored box and vertical launch systems, for example) are easier to count and lend credibility to such an arrangement. This could be supplemented by other measures to ease verification problems: forbidding testing and deployment of SLCMs from submarine torpedo tubes, providing for SLCM loading to take place in the open, and designating factories where SLCMs are built so that production can be determined more accurately.

Alternatively, SLCMs on ships or submarines could be counted against MIRV platform subceilings in increments of, perhaps, fifteen to one. Thus, a battleship with thirty-two SLCMs aboard would count as two MIRVed launchers. This counting system could be applied no matter what the mix of nuclear and conventional SLCMs on board.

More exotic means could be used to distinguish among SLCM types if, for example, nuclear SLCMs were restricted to certain launch platforms. Devices to detect gamma ray emanations from nuclear weapons could be periodically placed aboard ships not permitted to carry nuclear SLCMs. Special zones could be created within which SLCM-carrying vessels could not operate. Such zones would be similar to the SSBN-free zones or ASW-standoff zones that have been discussed within SALT from time to time. Historically, the Soviets have perceived it as being in their interest to create such zones, since they lagged behind the United States in ASW and submarine technology. Though the U.S. Navy can be expected to oppose SLCM-free ocean areas, an objective evaluation, outside of parochial interests, should be undertaken to explore the feasibility of this type of stability-enhancing arms control measure.

Conclusion

While many characteristics of the cruise missile and its deployment present challenges to existing means of verification, cruise missiles need not represent a hopeless task for arms control. Methods can be found to facilitate the monitoring of U.S. and Soviet cruise missiles and still allow their limited introduction into the military forces of the two sides.

This will require, however, that cruise missile advocates realize that deployment schemes that make arms control more difficult may also create uncertainties in the level of the threat. Moreover, questionable cruise missile missions that do little to increase strategic capabilities may do far more to erode strategic stability.

Any restrictions on cruise missiles must meet both the military and political requirements for verifiability. The military requirement is that limits be sufficiently verifiable to enable the United States to detect militarily significant clandestine deployments. This can be accomplished through counting rules that take such possibilities into account and through vigilant monitoring using presently available technical means. Though cruise missiles are easier to conceal than ballistic missiles, they are no more so than other weapons systems (antiaircraft missiles, tanks, and so forth) that we presently count with a great deal of precision. It would be extremely difficult and politically risky for the Soviets to conceal large-scale deployment of cruise missiles from U.S. intelligence. Should other means of verification (designated facilities, gamma ray detectors, FRODs, and other things) become available, they could supplement present means and perhaps allow more detailed restrictions.

Determining the political requirements for adequate verification is more difficult. It is probably safe to say that once the Soviets begin deploying them in quantity, modern cruise missiles may be used by opponents of arms control to sabotage strategic arms agreements. If the verification requirement becomes, in order to appease domestic political elements, the capability to detect a single Soviet SLCM on a single submarine, no foreseeable monitoring regime will suffice, and no treaty will be possible. The result will be a net loss for U.S. security. *(May 1983)*

Mobile Missiles and Arms Control
John C. Baker
Joel S. Wit

In recent years, as fixed missile deployments have theoretically become more vulnerable to attack, the United States and the Soviet Union have begun to emphasize land-based mobile missiles in theater and strategic nuclear roles. The Soviet Union began deployments of the mobile SS-20 intermediate-range missile in 1977, and NATO began deployments of mobile Pershing II and ground-launched cruise missiles in 1983. Now the Soviet Union has begun deployment of intercontinental-range mobile missiles—the SS-25 and, soon, the SS-X-24—and the United States is developing its mobile ICBM, the Midgetman. This trend toward mobile systems could continue and perhaps accelerate in the future.

Despite years of study and debate, the impact of mobile missile deployments on military planning and arms control is still controversial. Indeed, just as the United States is faced with key arms control and funding decisions with regard to mobile missiles, there seems to be considerable confusion on the issue. For example, while mobile missiles are thought by many to enhance nuclear stability, the Reagan administration recently proposed banning mobile ICBMs altogether. Yet one point about mobile missiles remains clear: their future will be shaped in large part by the kind of strategic arms control agreement, if any, the United States negotiates with the Soviet Union. The objective here is to examine the opportunities and problems posed by these new weapons and to offer suggestions for coping with both.

The United States and the Soviet Union first experimented with long-range mobile missiles during the 1960s. The first U.S. program, the mobile Minuteman, was seen as a hedge against the possible vulnerability of U.S. missile silos and submarine forces. Mobile Minuteman was to be mounted on railroad cars and moved at random over track in isolated areas. Up to three hundred rail-mobile ICBMs were scheduled to begin deployment in 1963.

By December 1961 the program was cancelled. Fear of the Soviet threat to U.S. strategic forces had waned, and the political, technical, and economic arguments against the missile were overwhelming. Many believed that mobile Minuteman was in fact more vulnerable than its silo-based counterpart because it could be barraged by high-yield inaccurate weapons. Some were concerned that the mobile Minuteman would be difficult to isolate from the public, leading to images of a garrison state. Finally, the mobile version cost two and a half times more than its silo-based counterpart.

The emergence of the anticipated Soviet threat following the SALT I Treaty led to the proposal of various mobile basing schemes for the MX missile. Once again, Pandora's box was opened. For almost a decade, U.S. administrations tried to balance a complex array of military, political, technical, and arms control considerations in devising a mobile basing plan. In the end they all failed, in part because of strong misgivings based on nonmilitary considerations, such as the negative domestic reaction to deployment of the MX in the western United States.

By comparison, a different set of factors have beset Soviet mobile missile developments. Soviet concerns about land-based missile vulnerability date back to the early 1960s, when their missile force was largely based on soft, above-ground launchers. Much of Soviet nuclear policy since that time has focused on reducing force vulnerability, in part by building more survivable weapon systems. Mobile missiles have been one of the possible solutions to this problem, although technical barriers, cost considerations, and even political factors may have had a major impact on Soviet programs.

For example, the first generation of Soviet mobile missiles consisted of two theater missiles, the SS-X-14 and SS-X-15, and possibly a mobile ICBM based on the SS-13. These weapons were clearly a response to the vulnerability of the older strategic and theater missiles with their fixed, above-ground launchers. Yet in the end the theater missiles did not become fully operational and only sixty SS-13s were deployed in silos. In large part, this failure seems to have been the result of technical difficulties with guidance systems and new solid-fuel rocket motors. However, the Soviet decision to forgo mobile missiles may also be attributable to ongoing alternative programs for silo and submarine-based missiles and to the unacceptably high costs of mobile missiles and their infrastructure when scarce resources were already heavily invested in other strategic programs.

The second generation of Soviet mobile missiles was a partial success. Once again, the new mobile ICBM, the SS-X-16, proved to be a technical failure. Furthermore, force survivability had greatly improved through continuing deployments in hardened silos, and new submarines made it entirely feasible to sacrifice the SS-X-16 in the SALT II agreement. On the other hand, the SS-20 mobile theater missile, a derivative of the SS-X-16, proved to be a technical success and began deployment in 1977.

Important recent developments have brought the subject of mobile missiles back into the limelight. In late 1983, the United States began development of a new single-warhead, small ICBM, popularly known as Midgetman. Development of the new missile resulted from the political stalemate over MX basing that was finally resolved in the 1983 report from the president's Commission on Strategic Forces (otherwise known as the Scowcroft Commission, after its chairman). The commission hoped that, in conjunction with properly designed arms control initiatives, moving to a single-warhead missile would promote strategic stability. The report also recommended that hardened silos and hardened mobile launchers be investigated for Midgetman basing.

Hardened mobile launchers have emerged as the prime basing mode, although advances in silo superhardening could present a competitive option. The mobile launchers would operate on large military reservations in peacetime. On advance warning, the force would disperse over larger areas, possibly beyond the reservations. Dispersal requires the Soviets to barrage large land areas to destroy the missile, a tactic that could prove prohibitive unless the Soviets greatly expand their warhead arsenal.

The development of Midgetman is just beginning. Problems that bedeviled previous U.S. mobile missile programs may eventually affect Midgetman. In the absence of an arms control agreement limiting the size of Soviet forces, Midgetman could be vulnerable to attack, regardless of countermeasures. The missile's mobility could raise environmental and other concerns among people living near proposed deployment areas. Also, several technical challenges in developing a small mobile ICBM must be resolved. For example, Midgetman is being designed to have a highly accurate guidance system that will enable it to strike hardened Soviet targets such as missile silos and C^3 installations. But the Air Force faces problems in building an affordable guidance and control system. Finally, the cost of a five-hundred-missile force, according to a General Accounting Office (GAO) report, could reach $44 billion, an exceedingly large amount of money for single-warhead missiles whose contribution to the overall U.S. force posture might be modest. For these reasons, Midgetman's eventual deployment is still in question.

New Soviet mobile missiles about to be deployed reflect a decade-old decision to procure more capable, more survivable systems as a "strategic reserve." (New submarines carrying MIRVed missiles also fulfill this requirement.) In part, they reflect a concern about the impending threat to Soviet strategic forces by increasingly accurate U.S. weapons. In the case of mobile missiles, this concern was sufficient to warrant a costly commitment to build and maintain a substantial support infrastructure.

The SS-25 ground-mobile ICBM, which became operational in late 1985, represents a logical continuation of previous Soviet efforts to develop mobile missiles. A single-warhead missile carried on a transporter-erector-launcher (TEL), the SS-25 is being deployed in bases similar to the SS-20 encampments. Indeed, in 1984 the Soviets began to convert SS-20 bases to house the new ICBM. Presumably, the new ICBM, like the SS-20, could either fire from its garage or "flush" from its base camps on warning into the surrounding countryside.

The second Soviet mobile ICBM, the SS-X-24, represents a departure from previous development efforts. This large, solid-fuel missile, armed with up to ten MIRVs, probably will be based in silos and on railroad cars. (Although much smaller than the SS-18, the missile's size and weight will still make transportation on a TEL difficult.) How the rail-mobile force will operate is unclear. It may be continuously on the move or, like the rail-mobile Minuteman, travel randomly between presurveyed launch sites. Presumably, the transporters will return on occasion to main bases to replenish on-board supplies. Apparently, the SS-X-24 program has experienced some difficulties. Several of the early flight tests are reported to have failed. Despite U.S. estimates, the Soviet ability to produce and deploy significant numbers of this large ICBM as a mobile system is questionable at this stage.

Mobile missiles pose a challenge for the dual goals of crisis stability and arms race stability. Like long-range cruise missiles, they highlight the fact that these two objectives are not always entirely compatible. Both weapons can enhance crisis stability but can also create new difficulties for negotiating verifiable arms agreements to control the arms race.

In theory, mobile missiles, by presenting undeniable uncertainties for the enemy's targeting efforts, can contribute to stability by improving survivability. However, what may be true as a general principle does not necessarily hold for specific mobile missile deployments. Each missile system must be evaluated according to its specific operational plans and its numerical relationship to the overall force posture.

For example, mobile missiles (Pershing IIs and GLCMs) will account for all the NATO INF deployments in Europe and would seem to make a significant contribution to force survivability. Yet by virtue of their forward deployment, they face a much broader range of nuclear and nonnuclear threats. While NATO plans to base the GLCM in hardened shelters, the Pershing II will continue to use relatively unsheltered facilities previously associated with the shorter-range Pershing IA missile. Like its predecessor, the Pershing II becomes a sitting duck. This situation highlights a potential instability caused by a mobile missile. The new, longer-range Pershing II is a critical target for the Soviet Union and is relatively vulnerable to a conventional attack by aircraft, short-range ballistic missiles armed with nonnuclear warheads, or even commandos.

In general, because they are deployed in the homelands of the United States or the Soviet Union, mobile ICBMs face a much narrower range of threats than forward-deployed mobile missiles like the Pershing II. Nevertheless, their dependence on warning to disperse might make these missiles vulnerable to "bolt from the blue" ballistic or cruise missile attacks from offshore submarines, particularly if the mobile missiles are routinely stationed or grouped around a home base and are therefore vulnerable to a "Pearl Harbor" type of attack. A futuristic attack alternative against mobile missiles would be to construct a satellite system to provide real-time target information or to deploy maneuverable warheads whose courses could be corrected at the end of their flights. However, such a system conceivably could be defeated by countermeasures, such as mobile launcher decoys. These are clearly worst-case scenarios and, on the whole, strategic mobile missiles seem to be more stabilizing than destabilizing.

Strategic mobile missiles are unlikely to account for a large percentage of superpower nuclear warheads in the near future, regardless of whether the United States and the Soviet Union continue to adhere to or abrogate the SALT II limits. Therefore the stability contribution of mobile missiles is greatest in the event of an arms control agreement that requires a reduction of MIRVed missiles and their warheads. The greater the percentage of mobiles in the ICBM inventory, the greater will be the strategic benefits of mobile missiles. This process is likely to last into the late 1990s and perhaps beyond.

The single-warhead Midgetman is regarded as the most stabilizing type of ICBM. However, placing additional, MIRV warheads on Midgetman would increase its contribution to overall force capabilities. Thus, greater numbers of survivable Midgetman warheads could increase the stability benefits of the missile. Of course, some argue that MIRVing mobile missiles will detract from their stability benefits by making them more attractive targets. Granted, though a mobile ICBM force with a limited number of MIRVed missiles is not as ideal as a mobile force with single warheads, such a force would certainly be more stabilizing than the present Minuteman and MX arsenal in fixed silos.

If mobile missiles offer some potential for improving stability, the price is likely to be in terms of further complicating the problem of reaching arms control agreements. Mobile missiles pose three particular problems for devising theater and strategic arms limitation agreements: (1) mobile launchers can be redeployed; (2) distinguishing between mobile theater and intercontinental missiles can be difficult; and (3) mobile systems create pressures to limit total missile inventories, both deployed and stored.

The first problem, that mobile missiles can be redeployed and therefore transferred in and out of different theaters, has already complicated previous negotiations to reach an INF agreement. In the INF negotiations, the United States has argued that any Soviet SS-20s in the Far East could be redeployed westward to cover targets in Europe. Consequently, the United States has been unwilling to agree simply to freeze the level of SS-20 missile deployments at Far Eastern bases. Instead, the U.S. position is that both sides must accept global limits on their INF deployments.

Second, negotiating arms control limits on mobile missiles is complicated by the fact that different types of mobile systems often use the same basic components, such as rocket stages or missile launchers. Under the SALT II Treaty at U.S. insistence the Soviets agreed to ban any deployment of the SS-X-16 mobile ICBM because it has two rocket stages in common with the SS-20 IRBM, which was not being limited. This problem of "commonality" threatened to complicate future treaty verification by making it difficult to distinguish clearly between these two mobile missiles. It could reappear in the future with new generations of Soviet IRBMs and ICBMs.

The third problem is that mobile missiles, because of their unusual refire capability, create pressures to limit total inventories of missiles in addition to launchers. The SALT I and SALT II agreements focused heavily on limiting deployed launchers, not the total number of missiles on each side. When the SALT I agreement was signed in 1972, the limitation on missile launchers, which could be readily verified using national technical means (NTM), was an effective surrogate for limiting usable missiles, which could not be easily monitored by NTM. This was true as long as only one missile could be fired from one launcher.

Over the next decade, this association between one launcher and one missile began to break down as a result of technological developments. Certain Soviet ICBMs, such as the SS-18, could be "cold launched" from their silos in a way that permitted them to be reused, although such a process would take days. Nevertheless, some U.S. experts worried that the Soviet Union might gain a strategic advantage over the United States by deploying these weapon systems, and the United States successfully insisted on provisions in SALT II designed to hinder reloading missile silos. Moreover, the dubious utility of possessing refire missiles for silos was highlighted in recent official testimony in which the U.S. Air Force explained its own lack of interest in procuring refires for the coldlaunch MX/Peacekeeper ICBM because of the difficulty of trying to reload silos in wartime. Presumably, this problem applies to the Soviet Union as well.

The Soviet SS-20 IRBM highlighted a new, more difficult side of the question of whether treaty limits should be expanded to include missile inventories. The U.S. intelligence community credits the SS-20 with a "refire" capability whereby extra missiles are maintained for each mobile launcher. Also, mobile missile launchers can be prepared to launch an additional missile in only a matter of hours, not days. Finally, some analysts argue that, unlike the reloading operation for a silo, which occurs at a known target, mobile launchers are likely to prove more survivable throughout a conflict. In short, mobile missiles challenge the earlier arms limitation assumption that, in practical terms, only one missile can be fired from each launcher. As a result, there has been renewed U.S. interest in limiting total missile inventories, both stored and deployed.

Yet, negotiating equal limits on total missile inventories in a future START or INF agreement would be a difficult task at best. One problem is where to begin counting missiles against threaty limits. Many solid-fuel ballistic missiles are not fully assembled until they arrive at their final deployment site. For example, the MX/Peacekeeper ICBM will remain in four separate stages until each is lowered into the underground missile silo.

Both countries typically produce a much larger number of missiles than are actually deployed. These extra missiles (or missile stages) are used for various types of reliability testing or operational flight tests. Placing equal limits on U.S. and

Soviet missiles assumes that the two countries employ similar practices for missile development, production, and testing. The Soviet Union historically has conducted more flight tests of its operational ICBMs than has the United States.

Monitoring total missile limits would apparently require very intrusive cooperative measures that go far beyond relying on national technical means. These intrusive measures would probably include a very detailed listing of all missile production facilities, the establishment of annual production quotas for weapon systems and their major subcomponents, and the extensive employment of human inspectors.

In sum, pursuit of limits on total missile inventories would be a complicated exercise that is probably not necessary for national security, given the limited military significance of the excess missiles. Mobile missile reloads seem to raise more concerns than are probably warranted and their dangers should be kept in context. This approach assumes that refires and stored mobile launchers have a potential for sudden breakout from treaty limits to gain political advantage, as well as a utility in fighting a nuclear war. Yet, it remains unclear what sudden political advantages could be gained that would outweigh the risks of breakout. The feasibility of prolonged nuclear war fighting and the utility of land-based mobiles in such scenarios is also open to debate. Storage and loading sites are likely to be destroyed in the earliest stage of a nuclear conflict, and the missile would be difficult to load and transport in a nuclear war environment.

Another important factor is that large military organizations have a tendency toward standardization, something that is not very compatible with establishing covert units. For example, the Soviet SS-20 and SS-25 missiles, like the GLCM and the Pershing II, reportedly employ central support bases for peacetime operations. Covert forces would also face serious constraints on realistic operational training, another basic military value. Finally, refires do not pose a first-strike threat. An arms control agreement that limits deployed weapons is the most important step toward enhancing stability and reducing each side's ability and temptation to launch a preemptive strike. Therefore, refires are not an obstacle to effective arms control.

Future U.S. policy must seek to maximize the potential benefits of mobile missiles, at the same time attempting to minimize potential problems. Such a policy can be ensured through certain unilateral and bilateral measures. First, U.S. decisions to proceed with the deployment of mobile missiles must be based on the judgement that these weapons make sense on their own merits. Second, the United States should seek negotiated arrangements with the Soviet Union designed to enhance the contributions of mobile missiles to stability, to minimize their political and economic costs, and to alleviate their potentially adverse impact on strategic arms control.

If the U.S. mobile missile effort is to stand on its own merits, it may require a thorough reexamination of the current Midgetman program. Already, questions are increasing as to the affordability and political acceptability of single-warhead ICBM. The program may soon be derailed altogether. The United States should seriously consider redesigning Midgetman to carry a small number, perhaps two or three, of MIRV warheads. This approach could retain the stability benefits of Midgetman while modestly increasing the number of survivable warheads based on mobile missiles. At the same time, it could minimize objections to the system based on cost-effectiveness and would be much preferable to the present force structure.

The United States should adopt unilateral measures to enhance the survivability of mobile missiles. For example, the vulnerability of Pershing II deployments to Warsaw Pact preemption using nonnuclear forces should be reduced by providing protective shelters similar to those designed for the European-based GLCMs. Mobile ICBMs deployed in the United States could necessitate improved warning capabilities around the periphery of the North American continent. In particular, since Midgetman is likely to be based in the Southwest, improved warning systems against low-flying, hard-to-detect cruise missile attacks from Soviet submarines off the West Coast should be an important priority.

Negotiated measures would seem to be indispensible for enhancing the potential benefits of mobile missiles and minimizing the potential problems. The best approach would be to seek limits on deployed mobile missile systems. They would be confined to restricted operating areas—designated deployment areas (DDAs)—established around peacetime mobile missile bases. For the United States, DDAs would substantially ease verification problems by creating large areas in the Soviet Union where mobile missile deployments would be prohibited. Merely detecting and discerning *any* mobile missiles in these prohibited areas would constitute a treaty violation. Within the DDAs themselves, additional cooperative measures could further enhance treaty monitoring. For example, operations in a manner to avoid detection or the use of camouflage could be prohibited.

This approach is not without its problems. One is the potential difficulty of devising acceptable DDAs given the distinctive types of mobile systems being pursued by the two superpowerrs. The hard mobile Midgetman is likely to require a smaller DAA to ensure acceptable survivability than the Soviet softmobile systems. To the extent that equivalency in DDAs is important, this could pose a negotiating problem. One solution would be to allow the United States an equivalent DDA that may encompass land it never intends to use in peacetime. Another major question is whether DDAs can be confined to areas small enough to improve treaty monitoring without adverse impact on the survivability of the mobile system.

Even with DDAs and other cooperative measures, monitoring the number of mobile missile systems is not likely to be done with the same certainty as monitoring fixed silos. The level of uncertainty involved is unclear; at the time of the 1974 Vladivostok accord, Secretary of State Henry Kissinger is reported to have stated that mobile launchers could be counted to within 25 percent of their real number using national technical means. During the SALT II hearings, Secretary of Defense Harold Brown acknowledged that "counting the number of mobile ICBM launchers is more difficult than counting silos, but it is a manageable task." Thus, in accepting this arms control scheme for mobile missile systems, any future administration will have to make a basic political decision on whether the stability benefits of mobile missiles outweigh the increased level of monitoring uncertainty they create.

In addition to negotiated DDAs, other bilateral measures might be necessary. Even if mobile ICBMs are deployed initially as a supplement to existing silo-based forces, arms control arrangements can ensure that ultimately they will become a substitute for fixed missile forces. An important step toward this goal might be to negotiate a ban on the deployment of new MIRVed ICBMs in silos after an agreed-upon date. These weapons represent the most destabilizing element of current U.S. and Soviet strategic forces.

Furthermore, the burden of deploying mobile missiles could be reduced significantly by negotiated measures that place restrictions on potential threats. For instance, reducing the permitted level of ballistic missile warheads would constrain the possibility of worst-case threats, such as barrage bombing, that affect the costs and political impact of mobile ICBM deployments. Similarly, limits on advanced-technology threats, such as missiles capable of in-flight retargeting, should be the subject of further examination.

Finally, efforts should begin now to encourage both sides to avoid deploying mobile missile systems in ways that seriously complicate the verification of treaty limits. While design practices can be altered to solve the problem of commonality mentioned earlier, it might prove useful to build into future agreements functionally related observable differences (FRODs) to distinguish between various mobile missile types that are similar in design. For example, mobile missile FRODs could be based on different characteristics of missile launchers or missile stages.

Mobile missiles are an important development. Over the next decade, deployments of these weapons are likely to continue, although the U.S. mobile Midgetman program still remains in doubt. The Reagan administration recently proposed a ban on mobile missiles, but such an agreement is unlikely since the Soviets appear seriously committed to deploying these weapons.

Mobile missiles have important implications for nuclear stability and nuclear arms control. While they are theoretically stabilizing, their actual impact depends on their location, the quantity deployed and on their operational characteristics. As a result of practical considerations, mobile missiles may greatly enhance stability, make a marginal contribution or even serve to reduce stability. While negotiating and verification problems should not be underestimated, reasonable and verifiable agreements are still possible.   *(November–December 1985)*

Midgetman: Our Best Hope for Stability and Arms Control

Albert Gore, Jr.

The Midgetman missile, proposed just two and a half years ago by the Scowcroft Commission, is now a well-evolved design ready to enter full-scale development, if the administration so recommends and if Congress agrees. This system is our best hope of settling the problem of intercontinental ballistic missile vulnerability in a manner that is intellectually legitimate and politically viable. Nevertheless, the Midgetman is now at risk. If it fails, the nuclear and arms control policies of the United States will be grievously damaged.

ICBM vulnerability, or more popularly, the "first-strike scenario," is the Gordian knot of arms control. For fifteen years it has ensnared U.S. planning for nuclear modernization and arms control policy. Though many analysts would simply dismiss the issue, no president has ever been able to deal with it so casually. As a matter of statecraft and political instinct, presidents reject the idea that the United States can safely concede even a theoretical first-strike capability to the Soviet Union.

SALT II resolved the first-strike problem in principle by means of a numerical equilibrium between MX missiles in protective shelters and the number of permitted Soviet warheads. But the treaty's political failure and the subsequent crisis over MX have ruled out a return to that particular solution. Moreover, policymakers have learned after examining some thirty-odd basing schemes for MX—that there *is* no single heavy missile basing mode with the inherent robustness to deal with improvements in Soviet missile accuracy.

The particular contribution of the Scowcroft Commission report was to break the usual confines of strategic analysis by looking at systems in combination with each other and with the Soviet threat. Midgetman, commonly presented as an arms controller's missile, in fact arose as the commission's answer to a military question: how to complicate the problem of an attacker to such an extent that he will be effectively deterred not only from striking at one particular U.S. weapon system, but from striking at all. That the answer happens to be a single-warhead missile in a hardened mobile launcher, and that this answer fits precisely into a larger concept of arms control, is an enormous stroke of luck for the United States. At last it has a serious weapon concept that works with, rather than across, the grain of arms control. There is hardly anything more rare.

"Price-to-attack" is a way to measure the degree of difficulty a Soviet planner will encounter if he tries to devise a first strike that works to his advantage. It asks what price the Soviet Union must pay—whether reckoned in throwweight or warheads—to destroy a stipulated percentage of U.S. ICBMs. The price to attack ICBMs based in silos grows steadily less as ICBM accuracy improves. Moreover, "returns" on this kind of Soviet "investment" grow in proportion as the United States loads its silos with MIRVed missiles. Midgetman, however, alters this reckoning profoundly.

If Midgetman is deployed in hardened mobile launchers (built to withstand blast pressures of 30 pounds per square inch) on just four existing military bases, the Soviet Union would have to attack with about one-half its present ICBM throwweight to destroy the system, even if the Midgetman launchers do not respond to the impending Soviet attack. If the launchers do respond by dispersing to an even larger area, then within fifteen minutes the price to attack will approach *all* Soviet heavy ICBMs. And if the launchers run for twenty to twenty-five minutes, the price then reaches out toward the combined throwweight of the entire Soviet inventory of ballistic missiles, both land- and sea-based. These calculations, supported by unclassified studies by the Congressional Research Service and by other studies in the executive branch, show that Midgetman, in comparison with the current U.S. ICBM force, exacts a much higher price to attack, particularly when faced with future improvements in Soviet missiles.

As a result, especially under SALT II limits, the Soviet Union would not have the means, even theoretically, to carry out a classic counterforce first strike. Moreover, any reductions below SALT levels would only reinforce this conclusion, even though the Soviets might still have residual advantages in ICBM throwweight and warhead numbers.

The mathematics behind these conclusions is not in dispute. Neither is there any question that by 1992 the United States can build and deploy the Midgetman and its hardened mobile launcher. What is now in doubt is whether the Reagan administration has the vision and steadiness to complete the missile program it agreed to begin, to recognize the implications for arms control, and to act upon them.

Just before the summit the president agreed to an arms control option proposing that all mobile ICBMs should be banned. Ostensibly, the grounds for this proposal were purely "arms control": namely, that any negotiated constraints on the two Soviet mobile ICBMs—the SS-X-24 and SS-25—could not be verified effectively.

In fact, the administration's real concerns are based on the near impossibility of keeping track of such systems well enough to target them. Unfortunately, in a less than perfect world, there is a choice to be made: either one trades off some of the requisites for nuclear war fighting in order to have arms control, or one trades off arms control to serve better the demands of a war fighting doctrine.

As it now stands, the administration's current proposal would lead to strategic forces much smaller but also much less stable than at present. Soviet silo-based ICBMs, after reduction, would be vulnerable to the upcoming U.S. Trident II (D-5) sea-launched ballistic missile, and U.S. ICBMs will still be vulnerable to Soviet ICBMs. These same forces with mobile components would be stable. In effect, the administration—for invalid reasons—has wrecked the logic of its own approach to deep reductions.

In my opinion, this instability at the core of the president's proposal is deliberately intended to make the Strategic Defense Initiative inescapable. The price tag for even an imperfect defensive system can now be guestimated, drawing on data in the so-called architecture studies now underway in the Pentagon: the price is quite literally in excess of $1 trillion. That particular model, it turns out, is not designed to defend the cities of the United States, but its strategic assets. In other words, it is in essence a system for the defense of the United States' land-based missiles.

The function of any such system is to frustrate Soviet planning by raising the price to attack U.S. missiles to irrationally high levels. The United States can produce this effect either by deploying Midgetman, at a cost of about $40 billion including manpower, or it can do it with SDI, at a cost of equal to half the national debt. Privately, the administration claims to doubt that Congress will continue its enthusiastic support for Midgetman because it is expensive. What must they think Congress will do when the price for SDI is broadly understood?

A number of design and mission problems associated with the Midgetman program are of legitimate concern and ought to be addressed before the United States makes its commitments final. Most of these questions have already been answered in a much delayed report, released in January 1986, from the secretary of defense to the Congress.

What we learn from this report is: (1) the United States can have the Midgetman as presently designed, or a somewhat larger version with penetration aids by 1992; (2) costs are coming down as a result of industry competition for Midgetman contracts and of the efforts to find savings through the use of existing facilities on military bases; (3) the Midgetman can coexist with the missions and the environments on existing military bases, causing no serious interruption to the former, or damage to the latter; (4) if the Soviet threat expands, more bases are available; (5) the Soviet threat would have to expand enormously to handle Midgetman's cost-to-attack characteristics; and (6) although MIRVed ICBMs are the cheapest way to build raw strategic inventory, Midgetman is the cheapest way to build *survivable* inventory.

The Scowcroft Commission report aspired to create a new political consensus on the objectives of nuclear modernization and arms control. Moderate Democrats and Republicans who joined in supporting the report's conclusions *are* what the president is talking about when he boasts of bipartisan support. All of us realize that the president can hardly propose anything at all in arms control that does not impinge on someone's conception of a vital national interest. But consensus is itself a strategic asset of enormous importance—not just to this president, but to the nation. What is now at issue, and what will soon be established, is whether the president really understands that.

It will help greatly if others who follow these issues as closely as do the members of the Arms Control Association also realize that what is at stake is one of the nation's most vital commodities: a clear, workable idea in the midst of an otherwise barren landscape. No one claims that Midgetman is perfectly conceived, just that it makes good sense. If we lose such an idea and the opportunities it represents, to what then shall we adhere with any hope of a successful outcome? *(November–December 1985)*

Midgetman: Superhero or Problem Child?
Jonathan Rich

Within the space of a year, the single-warhead intercontinental ballistic missile, known as SICBM (small intercontinental ballistic missile) or Midgetman, has been transformed from a theoretical concept to a major United States strategic nuclear weapon program. Previously the preserve of a specialized group of defense analysts, the Midgetman is now being propelled forward as a national priority initiative with a fiscal year 1985 budget of more than $700 million, an extraordinary amount for a one-year-old program.

The missile's almost universal popularity is linked to its promise of finally resolving the decade-long dilemma over how to assure that U.S. land-based missiles can survive a Soviet nuclear attack. Legislators from across the political spectrum have agreed that the prospect of one thousand or so survivable Midgetman missiles—probably based in mobile launchers in the Southwest—could significantly boost the nation's security and add stability to the nuclear balance.

However, the development of the Midgetman remains part of a fragile compromise engineered in 1983 by the president's Commission on Strategic Forces— the Scowcroft Commission—in which congressional support for procurement of the MX is tied to the Reagan administration's commitment to the SICBM and arms control. Whereas the administration and congressional conservatives believe that both missiles are necessary, some congressmen hope to replace the MX completely with the smaller missile. The outcome of this debate will center largely on the question of whether the two missiles offer distinct qualities, or whether the Air Force is in the process of developing two very expensive systems with redundant capabilities.

Furthermore, the raison d'être of the Midgetman—its survivability against any potential Soviet threat—seems by no means assured. Significant technical uncertainties still surround U.S. efforts to harden either silo or mobile launchers to the degree necessary to withstand a large-scale Soviet attack. Even if the desired degree of hardness is achieved, it may not be sufficient to assure adequate security against projected Soviet forces in the 1990s. Ultimately, the viability of a secure and affordable Midgetman force will hinge on the establishment of an appropriate arms control regime.

The Rise of Midgetman

The emergence of Midgetman marks a new phase in the evolution of U.S. strategic systems. During the 1960s, mobile strategic missiles were considered and then rejected as unnecessarily expensive and complex, especially in comparison with the seemingly invulnerable missiles based in underground silos. But as the United States and the Soviet Union improved the accuracy of their missiles and deployed multiple independently targetable reentry vehicles in the 1970s, the offensive capabilities of both sides dramatically increased, particularly against stationary targets like intercontinental ballistic missile silos. Strategic planners became concerned about the "window of vulnerability," or the long-term ability of silo-based missiles to survive a first-strike attack.

The Soviets sought to hedge against this threat through the development of their unsuccessful mobile ICBM, the SS-16. Meanwhile, the Carter administration attempted to assure the survivability of the MX by proposing the very expensive multiple protective shelter (MPS) system, whereby two hundred missiles were to be rotated within a network of 4,600 hardened concrete shelters. This and dozens of other methods for a mobile MX basing were inevitably confronted with the extreme difficulty of transporting and hiding a one-hundred-ton missile in an affordable system that would not be greatly detrimental to the environment.

Early proponents of the Midgetman, such as Jan Lodal and Henry Kissinger, offered the Singlet concept as a solution to this dilemma. Thousands of small, cheap missiles dispersed in mobile launchers or silos would present the Soviets with a much less critical target than one or two hundred MIRVed MX missiles. If accompanied by a Soviet move toward SICBMs and a suitable arms control framework, the missile would ultimately reverse the dangerous strategic environment created by MIRVs a decade earlier.

In March 1983 the Scowcroft Commission recommended the development of both the MX and a mobile, single-warhead missile, thereby raising the Midgetman from relative obscurity. The commission effectively closed the window of vulnerability by reaffirming the implausibility of a successful attack on the redundant, complementary ICBM bomber, and submarine forces of the U.S. triad. Yet the commission's report emphasized the complementary capabilities of the two missiles: the MX would have multiple, accurate warheads comparable with large Soviet missiles, and the Midgetman would assure land-based ICBM survivability. The commission took pains to clarify this synergistic relationship by arguing that two missiles in different basing modes would complicate any Soviet plans for an attack, while the development of the MX—which will threaten Soviet ICBMs— would give the United States leverage toward the establishment of an arms control agreement most suited to the deployment of the SICBM.

The recommendations of the Scowcroft Commission formed the basis for an historic compromise, in which congressional moderates conditionally accepted the MX in return for an administration commitment to the Midgetman and arms control.

To ensure that the administration and the Air Force maintained their side of the bargain, Congress amended the Department of Defense authorization bill, linking the deployment of the MX to the development and testing of Singlet components. Before the Air Force can deploy the first ten MX missiles, scheduled for December 1986, it must complete tests of Midgetman guidance and propulsion subsystems, as well as various basing mode subsystems. Congress also set an upper limit of 33,000 pounds on the weight of the missile to assure its mobility.

Development Program

The Air Force has embarked on a development and testing program scheduled to produce the first operational Midgetman missiles in 1992. The missile program will use many existing or modified components from the MX, while pursuing parallel developments of alternate systems. As presently envisioned, the Midgetman will be about 44 feet in length and 4 feet in diameter, with a range of 6,000 nautical miles. A payload capacity of approximately 1,000 pounds will allow it to carry one Mk21, a 300–500 kiloton warhead, ten of which are designed for each MX. The Air Force is using a lightweight version of the advanced inertial reference sphere (AIRS) employed on the MX as the baseline guidance system. Alternative systems, such as ring-laser gyroscopes and terminal guidance are also being pursued.

The basing mode is crucial to the success of the Midgetman. The Department of Defense is concentrating on the development of hardened transporter-erector-launcher vehicles. Planners hope that the design of highly blast-resistant vehicles will enable the United States to restrict deployment to Air Force bases and land areas allocated to the Defense Department. In recognition of the technical uncertainty facing this basing mode, the Air Force is also studying superhardened silos and deep underground basing as alternatives. A final decision on the basing mode will be made before full-scale missile development begins in 1987.

Problems with the Midgetman

Despite its propitious beginnings, the Midgetman faces a number of technical and logistical obstacles before reaching deployment. Guidance system, weight, propulsion, basing mode, and cost all represent interdependent areas of concern that must be addressed in a manner consistent with the underlying rationale for the missile: to provide a mobile or otherwise secure force of land-based ICBMs. Trade-offs must inevitably be made among cost, survivability, accuracy, and payload.

A good portion of the complexity, expense, and development time associated with the Midgetman stems from the decision to model it after the MX on a smaller, mobile scale. Taking its cue from the Scowcroft Commission, the Air Force has set out to develop a missile with "sufficient accuracy and yield to put Soviet hardened military targets at risk." The combination of a lightweight AIRS and the Mk21 warhead was an obvious choice to achieve this capability within the given time frame. But AIRS and, to a lesser extent, the Mk21 carry the double disadvantage of high cost and weight. Even the lightweight AIRS, at 300 pounds, is almost three times heavier than the Mark 5 guidance system used on Trident submarine-launched missiles. Advance in rocket propulsion and lighter engine components are thus required before a 30,000 pound missile can confidently lift this guidance and warhead package.

The decision to duplicate the MX hard-target capability has definite implications for U.S. strategic doctrine and arms control in addition to greater cost and complexity. A potential force of one thousand Singlets actually offers more versatility than the one hundred MX, because the Singlets can reach widely separated targets. The ten MIRVed warheads on each MX missile can only be targeted within a finite missile "footprint," or impact area. The dramatic increase in offensive capability that is expected through the combined deployment of very accurate MX, Midgetman, and Trident II missiles will give the United States enough counterforce capability to threaten—at least theoretically—all of the existing Soviet land-based forces. A program that promises to remedy U.S. survivability problems by putting Soviet strategic forces at risk is not likely to increase stability or the prospects for arms control.

Aside from guidance and propulsion, the two most serious obstacles facing the Midgetman are the closely related factors of cost and survivability. However constituted, the Singlet promises to be an enormously expensive proposition, with estimated acquisition costs for one thousand missiles and launchers ranging from $45 to $70 billion, depending on the basing mode. Twenty-year maintenance expenses could bring the total cost to almost $100 billion, according to the Congressional Budget Office. Much of the expense represents the result of the decision to return to less cost-effective, single-warhead missiles. While the Air Force is seeking to reduce the number and high cost of operations and security personnel associated with the SICBM, the expense of acquiring a thousand separate propulsion, guidance, and control systems will remain. Cost is also driven by the technological challenge of assuring survivability against the potential threat of thousands of very accurate Soviet warheads.

Hardened Launchers

Deployment in ordinary silos, superhard silos, "soft-mobile" trucks, and "hard-mobile" launchers have all been considered for Midgetman basing. Missiles based in soft-mobile vans traversing the nation's vast highway system offer the unique advantage of almost total invulnerability, but this mode has been practically eliminated as an option because of command and control difficulties and fear of accidents. The possibility of deploying thousands of Singlets in ordinary silos has likewise been rejected, largely on the basis of cost and the concern that even a large force could eventually be overwhelmed by Soviet MIRVs.

For these reasons, the Air Force is concentrating on the development of hardened transporter-erector-launchers (TELs) and superhard silos, particularly the former. Hoping to maintain high security while avoiding the potential pitfalls of political and environmental opposition, the Air Force currently plans to restrict Midgetman deployment to mobile launchers roaming over bases in the southwestern and western United States. More specifically, the Defense Department envisions using about twelve thousand square miles of its land, which represents most of the suitable terrain within the five largest military reservations in the U.S. mainland.

Mobile launcher survivability is calculated as a function of the total expected megatonnage dropped on a given basing area and the hardness and numbers of the launch vehicles. The harder or more capable the TELs are of withstanding the effects of nuclear blasts, the less land is required to ensure that a substantial percentage will survive against a Soviet nuclear barrage. For example, if the Soviets launched most of their large SS-18 ICBMs, carrying as many as three thousand 500-kiloton warheads, Midgetman launchers would have to be hardened to withstand overpressure blasts of at least 30 pounds per square inch (psi) in order to assure even a minimal level of survivability within the currently projected basing area. The Air Force plans to deploy missiles outside the bases in times of crisis. But even hardened to 30 psi, the one thousand TELs would have to be spread over twenty-four thousand square miles—or twice the envisioned basing area—to guarantee the survival of more than 50 percent of this force.

As the Air Force attests, attaining hardness levels of 30 psi and more presents a considerable technological challenge. An M-60 tank, for example, can be disabled by an overpressure of 10 psi. Even if the TEL is not destroyed, overpressure damage may impair its function. The viability of mobile launchers also will hinge largely on the ability to prevent them from turning over during the blast wave passage and the high velocity winds accompanying a nuclear detonation. The multiple requirements for low profile, structural strength, and a near-perfect seal with the underlying terrain have prompted a number of futuresque launcher models employing various sealing mechanisms and anchoring devices. Whether any of these can withstand winds of greater than 600 miles per hour has yet to be determined.

The development of "superhard" silos capable of withstanding all but a direct hit is also a precarious technological undertaking. Although recent test results have been promising, advances in silo hardening techniques may be outpaced by expected improvements in Soviet missile accuracy.

Failure to achieve the desired hardness for either basing mode will probably force the United States to expand the basing area of mobile launchers onto private land or else turn to an alternative system, such as "soft-mobile" trucks. Either alternative is likely to precipitate considerable controversy and political opposition of the magnitude that greeted the Carter administration's MPS basing scheme. An increase in the number of launchers—aside from the considerable expense—would be of little consequence if a Soviet barrage could already destroy most of the launchers within the projected basing area. As a final option, a combined force of mobile and silo-based Singlets could increase survivability but would involve significant additions in expense and operational complexity.

The Arms Control Alternative

The only practical alternative to these equally unsavory choices is an arms control regime that reduces the potential threat to U.S. ICBMs. Even if the desired hardness is attained, arms limitation is a prerequisite for the long-term security of an economical SICBM force.

The Midgetman will not be introduced until 1992, at which time it could face a significantly more dangerous strategic environment. Both the United States and the Soviet Union are in the process of testing new MIRVed ICBMs, in addition to mobile SICBMs. In the present political climate, this widespread expansion of offensive nuclear capabilities seems unlikely to be restricted by arms control. Although SALT II places a ceiling on ICBM launchers and limits the United States and the Soviet Union to one new type of ICBM, the current administration does not appear inclined to extend the treaty, which expires in 1985. Meanwhile, both sides are dramatically increasing their ballistic missile defense efforts, giving additional impetus to the development of more capable and numerous offensive weapons.

Without arms control, even the most optimistic calculations about launcher hardness and secure missile basing modes are no match for the potential threat of future Soviet forces. A sizable deployment of the Soviets' ten warhead SS-X-24 ICBM—in addition to the existing or an expanded force of SS-17s, SS-18s, and SS-19s—would pose a severe threat to a mobile or stationary Midgetman force. A doubling in the number of warheads that the Soviets could be expected to target against mobile launchers could reduce a 50 percent missile survivability ratio to almost zero. An expansion in Soviet strategic capability could also endanger hardened or superhardened silos. The combination of increased accuracy and yield that could be allocated per target would probably counter any potential gains in harder silo construction.

A restrictive arms control agreement could provide a secure environment for the deployment of only several hundred Singlets, thereby allowing a much cheaper and less threatening ICBM force. Arms control is also mandated by the fact that the Soviet Union holds several advantages over the United States in the deployment of mobile missiles. The Soviets' larger territory and lack of political opposition will give them more flexibility in their basing schemes. The effect of a Soviet barrage on mobile SICBMs is primarily a function of the total megatonnage, or the explosive power that can "sweep" a given basing area. Soviet MIRVed ICBMs, with their large number of powerful warheads, currently constitute the greatest threat in this regard. The safety of hardened silos is likewise contingent on restricting the number of high-yield MIRVed warheads. Specifically, U.S. negotiators will need to seek a framework that restricts strategic launchers to at least current levels while decreasing the SALT II sublimits on MIRVs and new large missiles.

Conclusion

As much as to arms control, the fate of the Midgetman is intricately linked to that of the MX. Congress will ultimately have to decide whether the SICBM is to complement or replace the controversial MX. In many respects, the present SICBM is a duplication of the larger MX. On the basis of cost alone, it is questionable whether the nation will wish to acquire the full complement of both missiles in order to bolster what is arguably the most problematic and vulnerable leg of the strategic triad. Equally important, a decision to proceed with two new ICBMs, rather than with the one allowed by SALT II, would probably undermine any possibility of extending the treaty when it expires next year.

The dramatic increase in the U.S. ability to threaten hardened Soviet military and command targets expected through the introduction of the MX, Midgetman, and Trident II may, in the view of some analysts, prove useful in driving the Soviets toward the bargaining table. It is more likely to motivate a large-scale strategic expansion of Soviet forces, which, if not checked by arms control, will seriously threaten the security of any U.S. SICBM force. In this regard, the supposed synergy between the MX and Midgetman seems without basis. The deployment of one to two hundred MX missiles, which are no more survivable than existing Minuteman ICBMs, would do little to alter theoretical Soviet first-strike scenarios. The actual introduction of the MX, however, will probably decrease the willingness of the Soviets to agree to a reduction in MIRVs.

Despite its evident potential, the Midgetman is no panacea for the many problems connected with ensuring land-based missile survivability. The limitations of technology, cost, and available land will place inevitable constraints on the numbers and invulnerability of launchers within any basing mode. As the Scowcroft Commission has made clear, the theoretical vulnerability of U.S. ICBMs poses little danger to the overall capability of U.S. retaliatory forces, which is firmly based on the strength of the U.S. strategic triad. Yet as long as both nations continue to field MIRVs of enormous destructive potential, the security of land-based forces is likely to remain in jeopardy. Ultimately, the survivability of U.S. ICBMs—as well as the stability of the nuclear balance—will best be served by a willingness to engage in constructive arms control.   *(May 1984)*

Counterforce at Sea: The Trident II Missile
Robert S. Norris

Nuclear missile submarines traditionally have been viewed as "good" nuclear weapons because their invulnerability at sea provides an assured retaliation to Soviet nuclear attack, and they do not pose a threat to the Soviet nuclear force structure. Until now, this view of submarines has been justified, but the future role of submarines will change in a critical way if, in the fiscal year 1987 military budget, Congress decides to begin procurement of Trident II sea-launched ballistic missiles (SLBMs). Like its SLBM predecessors, the Trident II will provide the United States with an invulnerable retaliatory nuclear force, but its high accuracy and powerful warheads will for the first time enable U.S. submarines to threaten Soviet missile silos and other hardened military targets. The result will be a far more dangerous strategic environment, all at great financial expense.

Fortunately the U.S. SLBM modernization program provides an attractive and far less expensive alternative. The Trident I missile, already being deployed on U.S. submarines, offers more security at a savings of $35–$40 billion. But this argument is almost never heard. With over $7 billion appropriated so far (almost all for research and development), Trident II has had an easy time on Capitol Hill. Congress is normally hesitant to deny money for research and development programs because this stage is mistakenly seen as benign or worthy of support for what it may bring in the future. By the time money must be voted to buy the weapon, so much momentum has been generated and so much pressure brought to bear by various constituencies that the weapon's purchase becomes inevitable.

The Navy's Trident II has kept a low profile. Like all weapons systems it has been subjected to the normal oversight and authorization process, which deals with programs piecemeal and in isolation. But the comprehensive picture rarely comes into view and the large questions have not been asked. What is the total scope and cost of the program? What military role will Trident II play and how will it fit with other strategic and nonstrategic nuclear weapons? How will the Soviet Union perceive it? What are the arms control implications? And how do we rate the alternatives? It is time to address these questions.

The Trident II (or D-5) missile is part of the larger Trident weapon system that includes *Ohio*-class submarines, Trident I (or C-4) SLBMs, and the bases and shore facilities that support them. By the year 2002, according to one Navy chart, a fleet of twenty-four *Ohio*-class submarines, operating from bases in Bangor, Washington, and Kings Bay, Georgia, will carry 576 Trident II SLBMs, with approximately 5,184 nuclear warheads. (See figure 3–1.)

With the submission of the fiscal year 1987 military budget, the Navy will request funds to buy the first batch of an estimated 958 Trident II missiles, including those used as spares and for tests. The total bill for the missiles and warheads, assuming a force of twenty-four submarines, will be approximately $52 billion, with budget requests over the next decade averaging at least $3.5 billion a year. (See table 3–1.) The submarines and other parts of the program will cost an additional $51 billion. (See table 3–2.) Conceivably, the Navy will want more than twenty-four submarines.

The overall Trident program is quickly moving forward. Twelve Poseidon submarines have been converted to carry the Trident I missile. These subs will be retired by the end of the century and replaced by *Ohio*-class subs. To date, thirteen *Ohio*-class submarines have been authorized in fiscal years 1974 through 1986. The fourteenth will be requested in the FY 1987 budget, and a request for one submarine a year can be expected at least through FY 1993 and probably to 1997 or beyond. The sixth submarine, the USS *Alabama*, will be deployed early in 1986. The seventh, the USS *Alaska*, began sea trials on September 18, 1985, and the eighth, the USS *Nevada*, was launched on September 14, 1985. The first eight submarines are being equipped with Trident I SLBMs and will be retrofitted with Trident II missiles starting in 1992. The ninth *Ohio*-class SSBN will be the first to carry Trident II missiles, with a scheduled initial operation date of December 1989.

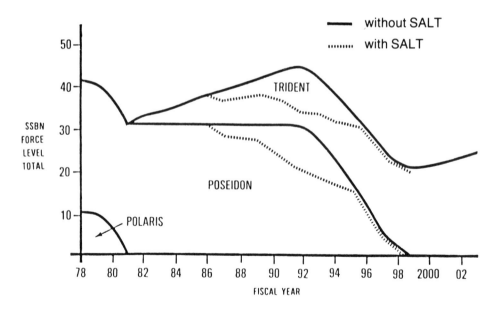

Source: U.S. Navy.

Figure 3–1. SSBN Force Levels

Table 3–1

The Cost of Trident II

The Trident II missile will be the most expensive strategic weapon the United States has ever bought. The table below shows the Navy's cost estimate (as of April 17, 1985) for 790 missiles for seventeen submarines.[a]

Fiscal Year	RDT&E	Procurement	Military Construction	Total
1983 & prior	681.7	—	—	681.7
1984	1,452.7	—	79.3	1,532.0
1985	2,035.4	162.9	82.4	2,280.7
1986	2,156.2	582.0	144.1	2,882.3
1987	1,713.7	1,865.6 (27)	37.3	3,616.6
1988	1,232.1	2,668.7 (72)	13.1	3,913.9
1989	732.1	2,788.8 (72)	25.8	3,537.0
1990	372.7	2,719.6 (72)	108.9	3,201.2
To completion	—	16,286.0 (517)	189.4	16,475.4
Total	10,376.9 [b]	27,063.6 (760) [c]	680.3	38,120.8 [d]

Source: "U.S. Navy Trident II Missile Data Sheet" reprinted in Jonathan E. Medalia, *Trident Program*, Congressional Research Service, Issue Brief IB73001, June 27, 1985, appendix A.

[a]In millions of current dollars.

[b]Includes funds for thirty research, development, testing, and evaluation (RDT&E) missiles. The first of approximately twenty flat-pad test launches is planned for January 1987 from Cape Canaveral. The other ten R&D missiles will be fired from an SSBN beginning in March 1989.

[c]Figures in parentheses refer to number of missiles. A force of twenty-four SSBNs would require approximately 958 missiles, bringing the total cost to $46.2 billion, based on a unit cost of $48.3 million per missile.

[d]This figure does not include Department of Energy costs. For 958 missiles, an additional $4–$5 billion of Department of Energy costs must be added for some three thousand W88 warheads.

Full program costs and fleet size are sometimes difficult to compute. The Navy stopped reporting at the end of 1984 the $17 billion cost of the first eight Trident submarines in its quarterly Selected Acquisition Reports to Congress, the key book-keeping account Congress uses to keep track of weapon costs. Dropping this item from the report makes the program seem cheaper. The cost of warheads produced by the Department of Energy is also frequently overlooked. Each Trident I W76 warhead is estimated to cost approximately $650,000. Over three thousand warheads comes to $2 billion. The cost for an approximately equal number of larger Trident II W88 warheads is $4.5 billion.

The Navy has not yet publicly stated exactly how many submarines it wants and has benefited by being vague about ultimate fleet size. Its refusal to tell Congress and the public has led to confusion over the scope and cost of the program. If the Navy had originally stated that Trident was going to be the costliest strategic weapon program ever and that the total bill would be more than $100 billion, more notice might have been taken. As it has turned out, the Navy has incrementally added a submarine a year, divided the program into several elements, not included all costs in the estimates it does provide, and never answered the question of how large a force it wants or how expensive it will be.

Table 3–2
Trident Program Costs
($ billions)

24 SSBNs[a]	$ 45.2
958 Trident II SLBMs	$ 46.2
6,500 warheads for Trident I and II[b]	$ 6.6
Backfits for Trident I and Trident II[c]	$ 5.5
Total	$103.5

[a]Includes 595 Trident I SLBMs and bases at Bangor and Kings Bay.

[b]Department of Energy costs.

[c]Trident I on 12 Lafayette/Franklin SSBNs ($3.6) and Trident II on eight Ohio SSBNS ($1.9).

SLBM capabilities have improved significantly since the first nuclear missile submarine, the USS *George Washington*, was deployed in late 1960. The *George Washington* carried sixteen Polaris A-1 missiles, each with a 1,200-nautical-mile range and a single warhead with a circular error probable (CEP), the common measure of missile accuracy, of 1 nautical mile. *Ohio*-class submarines will eventually be equipped with twenty-four Trident II missiles, each capable of delivering some eight to fourteen multiple independently targetable reentry vehicles over 4,000 nautical miles to land within approximately 500 feet of their targets. (Clarence A. Robinson, Jr., "Congress Questioning Viability of MX ICBM," *Aviation Week and Space Technology*, March 22, 1982, p. 18. Also, U.S. Congress. Congressional Budget Office, *Modernizing U.S. Strategic Forces: The Administration's Program and Alternatives*, May 1983, p. 84). (See table 3–3.)

Rear Adm. William A. Williams, former director of the Navy's Strategic and Theater Nuclear Warfare Division, told Congress in 1981, "The Trident II missile will add an entirely new dimension to our sea-based capability" (U.S. Senate Armed Services Committee, *Strategic Force Modernization Programs* (Washington, D.C.: U.S. Government Printing Office, 1981, p. 187). That new dimension, and Trident II's most significant characteristic, will be the ability to hit the hardest of Soviet targets in fifteen minutes or less after being launched.

The pursuit of ever more accurate ballistic missiles has been a continuing imperative for three decades, driven by technological advances and precision targeting requirements of nuclear war plans. Trident II's capabilities can be largely attributed to an eight-year Improved Accuracy Program, in which more than eight hundred techniques were proposed and reviewed. It will employ improved submarine navigation and missile guidance systems, including an enhanced stellar inertial guidance system, wherein the missile fixes its position by the stars to correct its flight. Improved submarine navigation and stellar guidance systems aid in increasing SLBM accuracy by adjusting for position problems inherent in submarine launches. Research on a maneuvering reentry vehicle is funded and could be a future option.

Table 3–3
Characteristics and Capabilities of U.S. SLBMS

	Polaris A-1	*Polaris A-2*	*Polaris A-3*	*Poseidon C-3*	*Trident C-4*	*Trident D-5*
Length (feet)	28.5	30.75	32.3	34.1	34.1	44.5
Diameter (inches)	54	54	54	74	74	83
Weight (lbs.)	28,500	30,000	35,700	65,000	73,000	130,000
Throwweight (lbs.)	c.1,000	c.1,000	1,100	3,300	2,900	5,075
Range (nautical miles)	1,200	1,500	2,500	2,500	4,000	4,000+
Reentry vehicles (average)	1 MK 1	1 MK 1	MRV x 3 MK 2	MIRV x 10 MK 3	MIRV x 8 MK 4	MIRV x 10–12 MK4/ 8 MK5
Warhead/yield (kilotons)	W47/600	W47/800	W58/200	W68/50	W76/100	W76/100 W88/475
RV weight (lbs.)	875	c.875	c.250	c.200	212	c.440(MK5)
CEP nm/ft	1/6,000	.5/3,000	.5/3,000	.28/1,700	.27–.125/ 1,640–750	.07–.10/ 425–600
Dates deployed	11/60–10/65	6/62–11/74	9/64–2/82	3/71–	10/79–	12/89–

Missile lethality is also determined by warhead yield. High precision in conjunction with high explosive power will greatly increase the probability of destroying even very hard targets. The Navy has decided to use two reentry vehicles on Trident II missiles: the new 475-kiloton Mk5/W88 and the 100-kiloton Mk4/W76, currently used on the Trident I. (Clarence A. Robinson, Jr., "Parallel Programs Advance Small ICBM," *Aviation Week and Space Technology*, March 5, 1984, p. 17). Each D-5 missile will carry only one type of warhead, though the warhead complement on individual submarines will vary. SSBNs can be loaded differently to fit the complex targeting requirements of the Single Integrated Operational Plan, the central U.S. nuclear war plan. Combining heavy and light warheads with different yields on the same launch platform gives war planners great flexibility.

The number of warheads carried on the Trident II missile will depend on the missile's range. During early stages of development the Navy considered giving the D-5 missile a range of up to 6,000 nautical miles, but decided to increase payload instead. Some congressmen mistakenly believe Trident II is programmed for a greater range than Trident I and argue vociferously that the United States needs it for that reason (see for example, Rep. Dickinson, *Congressional Record*, June 19, 1985, H4466, and Rep. Stratton, *Congressional Record*, May 17, 1984, H4116). By reducing the number of reentry vehicles the range of both missiles can be increased to 6,000 nautical miles, but at full payload both have approximately a 4,000-nautical-mile range. As Admiral Williams told Congress, "The C-4 has a very comfortable range" (U.S. Senate Armed Services Committee. *Strategic Force Modernizations Programs*, p. 167).

Even if the range of the Trident II is established, the number of warheads it will carry is still difficult to estimate because of the mix of reentry vehicles, but for illustrative purposes several reasonable assumptions can be made. The D-5

A Soviet Trident II?

Most milestones of the nuclear arms race achieved first by the United States were eventually matched by the Soviet Union. How soon will the Soviets have a comparable SLBM force equivalent to the Trident II? From the available evidence, it appears that the United States is at least a decade ahead.

The current most advanced Soviet MIRVed SLBM is the SS-N-20, sixty of which are now on three Typhoon SSBNs, a submarine sometimes compared to the U.S. Ohio-class SSBNs. The SS-N-20 is comparable to the Trident II in some characteristics, notably fuel, length, weight, range, and throwweight. However, in the most significant area, accuracy, the Trident I is twice as accurate as the SS-N-20, and the Trident II is planned to be four times as accurate.

A new SLBM, the SS-NX-23, is now being flight tested and is expected to enter the Soviet force in early 1987. It is planned for Delta IV SSBNs and may replace the SS-N-18 on Delta IIIs. Both the SS-N-18 and SS-NX-23 are liquid fueled, a hallmark of Soviet ballistic missile technology, but generally considered to be inferior to solid-fuel propulsion. The CEP estimate for the SS-NX-23 is approximately the same as that for the U.S. Poseidon SLBM.

Given past Soviet practice, both the SS-N-20 and the SS-NX-23 are likely to be modified and improved by the end of the decade. But even if those modified missiles become twice as accurate, they will still be only half as accurate as the Trident II.

A possible candidate for a Soviet Trident II may be a new missile for a new class of SSBN. According to the 1985 National Intelligence Estimate, a new class of SSBN is projected to be launched in the early 1990s, though there was no mention of a new SLBM in development. By the mid-1990s, the NIE projects that the Soviets might have four hundred warheads on the new class of SSBN (or forty missiles on two boats). Even if that timetable is kept and a new missile as accurate as Trident II is introduced, a Soviet Trident II force will be at least a decade behind that of the United States.

Estimated Characteristics and Capabilities of Current Soviet MIRVed SLBMs

	SS-N-18	SS-N-20	SS-NX-23
Length (feet)	46.25	49.2	55.6
Diameter (inches)	72	87	71
Weight (lbs.)	44,000–67,200	134,400	78,400
Throwweight (lbs.)	1,800–2,900	5,600	3,360
Range (nautical miles)	3,500–4,300	4,480	4,590
Reentry vehicles	single, 3 or 7 MIRV	6–9 MIRV	6+ MIRV
Yield (kilotons)	450 (single) 200 (MIRV)	200+	250
CEP (nm/ft)	.76/4,620	.27–.3/ 1,640–1,825	.32/1,950
Submarine	Delta III	Typhoon	Delta III/IV
Initial operational capability	1978	end 1983	1987
Fuel	liquid	solid	liquid

By Jeffrey I. Sands and Robert S. Norris. Jeffrey I. Sands is a former research associate with the Natural Resources Defense Council.

on average will probably carry at least a dozen of the smaller Mk4s or eight Mk5s. The majority of the missiles, perhaps a three-to-one ratio, will be loaded with the heavier Mk5s, because if more Mk4s were used the Navy would be seen as undercutting its case for the Mk5, if not for the whole Trident II program.

Based on these assumptions, an average Trident submarine would carry 216 warheads. A force of twenty-four submarines would carry 5,184 warheads. These figures represent a several-fold increase in the number of U.S. ballistic missile warheads available to strike Soviet hard targets. About two-thirds of the fleet would routinely be on patrol, giving the United States a significant counterforce capability at sea at any given time.

Trident II by itself may not be enough to disarm the Soviet Union, but in concert with other strategic and nonstrategic programs, all with high accuracy, it will create an entirely new strategic condition. Trident advocates choose to see the missile in isolation, whereas in fact it will be integrated in war plans with the MX, Pershing II, Midgetman, stealth cruise missiles and bombers, and eventually British Trident II forces. Hence, the Soviet Union will soon be faced with large numbers of weapons capable of threatening their fixed, hard, military targets, including nuclear forces and command, control, and communications facilities. Added to this "hard-target kill" capability, Trident II missiles will have the short—approximately fifteen minute—flight time shared by all SLBMs. An improved fire control system will also allow the submarines to launch larger salvos more quickly. Some estimate that all twenty-four missiles of a Trident sub could be fired in less than ten minutes. These factors undoubtedly paint a threatening picture in the minds of the Soviets: large numbers of hard-target warheads arriving with little warning or time to evaluate an attack and make decisions.

Under these conditions, the Soviets must consider the possibility of a U.S. preemptive first strike. Indeed, the United States has not repudiated such an option, and pressures could build during a crisis that might force such a decision. From the Soviet viewpoint, this problem is accentuated by U.S. intentions to "render ineffective the total Soviet (and Soviet-allied) military and political power structure through attacks on political/military leadership and associated control facilities," as was stated in Pentagon policy guidance (Richard Halloran, "Pentagon Draws Up First Strategy for Fighting a Long Nuclear War," *New York Times*, May 30, 1982, p. A12). U.S. nuclear forces could quickly knock out Soviet command centers and communications installations, weakening the Soviet ability to retaliate. Under this "decapitation" scenario, the possibility of restraining or terminating a conflict before it fully escalates would be remote, because Soviet leaders would be unavailable or unable to negotiate an end to the fighting.

The most logical, if dangerous, Soviet response is to implement procedures to launch-under-attack or on-warning so that their nuclear forces would not be destroyed. In the face of more accurate ballistic missiles the trend on both sides has been to move in this direction. The Soviets issued warnings that they would be forced to adopt such options in response to the deployment of Pershing II. The

United States has repeatedly stated that "launch-on-warning is an option we have and must maintain" (U.S. Senate Armed Services Committee, *FY 1982 Department of Defense Authorizations*, part 7, p. 3834), and that it enhances deterrence by keeping the Soviets uncertain about what the United States would do. Even more ominous is the prospect that such U.S. counterforce capabilities could increase the Soviet incentive, in an intense crisis, not only to launch first, but to launch a lot for fear the United States was about to do so. This "hair trigger" situation, which each superpower is forcing upon the other, heightens the risk that war will start inadvertently through accident or miscalculation. The deployment of Trident II will intensify this situation.

Another Soviet response would be to restructure their nuclear forces in more survivable basing modes, placing greater emphasis on sea-based and land mobile-based systems. The Soviets are in fact already moving in this direction. But having just completed a huge investment in large, fixed ICBMs—missiles that intimidate the United States and symbolize to the Soviets their arrival as a superpower—the Soviet Union is likely to keep them around for some time. For the foreseeable future, additional survivable Soviet nuclear forces will only augment their current fixed one.

A number of important arms control considerations should also figure in the Trident debate. The most immediate implication of the overall Trident program is that, to stay within a critical SALT II sublimit, the United States must dismantle MIRVed missiles as new *Ohio*-class submarines are added to the fleet. The United States would have exceeded the 1,200 MIRVed missile sublimit when the seventh Trident sub, the USS *Alaska*, began sea trials in September 1985, but President Reagan chose to stay within the limit temporarily by dismantling a Poseidon submarine. Figure 3–1 shows U.S. SSBN force levels, with and without SALT, to the end of the century. The Navy projects that the Trident program will continue unabated even with SALT II limits, although compensating Poseidon retirements will come at a faster rate if SALT II is retained. Whether President Reagan will continue to dismantle older Poseidons as new Tridents are deployed is unknown, particularly after the SALT II limits officially expire on December 31, 1985.

The United States has good reason to stick with SALT II. The agreement provides for a substantial SSBN force while placing limits on U.S. and Soviet strategic launchers. Though Trident II is not specifically affected by the SALT II Treaty, the missile may create problems for the Navy if SALT II counting rules are applied in a future deep-reductions agreements. The SALT II agreement determined that a missile would be counted as carrying the maximum number of warheads used in the missile's tests. Under this rule, if the D-5 were tested with twelve warheads it would be counted with twelve, even if most D-5 missiles carried only eight or fewer warheads. *Ohio*-class submarines, carrying twenty-four missiles as opposed to the Poseidon's sixteen, would quickly run up against the warhead limits of a START-type agreement, meaning that only a small fleet of Trident submarines could be deployed. Under the proposals now being offered by the United States and the Soviet Union, the United States will only be allowed to have ten or twelve Trident subs, with six or seven on patrol at any one time. If the antisubmarine warfare threat to SSBNs becomes more serious, then the Navy may find it has placed too many eggs in one basket.

All of these computations may be academic. If SALT is allowed to expire and new agreements are not reached, Trident II and other nuclear systems will go forward with no restrictions at all. Current Reagan policies appear to preclude an arms control deal with the Soviets in the near future. In those technologies in which the administration claims that the United States is behind (for example, ICBMs, antisatellite weapons, nuclear testing), whatever the evidence to the contrary, the administration is unwilling to negotiate until the United States catches up. In those technologies in which the United States is markedly ahead (for example, SLBMs), the administration does not want to negotiate away an advantage.

An alternative to the Trident II exists: the Trident I. The Navy has sought to downplay the improvements that have been incorporated into the Trident I because of the troubling questions it could raise about the need for Trident II. The Trident I also benefited from the Improved Accuracy Program. According to *Aviation Week and Space Technology*, "Guidance accuracy for the C-4's Mk4 reentry system is . . . under 1,000 feet circular error probable at 4,000 nautical miles, well below the 1,500-feet goal" (May 30, 1983, p. 41). At ranges less than 4,000 nautical miles the accuracy is even better (U.S. Senate Armed Services Committee, *FY 1985 Department of Defense Authorizations*, part 7, p. 3426). A Pentagon report to Congress stated that "Trident I missile system accuracy is now about the same as Minuteman III operational accuracy" (William M. Arkin, "Sleight of Hand with Trident II," *Bulletin of Atomic Scientists*, December 1984, p. 6). Trident I tests during 1983 consistently achieved CEPs of 750 feet (see Arkin, "Sleight of Hand," p. 6). Many in Congress are apparently unaware of these developments and the Navy is doing little to advertise them, for it would raise the central question over the wisdom of spending $50 billion to gain a better accuracy of a few hundred feet.

Trident I's accuracy is sufficient to meet many of the Navy's targeting needs, but its lower-yield warhead does not pose the silo-busting or decapitation threat of the Trident II. It is already deployed on seven *Ohio*-class SSBNs and has been retrofitted on twelve Poseidon SSBNs. Of the current 648 SLBMs, 55 percent are Trident I missiles and seem to be satisfactory to the Navy. They are as survivable as Trident II, mostly paid for, and far cheaper to outfit on the rest of the *Ohio* fleet. At $19 million each, instead of $48 million for each Trident II missile, the cost to outfit sixteen more *Ohio*-class SSBNs with Trident I would be $10 billion for missiles and warheads. In a time of soaring deficits and level military budgets, a $35–$40 billion savings is not insignificant.

Unfortunately, too little attention is being paid to the Trident story. The Navy's submarines are not as controversial as the major Air Force weapons, and, because submarines are not land based, they are less of a "backyard" issue. In Congress, Trident II has acted as a safety valve in the heated politics of the MX missile. It has allowed many congressmen to appear tough on defense issues by voting *for* something after voting against the MX.

It is time to reevaluate Trident II, its role in the evolving U.S. counterforce strategy, and its impact on U.S. security. Under the Reagan administration the chief rationale for Trident II has shifted from the traditional argument of SSBN survivability to the "need" for large amounts of hard-target kill capability, defined now as the sine qua non of deterrence. U.S. security is presumably enhanced the more the Soviet Union is threatened. The real rather than the intended result of such logic will be that both sides will end up less secure. Advocates never tire of saying how counterforce strengthens deterrence, but never ask if too much weakens it. With Trident II's addition, the erosion of deterrence will fully set in. Though time is short, an outright ban on Trident II and on a future Soviet counterpart in an arms control deal would make both nations more secure.   *(September 1985)*

Why We Need Counterforce at Sea
Walter B. Slocombe

No nuclear weapons system, and indeed no old one, can in any fundamental sense be considered a "good" thing. However, generalized attacks by advocates of arms control on the Trident II, D-5 program are overstated and misdirected.

From the arms control and stability point of view, the desirable attributes of a nuclear weapons system should be that it is *survivable* so that there is no incentive to attack it, readily *verifiable* so that it can unambiguously be taken into account in agreements (and, indeed so that even without agreements it does not lend itself to uncertainty about the size of the other side's force), and finally, that its capability is *not such as to present an avoidable threat* to the other side's deterrent forces, which could create an incentive to attack in a crisis.

The Trident II missile, like its submarine-launched predecessors, is conceded by even its severest critics to satisfy the first two criteria, but it is denounced for violating the third by bringing to the submarine force a degree of accuracy sufficient to threaten Soviet silos, missile launch-control facilities, nuclear storage areas, communication centers, and other hardened targets.

No doubt we would all be better off if no nuclear systems had such capabilities. But the hard fact is that guidance technology has reached the point where all new systems will inevitably have substantial hard-target capability, or at any rate will be perceived to have it by those against whom they are aimed. Possession of this capability by intercontinental-ballistic missiles in fixed launchers is, of course, one of the main strategic stability problems of the age. Perhaps less well recognized is that bombers, which have long had high accuracy with gravity bombs, will have even better accuracies in the coming years with cruise missiles and other high-precision standoff weapons. Indeed, some argue that guidance accuracies will improve to a point when attacks on hardened facilities with conventional weapons will become feasible. It is, therefore, scarcely surprising that any newly developed submarine missile will have greater accuracy than its predecessors.

If one judges, as have successive U.S. administrations—though many have disputed this view—that some degree of capability to attack the full range of targets in the Soviet Union is useful and even critical for deterrence, this capability should surely rest in the most survivable parts of the deterrent force, precisely to avoid incentives or pressures for preemption in a crisis.

But whatever the utility of survivable hard-target forces to stability and deterrence, and some would count it substantial, an effort to design strategic systems deliberately to have less than attainable accuracies is likely to prove futile, if only because the adversary would probably not believe that the effort had been successful. The recent U.S. controversies about the exact accuracy of Soviet ICBMs are sufficient evidence of this.

It is sometimes argued that the accurate submarine-based missile force is likely to "drive" the Soviets into a launch-on-warning or launch-under-attack strategy because of the threat to their heavy investment in vulnerable fixed ICBMs. In a sense this is simply a special case of the argument that quick hard-target capability makes fixed forces vulnerable; whether the missiles that carry the capability are in submarines is irrelevant.

What is usually missed in the analysis, however, is that a launch-under-attack policy is an extraordinarily unsatisfactory one for the side relying on it, as well as dangerous for everyone else. Warning times are certainly short—no more than thirty minutes—and are subject to being cut virtually to zero. A launch-under-attack system exacerbates the vulnerability of forces it is intended to offset by itself being vulnerable to any action that can prevent such a prompt decision. Moreover, in any political system, and very much so in the Soviet one, the degree of predelegation or predecision necessary for a launch-under-attack policy poses the most fundamental issues of political control and legitimacy.

In short, any country that finds itself in the position where its forces are so vulnerable—to submarines, ICBMs or anything else—that it must regard launch-under-attack as a necessary part of its deterrent strategy, rather than simply an inevitable possibility whose existence makes some contribution to the uncertainties facing an aggressor, will, in its own interest, quickly take action to correct the problem by restoring the survivability of its force.

While the Soviets occasionally talk about launch-on-warning as a way to offset U.S. threats to their ICBMs (and, indeed, recommend the policy to us), they are ensuring that they will not have to rely on any such policy in the future. They have their own very substantial submarine deployment program, which is continuing apace, and they, unlike the United States, are moving promptly to offset the vulnerability of their fixed ICBM force by the deployment of modern, highly capable, mobile ICBMs. That process, taken in Soviet self-interest, will ensure that neither D-5 nor any other U.S. program will give the United States a credible threat of wiping out the Soviet deterrent. Given modern technology, some capability against some elements of the Soviet force is inevitable and may be useful as part of a countervailing strategy for deterrence of less than all-out strikes as well as deliberate total destruction.

In short, D-5's contribution to the vulnerability of the Soviet force—whether described as part of a general increase in U.S. hard-target capability or as an incentive for launch-under-attack—is not a major departure, for it is the product of a single factor, the general improvement in accuracies. The Soviets are already acting to reduce the overall vulnerability of their forces. These effects of D-5 by no means offset its very important potential contribution to the long-run survivability of a key element in the U.S. deterrent force.

Those concerned with the stability of the nuclear balance should not focus on a Canute-like effort to hold back the tide of greater accuracy but should emphasize the need to place these highly accurate systems in survivable basing modes. From this perspective, opponents of the vulnerably based MX missile can quite logically support the D-5. For, in contrast to a vulnerable MX, D-5 will provide the United States with the full range of deterrent capabilities without the high costs and risks to stability of concentrating those capabilities in highly vulnerable deployments.

Indeed, the D-5 program as it is evolving must be monitored carefully to ensure that proper weight is given to survivability. One of the great potential advantages of the D-5 relative to its Trident I, C-4 predecessor is the inherent extra range capability of the larger and more powerful missile. This capability can be converted either into greater range to be used to expand the ocean area in which the submarine can hide, or into extra throwweight to be used either for more warheads or for larger and heavier ones with greater yield. Evidently Navy planners have opted, at least initially, to use the extra capability chiefly for more reentry vehicles and greater yield rather than for more range.

As a short-term measure, this decision can be defended as a reasonable judgment that Trident I ranges are now sufficient to battle Soviet antisubmarine warfare efforts for the foreseeable future, so there is no need to opt for greater range at this point. But the program should at a minimum be structured to maintain the option to add range in the future by deploying lighter or reduced numbers of reentry vehicles.

Similarly, current support for the Trident II should not entail an open-ended commitment to build very large Trident submarines of present designs. Under currently foreseeable conditions, there are certainly valid arguments for the economies of scale and exploitation of experience that are involved in continuing to build submarines of the large and proven *Ohio* class. However, it would be the height of irresponsibility not to begin thinking seriously now about alternative forms of sea-basing for missiles.

If these long-term survivability concerns are met, as Congress should ensure that they are, the D-5 is an excellent investment from the point of view of survivability, which ought to be the hallmark of a strategic program motivated by arms control and stability. Its added hard-target capability is an inevitable aspect of virtually any new missile and, in view of current Soviet programs for added survivability, will by no means give the United States anything like a disarming option against the Soviet Union.   *(September 1985)*

Bean-counting and War-gaming: How to Analyze the Strategic Balance
Marie M. Hoguet

Sooner or later most discussions of the arms race lead to the question of "who's ahead"—which side has more, or bigger, or better nuclear weapons; whose buildup has been more unprecedented; and what it all means for U.S. defense policies. Many teachers and students have seen graphs and charts comparing the numbers of U.S. and Soviet intercontinental ballistic missiles, submarine-launched ballistic missiles, warheads, bombers, and so on.

Comparisons of U.S. and Soviet nuclear forces are both inevitable and necessary in considering the relative strengths and weaknesses of the United States. But very often they are misleading because they omit so much relevant information and fail to disclose their underlying assumptions. They tend to give an incorrect impression of precision where in fact it is impossible to be precise.

There are two basic approaches to comparing U.S. and Soviet nuclear forces. The first and more familiar approach compares the characteristics and destructive potential of the two sides' weapons. Sometimes called "bean-counting," it looks at specific weapons or characteristics of weapons and attempts to show, often in graphic form, what the United States and the Soviet Union each has in the discrete categories. This approach provides a static picture, a snapshot, of the various components of each side's forces at a particular time, in peacetime. Or it can provide a picture of the change in the quantity of these components over a certain period of time. This approach does not, and cannot, show how these components would interact in a war, or what extrinsic factors would affect their performance or importance in actual combat.

Let us look at one of the more frequently encountered comparisons—the one between U.S. and Soviet ICBMs and SLBMs—and note some of its limitations. A typical graph depicts a small forest of the many different kinds of Soviet missiles and a more modest array of the U.S. missiles. It will show that Soviet ICBMs and SLBMs are larger, more varied, and more numerous than their U.S. counterparts.

One's intuitive conclusion, on seeing such a graph, would be that the Soviets are better armed and stronger.

But this sort of graph does not reveal that U.S. Minuteman missiles, which make up the vast bulk of the nation's ICBM arsenal, are smaller because superior technology in miniaturizing explosive devices and guidance systems and in using more efficient, less bulky solid-fuel propellants allowed the U.S. deliberately to scale down the size of its missiles. (If size itself were important, the U.S. would not be phasing out of its arsenal its largest ICBMs, the gargantuan Titans.) Nor does such a graph show that the variety of the Soviet Union's ICBMs and SLBMs is in no small part attributable to the Soviets' persistent problems in producing one reliable model in which they have confidence. This graph gives no indication, moreover, of the qualitative differences between the Soviet and U.S. ICBMs and SLBMs— differences that are at least as significant as differences in quantity, size and variety. For example, a submarine's ability to glide silently through the water and thus evade detection and destruction is a critically valuable feature. And the United States' SLBM-carrying submarines can move much more quietly than Soviet submarines.

One frequently sees charts showing the relative increase in the number of U.S. and Soviet ICBMs and SLBMs over a particular span of time. This too can create a misleading effect. A graph showing the tremendous growth in the number of Soviet missiles and the much lower growth of the U.S. arsenal from 1970 to 1980, for example, suggests a truly alarming Soviet buildup. However, a graph including the period from 1950, say, to 1980, would reveal that the United States too engaged in an enormous buildup—but in the decades preceding the Soviet effort. The point here is simply that the choice of period can radically alter the message of a graph comparing quantities of weapons over a span of time.

Another common way of comparing nuclear forces is by counting the number of warheads. Initially, both U.S. and Soviet missiles carried only one warhead apiece. Each missile could therefore be aimed at only one target. In the early 1970s, however, first the United States and then the Soviet Union mastered the technology of multiple independently targeted reentry vehicles, or MIRVs, which allows one to load onto a single missile a number of warheads, each of which can be programmed to strike a different target. (The reentry vehicle of a missile basically contains the explosive device or warhead.)

By now, most of the superpowers' missiles are MIRVed, carrying between three and fourteen warheads on each missile. Counting each side's ICBMs and SLBMs has therefore become an even less useful exercise than before, because it does not tell one how many bombs each side can deliver with these systems. So graphs comparing the number of deliverable warheads have become more common.

This measure, however, has its own limits. It is very difficult to determine just how many warheads the various delivery systems actually carry. The Strategic Arms Limitation Treaty of 1979 between the United States and the Soviet Union (SALT II)—signed, unratified by the United States, but observed by both parties) put ceilings on the numbers of reentry vehicles that ICBMs and SLBMs may carry. But in order to make their forces as versatile as possible, both the United States and the Soviet Union deploy their missiles with differing numbers of warheads, as well as differing megatonnage, range, and guidance systems. Thus in many cases missiles carry fewer than the maximum permitted them by SALT II. Bombers too vary in the number and kinds of warheads they carry. Comparisons of each super-power's warheads can therefore be based only on educated guesses.

Comparisons of numbers of warheads, like comparisons of delivery systems, also do not tell one about qualitative differences. The effectivess—that is, the destructive potential—of a weapon is a function of the weapon's explosive power and its accuracy and must be judged in relation to the kind of target it is intended to destroy. A weapon with a certain combination of explosiveness and accuracy may be devastating against a "soft" civilian or military target such as a city or a submarine base, but ineffective against a "hardened" target such as a missile silo or a command-and-control bunker buried deep in reinforced concrete and steel. The importance of accuracy is thus especially great in relation to hard targets, which are built to withstand enormous explosions unless they occur almost precisely on point. *Accuracy*, therefore, is a key variable in comparing U.S. and Soviet forces.

Like the number and distribution of each side's warheads, however, accuracy can only be estimated. These estimates are based on observations of test firings of missiles. But there are too few tests for any particular model to permit an exact evaluation of its accuracy; the tests cannot be conducted over the path that the missile would have to follow if it were ever actually used; and weather and wartime conditions can also cause unpredictable variations. In addition, when observing Soviet missile tests, we cannot be sure how accurate the missiles are because we do not know the precise point at which they are aimed. And since estimates of accuracy are in turn used in other, more complex qualitative measurements of weapons' capabilities, the uncertainties inherent in assessments of accuracy are compounded in any subsequent measurements.

Bean-counting and qualitative measurements can be useful when the limitations both of the underlying data and of the significance of the comparisons are kept in mind. As former Defense Secretary Harold Brown pointed out in the 1982 Annual Report of the Defense Department, however, these measures are isolated "from 'real world' factors inherent in any actual attack situation."

The second basic approach to weighing U.S. and Soviet nuclear forces seeks to approximate, in a very theoretical way, what could happen in "actual attack situations." It attempts to predict, through a series of calculations—computer war games—how the superpower forces would interact in a nuclear war. These are often called force exchange comparisons, and they seek to measure the ability of one side to attack military targets of the other side, the ability of the other side to retaliate, and the outcome of the exchange. Force exchange analysis allows a more sophisticated comparison of the two sides' forces, but it depends entirely on the validity of the many underlying assumptions.

Sometimes these assumptions are stated explicitly. For example, one scenario seeks to determine the outcome of a surprise nuclear attack. It assumes that at the time of the attacker's initial strike, the other side's forces are on normal peacetime alert during which certain percentages of its ICBMs, SLBMs, and bombers are kept fully readied to respond to the attack. Another scenario assumes that the other side has received warning of a likely attack and thus has readied a higher percentage of its forces to survive and retaliate. Many other factors, however, may enter into the calculations but are unlikely to be articulated.

Furthermore, as Harold Brown noted in the 1982 DOD Annual Report, force exchange analysis also omits from its calculations certain "real, important, yet hard-to-quantify factors such as leadership, motivation, C^3, training and maintenance." It does not attempt to treat the military and political context in which such exchanges occur, or the military plans and tactics that would of course come into play in any real combat situation.

Beyond these important but unquantifiable factors is yet another range of very significant elements in comparing the military capabilities of the two super-powers. Alliances, industrial capacities, natural resources, population, geography, national morale, and political leadership and values all must figure in any realistic consideration of two potential adversaries' ability to wage war against each other. And although it is impossible to quantify these factors in a way that relates them meaningfully to an overall military balance assessment, they must nonethless be borne in mind. Similarly, one must remember that while force exchange analyses have an artificial, even surrealistic, air, they are not merely theoretical constructs. Although abstract themselves, these analyses are based on real weapons—and weapons so powerful and so numerous that, if ever used, they would only serve, in Winston Churchill's oft-quoted phrase, to "make the rubble bounce."

This quick overview is intended only to suggest that the various ways of attempting to determine the relative strengths and weaknesses of the U.S. and Soviet nuclear forces all have limitations in both their methodology and their application. In the face of such uncertainties, how is the layman to regard such comparisons? It may be helpful to remember several general caveats.

First, no single quantitative measure or set of measures can give a true picture of the two sides' capabilities. At best they can be only pieces of a very large and complex mosaic. Second, the quantities themselves are in many cases subject to uncertainties and often inherently so. Third, the scenario-based force exchange comparisons depend totally for their validity on their underlying assumptions, and unless one is aware of them—or at least of the fact that these assumptions loom under the surface—one has almost no way of knowing how meaningful the comparison is. Finally, it is always useful to ask what the purpose of the presentation of the chart or analysis is, and what message it is being used to convey.

With all these cautions, however, it is possible nonetheless to make some judgments about overall relative U.S. and Soviet nuclear capabilities. In the words of one authority, Raymond L. Garthoff of the Brookings Institution:

In the most basic sense, strategic parity between the United States and the Soviet Union has existed, and will continue to exist, so long as each has the recognized capability to deal the other a devastating retaliatory strike after receiving a first strike. The common wisdom that under such circumstance the leaders on each side will be deterred from starting a war or even knowingly courting high risks of war is more solid than the sophisticated assumptions of scenarios in which these leaders would be attracted by arcane calculations of theoretically possible residual advantages after the first, second, or third strategic exchange. This general existing parity of nuclear retaliatory capacity, and the resulting mutual deterrence, is not the delicate balance sometimes depicted.[1]

(June 1984)

Note

1. Raymond L. Garthoff, *Perspectives on the Strategic Balance* (Washington, D.C.: The Brookings Institution, 1983), p. 5.

4

Nuclear Proliferation and Testing

Since World War II, the United States has pursued policies and engaged in international negotiations to prevent the spread of nuclear weapons to additional states. Among the notable nuclear nonproliferation achievements to date are the establishment of the International Atomic Energy Agency in 1957, the 1967 Treaty for the Prohibition of Nuclear Weapons in Latin America (Tlatelolco Treaty), and the 1968 Nonproliferation Treaty (NPT).

As is described in articles by administration officials Richard T. Kennedy and Lewis A. Dunn, the Reagan administration has been supportive of nonproliferation efforts. Although some critics, such as Peter Clausen, find serious faults in the administration's nonproliferation policy, others, such as Leonard Spector, cite "notable successes." One test of the administration's nonproliferation policy came in August and September of 1985, when 86 of the 130 nations party to the Nonproliferation Treaty met in Geneva for the third review conference of the agreement. As Dunn notes, many observers "feared that the 1985 conference, like that of 1980, would break down in acrimonious disagreement." According to some reports prior to the review conference, the non-nuclear nations were prepared to criticize the superpowers severely for their failure to take effective measures toward nuclear disarmament and the United States in particular for its refusal to negotiate a comprehensive test ban treaty, as called for by the NPT. As it turned out, the conference delegates adopted a consensus Final Declaration that strengthened the nonproliferation regime. The conference was viewed by most observers as a success, and the United States was given much of the credit.

The Nonproliferation Treaty urges its parties "to seek to achieve the discontinuance of all test explosions of nuclear weapons." Indeed, although a comprehensive test ban (CTB), if achieved, would have its greatest effect on the arms competitions between nuclear weapon states, it has also been widely regarded as a partial measure for nonproliferation. The superpowers made progress toward a comprehensive test ban treaty in the late 1970s, but after the Soviet invasion of Afghanistan and the suspension of the SALT II ratification process, the negotiations slowed to a near stop. The Reagan administration, reversing the position of U.S. presidents since Eisenhower, never resumed CTB negotiations and has opposed as contrary to U.S. security interests further efforts to achieve one. The administration has essentially argued that the United States must continue nuclear tests to maintain the effectiveness of its nuclear weapons stockpile and to develop new weapon technologies. The Reagan administration is also the first to view a CTB as detrimental to the cause of nonproliferation. An administration policy statement released in April 1986 argued that a ban on nuclear testing could push non-nuclear nations to develop their own nuclear weapons. A CTB, the administration argued, could decrease confidence "in the credibility of the U.S. nuclear deterrent," leading non-nuclear nations "to carefully reassess their national security calculations. In that context their adoption of nuclear options cannot be excluded."

Nevertheless, several test ban agreements are still in effect. In 1963 the United States, Soviet Union, and Great Britain signed the Limited Test Ban Treaty (LTBT), which bans all but underground nuclear test explosions. With the notable exception of three nuclear-weapon nations—France, the People's Republic of China, and India—most nations of the world have joined the treaty. The United States and the Soviet Union signed two test agreements in the mid-1970s: the Threshold Test Ban Treaty (TTBT), limiting test explosions to a yield of 150 kilotons, and the Peaceful Nuclear Explosions Treaty (PNET). Both agreements remain unratified, but the parties have made clear their intentions not to act inconsistently with the agreements as long as the other side does likewise.

The Reagan Nonproliferation Policy
Peter Clausen

The Reagan administration arrived in office with a sweeping critique of its predecessor's nuclear nonproliferation policy. While defining nonproliferation as "a fundamental national security and foreign policy objective" and affirming support for such basic institutions as the Nonproliferation Treaty and the International Atomic Energy Agency, the new administration took issue on both practical and philosophical grounds with key elements of U.S. policy as it had evolved during the late 1970s. As outlined in a July 1981 White House statement and in subsequent administration testimony, the Reagan policy was to be based on three general guiding principles.

First, in nuclear energy cooperation, the emphasis would be on "reliable supply" and on the return of the United States to the international mainstream following the ambivalence and restrictions of the Carter years. This meant that the Carter (and Ford) preoccupation with the dangers of plutonium fuel cycles would be dropped; that cooperation would be preferred to denial of technology as a strategy for controlling proliferation risks; and that U.S. nuclear exports would be enthusiastically promoted.

Second, whereas the Carter policy had focused on slowing the spread of nuclear technology, the Reagan administration would address the underlying security incentives that prompt states to seek nuclear weapons in the first place. Through revitalized alliances, arms sales, and a stronger overall defense posture, the United States would attempt to reassure potential proliferators whose insecurities had in some cases been aggravated by post-Vietnam inhibitions and vacillations in U.S. foreign policy.

The third guiding principle was that nonproliferation policy must in large measure be a country-by-country undertaking. Highly critical of the alleged "universalism" of the Carter policies, and in particular of the sometimes rigid formulations of the 1978 Nuclear Nonproliferation Act (NNPA), the Reagan administration proposed a more differentiated, country-specific approach. This meant not only that countries would be treated differently according to the risk that they might acquire nuclear weapons, but also that nonproliferation would be integrated into broader U.S. security calculations rather than treated as an end in itself.

The administration has shown, perhaps inevitably, more continuity with the policies it inherited than might have been expected. Bureaucratic momentum, legislative constraints, and the intractabilities of the nuclear export market have frustrated any wholesale translation of the Reagan strategy into reality.

Nevertheless, there have been significant changes, in both tone and substance, and on the whole these have been faithful to the administration's original design. But the result has not been a more realistic or effective nonproliferation policy. On the contrary, the Reagan policy to date raises serious questions about the validity of its underlying assumptions and ultimately about the seriousness of the administration's professed concern about proliferation. While it is obviously too early to render a final judgment, a midterm appraisal of the policy in three areas—the plutonium economy, nuclear exports, and security relations—suggests that the Reagan administration has hastened the erosion of important nonproliferation standards while failing to deal effectively with specific cases of threatened proliferation.

Reprocessing and Plutonium

The dangers of a plutonium economy, in which weapons-usable plutonium would become widely used as a nuclear fuel, were central to the Carter administration's analysis of the proliferation threat. The resulting U.S. efforts to restrict reprocessing (whereby plutonium is separated from spent reactor fuel) and to postpone the commercial use of plutonium led to sharp conflicts with U.S. allies who viewed plutonium-fueled breeder reactors as a key future energy source.

The immediate focus of this controversy was the exercise of U.S. approval rights over the reprocessing of nuclear fuel exported from the United States. Most of the U.S. nuclear cooperation agreements with foreign countries provide for such rights, and the NNPA requires that the United States seek to renegotiate those (notably the one with the European Community) that do not. The Carter administration used these approval rights as a lever to dissuade U.S. nuclear customers from early commitments to plutonium. While requests to reprocess U.S. fuel were never actually denied, they were subject to a lengthy case-by-case review process—causing much friction with Japan in particular—and the United States reserved a veto over any use of the separated plutonium itself.

In hopes of restoring allied nuclear harmony, the Reagan administration has declared that it will not "inhibit or set back" breeder and reprocessing programs in advanced countries that do not themselves pose proliferation risks. It intends to accommodate such programs by negotiating "programmatic" arrrangements providing for long-term advance approval for reprocessing of U.S.-supplied fuel and for use of the resulting plutonium. The new approach is explicitly discriminatory: officials have indicated that in practice it is meant only for Japan and the European Community countries.

In judging the implications of this policy, it should be noted that its near-term effects may be relatively modest. Both the administration and its critics have tended to exaggerate the momentum of progress toward plutonium use in the industrial countries—the former claiming that the new U.S. policy merely "accepts reality" in the face of firm allied commitments, and the latter implying that the policy will unleash a sudden flood of plutonium.

In fact, the outlook for widespread plutonium use in the foreseeable future is exceedingly dim regardless of U.S. policy. Not only is the future of nuclear power itself in doubt in several countries, but declining uranium prices have drastically undercut the commercial prospects for a transition to plutonium fuels. In this context, the immediate effect of the Reagan policy is primarily symbolic: it puts the United States on the side of beleaguered nuclear establishments in Europe and Japan and may thus have a marginal legitimizing effect on their troubled programs.

The more significant issue raised by the Reagan plutonium policy is its impact on the politics of the international nonproliferation regime. The administration argues that this impact will be beneficial in that an accommodation of domestic nuclear plans in Europe and Japan will elicit stronger allied cooperation on questions of safeguards improvements and nuclear export controls. This linkage is doubtful, for reasons to be discussed later. It is much more likely that the new plutonium policy will handicap future efforts to strengthen the nonproliferation regime.

The key problem is of course the overtly discriminatory nature of the U.S. approach, which suggests a double standard for plutonium use. In assuming that such an approach can be sustained politically, the Reagan administration differs from its predecessor. The difference is not in the fact of discrimination itself. The Carter administration did not rule out an accommodation with Europe and Japan on plutonium (and was moving in that direction during its final year), but it attached great importance to the problems of precedent and legitimacy this raised for the regime. It therefore devoted considerable effort, especially in the international nuclear fuel cycle evaluation (INFCE) to the development of reasonably objective economic and technical criteria by which plutonium use could be judged as more or less sensible.

The point of this effort was to build a set of presumptions about plutonium that would de facto confine it to the breeder programs of the advanced countries while avoiding an explicit double standard. In particular, the United States sought to narrow the grounds for reprocessing by challenging the conventional wisdom on the economic benefits of plutonium recycling in existing thermal reactors (which gives any country with nuclear reactors, rather than just those few with breeder programs, a pretext for using plutonium) and the need for reprocessing as a step in nuclear waste management.

U.S. success in INFCE was modest but not negligible. A foothold was gained for subsequent consensus building, especially on the thermal recycling issue. However, the Reagan administration has chosen to see INFCE as an unqualified rejection of the Carter policy and thus has ignored points that could be useful in supporting a differentiated approach to plutonium use. Instead, it has opted for blanket approval of the use of U.S.-origin plutonium in European and Japanese nuclear programs, including recycling in thermal reactors. Seen in conjunction with a domestic nuclear policy aimed at subsidizing the creation of a U.S. plutonium industry in defiance of all market signals, the approach strongly suggests that "anything goes" for countries that fall within the privileged circle. The problem of precedent is dismissed by denying any link between plutonium use in the industrial countries and proliferation threats elsewhere, and by asserting that other claimants to favored treatment (such as South Korea and Taiwan) will simply be refused. The administration's complacency on this issue is curious given its emphasis on the limits of unilateral U.S. nuclear leverage and the importance it places on the U.S. reputation as a reliable supplier.

In effect, then, the Reagan plutonium policy simultaneously makes discrimination more explicit and erodes the kinds of criteria that would be most helpful in defending such discrimination. This will at the very least raise the political costs of "saying no" to third world countries interested in plutonium and may as a result increase pressures to bend the policy to accommodate new countries in the future.

"Reliable Supply" and Nuclear Exports

"Reliable supply," which dominates the administration's philosophy of nuclear cooperation and exports, has become a kind of code phrase in nonproliferation debates. To critics, it is little more than a self-serving rationale for promoting exports. To the administration, it signifies a return to the logic of the original "nuclear bargain"—cooperation in return for safeguards and other nonproliferation assurances— following the trend toward denial during the late 1970s. It also signifies a strong correlation between the U.S. role in international nuclear commerce and U.S. influence on behalf of nonproliferation goals. In the words of Deputy Energy Secretary

W. Kenneth Davis, "We used to be the leader in the world, developing safeguards, developing international agencies, developing the whole process. We were the leaders because we were the leaders in international trade related to nuclear power. We lost a substantial part of our leadership in technology under the previous administration."

As this statement suggests, there is a strong element of nostalgia in the reliable supplier theme—a harking back to the early days of the civil nuclear era when the United States dominated (and in some areas monopolized) a growing international market and took the lead in putting in place the key institutions of the regime. There is also a tendency to attribute the decline of the U.S. market position in the 1970s to changes in nonproliferation policies rather than to structural causes and to the inevitable rise of competing suppliers. While it is doubtful that many officials really believe the U.S. dominance of the 1950s and 1960s can be restored, it is revealing that the administration's model of nuclear affairs and its premises about nuclear influence relationships are drawn from that era.

It scarcely needs to be emphasized that the current nuclear market bears little relation to the administration's nostalgic ideal. First, it is a buyer's market, in a deep recession with no end in sight. Suppliers of fuel and technology, already faced in most cases with stagnant domestic markets, compete for a steadily dwindling number of export orders. Second, this shrinking market is strongly skewed on the customer side toward countries in the proliferation "gray zone" (like Argentina, South Korea, Taiwan, and Brazil), which, by virtue of their past behavior or suspected motives, rank on the list of possible future proliferators. In this environment, "reliable supply" is a doubtful instrument of influence or control.

Particularly dubious in the current market is the administration's equation of a stronger U.S. commercial role with enhanced influence in shaping the rules of the regime. Despite administration rhetoric that treats a U.S. "return to the game" as a kind of public good, any recovery of ground lost by the United States during the last decade must obviously come at the expense of the other suppliers. The supplier game is a mixed-motive one: while U.S. allies will certainly welcome a more benign U.S. attitude toward their domestic programs, they can hardly be expected to applaud a U.S. determination to compete more aggressively for the few prospective orders on the world market.

Contrary to administration arguments, then, U.S. export ambitions could well make the other suppliers less receptive to appeals for collective restraint on behalf of nonproliferation interests. The resulting danger of an unraveling of restraint is particularly worrisome when U.S. competitiveness is accompanied by a new flexibility on the issues of sensitive technology exports and safeguards conditions.

Sensitive Technology Transfer

According to the July 1981 White House statement, the United States "will continue to inhibit the transfer of sensitive nuclear material, equipment and technology, particularly where the danger of proliferation demands." This somewhat ambiguous formulation foreshadowed a lifting of the long-standing embargo on U.S. exports of reprocessing and enrichment technologies and its replacement by a more differentiated approach based on perceptions of proliferation risk. Subsequently, the administration announced that it would consider requests from U.S. firms to export reprocessing technology to Japan and Western Europe, apparently with the immediate aim of enabling the Bechtel Corporation to compete for a role in Japan's planned commercial-scale plant. In addition, the administration took the major step of offering to share highly classified U.S. gas centrifuge technology with Australia for a joint enrichment venture in that country.

Both decisions were regarded by the administration as important to reestablishing U.S. international leadership in nuclear technology and commerce. In the enrichment case, the United States was competing against France and the Urenco consortium for a partnership with Australia in what was seen as a high-stakes game for position not only in the depressed enrichment services market but also in future reactor sales. (Ultimately, Australia selected Urenco, whose centrifuge technology has already "proliferated" to Pakistan via security lapses at the consortium's Dutch facility.)

Neither Japan nor Australia can be considered a proliferation risk, and in neither of these cases did the United States initiate the sensitive technology bidding. Nevertheless, the U.S. decision to join in is significant. As with plutonium use, the question arises whether a discriminary approach can be sustained or whether lines will prove blurry and flexible in practice. There are two reasons for pessimism here. First, in a competitive market where each supplier has its own favored export technologies and where most customers do not fall into clear-cut risk categories, consensus on where to draw lines will be difficult to achieve. There is little reason to believe that U.S. distinctions will be readily accepted as a basis for regime rules. Second, the prospects for consensus are even dimmer if the United States itself is perceived as opportunistically flexible.

Here, the Mexican case is suggestive. In 1981, Mexico solicited bids on a major nuclear development program, making clear its interest in acquiring fuel cycle technologies as well as reactors. This prospective "deal of the century" set off a furious competition among the supplier countries and posed a clear and present danger to the fabric of collective restraint. The United States faced a dilemma: how to keep U.S. firms in the running (three U.S. vendors were competing for the sale with strong government backing) without making an explicit commitment to technology transfer that could trigger a collapse of supplier restraint.

In the end, the United States maintained a calculated ambiguity about near-term technology transfer, while hinting broadly that over the longer term anything was possible. The administration did not attempt to develop a consensus among suppliers, dismissing such an effort as "counterproductive." A January 1982 letter to the Mexican government offered U.S. assistance in assessing Mexico's requirements in the reprocessing and enrichment fields, held out the prospect of future cooperation in these fields, and invited Mexican participation in U.S. breeder and reprocessing programs.

The abrupt suspension of the Mexican program due to the country's economic crisis left unclear what the final outcome of the bidding would have been. But the open-ended character of the U.S. offer invites skepticism about the administration's intension to draw firm lines where sensitive technology is concerned and constitutes a warning signal for future cases.

The Mexican case underscores the potentially self-defeating nature of a U.S. bid to recapture nuclear influence through a stronger presence in the international market. Too aggressive an export posture may weaken those very nonproliferation standards on behalf of which the hoped-for influence is to be exercised. In showing a willingness to "play the game," the administration undercuts the U.S. claim to leadership (for example, the strengthening of controls on dual-use technologies) and invites the suspicion that it is in fact ambivalent about that claim: nostalgic for the days of U.S. predominance but tempted to use the loss of primacy as a license to behave like an ordinary supplier. Such an abdication would have very damaging consequences for the regime. While it is true, as the administration often points out, that the United States cannot unilaterally make the rules through the power of its own example, it is equally true that a negative U.S. example can very quickly erode the rules.

Full-Scope Safeguards

This problem of erosion is illustrated with particular force in the issue of "full-scope" safeguards—that is, the NPT requirement that nonnuclear-weapon states accept safeguards on all their nuclear activities rather than just on those involving imports. Here, administration actions have compromised, perhaps irretrievably, the chances of upgrading nonproliferation standards on an issue bearing directly on several of the problem cases of the regime—those countries that have refused to sign the NPT but that continue to benefit from outside assistance to their nuclear programs.

A full-scope safeguards requirement was imposed by the NNPA on U.S. nuclear customers (following a two-year grace period that has now expired), and during the Carter administration the United States lobbied hard for other suppliers to apply a similar condition to their own exports. While paying lip service to this effort, the Reagan administration has shown little inclination to make it a priority except in regard to Pakistan. On the contrary, the administration has contrived to let three key targets of the NNPA cutoff provision—India, Brazil, and South Africa—escape the law's consequences through surrogate fuel supply arrangements.

In the Indian case, the United States has arranged for France to assume the U.S. role in supplying enriched uranium for the Tarapur reactor. As a result, the country whose explosion of a nuclear device in 1974 largely inspired the NNPA full-scope safeguards provision (and which has not renounced future tests) will continue to receive fuel as if the law had not been passed. Moreover, India has made clear that it retains the option of reprocessing the U.S. fuel already supplied. The United States has argued that the original Tarapur agreement gives it a veto over such reprocessing, but India disputes this interpretation, and the administration declined to press the issue in connection with French deal.

Brazil, another U.S. customer that has not accepted full-scope safeguards, has been granted a "suspension" of its U.S. enrichment contract, enabling it to arrange an alternative fuel supply for the Angra I reactor without incurring the financial penalty this would normally entail. Finally, South Africa has obtained enriched uranium from Europe to start up its Koeburg reactors, in a deal brokered by U.S. firms with at least the passive assent of the administration. According to reports, the quantity of fuel involved will be adequate to run the reactors until South Africa is able to furnish fuel on its own from the unsafeguarded enrichment plant at Valindaba.

In each case, nonproliferation arguments have been advanced for circumventing the clear intent of the NNPA. The preservation of a supply link, it has been said, prevents a rupture that might leave fewer constraints on the recipient state, and buys time for a possible future settlement of safeguards and other nonproliferation issues. In none of the cases, however, does such a resolution appear at all likely. Instead, one is left with the uncomfortable feeling that it is the recipients who have bought time—for their own purposes—while the United States has surrendered whatever slim leverage the withholding of cooperation gave it.

The Security Dimension

Perhaps the most encouraging aspect of the policy outlined by the administration in July 1981 was its emphasis on the strategic dimension of nuclear proliferation. This emphasis suggested not only that greater attention would be given to the security motives driving the spread of nuclear weapons, but also that nonproliferation would be approached as an integral part of U.S. national security policy. Moreover, there were grounds for expecting that the Reagan administration—being less ambivalent about arms sales and the projection of U.S. power, and more favorably disposed toward a number of conservative regimes with which the United States had strained relations during the Carter years—would in fact handle this side of the problem more effectively than did its predecessor.

This ground has proven trickier than the administration might at first have thought, however. The record so far indicates that the proliferation threat will not yield easily to a reawakened U.S. strategic posture, for reasons having to do both with the intractability of proliferation motives and with tensions between nonproliferation and other U.S. objectives, including the containment of Soviet power. While in theory containment and nonproliferation appear mutually reinforcing—especially in cases as those of Pakistan, Taiwan, and South Korea—in practice the situation is considerably more complex, and the impact of U.S. security policies on proliferation dynamics is far from straightforward.

The difficulties are evident in the case of Pakistan, which is the closest thing to a test case of the Reagan approach. The administration has resumed military and economic aid to Pakistan—in the form of a $3.2 billion package including forty F-16s—following the 1979 cutoff under the Symington Amendment to the Foreign Assistance Act. (The latter, which was waived in order to allow the resumption of aid, prohibits assistance to countries acquiring unsafeguarded enrichment facilities.) Although its main purpose is to strengthen the U.S. strategic position in Southwest Asia in the wake of the Soviet invasion of Afghanistan, the administration hopes that this security relationship will also moderate Pakistan's nuclear incentives. However, the linkage is a weak one. The administration failed to obtain a cessation of the Pakistani nuclear weapons program as a condition of aid, and all indications are that the program is in fact continuing. Thus the U.S. strategic embrace runs the risk of seeming to legitimize Pakistan's nuclear ambitions and —given India's concern about the F-16s—may actually feed the regional rivalry from which those ambitions stem. The best that can be said is that the aid package gives Pakistan a strong incentive to refrain from a nuclear test that would probably provoke another cutoff by the U.S. Congress.

The ambiguous effects of containment policies on proliferation motives are also seen in East Asia. Despite its strong rhetorical declarations of support for Taiwan, the administration has accepted the anti-Soviet logic of continuing the process of U.S.-PRC (People's Republic of China) normalization. Following this logic, it has lifted the ban on sales of lethal weapons to the PRC, decided against the sale of advanced F-5G fighters to Taiwan, and agreed to limit and eventually reduce arms transfers to the latter. As a result, the intended reassurance of Taiwan has been frustrated, and its sense of isolation and insecurity increased. In the case of Korea, there would seem to be less danger of containment and nonproliferation goals running at cross-purposes. Even here, however, one can predict that U.S. pressure for a more expansive Japanese security role in the Pacific will be seen by Korea as having at least mixed implications for its own security interests.

Argentina offers a final illustration of how global U.S. calculations can frustrate expected improvements in relations with potential proliferators. Not only did U.S. support for Britain during the Falklands war cut short the administration's hoped-for U.S.-Argentine rapprochement, but Argentina is generally assumed to have emerged from the war more disposed than ever to keep the nuclear option open.

The point of these examples is not that nonproliferation interests should always dominate U.S. decision making. It is simply that the integration of nonprofileration into security policy is easier said than done. It requires a sustained, high-level effort to think through the national security significance of proliferation and to define a coherent strategic attitude toward it.

Unfortunately, there is little evidence that the Reagan administration has undertaken such an effort. Indeed, senior U.S. officials have largely ignored the issue except in connection with Pakistan. The result has been that nonproliferation considerations, rather than being consciously traded off against other interests, tend either to fall between the cracks or to be used as post hoc justifications for policies pursued on other grounds. In these circumstances, the administration's country-specific approach to nonproliferation can all too easily become mere opportunism, serving short-term commercial and diplomatic convenience rather than long-term U.S. national interests. *(December 1982)*

Nonproliferation Policy: An Exchange
Richard T. Kennedy

The following letter was submitted by Richard T. Kennedy, U.S. Representative to the International Atomic Energy Agency, in response to Peter Clausen's article, "The Reagan Nonproliferation Policy."

Peter Clausen's article, "The Reagan Nonproliferation Policy," perpetuates a number of misconceptions about the design and pursuit of a sound nonproliferation strategy. If we are to pursue successfully the types of institutions and practices needed to control the further spread of nuclear weapons, those very misconceptions must be understood and dispelled.

Implicit within Dr. Clausen's critique is a view of nonproliferation strategy as a matter of "either/or." Efforts to restore the reliability of the United States as a nuclear supplier are set against a posture of nonproliferation restraint; cooperation with other countries is contrasted with a policy of technology denial; measures to reduce countries' motivations for acquiring nuclear weapons are compared with steps to check the spread of nuclear technology; and adaptation to the use of plutonium as a fuel by Japan and the European community countries is opposed to concentration on the dangers of a so-called plutonium economy.

But design and pursuit of a sound nonprofileration strategy is not a matter of either/or. To put in place the defense in depth that the threat demands, a variety of approaches and initiatives must be pursued.

Efforts are needed to slow the spread of sensitive technology and to make it technically more difficult for a country to acquire the materials and facilities for making a nuclear explosive. This is the course pursued by this administration in close consultation and cooperation with other supplier countries. Denial alone, however, cannot succeed. The global process of industrial development and economic change makes technology denial a wasting asset in the nonproliferation arsenal. Such steps can only buy time. The United States must use that time wisely. It needs to encourage leaders of countries that might be contemplating acquisition of nuclear weapons to ask whether that course of action would serve their long-term security interests. The political, economic, and security influence of the United States also must be brought to bear to strengthen alternative means of providing security and get at the roots of regional tension.

Neither is the either/or approach adequate to deal effectively with the problem of plutonium use. There is no question that plutonium, the substance of nuclear weapons, is a dangerous material. Yet Japan and the Euratom countries believe that its use as a fuel will be needed for their energy security. The past preoccupation with the plutonium economy and the grudging, drawn-out process that was pursued in approving reprocessing served mainly, as Dr. Clausen so rightly notes, to cause "much friction" with Japan while having little, if any, impact on its plutonium fuel program. If the United States is to control the dangers of plutonium and en-sure the tightest standards and procedures for its use, it needs to work with, not antagonize, Japan and the Euratom countries. Without their cooperation, the United States will have little influence on their programs. And this is particularly true since an increasing amount of the spent fuel available to them is not subject to formal U.S. controls.

A second misconception in Dr. Clausen's approach is the belief that withholding U.S. cooperation somehow provides "leverage." Of course, there are both legal and policy limits to the extent of U.S. cooperation with other countries. Clearly, the United States has no intention of being a reliable supplier to unreliable countries. At the same time, efforts to coerce other countries to adopt U.S. policy preferences or to accept U.S. demands are most likely to be unavailing. Experience has shown that such efforts engender suspicion, excite national passions, and make more difficult the discourse without which the United States will be unable to win international support for the nonproliferation regime it seeks. Simply put, without cooperation we shall be doomed to fail.

Yet another misconception is that acceptance of practical if limited gains necessarily entails a sacrifice of U.S. nonproliferation principles. Yet precisely the opposite is true. For if the principle is that we must strive continuously to achieve an ever more encompassing nonproliferation regime, each step that can be achieved is a step on that road. Striking a bargain now with advanced nuclear countries such as Japan to influence their use of plutonium a decade hence is a case in point. Preservation of IAEA (International Atomic Energy Agency) safeguards on Tarapur, made possible by the waiver of that portion of the 1963 agreement that obligated India to buy fuel solely from the United States is another. And we must ask whether long-term U.S. objectives are served best by the nation's cutting all ties with countries that refuse to accept full-scope safeguards. Or are U.S. objectives likely to be better served by the United States' finding limited areas for cooperation in an effort to encourage their acceptance of more comprehensive safeguards and binding pledges not to acquire nuclear explosives.

Sheer pragmatism alone, however, will not and cannot suffice. A comprehensive nonproliferation policy must be grounded in sound guidelines and principles.

President Reagan enunciated just such a set of guidelines and principles in July 1981. They provide the essential road map for the achievement of long-term U.S. nonproliferation goals. They provide the basis for those judgments that must inevitably be made as the United States pursues those goals. For there will be those cases in which the United States must decide whether a limited gain is a genuine advance. Nonetheless, to allow the "best" to become the enemy of the "good" is to risk sacrificing sound achievement on the altar of theological principle.

Preventing the spread of nuclear weapons will remain one of the most urgent and important national security problems in the decades ahead. As President Reagan has said, it would be a tragedy were we to succeed in reducing Soviet and U.S. nuclear arsenals only to see those weapons spread to still other regions of the world. Nonetheless, to put in place an effective regime of nonproliferation institutions, norms, and practices, the United States needs the support of other countries. Winning that support and achieving U.S. goals demands that the United States bring its case to those countries, putting aside past misconceptions, seeking instead to convince them that their long-term security and well-being will be best served by cooperating in building a sound and comprehensive nonproliferation regime.   *(June 1983)*

Nuclear Proliferation after Osirak
Richard K. Betts

On June 7, 1981, Israeli planes executed the first overt military attack in history on a nuclear facility, destroying Iraq's Osirak research reactor. While most nations condemned the Israeli strike as aggressive, unnecessary, or at least premature, Prime Minister Menachem Begin justified it as a defensive action required to assure his country's survival. The Israeli attack thrust the issue of nuclear proliferation into public consciousness more forcefully than any event since the Indian nuclear test of 1974. The incident also highlighted the inadequacies of some prevalent approaches to dealing with the danger of proliferation.

Prevention Attack: Effective or Counterproductive?

Some observers have noted ironically, if not cynically, that Israel has shown that it has the most serious nonproliferation policy of any nation. It is not clear, however, that destruction of Osirak will actually solve the problem of Iraq's potential acquisition of nuclear weapons. Indeed, it is possible that the attack could ultimately make the danger to Israel even greater.

If Iraq had been on the verge of building nuclear weapons with fissionable material derived from the reactor, the raid might be considered at least a short-term "solution" to Israel's security problem. But most experts agree that the Iraqis would have needed several years to obtain significant amounts of usable plutonium from Osirak and even then would have had to operate the reactor in a way that would have alerted observers. To build a bomb sooner, Iraq might theoretically have diverted a fuel charge (like other research reactors, Osirak was to use highly enriched uranium). This would not be the most sensible route for gaining a serious nuclear weapon capability because it would leave the reactor inactive and would alert France or other suppliers to the breach of safeguards agreements and Nonproliferation Treaty commitments while leaving Iraq with probably only one very small bomb. Thus it is doubtful that the Israeli attack was necessary even as a short-term solution.

For the longer term, Israel's action may have a boomerang effect. The attack dramatized the issue of nuclear weapons for the Arabs and provided a challenging slap in the face that creates even greater incentives for them to develop such capability. Suspicions that Iraq was previously committed to a nuclear weapons program may well have been justified—and certainly no prudent Israeli defense planner could have assumed otherwise—but at least it was not certain before June 7. Iraq was a party to the NPT and had accepted extensive safeguards on its nuclear installations (International Atomic Energy Agency inspections were interrupted after the outbreak of the war with Iran, but only temporarily).

Prime Minister Begin claimed that President Saddam Hussein had criticized the earlier small and ineffective attack on the reactor by what were assumed to be Iranian aircraft on grounds that Iraq's nuclear program was directed against Israel rather than Iran, but it was later revealed that Hussein had not made the statement. A week *after* the Israeli raid, however, Hussein proclaimed openly that peace-loving nations "should assist the Arabs . . . to obtain the nuclear bomb in order to confront Israel's existing bombs." And in July, Saudi Arabia offered to finance the rebuilding of Iraq's reactor.

If the strike against Osirak damaged Iraq's capabilities to produce nuclear weapons only in the near future but dramatically enhanced interest in a nuclear option throughout the Arab world, did Israel reduce the threat to its security or increase it? Moral questions aside, it is hard to imagine that Israel could periodically mount similar operations against all the potentially threatening nuclear programs that could be undertaken by its numerous enemies. Even if feasible, this strategy would drastically aggravate Israel's political isolation, which is the country's basic security problem.

A Precedent?

Destruction of Osirak could have implications for nonproliferation beyond the region of the Middle East. As the first instance of a forcible preventive option, it suggests that other threatened countries might now more readily consider similar actions. On the other hand, an optimistic view would be that the precedent might inhibit proliferation by dissuading some countries from developing nuclear capabilities that could provoke preemption by their enemies. Both possibilities are real, although they may be overestimated. The probabilities differ according to particular cases, where the combinations of capabilities and incentives for nuclear proliferation differ.

In Africa the precedent will probably have only modest impact. South Africa's nuclear capabilities are already so highly developed (indeed, Pretoria may have tested a bomb in the South Atlantic in September 1979) and so well protected that they could not easily be destroyed by military action. The event might, though, increase Nigeria's interest in a nuclear capability. In East Asia, Taiwan has too many reactors operating or under construction for the Chinese government in Beijing to have high confidence in the effectiveness of an aerial attack with conventional munitions.

India, however, could be tempted to try to destroy the threatening elements of Pakistan's nuclear program—the enrichment and reprocessing plants under construction—especially if there is another conventional military conflict between the two nations. India and Pakistan have fought three wars against each other since they gained independence. Unresolved territorial disputes, combined with lingering religious and ethnic animosities that resemble those in the Middle East, offer the potential for such a clash. Because of this heritage of conflict, though, strategists in New Delhi did not need any lessons from the Israelis to suggest the option of preventive action.

All in all, the precedent-setting character of the strike against Osirak is disturbing, but it may be less significant than the way in which the attack underlines the inadequacies of the institutions, policies, and agreements that have constituted the dominant approach to nonproliferation.

The Nonproliferation Regime

Iraq had adhered to the NPT and accepted safeguards on its nuclear facilities, and no evidence has been cited that Baghdad was engaged in clandestine commerce in sensitive components. Yet Israel still felt threatened. It is true that Baghdad's fuel contract with Paris was not as "safe" as nonproliferation advocates wanted, since it provided for highly enriched uranium fuel charges rather than for the "caramel" fuel (unsuitable for incorporation in a weapon) that the French belatedly tried to substitute. But in regard to constraints against diversion of *plutonium* from the reactor, which was the target of the Israeli attack, Iraq's program was quite controlled in terms of current supplier guidelines and treaty requirements. The incident of June 7 suggests, therefore, that in the most politically volatile regions—which should be the ones of most concern—the current regime may not provide a guarantee against nuclear weapon proliferation that satisfies insecure nations.

Adherence to the NPT is desirable since it indicates that the nation ratifying the treaty has no near-term plan to develop nuclear weapons. Nations rarely undertake legal commitments that they intend to violate soon. But the treaty does not ensure innocent intent, as Israel's suspicions demonstrate, and it can legally be abrogated after three months' notice. Nor does the NPT prevent acquisition of the technical capabilities for a bomb, since it does not forbid importation or indigenous development of enrichment or reprocessing facilities. Leaving aside the controversial issue of effects on U.S. deterrent capabilities, the Comprehensive Test Ban (CTB) Treaty also would certainly not hurt, but cannot be a great comfort to nonproliferationists. First, it would be a near miracle if the CTB is concluded, given the current state of East–West relations and the policy of the Reagan administration. And second, adherence to the CTB would simply reflect a nation's lack of interest in testing a nuclear weapon. A country bent on testing a device would not become a party to the treaty; by definition it is those countries, not the ones that willingly accept restraints, that represent the proliferation problem. A nonproliferation regime is only as good as its members. (One potential benefit of a CTB, however, could be as a hedge against a change of government policy. If a probomb faction came to power in a country that had previously ratified the treaty it would be more inhibited than if it did not have to break a legal commitment in order to test a device.) And like the NPT, a CTB would not preclude an untested "bomb in the basement."

As long as member states do not make an issue of Article IV of the NPT—which stipulates their right to "the fullest possible exchange of equipment"—restrictive guidelines of the nuclear suppliers group will make it difficult to obtain facilities for producing fissionable material. But the difficulty may not be insurmountable for the most worrisome countries—those bent on obtaining the weapons option. Pakistan succeeded in importing numerous components for its secret enrichment plant through various subterfuges in a number of countries, and Switzerland openly engaged in such trade, arguing that the particular components were not on the list of items prohibited by supplier agreements.

Tighter restraints on supply can raise the cost and prolong the time necessary for a nation to acquire fissionable material. For countries that want nuclear weapons for prestige purposes, this may make the price high enough to dissuade them. But in a world in which the requisite scientific information is now so widely dispersed, most nations desperate enough to take the risks and sacrifices will eventually be able to get a bomb by hook or by crook. Desperation comes from insecurity. A serious nonproliferation policy, therefore, must address security problems.

Strategic Solutions

Reducing a nation's vulnerability sufficiently to make a nuclear deterrent unattractive can pose difficult choices. To keep South Korea from attempting to develop a nuclear option, maintaining the U.S. military presence as a reassuring deterrent against

North Korean attack is the best solution. In Pakistan, a large improvement in conventional defenses would be the only hope for a quid pro quo sidetracking of enrichment and reprocessing efforts. In the late 1970s this option contradicted President Carter's arms transfer policy and his diplomatic tilt toward India, until the Soviet invasion of Afghanistan overrode those concerns. The principal danger to Pakistan, however, is still India. And improved conventional forces that reduce apprehensions in Islamabad will increase them in New Delhi—perhaps pushing the Gandhi government closer to deployment of a nuclear force of its own. The ideal solution would be resolution of the political antagonism between the two countries, but that is no more likely than ending the East–West conflict.

Political problems in the Middle East are equally intractable. Facing numerous enemies committed to its extinction, Israel will not give up its own nuclear option. The only hope for inducing an Israeli government to do so would be to offer an absolutely credible U.S. security guarantee. That sort of credibility would probably require stationing U.S. troops in the country, committed to combat against any Arab invader, as a deterrent. If this were ever to be feasible (or justifiable), it would probably have to be coupled with Israeli withdrawal from territories conquered in 1967 (the Golan Heights and the West Bank). Israeli leaders prefer to rely on their own forces, buttressed by control of the conquered buffer zones, as well as U.S. arms supplies and financial subsidies. U.S. leaders have been equally reluctant to make a commitment as credible as the one extended to NATO.

The result of that unwillingness on both sides, however, leads to other complications in U.S. policy that overlap the nuclear proliferation issue—for example, controls on transfers of conventional weapons. Israel used U.S.-supplied aircraft to destroy Osirak, despite contractual requirements that the planes be used only for "defense." After the raid, Secretary of State Alexander Haig reportedly considered demanding that Israel consult with Washington in the future before using U.S.-supplied aircraft for such attacks. Prime Minister Begin insisted that no nation can entrust decisions on its security to another. Given traditional U.S. unwillingness to exert brutal pressure on Israel, this may be just as well; Washington could find itself implicated more directly in any Israeli actions considered aggressive by the rest of the world. Yet if Washington were to pressure Israel (with threats to cut off arms or aid), without providing a satisfactory security guarantee, this would increase Israel's reliance on the nuclear option. For the Middle East, moderate changes in U.S. policy are unlikely to avert nuclear spread. A dramatic change in commitments would be necessary.

Inducements and Sanctions

To go beyond the limited effectiveness of controls on commerce in sensitive nuclear power facilities and on the operation of reactors, a vigorous nonproliferation policy requires measures to convince countries contemplating a nuclear weapons option that they will be more secure without it than they are at present, or that they will suffer if they pursue the option. Given the political complexity and delicacy of particular cases, this is best done through quiet but firm diplomacy rather than through sweeping formulas designed to apply to all. For Pakistan, U.S. aid to improve conventional military capabilities should be offered, but only on the condition that Islamabad refrain from developing fissionable material. It is too late to apply this formula to Israel, but if the U.S. government has the political will, the condition of refraining from any deployment or test of nuclear weapons could still be stipulated. The threat of trade sanctions might be applied to the same end in regard to South Africa, and Taiwan could be informed that any nuclear weapons program would bar future U.S. arms sales.

Such measures would be unpleasant to implement, because the United States has reasons to preserve what leverage it has to deal with numerous other interests it has in relations with those countries. The issue is simply how important nonproliferation is compared to other issues. If the importance is high, Washington must be willing to pay a price. It is unrealistic to expect that insecure nations will sacrifice the option of a nuclear deterrent if the United States is unwilling to sacrifice much to convince them.   *(September 1981)*

The Reagan Record on Nonproliferation: Some Achievements, But Growing Dangers
Leonard S. Spector

On November 1, 1984, George Shultz, in the first address by a secretary of state devoted exclusively to nuclear nonproliferation, declared that the administration's policy to curb the spread of atomic weapons has worked well: "The struggle we are waging is not on the battlefield. It goes on in the quiet of diplomatic chanceries, at meetings of technical experts, and in safeguards laboratories. Success is measured not in terms of territory liberated or new allies gained, but rather in terms of confidence established, restraints voluntarily accepted, and destabilizing military options forgone. By these measures, our nonproliferation policy has been a success."

From one perspective, Shultz's assessment is correct: U.S. nonproliferation policy has achieved several notable successes in the past four years. But these have been overshadowed by the progress the majority of emerging nuclear states seem to have made toward building or expanding nuclear weapons capabilities.

South Asia

Pakistan has reportedly been seeking to develop nuclear weapons since at least 1972 but has lacked a source of nuclear weapons material. Since the late 1970s Pakistan's efforts to produce this commodity have been concentrated on completing a uranium enrichment plant at Kahuta. This facility, not subject to International Atomic Energy Agency (IAEA) inspection, is believed to be based on designs stolen from a similar plant in the Netherlands and on hardware imported, often illegally, from the West.

The Carter administration tried with some success to work with other nuclear supplier countries to close the hardware pipeline. The Reagan team has expanded and formalized the supplier understandings, a worthy accomplishment. The centerpiece of Reagan nonproliferation efforts in Pakistan, however, has been a six-year, $3.2 billion package of economic and military assistance, including forty F-16 fighterbombers. Although the aid was offered to bolster Pakistan against the threat of Soviet troops in Afghanistan, administration officials have argued that conventional military aid will dissuade Pakistani President Zia from pursuing a nuclear arms policy by giving him an alternative way to protect his nation's security. Washington has also advised Islamabad that the assistance will be terminated if Pakistan detonates a nuclear device. So far Pakistan has not taken this step. It is difficult to assess the deterrent effect of the Reagan policy, however, since Islamabad has lacked the necessary nuclear weapons material.

Moreover, even though it has not detonated a nuclear explosive, Pakistan has made significant progress over the past four years toward acquiring the capability to produce one. According to announcements in 1984 by Pakistani officials and the statements of administration sources disclosed by the press and by Sen. Alan Cranston, Pakistan has partly completed the Kahuta enrichment facility and may actually have produced some small quantity of the weapons-grade uranium. (Senator Cranston put its output at 15 kilograms of highly enriched uranium per year, enough for perhaps one Hiroshima-sized bomb.)

During the past four years Pakistan is also reported to have conducted significant work on designing nuclear weapons. Indeed, recently a Pakistani businessman pleaded guilty to attempting to smuggle high-speed electronic switches from the United States apparently for use in nuclear weapons, leaving little doubt that Pakistan's pursuit of nuclear armaments continues. Since 1981 China is also believed to have provided Pakistan with sensitive nuclear weapons design information, including details of the bomb used in China's fourth test, in 1966.

Thus, despite the Reagan administration's modest successes, Pakistan is now closer to realizing its nuclear ambitions than ever before and is on the verge of joining India, South Africa, and Israel as a de facto nuclear weapon state.

The Reagan team may have fared somewhat better with India, which conducted a single nuclear test in 1974 but has apparently refrained from manufacturing nuclear arms ever since. In 1982, the administration succeeded in defusing an increasingly bitter dispute with New Delhi over nuclear fuel exports for the U.S.-supplied Tarapur reactors. India had threatened to abrogate the 1963 U.S.-India nuclear accord, with its numerous nonproliferation restrictions, in 1981 because of the impending suspension of U.S. nuclear fuel shipments. (This was required by the 1978 Nonproliferation Act to penalize India for refusing to place certain of its nuclear installations under IAEA inspection.) After considerable behind-the-scenes negotiations, said to include a U.S. threat to deny India access to Export-Import Bank and multilateral financial institution credits, India agreed to accept France as a substitute supplier, while maintaining all the nonproliferation controls in the U.S.-India accord over the Tarapur plants and their fuel.

Though critics charged that the arrangement improperly protected India from the fuel cutoff intended by the Nonproliferation Act, the episode did help improve overall U.S.-India relations. Moreover, these negotiations coincided with 1981 reports that India was readying a second nuclear test. Reagan administration diplomacy during this period undoubtedly contributed to New Delhi's decision not to conduct additional nuclear explosions, an accomplishment of considerable proportions.

India has nevertheless taken major steps, like Pakistan, to expand its nuclear weapons production capabilities. In mid-1984 New Delhi inaugurated the Madras I nuclear power plant, the first in India not subject to IAEA inspection. If spent fuel from this facility were reprocessed at the Tarapur reprocessing plant, where IAEA safeguards apply only when IAEA-safeguarded fuel is present, India could produce enough plutonium for perhaps a dozen nuclear weapons per year and could use the material for this purpose without violating any legal restrictions. The Tarapur reprocessing plant began full-scale operations (using safeguarded fuel) in 1982.

In addition, India has apparently completed the refurbishing and expansion of its reprocessing plant at the Bhabha Atomic Research Center, although it is not clear whether this facility has begun operating. The installation is intended to reprocess fuel from India's Canadian-supplied Cirus reactor, which produced plutonium for the 1974 test, and from the larger R5 reactor, to be commissioned shortly. None of these facilities is covered by IAEA safeguards, leaving India free to use any plutonium that these reactors produce—perhaps enough for five additional weapons annually—for nuclear arms.

In all, the United States may so far have averted the most serious proliferation dangers in Pakistan and India, but it has not been able to forestall the continued growth of the two nations' nuclear weapons potential. Moreover, as Pakistan moves closer to possessing nuclear weapons, pressures on India to reactivate its own nuclear explosives program will mount, threatening a highly dangerous regional nuclear arms race.

China

The administration has come close to an important achievement in its nuclear dealings with China. Holding out the prospect of extensive civil nuclear trade, Washington helped persuade Peking to join the International Atomic Energy Agency and to adopt one of the basic export rules of the other nuclear supplier countries: requiring IAEA inspection of any exported nuclear equipment and material. This led to the initialing of a U.S.-China nuclear trade pact during President Reagan's April 1984 trip to Peking. Despite these positive developments, however, China has reportedly continued to assist Pakistan's uranium enrichment activities at

Kahuta. In response, the administration has suspended the statutory review process necessary to bring the U.S.-China accord into force. Thus while China's adoption of a strict nonproliferation policy may eventually become the greatest achievement of the Reagan team, for now the administration cannot claim a victory. Indeed, China's reported aid to Pakistan since 1981 has been highly injurious to U.S. nonproliferation interests.

The Middle East

The Reagan record is equally mixed in the Middle East. Iraq, Libya, and Israel are generally regarded as the countries of prime proliferation concern.

Iraq has apparently ceased to be a major focus of U.S. nonproliferation activity ever since Israel destroyed Baghdad's principal research reactor in 1981. Nevertheless, according to a dossier compiled by an Italian prosecutor, Iraq may have been negotiating during the early 1980s with a thirty-man Italian arms smuggling ring to purchase 34 kilograms of plutonium, enough for possibly six Hiroshima-sized bombs. The ring was broken before the alleged transaction was consummated. If the facts as reported are true, they would indicate that Iraq has been engaged in a clandestine, if unsuccessful, nuclear weapons program in violation of its Nonproliferation Treaty pledges. This would be a serious blow for the Reagan administration, which has not taken these allegations seriously and which recently restored full diplomatic relations with Baghdad.

Reagan officials have been more aggressive in dealing with Libyan nuclear activities. Like Iraq, Libya is far from having the capability to produce nuclear arms and is a party to the Nonproliferation Treaty. Nonetheless, in 1984 the administration intervened forcefully with Belgium to forestall a major nuclear trade agreement under which it was to provide Libya extensive technological assistance for Tripoli's nascent nuclear energy program. While the deal would not have contributed directly to a Libyan nuclear weapons effort, it would have assisted Tripoli in building a nuclear infrastructure that might some day have been turned to this goal. Given past reports of Libya's interest in nuclear arms, its interventionist foreign policy, and its support for international terrorism, Washington's initiative appears well taken and, to date, successful.

Israel has not conducted a nuclear test but is widely believed to have had a small undeclared nuclear arsenal since the late 1960s or early 1970s. There has been no public evidence of any Reagan administration effort to curtail Israel's presumed nuclear weapons activities, however, and indeed, Reagan officials (like their predecessors) have sought to keep the issue of Israeli proliferation out of the spotlight. When the Reagan State Department provided a list of Israeli nuclear facilities for the Senate Foreign Relations Committee in June 1981, for example, it omitted the presumed reprocessing plant most other observers—including, apparently, the CIA—believe is the keystone of the Israeli nuclear weapons program.

Similarly, although U.S. aid to Israel has increased substantially since 1981, judging by the public statements of U.S. nuclear officials, this aid relationship has not been linked to curbs on Israel's reported nuclear activities—a sharp contrast to the open and repeated connection made between U.S. aid to Pakistan and the latter's nuclear weapons program.

If widely accepted reports are accurate that Israel now possesses a nuclear weapons capability based on plutonium produced in the Dimona reactor and reprocessed at the site, Israel may have been able to produce some 36 kilograms of plutonium over the past four years. This would be enough for perhaps seven additional weapons, a significant increase of an arsenal said to be in the ten to twenty range as of 1981. Moreover, if the Dimona reactor was enlarged to 70 megawatts in 1980, as some have reported, its total output in the past four years might have been 100 kilograms of plutonium, sufficient to double Israel's supposed preexisting arsenal. The dangers of Israeli nuclear arms may thus have increased significantly during the Reagan years.

South Africa

South Africa appears to have gained a nuclear weapons capability in the mid-1970s based on highly enriched uranium produced in its pilot-scale uranium enrichment plant at Valindaba. U.S. nonproliferation officials have argued that the key to reducing pressures for nuclear weapons in South Africa is movement toward the regional settlement long promoted by the administration. In the meantime, the administration has agreed to certain limited nuclear transfers to Pretoria, in the hope of gaining its acceptance of stricter nonproliferation controls.

Despite these conciliatory gestures, Pretoria continues to reject IAEA inspection of the pilot-scale uranium enrichment facility critical to its current nuclear weapons capability. It has agreed only to discuss with the IAEA the inspection of a second facility, a semi-industrial-scale enrichment plant now being built. South Africa has pledged, also in response to U.S. overtures, that it will subject any future uranium exports to IAEA monitoring, consistent with the policy of other nuclear suppliers. Pretoria's past actions raise questions about its recent declarations, however. South Africa has given similar pledges since the 1950s but may have violated them by supplying unsafeguarded uranium to Israel, probably sometime between 1955 and 1965.

Moreover, assuming that during these years of negotiation South Africa used its Valindaba pilot-scale enrichment plant to produce highly enriched uranium at the plant's reported maximum rate of 50 kilograms per year (enough for two to three sizable weapons), Pretoria may have nearly doubled its stockpile of nuclear weapons material since 1981. The overall threat posed by the South African nuclear program may thus have substantially increased since the Reagan team took over.

Latin America

The Reagan administration has also sought to restore a dialogue on nuclear matters with Argentina and Brazil by acquiescing in a series of lesser nuclear transfers to them. Both are building facilities that could provide nuclear weapons capabilities by the end of the decade.

Any improvement in U.S.-Argentine relations resulting from this policy, however, was undoubtedly wiped out by U.S. support for Great Britain in the Falklands crisis. Moreover, in November 1983, just prior to the inauguration of President Raul Alfonsin, the head of Argentina's nuclear program announced that Buenos Aires had for five years been secretly constructing a uranium enrichment plant at Pilcaniyeu that would, in principle, be able to produce enough highly enriched uranium annually for five or six nuclear weapons by 1985. Argentine officials insisted that the plant had been built to produce non-weapons-grade enriched uranium for Argentina's nuclear reactors. The secrecy with which the plant was constructed, Argentina's unwillingness to place it under IAEA inspection, and the fact that the plant's stated capacity is many times larger than the apparent need of the Argentine nuclear energy program, however, strongly suggest that the plant was built as a step toward development of a nuclear weapons capability, probably in response to Brazil's uranium enrichment efforts initiated under the latter's 1975 deal with West Germany. The November 1983 announcement made clear that any nuclear rapprochement with Washington had done little to restrain the Argentine nuclear program.

The Alfonsin government has largely embraced the nuclear policies of Argentina's former military leaders, continuing to support completion of the Pilcaniyeu enrichment facility and a second installation capable of producing nuclear weapons material, the Ezeiza reprocessing plant. Alfonsin has similarly maintained Argentina's refusal to ratify the Nonproliferation and Tlatelolco treaties, which would require Argentina to place all of its nuclear installations under IAEA safeguards.

The Reagan administration has fared little better in Brazil, where despite improving ties in nuclear and other fields (such as the signing of a military coproduction agreement in June 1984), Brazil has continued to pursue unsafeguarded research on uranium enrichment at two of its principal nuclear research centers, as well as safeguarded reprocessing and enrichment installations under its 1975 nuclear pact with West Germany. After Argentina's announcement of its secret enrichment plant in November 1983, a number of Brazilian military officials declared that their nation's unsafeguarded enrichment activities would be accelerated and openly pointed to the military potential of this technology by stressing that it would provide Brazil with a nuclear weapons capability by 1990.

The intensity of the Argentine-Brazil nuclear rivalry has thus sharply increased over the past several years, notwithstanding Reagan administration nonproliferation efforts.

While some details remain murky, the overall trend of proliferation in the first Reagan term is clear. The Reagan team can claim a number of achievements, but in region after region proliferation dangers have grown. This trend seems likely to persist. Judging from the first Reagan term, the administration has apparently decided, if only implicitly, that other U.S. foreign policy interests—in particular, meeting the Soviet challenge—will take precedence over nonproliferation in U.S. dealings with the emerging nuclear states. The last four years, for example, have seen U.S. efforts to buttress Pakistan against the Soviet presence in Afghanistan; to dissuade India from moving farther into the Soviet orbit; to build Israel into a "strategic ally"; to improve ties with Soviet-supported Iraq; to support South Africa as a bastion of anti-Communism in its region; and to shore up relations with friendly governments in Argentina and Brazil at a time of increasing Soviet activity in the western hemisphere. All of these initiatives would undoubtedly be set back by the tensions that a "no holds barred" U.S. nonproliferation effort would likely engender.

Such factors make it improbable that the administration will substantially intensify its nonproliferation efforts with respect to these countries, particularly in the continued absence of dramatic new developments such as a Pakistani nuclear test. The likely result will be gradually worsening regional nuclear tensions, while the United States concentrates, one hopes with success, on strengthening elements of the international nonproliferation regime, such as the International Atomic Energy Agency, and on averting the most severe near-term acts of proliferation, such as nuclear testing or the open declaration by an emerging nuclear state that it possesses nuclear arms.   *(January 1985)*

Standing Up for the NPT
Lewis A. Dunn

The third conference to review implementation of the Treaty on the Nonproliferation of Nuclear Weapons (NPT) was held from August 27 to September 21, 1985, in Geneva. With 86 of the 130 parties present, the Review Conference successfully concluded at 5:20 A.M. on Saturday, September 21. Confounding many observers who feared that the 1985 conference, like that of 1980, would break down in acrimonious disagreement, it adopted a consensus Final Declaration that strengthens global nonproliferation efforts.

What were the themes of the debate? What was gained for nonproliferation? What were the key obstacles? Why was success achieved?

The national statements given during the first ten days of the conference repeatedly voiced strong support for the treaty, as well as concern about the dangers of nuclear proliferation for regional and global security. They stressed as well support for the International Atomic Energy Agency (IAEA), both in operating safeguards to detect misuse of peaceful nuclear cooperation and in helping countries gain the benefits of the peaceful atom. The considerable assistance already provided to developing countries in the peaceful uses of nuclear energy was recognized, but there were calls, too, for stepped-up cooperation and aid. Not least among these basic themes of the plenary debate was a broad sense of disappointment, shared by the United States, at the slender progress made in achieving the arms control and disarmament objectives of Article VI of the NPT.

The results of the conference strongly served U.S. nonproliferation objectives. On the broadest plane, the NPT emerged with an aura of success, strengthened, not weakened, by an honest and balanced review. The recognition in all quarters that the NPT is an arms control success underscored the vitality of the treaty, a vitality already enhanced by the addition of a dozen countries in the past year and a half, bringing the total number of parties to 130. As a result, the international norm of nonproliferation has been buttressed; it has become politically harder for countries to set out on the path to acquire nuclear explosives.

Many specific elements of the consensus Final Declaration are equally a nonproliferation plus. For example, the declaration affirms the parties' commitment to the NPT and their belief that it is essential to international peace and security. The Final Declaration also stresses the importance of the treaty's provisions for peaceful nuclear commerce. IAEA safeguards are strongly supported, as are efforts to improve their effectiveness.

With a view to the treaty holdouts, the Final Declaration calls on the parties in their nuclear export policies to take effective steps toward achieving IAEA safeguards on all peaceful nuclear activities in nonnuclear weapon states not party to the NPT; this clearly tilts in the direction of a supplier commitment to so-called full-scope safeguards as a condition of nuclear supply. From a different tack, heightened coordination among the parties to convince nonparties to join the NPT is envisaged, while the declaration also warns that any further detonation of a nuclear explosive by a nonweapons state would be a most serious breach of the nonproliferation objective and would increase the danger of nuclear war.

What did not happen also reflects the cooperative and constructive approach that characterized the review. There were no threats to withdraw from the NPT, and no party proposed amendments to the treaty. The claims of some nonparty observer states that the NPT served only the interests of the nuclear weapon states were rejected by their nonaligned targets, and the efforts of some nongovernmental organizations to provoke confrontation over disarmament issues at the risk of damaging the treaty failed to gain support.

Before a final consensus could be achieved, however, several obstacles had to be overcome. On the next to last day, an accommodation was reached on how to treat the matter of a comprehensive ban on nuclear testing. Here, there was an honest difference on whether negotiations on and conclusion of a CTB should be the next step toward the shared goal of nuclear disarmament. The language that was worked out reflected the strong concern of the great majority that such negotiations should resume in 1985, but it also reflected the U.S. conviction that deep and verifiable reductions of existing nuclear arsenals must take priority. Several countries, nonetheless, left disappointed that more far-reaching results were not achieved on the nuclear arms limitation and disarmament objectives of Article VI.

Even after the CTB issue had been resolved, the work of the conference was threatened by the intrusion of regional political issues. Iraq did not drop its demand that the conference condemn Israel's 1981 attack on Iraq's nuclear research reactor until the final night of the conference, in the face of strong U.S. resistance. Similarly, a group of Arab and African countries refused to modify its position that the conference demand a cutoff of all nuclear cooperation with South Africa and Israel until the final round. Instead, the conference simply noted concerns expressed about these matters.

Finally, just when all matters seemed successfully resolved, a truly eleventh-hour clash between Iran and Iraq threatened to prevent consensus adoption of the document. Iraq demanded that the Final Document contain a reference to its concern about attacks against its nuclear reactor; Iran opposed that reference. But under pressure from the nonaligned, these two countries compromised and agreed not to block consensus in the early hours of Saturday morning, September 21.

Many factors contributed to the successful outcome of the 1985 Review Conference. For more than two years the United States had been actively preparing for the conference, consulting closely with U.S. allies, with the Soviets and the socialist group, and especially with the nonaligned and neutral countries. Both the United States and the Soviet Union steered clear of polemical exchanges at the conference, guided by their common interest in a strong NPT.

Memories of 1980 also played a role. At that second Review Conference, confrontation prevailed and agreement was not achieved on a final document. Many countries, this time, were concerned that a similar breakdown of consensus would damage the NPT itself.

But the most important key to success is found elsewhere. It was most evident during that long closing session when the parties, especially the nonaligned, stood up for their treaty and kept it from becoming a political hostage to the Iran–Iraq dispute. The key to success was the recognition by all parties of the common ground that binds us together: All parties have a vital security stake in the NPT; the NPT is too important to risk damaging to make a political point. For without the treaty, the world would be a more dangerous place, and all countries would be less secure.

Momentum is now with the NPT. In an honest review, the treaty stood on its merits as an unquestionable arms control success. What is necessary now, in the words of Review Conference President Mohammed Shaker, is "to build on its successes, not belittle them." To do so will keep the momentum behind the treaty, and support our nonproliferation objectives in the years ahead.   *(October 1985)*

Small Nuclear Forces
Rodney W. Jones

Since China became the fifth nuclear weapons power twenty years ago, there has been a welcome lull in declared nuclear proliferation. But during that interval, the spread of nuclear weapons capabilities has continued, especially among those countries that rejected the 1968 Treaty on the Nonproliferation of Nuclear Weapons. Of the latter, India actually detonated a nuclear explosive device in May 1974. Meanwhile, Israel earned the reputation of having acquired unseen a "bomb in the basement," and by the end of the 1970s South Africa, Pakistan, and Argentina each appeared near the nuclear weapons threshold. Judging by these trends, it seems reasonable to expect that other nuclear powers could materialize before yet another two decades have elapsed, introducing new dangers to international security that have yet to be properly understood.

Most of those developing countries that could go nuclear would be able at first to acquire only "small nuclear forces," containing between a handful and a few dozen early-generation atomic bombs. Small nuclear forces (SNFs) on this scale would be dwarfed, of course, by the thousands of nuclear and thermonuclear warheads in the superpower arsenals. Though far less sophisticated than the nuclear forces of the superpowers, even one SNF with a handful of Hiroshima-sized nuclear weapons would profoundly disturb the stability of a neighboring region. Emerging nuclear powers equipped with SNFs could have a dangerous impact on global strategic conditions and on the broader arms control environment.

New Bombs

Which Middle Eastern and South Asian countries could acquire SNFs? What might such SNFs look like? What consequences would they have for the region? The states leading the regional nuclear trends are easily identified. In technical capacity, Israel, India, and Pakistan each stands out. Israel reputedly could deploy an SNF on short notice. India could resume explosive tests, "weaponize" unsafeguarded plutonium stocks, develop an SNF of several dozen warheads within two or three years, and perhaps field a long-range nuclear force in the 1990s. Pakistan, by working with enriched uranium as well as plutonium, might be able to deploy an SNF before 1990.

Nuclear capabilities might also have appeared in the 1980s in Iraq and Iran if it had not been for political and military conflict in those countries, namely, the

Iranian revolution of 1979, the prolonged Iran–Iraq War, and the 1981 Israeli air strike on the Iraqi Tammuz I (Osirak) reactor. In both countries, revived nuclear programs could still lead to SNFs in the 1990s. Libya remains a cause for long-term concern, while Egypt, though presently dedicated to nonproliferation, might find it difficult to abstain if an Israeli SNF or Arab state SNFs elsewhere become certain.

Nuclear Delivery Systems

It was once assumed that getting nuclear-capable delivery systems would present a major obstacle for developing countries and would therefore provide an indicator of proliferation intent. Here the conventional wisdom may need to be rethought. The accelerated transfer after 1970 of conventional weaponry has made high-performance, nuclear-capable, tactical aircraft (for example, the MiG-23, F-16, Mirage-V and Jaguar) available to all of the states in the region that have SNF potentials. With minor modifications, such aircraft already are able to deliver nuclear-dimension payloads over ranges of several hundred miles, ranges that are "strategic" within the local contexts of the regions involved. Moreover, conformal fuel tanks and air-refueling capabilities can be expected to extend tactical aircraft delivery ranges in the 1990s to distances of about a thousand miles. Several countries also have bomber aircraft with such range today. Thus, there may be little or no lead time between acquiring atomic weapons and equipping them with fairly sophisticated delivery systems.

While aircraft delivery systems are likely to be the initial choice of planners for SNFs, short-range and medium-range ballistic missile systems that could also deliver nuclear warheads are being transferred into the Middle East and could provide certain SNF deployment options. The Soviet Union sold conventionally equipped, dual-capable battlefield missiles to Egypt before the 1973 war and lately supplied modern dual-capable surface-to-surface (SSM) and surface-to-air (SAM) missiles to Syria and Iraq. This year the Soviet Union reportedly even offered to assist India with the acquisition of intermediate-range ballistic missiles. Israel and, until recently, Egypt have had their own dual-capable SSM development programs. India's space program—which has benefited more from U.S. and European than Soviet cooperation—is believed to be capable of developing a long-range missile capability in the 1990s.

Missile delivery systems might be sought for an SNF to signify added psychological potency and, supplemented with aircraft, greater SNF flexibility and perhaps survivability. The spread of missile delivery systems would eventually make some potential SNF powers capable of posing strategic threats to extraregional powers, with implications for global stability.

New Equations for Conflict

Efforts by SNF powers to overcome technical asymmetries or new vulnerabilities posed by an SNF opponent would also intensify conventional arms acquisition and thus conventional arms races, both to improve deterrence and to keep the presumed threshold of nuclear first-use high. Moreover, as states try to master SNF capabilities, we can expect to see more preventive military strikes—illustrated by the Israeli attack on Osirak in 1981—as states resort to conventional force in hopes of preventing irreversible SNF proliferation. Finally, it should be recognized that just as Iraq resorted to chemical warfare against the massed invasion forces of a revolutionary Iran, any nonnuclear state threatened by an SNF may acquire chemical and bacteriological weapons as an alternative means of deterrence, accelerating the proliferation of other weapons of mass destruction.

SNF capabilities within the region could threaten the survival of certain local states or put Persian Gulf oil supplies in sudden jeopardy. Nuclear attacks could be far more decisive and devastating in a few hours than the conventional attrition that has already cost Iraq and Iran several hundred thousand lives over more than four years. One can only wonder how the course of this war might have changed if either or both had recourse to SNFs.

Regional SNFs could also be destabilizing to Western Europe, to NATO, and ultimately to the East–West balance. NATO members are only now coming to grips with so-called out-of-area contingencies arising from the disruptions of Middle East oil supplies, (for example, results of the Iraq–Iran war) and have yet to face the complications, SNFs would introduce. One possible effect of SNFs' emerging in the Middle East would be to revive thinking in the countries of southern Europe about independent nuclear capabilities, with dangerous implications for the opposed alliance systems and the superpowers. Other complications from regional SNFs could flow from Soviet reactions, where geographical proximity could put Soviet territory within nuclear range, increase Soviet uncertainty, and excite new interventionist tendencies.

Most important of all, SNFs in the Middle East and South Asia would increase the potential for catalytic nuclear warfare in situations of crisis or confrontation between the superpowers. The strategic stakes the West has in the free flow of oil from the region, combined with Soviet geographical proximity, requires the maintenance of U.S. rapid-deployment forces for emergencies. Timely and effective U.S. response to a crisis arising from the disruption of oil or from Soviet military intervention in the region could be hampered by SNF threats against states whose support is needed for logistical purposes. Moreover, nuclear threats or strikes by SNF powers against local targets, against the forces of either superpower, or even in the vicinity of the forces of a superpower, could greatly increase the risks of miscalculation, confrontation, and escalation of force between the superpowers. The close relationships between the superpowers and potentially nuclear client-states in the region add to the risks of confusion.

Preventing SNFs

Improved nonproliferation policies and greater international efforts in support of existing institutions for this purpose are vitally needed. Efforts might include upgrading the effectiveness of international safeguards on the nuclear fuel cycle. Wider adherence to the NPT or development of new nuclear-free zone institutions could reassure nations in regions where SNFs are likely to evolve. Other efforts would include further refinement and multilateral coordination of nuclear export controls, particularly on sensitive technologies. Fresh attention needs to be given to controlling exports of nonnuclear technologies and conventional military systems, especially in the aerospace fields, to limit the opportunities for easy conversion to SNF delivery purposes and to limit the range of dual-capable systems so as to discourage acquisition of truly strategic capabilities.   *(June 1984)*

Lessons from the Past: The Limited Test Ban Treaty and the Future of Arms Control
G. Allen Greb

In 1963, the United States, the Soviet Union, and the United Kingdom reached agreement on the Limited Test Ban Treaty (LTBT), which prohibits nuclear testing in all environments—the atmosphere, the oceans, and outer space—except underground. Hailed as the first significant arms control agreement of the nuclear era, the LTBT has achieved many of the objectives set out by its original proponents. It virtually eliminated the health hazards associated with radioactive fallout from atmospheric tests; it encouraged better East–West relations; and it set the stage for the negotiation of other important international treaties, most notably the 1968 Nonproliferation Treaty.

Still, the LTBT has failed in what many proponents saw as one of its major goals: the curtailment of superpower competition in the arms race. Both the United States and the Soviet Union have carried out extensive underground test programs since 1963. In fact, they have dramatically increased the rate of nuclear testing since the LTBT went into force, which has permitted nearly unrestricted weapons development by both powers. Moreover, we still do not have the logical successor to the LTBT, a comprehensive test ban (CTB), nor has the United States ratified the 1974 Threshold Test Ban Treaty or the companion 1976 Peaceful Nuclear Explosions Treaty.

Kennedy, Khrushchev, and Calamity

The political climate in 1963 was especially conducive to arms control negotiations in general and to test ban talks in particular. Pushed and pulled by a number of forces, President John Kennedy and Chairman Nikita Khrushchev had by then personally committed themselves to achieving some kind of limits on the super-power nuclear arms competition. Kennedy and Khrushchev already shared concerns about the high costs of the arms race and about the spread of nuclear weapons to other nations. More important, these leaders had just experienced the 1962 Cuban missile crisis, which, as Glenn Seaborg stresses in his book about the test ban negotiations, made a deep psychological impression on them both. "That brush with calamity," Seaborg writes, "seemed to forge a bond between them." Nuclear war no longer appeared only an abstract threat but a very real and imminent possibility.

Testing the Test Ban

It was natural, moreover, that Kennedy and Khrushchev should focus on a test ban as the immediate means to lessen the risks of nuclear holocaust. During the previous administration, President Eisenhower had set the tone of concern about nuclear weapons and had suggested a test cessation as an important first step to reduce the nuclear threat. Although ultimately not successful, Eisenhower and Khrushchev initiated formal negotiations on a CTB and imposed a complete test moratorium in 1958 that lasted for almost three years. The LTBT of 1963 can in large measure be viewed as the culmination of this earlier set of negotiations.

In addition to this legacy of strong official interest at the highest levels in a test ban, widespread popular concern over the issue had been growing steadily since the U.S. Bravo test of 1954. Public concern centered not on arms control considerations but on the dangers of radioactive fallout. As persuasive scientific evidence accumulated about the possibility of environmental and genetic damage from fallout, the worldwide clamor against testing intensified, reaching a peak in the early 1960s.

Against this background, President Kennedy announced in his famous American University speech of June 1963 that U.S., Soviet, and British delegations would meet in Moscow to negotiate a CTB. Despite the concert of official and public interest, however, the parties could forge only a partial test ban agreement. The brief negotiations underscored not only long-standing East–West differences on the question of verification, but also important internal roadblocks to the entire negotiating process. Within the United States, as in the Soviet Union, important constituencies remained opposed to the idea of a test ban. Many of these opponents saw any discussions with the other side as a zero-sum game: if the United States was ahead of the Soviets in weapons development, it must continue to stay ahead; if behind, it must strive to catch up. Presidents Eisenhower and Kennedy, aided by public support, were able to overcome this narrow outlook and argue that security could be sought through cooperation as well as confrontation. Yet strong opposition entrenched within the government bureaucracy greatly restricted their range of options on test ban policy, a problem exacerbated by certain unique aspects of the American political process.

Opposition

Among all the governments of the world, only the United States requires a two-thirds vote in the Senate for ratification of any treaty. A small swing element of Congress (as few as five or six senators), therefore, can have an inordinate influence on the course of U.S. foreign policy. The president and his national security leadership must keep this in mind at every stage of the negotiating process, especially when dealing with such an inherently controversial subject as arms control. President Kennedy certainly felt such constraints in 1963 as the uniformed military, scientists at the weapons' laboratories, Atomic Energy Commission officials, and prominent members of the Senate all voiced objections to a CTB.

These domestic political considerations weighed heavily in the administration's decision to accept the Soviet offer of an LTBT in lieu of a more comprehensive agreement. Even after the LTBT had been negotiated, President Kennedy felt compelled to offer, as he put it, "unqualified and unequivocal assurances" to those who might still have reservations about the treaty. These included safeguards—for example, underground testing would be "vigorously and diligently carried forward" and the government would "maintain strong weapons laboratories in a vigorous program of weapons developments"—that ensured strong Senate support (the treaty was ratified by a vote of eighty to nineteen), yet at the same time virtually guaranteed that President Kennedy's long-term goal of limiting the arms race would be postponed indefinitely.

Negotiability

In fact, much has happened in the twenty years since the LTBT went into effect to destabilize rather than stabilize the superpower relationship, to increase rather than decrease the risks of nuclear war. Yet there are important lessons to be learned from the LTBT experience that can directly benefit arms control today. One relates to what can be termed the "negotiability" of agreements. Any treaty must be negotiated within a reasonable period of time; if the process takes too long, the measure being sought most certainly will be doomed to failure. This process must include a realistic assessment of what is acceptable to the other side, in addition to one's own security goals and objectives. During a drawn-out negotiation, treaty opponents at home invariably have a chance to marshal their forces. Lengthy negotiations also can fall victim to shifts in political leadership. Finally, events external to the negotiations can have a negative impact as well.

As a partial measure, the LTBT was eminently negotiable. By sidestepping the thorny problem of verification, the parties in Moscow produced a completed document in less than a month. Even then, it took considerable effort on President Kennedy's part to allay domestic criticism (an effort perhaps taken too far with his set of "assurances" to opponents). Although the historical record is not as clear,

Khrushchev apparently had similar problems to contend with from within the Soviet bureaucracy.

The ultimate success of this effort stands in sharp contrast to the ponderous and prolonged SALT II talks, which culminated in a treaty that has yet to be ratified by the United States. During these negotiations, domestic critics were able to organize themselves as the Committee on the Present Danger and mount a well-coordinated anti-SALT campaign. Then in 1979, long after most officials believed SALT II would be in place, a series of international crises, capped by the Soviet invasion of Afghanistan, led President Carter to withdraw the treaty from Senate consideration.

This brings us to an important corollary lesson: in the West, both a determined national security leadership and an interested public are necessary for progress in arms control. Neither by itself is enough. In 1963, historical forces merged to provide this dual constituency. The president stood firmly behind a test ban at the same time that American and international public opinion pushed for an end to atmospheric tests. The result was the LTBT. This joint public-official momentum carried through the era of détente and reached an apogee with the SALT I ABM Treaty and Interim Agreement. The Senate ratified these agreements by the resounding vote of eighty-eight to two.

Since the mid 1970s, however, these forces have been out of phase. President Carter, for example, came to office in 1977 firmly committed to a full program of arms control. By then, however, the American body politic had become complacent toward such issues. Apathy soon turned to active hostility because of the rapid deterioration in U.S.-Soviet relations. The public reaction (or, more appropriately, nonreaction) to SALT II is well documented; less known is the almost total lack of response to the separate tripartite negotiations on a CTB held in Geneva between 1977 and 1980. Herbert York, chief U.S. negotiator and ambassador to those talks, recalls that very few people outside the inner circles of government even knew that the negotiations were actually taking place. In fact, many assumed that York's connection was to SALT rather than to CTB.

The situation today is nearly reversed. While official resolve appears to be at one of its lowest points in the nuclear era, there is, as existed in the early 1960s, a tremendous mobilization of forces outside of government concerned about nuclear arms control. Responding to ongoing nuclear modernization programs and to the rhetorical exuberance of the Reagan administration, Europeans and Americans have demonstrated a renewed interest in nuclear questions. In Europe, the rise of public concern has taken the form of mass protests and new political parties. In the United States, it has coalesced around the nuclear freeze movement.

The Public Factor

Introduced in the spring of 1980, the freeze in its most common manifestation calls for a bilateral and verifiable halt to the production, testing, and deployment of superpower nuclear weapons. It has engaged nearly all segments of society— professional groups, scientists, churches, and the press—in a sustained debate over its merits and the government's nuclear and defense policies in general. Both freeze advocates and more "traditional" arms controllers, whether they like the freeze idea as a negotiating initiative or not, agree that the new public involvement has created a climate in which arms control can again succeed if the political will is there on the part of West and East.

Increasingly, all nuclear decisions—whether they involve introducing new systems, modernizing old ones, or proposing arms control measures—will be subject to intense public debate and scrutiny. Unlike the 1960s, moreover, public engagement in such policy issues is likely to endure into the future. As former Secretary of Defense Harold Brown put it, "The thirty-year diffusion of nuclear policy consideration and formulation from official through academic and intellectual to journalistic and public circles is now irreversible."

The arms control challenge for the 1980s, then, is first and foremost one of education. National security cannot and should not be left to the "experts" alone; rather, we should strive for a consensus among decisionmakers, professional analysts, and well-informed citizens. If we are to go beyond the promise of the LTBT and the other arms control agreements of the past, it is essential to promote communication and understanding among these groups about U.S. policies and those of the Soviet Union. As this knowledge gap is narrowed, prospects for effective arms control will grow in direct proportion.   *(October 1983)*

The Comprehensive Test Ban Negotiations: Can They Be Revitalized?
Barry M. Blechman

Background

For more than ten years the primary symbol and substance of efforts to control nuclear arms has been SALT—the U.S.-Soviet talks to limit strategic weapons. In an earlier period, however, the centerpiece of arms control was a different set of negotiations—those for a comprehensive ban on tests of nuclear weapons. Beginning in the latter part of the 1950s, determined efforts were made to reach such an agreement. Once-promising negotiations stalled in the early 1960s, however, ostensibly over questions of how a test ban would be verified, more likely as a result of foundering East–West relations connected with the Berlin situation.

Even so, talks continued, and in 1963, when U.S.-Soviet relations improved following the Cuban missile crisis, political developments again were reflected in the test ban negotiations. Within two months of President Kennedy's speech at American University signaling the United States' desire to move away from cold war confrontation, the United States, the Soviet Union, and the United Kingdom had agreed to a treaty prohibiting tests of nuclear weapons in the atmosphere, underwater, and in outer space; tests underground were still permitted.

This limited test ban treaty, known as the LTBT, alleviated the potential physical consequences of nuclear tests—poisoning of the atmosphere and higher rates of birth defects and other harmful medical effects among those exposed to radioactive fallout. It also had positive military and political effects, curbing tests of very large weapons and other types of military experimentation, as well as ushering in an era in which the potential of arms control to enhance national security was viewed positively. Negotiations proceeded successfully on several other arms control agreements in the wake of the LTBT, culminating eventually in the 1968 Nonproliferation Treaty and the beginning of SALT.

Still, the LTBT could not deliver the full range of political and military benefits that would be expected from a comprehensive test ban. Since 1963, both the United States and the Soviet Union have continued to test nuclear weapons extensively. The United States has carried out well more than four hundred tests of nuclear devices since the LTBT was signed, while nearly three hundred tests have been reported for the Soviet Union, all underground. In the most recent years, the annual number of reported Soviet tests has exceeded the number of announced U.S. tests. Other nations, of course, also test nuclear weapons. The French have carried out about eighty tests since their first nuclear explosion in 1961; British nuclear weapons are tested occasionally at the U.S. underground test site in Nevada. China also tests nuclear weapons, having completed more than twenty-five such tests since its first explosion in 1964. Indeed, both China and France have refused to sign the LTBT and, although France has tested only underground since 1974, the Chinese continue to test in the atmosphere, a practice that results in radioactive contamination in the United States and other nations. (All test data are extrapolated from the 1980 edition of the *SIPRI Yearbook of World Armaments and Disarmament*. It is the practice of the U.S. government not to announce either its own or other nations' tests below a certain explosive yield. The Soviet Union generally does not announce any nuclear tests.)

Negotiation of a comprehensive test ban, known as CTB, thus has remained high on the agenda of uncompleted arms control efforts; relevant discussions have taken place throughout the 1970s, in various formats, in association with the Geneva-based Committee on Disarmament. In 1974 the United States and the Soviet Union completed an agreement that represented additional progress toward an end to all nuclear testing. The Threshold Test Ban Treaty (TTBT) specified that no nuclear weapon would be tested underground whose explosive yield exceeded 150 kilotons. To ensure that it could be verified, the treaty provided for the exchange of geophysical and geological data between the signatories, the exchange of precise yield and location data for two past tests at each test site so that the instruments each signatory would use to verify the treaty could be calibrated, and the reporting of all future tests. It also stated the intention of the two nations to reach a second agreement placing limits on underground nuclear explosions for peaceful purposes. This second agreement, known as the Peaceful Nuclear Explosion Treaty (PNET), was completed in 1976. In addition to imposing a 150-kiloton ceiling on the yield of all single nuclear explosions at locations other than test sites, it provided for the exchange of even more data and specified that under certain circumstances observers from the other signatory could inspect preparations for peaceful nuclear explosions and even place sophisticated instrumentation at the site. Soviet agreement to the PNET represented an important concession, as the Soviet Union had maintained for a time that these types of nuclear explosions should not be restricted like explosions at weapon test sites. Moreover, the verification procedures specified in both treaties, particularly those permitting on-site inspections, were unprecedented. Both treaties were submitted to the U.S. Senate in 1976, but neither has yet been ratified.

In 1977 the United States, the Soviet Union, and Great Britain initiated a new round of talks to conclude a comprehensive test ban. These negotiations proceeded fairly rapidly and made good progress for the first year or two, but subsequently bogged down as U.S.-Soviet relations worsened in the wake of the Soviet and Cuban intervention on the Horn of Africa, events in the Middle East and Latin America, and most important, the Soviet occupation of Afghanistan.

Incentives and Problems

Emphasis on a comprehensive test ban is not misdirected; a case can be made that a complete end to nuclear testing might do more to reduce the risk of nuclear war over the long term than would any limitations on nuclear forces that realistically might result from SALT. The benefits of a comprehensive test ban would be felt both directly and indirectly.

Presently, it is the common practice of the great powers to test both nuclear warheads with new characteristics, such as the neutron warhead, and warheads based on familiar technologies but modified for new delivery systems, before introducing them into operational forces. While greater reliance on such techniques as computer simulations might reduce perceived requirements for this developmental testing, it is hard to imagine the armed forces of any nation having confidence in new weapon systems without some tests involving nuclear explosions. Thus, if they could agree to a comprehensive test ban, the United States and the Soviet Union in effect would be agreeing to constrain the qualitative arms race. This would put a cap of sorts on the overall strategic competition and, particularly if combined with quantitative limits negotiated in SALT, could contribute to a more stable military balance between the two.

Freezing the design of nuclear warheads might be particularly advantageous to the United States, which is presently believed to be ahead of its rival in such characteristics as weight-to-yield ratios. Continued testing might be particularly important to the Soviet Union if it wished to deploy larger numbers of warheads on its missiles, especially its submarine-launched ballistic missiles.

Indirectly, the achievement of a comprehensive test ban could have important effects on the danger that additional nations will deploy nuclear weapons. If the United States and the Soviet Union could agree to and ratify a comprehensive test ban, they would be in a position to exert considerable political pressure on other nations to adhere to it. Particularly high on the list of potential signatories would be near-nuclear powers such as Brazil, India, Israel, and South Africa, which have refused to ratify the Nonproliferation Treaty but have committed themselves to subscribe to a CTB by ratifying the Limited Test Ban Treaty. If nations like these could be persuaded to ratify a comprehensive test ban and thus to refrain from actually demonstrating a nuclear weapons capability, the effects of whatever research and development they still carried out could be mitigated.

Moreover, if a comprehensive test ban is not achieved reasonably soon, there is a serious risk that the nonproliferation regime that has been put into place so painfully, the whole system of controls on the movement of nuclear materials and limits on the export of certain items that are necessary for the production of nuclear weapons, would begin to unravel, eventually leading to defections from the Nonproliferation Treaty. The essence of that treaty is a bargain between the existing nuclear powers and the nonnuclear nations. The latter pledged to forbear in the development of nuclear weapons and to accept controls over various aspects of their use of nuclear power for peaceful purposes to make possible verification of such forbearance. In exchange, the nuclear powers pledged to continue good faith negotiations toward containing the nuclear arms race and nuclear disarmament. This commitment generally is interpreted to include the complete end of nuclear testing.

Of course, a nation's decision whether or not to develop nuclear weapons depends on many factors, and drawing attention to this commitment well serves the interests of the nonnuclear powers. Still, it is clear that given the positions already taken, it would be increasingly difficult to hold on to what progress has been made in limiting the further proliferation of nuclear weapons in the absence of further significant progress toward a CTB, particularly if the nuclear powers also were not making progress in limiting the size of their nuclear arsenals in SALT. A breakdown of the nonproliferation regime, of course, and each entry of a new nation into the nuclear club, implies a greater risk of a crossing of the nuclear threshold, and the incalculable dangers of a world in which nuclear weapons had become the common currency of warfare among nations.

Why hasn't it been possible to make more progress toward a comprehensive test ban? Substantively, three problems seem to have provided the greatest difficulties for the negotiations.

First, throughout the history of test ban negotiations, establishing procedures to verify adequately an agreement has been a central issue. This obviously is more of a problem for the United States than for the Soviet Union, as the latter's closed society and the extraordinary secrecy attending anything even remotely connected with Soviet defense programs would make it difficult for the United States to be confident that the Soviet Union was adhering to negotiated restrictions.

An important breakthrough in the verification problem was made during the latest phase of the talks in 1978, when the Soviet Union accepted, in principle, an intrusive set of verification procedures proposed by the United States and Great Britain. These procedures would feature the construction of stations on each of the three nations' territories to monitor seismic waves and transmit that data, encrypted in such a way as to assure that they could not be tampered with, to the other signatories. At the same time, the Soviet Union also agreed to on-site inspections to buttress the value of the data provided by the seismic stations in particular circumstances. Soviet acceptance of these procedures in principle, of course, did not mean that final agreement necessarily would be achieved. And details of the verification provisions of a comprehensive test ban treaty were the subject of painstaking negotiations for the next two years. Still, this Soviet acceptance of the need for "heroic" verification procedures was a real breakthrough in the more than twenty-year history of test ban negotiations.

Even so, not all U.S. commentators are satisfied with the verification procedures outlined in the negotiations, arguing that the Soviet Union could still find ways to circumvent the test ban clandestinely. Various scenarios have been suggested in which, it is maintained, it would be possible for the Soviet Union to carry out nuclear tests—at least at relatively low yields—even under a CTB with extensive verification procedures. This is a technical issue that clearly requires dispassionate study and informed public debate.

Second, there is the problem of how to assure the reliability of existing nuclear weapons without an ongoing test program. Although much can be done short of actually exploding a weapon drawn from the stockpile to assure that nuclear weapons would still work if needed, such as the visual and electronic inspection of various components, critics of a CTB maintain that as time passed without tests, decision-makers in the United States and abroad would lose confidence in the effectiveness of the nuclear arsenal. For example, they maintain, even if defective components were identified and replaced without exploding a bomb, one could not be confident that the replacements had been constructed properly or that they meshed properly with the older components of the weapon. Since nuclear weapons exist primarily to deter war, the argument continues, erosion of confidence in the nuclear arsenal would lead to more unstable international relations.

Others point out that the United States, at least, had never done very much if any testing solely to check reliability until critics of the CTB negotiations found that weapons reliability was a potentially effective argument against the treaty. They maintain that problems such as the one just mentioned are unlikely to occur. Moreover, they assert, there is no reason why whatever problems were detected in the nuclear weapons stockpile could not be diagnosed and corrected, with high confidence, without actually testing a repaired weapon. Furthermore, they maintain, reliability could be improved even beyond its present high levels if certain steps were taken: parts and special materials could be stockpiled, quality control procedures during weapons fabrication could be tightened, documentation of design and engineering decisions could be improved. And finally, reliability could be made a more important criterion in the design of new weapons.

In fact, the reliability problem is only the public manifestation of a deeper issue. Some critics of the CTB worry about the feasibility of maintaining a viable nuclear weapons development and production establishment without a test program. Under a CTB, they fear, it would become increasingly difficult to recruit and retain qualified physicists, engineers, machinists, and other skilled personnel to work in nuclear laboratories and other facilities. Over time, they argue, this U.S. capability would atrophy. This is a deeply held conviction, and it is difficult to analyze objectively or empirically. The central questions are how important a continuing test program is for the viability of the whole U.S. nuclear establishment, and whether compensatory programs could not make up for whatever difficulties were caused by a test ban.

One way around some aspects of the reliability issue would be to permit some nuclear explosions—in other words, to negotiate a new but much lower threshold test ban. A limit in the very low kiloton range on the explosive yield of nuclear tests, some argue, would permit reliability testing of the fission triggers of nuclear weapons. Those who oppose such a low threshold treaty, on the other hand, maintain that exceptions to a comprehensive test ban would mean loss of the expected benefits of a CTB for military stability and for nonproliferation, and therefore would make such a treaty much less useful than a comprehensive test ban.

Finally, there is the problem of the nuclear powers that have refused to take part in test ban negotiations. Without the participation of France and China there would be obvious limits to the willingness of the other nuclear powers to continue to suspend nuclear tests. Most pointedly, the Soviet Union could not be expected to refrain from advancing its nuclear capabilities indefinitely if China continued to improve its nuclear posture. The solution to this problem obviously lies in negotiating a treaty that would be in effect only for a specified period of time; the appropriate length of time, however, and the terms under which the treaty would be reviewed, amended, abrogated, or renewed at the expiration of that period, constitute difficult questions.

A New Approach

Of all the issues that led to bureaucratic infighting within the Carter administration, none prompted so vicious a brawl, for so long, as the comprehensive test ban negotiations. The 1977 and 1978 Soviet agreement in principle, first to include peaceful nuclear explosions in a CTB and then to "heroic" means of verification, made achievement of a comprehensive test ban appear feasible. Following this, critics

214 · The Race for Security

within the bureaucracy rallied to force changes in the U.S. negotiating position on some issues and to make it impossible for the United States to take a position on others. Opposition to the treaty came largely from the Joint Chiefs of Staff, the two nuclear weapons laboratories, and the Department of Energy. (The two U.S. nuclear weapons laboratories, Los Alamos National Scientific Laboratory and Lawrence Livermore National Laboratory, are formally part of the University of California system, but they are financed by the U.S. government.) They were abetted in their efforts to slow the negotiations by several congressmen who were kept well-informed about executive branch decision making. Interestingly, elements of the British Defence Ministry aided these internal U.S. critics through their own political channels because they feared that a comprehensive test ban would interfere with efforts to develop the next generation of British nuclear weapons.

Opposition to the test ban derives from a number of factors. Certainly, many of the critics are sincerely concerned about verification and/or weapons reliability. Yet there are unspoken reasons for opposition as well—reasons that are related precisely to the importance of the test ban. In a sense, a complete test ban would embody a serious decision to move farther away from reliance on nuclear weapons for the nation's security. Obviously, nuclear weapons—tens of thousands of nuclear weapons—would exist long after such a treaty had been completed, but by agreeing to the prohibition on nuclear tests and thus to limits on their ability to develop new types of nuclear weapons the signatories would be indicating their determination eventually to end this state of affairs. This implication of a CTB is well understood by those involved in the issue, even if it is generally not discussed; it is, after all, one of the reasons why the CTB is so important for efforts to stem nuclear proliferation.

From the critics' perspective, such an objective would not be consonant with U.S. security interests. For one thing, some believe that the future is too uncertain for the United States to accept such a restriction. Under some circumstances, they argue, the United States may have to carry out additional tests to analyze nuclear effects on ballistic missile defenses or develop new warheads with special characteristics to counter threats that simply cannot be foreseen at present. Moreover, they believe, these contingencies aside, the United States cannot compete effectively with its adversary in maintaining conventional military strength because a democratic political system will not sustain the economic burden necessary to do so for very long, at least not in peacetime. Consequently, the argument continues, when push comes to shove, the United States has in the past relied, does so at present, and will continue in the future to rely on nuclear weapons, on the threat of nuclear war, to protect its security. Consequently, the CTB, because it symbolizes deemphasis of nuclear defense, would not be in the United States' interest even if technical questions such as reliability and verification were resolved successfully.

The contrary arguments are direct and to the point. "Yes," supporters of the CTB maintain, "the threat of nuclear war may have contributed to the avoidance of direct attacks on the United States and its major industrial allies so far, but there is no certainty that deterrence based on the fear of nuclear Armageddon can last indefinitely." Moreover, they argue, nuclear capabilities have proved ineffective or irrelevant in defending U.S. interests in the Middle East, Southeast Asia, and elsewhere. Most importantly, they maintain, as generations grow up for whom nuclear weapons are only a normal part of the reality they have always experienced and for whom therefore nuclear weapons have lost their special terror, the risk of a nuclear exchange will grow larger. As nuclear capabilities spread to additional nations, the risk of nuclear war—through the action of a madman, through accident or miscalculation, or because of a desperate bid to save a deteriorating national or personal position—will increase dramatically. And once the forty-year-old sanction against the use of nuclear weapons is broken, the consequences are incalculable. For this reason alone, the argument continues, the nation's security and the well-being of future generations can only be protected by moving, through negotiations, to less and less dependence on nuclear weapons, at the same time making whatever economic sacrifice may be necessary to maintain adequate conventional military strength.

Is there a middle course between opponents and supporters? Can a strategy be devised that would permit sufficient movement toward a comprehensive test ban so as to obtain its hoped-for positive effects on the risks of proliferation and the balance of military forces between the United States and the Soviet Union, yet would also buy time to permit the substantive and symbolic issues besetting the negotations to be resolved? I think so.

Such an approach would begin by renewing efforts to ratify the Threshold Test Ban and Peaceful Nuclear Explosion treaties. These two treaties have never been very popular, being opposed by critics of a comprehensive test ban as first steps toward the wrong objective, and being disliked by those in favor of the CTB as an inadequate substitute for a true ban on all nuclear testing, which would weaken political support for a CTB. Most importantly, from this perspective, the TTBT and PNET are opposed because, it is believed, they would not help to stop proliferation. As far as the nonnuclear powers are concerned, continued nuclear testing, even at lower yields, is an inadequate substitute for a comprehensive test ban. Nonetheless, the Nixon and Ford administrations saw the two treaties as better than nothing. I agree.

Ratification of these treaties could have important beneficial effects. It would show considerable progress toward the goal of a comprehensive test ban. More important, the treaties have important provisions that could alleviate some of the uncertainties in the United States about the Soviet Union's nuclear test program. The exchange of geological and geophysical data, the provision of data about past tests to permit calibration of seismometers, and the required reporting of all future nuclear tests and their coordinates would greatly aid U.S. efforts to monitor the Soviet nuclear test program. This would be of some political benefit itself. Ratification of the treaties could also help to resolve some uncertainties about the possibilities of verifying a CTB. And the detailed verification procedures contained in these treaties could be important precedents for future efforts to limit nuclear arms.

Second, the United States could take unilateral measures to put itself in a better position to contemplate positively the comprehensive end to nuclear testing. Resources devoted to the monitoring of worldwide nuclear tests could be enhanced, for example. It is rather surprising that nearly two years after the mysterious event near South Africa in September 1979 the United States apparently still has not taken steps to improve its ability to monitor nuclear tests in the atmosphere. Additional funds could also be spent on modernizing seismic verification systems, as well as on improving the methods used to analyze the data produced by seismic devices. Some suggest that a joint effort be undertaken with the Soviet Union to build and operate a prototype of the station that would be used to verify a CTB. And steps could be taken to minimize any risks of a long period of no nuclear testing, such as instructing the nuclear laboratories to give stockpile reliability a higher priority in their future efforts.

Third, under this new approach, the comprehensive test ban negotiations would be resumed, but the U.S. objective would be scaled down substantially. In effect, the new purpose would be to negotiate an interim agreement, a much improved threshold test ban, which could preserve and impart momentum to a process that eventually might lead to the end of nuclear testing. As such, an interim agreement might garner some of the political benefits of a CTB, particularly as concerns proliferation, or would at least avoid the adverse repercussions of a breakdown of the negotiating process. Even so, an interim agreement would permit continued evaluation of the questions that cause some to oppose CTB and would not commit the nation to a definite schedule for achieving a total ban on nuclear tests.

1. The interim agreement would include restrictions on the number and yield of nuclear tests permitted each signatory each year; these limitations would become tighter gradually over a period of time. In other words, the treaty would enforce the gradual tapering down of the nuclear powers' test programs. The number of tests permitted each year might begin at roughly the average of the two sides' present levels, scaling down to a relatively low number over the lifetime of the agreement. The permitted yield of tests might begin at the 150 kilotons permitted the TTBT and scale down to the very low kiloton range said to be necessary for some aspects of reliability testing.

2. The interim agreement also would include extensive verification procedures, including a network of seismic stations. This could both build confidence in the effective functioning of the interim agreement itself and provide data and operational experience to ease concerns about verifying a permanent CTB. Judging from past Soviet attitudes toward verification, they may be reluctant to agree to extensive verification procedures in an interim agreement. The Soviets must come to understand, however, that given their penchant for secrecy, these provisions would be necessary for political acceptance of this and any future test ban in the United States.

3. The agreement would terminate automatically after a relatively long interval of time, say ten years, and the conditions and terms for its possible renegotiation

would be put in neutral language. In short, as much as possible, the interim agreement itself should not prejudice the case for or against a permanent comprehensive test ban. Also, a provision permitting abrogation of the treaty before the end of its planned lifetime would be included, so as to protect each nation's security in the event of unforeseen contingencies.

Conclusion

Essentially, what such an interim agreement would do would be to buy time so that the issues that currently make it difficult to negotiate a permanent comprehensive test ban could be resolved, and at the same time obtain some of the benefits of a CTB—or at least avoid some of the risks of an evident freeze in the negotiating process. The installation of seismic stations and their operation during the period of this interim agreement could help to ease concerns about the verifiability of any comprehensive test ban. It would provide the signatories with extensive seismic data and operational experience and would thus facilitate careful study of the reliability and confidence that could be invested in the data that came from such stations. Moreover, the time provided by an interim agreement would permit study of and debate about the reliability issue. Views have been expressed as to whether testing is necessary to assure the reliability of nuclear weapons and the viability of the nuclear weapons establishment; an interim agreement would make it possible to explore such questions further. Finally, an interim agreement would provide added time during which the other nuclear powers might decide to join in a comprehensive test ban. Over the course of an interim agreement, for whatever reasons, China and France conceivably could change their positions on a CTB. They may not, and in that eventuality the Soviet Union, and Great Britain would have to determine whether to go ahead with a permanent test ban, but at least there would be an opportunity to test these possibilities.

The three-part proposal outlined here would move toward the complete end to nuclear testing but, in many ways, would represent only half a loaf. It would not make the achievement of a comprehensive test ban a certainty. Nor would it incorporate substantial enough progress for some of the more outspoken critics of the nuclear powers. Still, it does move in the direction of a CTB and contains elements that could impart enough momentum to the process that none of the signatories would view their backing out of future negotiations as a cost-free exercise.

Most importantly, while making some progress, and thereby perhaps alleviating the dangerous consequences for nuclear proliferation of a total breakdown of test ban negotiations, an interim agreement would provide the opportunity to resolve the two most pressing issues: Can U.S. nuclear weapons be maintained reliably without tests? Can a test ban be verified with adequate confidence? These are not trivial questions. They cannot be resolved without a determined national effort, nor can they be settled without the time that would be made available by an interim agreement.   *(June 1981)*

Limits on Nuclear Testing: Another View
William Epstein

A growing controversy is brewing over whether the United States should ratify the 1974 Threshold Test Ban Treaty and the 1976 Peaceful Nuclear Explosions Treaty. The two treaties were submitted to the Senate in 1976, but the Senate—in my view wisely—has refrained from ratifying them. In the meantime, both the United States and the Soviet Union announced that they would continue to abide by the treaties while they proceeded to negotiate a comprehensive test ban (CTB).

In confirmation hearings for their positions at ACDA, former ACDA director Eugene J. Rostow and START negotiator Gen. Edward L. Rowny advocated the ratification of these two treaties. Their approach views the problem of nuclear testing and its impact on nonproliferation in almost exclusively U.S. or U.S.-Soviet terms, instead of in terms of how the potential nuclear proliferators might react. Unfortunately, it also shifts the emphasis away from a CTB by giving formal legal sanction to continued testing.

The advocates of ratification fall into what I regard as the error of accepting the views of military men and of those scientists at the Los Alamos and Livermore laboratories who want to continue what they call "reliability" or "confidence" testing to ensure that the nuclear warheads will continue to explode as intended.

To deal with the latter point first, we must recall the views of many scientists who insist that reliability testing is not necessary to maintain confidence in nuclear weapons. They go further and say that if there is deterioration in some components of nuclear weapons, it would affect both Soviet and U.S. weapons about equally. If there were, therefore, any lessening of confidence in the reliability of these weapons, it would tend to lessen the temptation by either side to risk a first strike, and it would certainly downgrade confidence in any counterforce capability. This would provide greater rather than less stability for mutual deterrence. The international group of experts that prepared a report on a CTB in 1980 at the request of the United Nations General Assembly stated on this specific point: "Moreover, experts who have studied the problem consider that the less confidence there is in nuclear weapons, the less would be the temptation to rely on them" (Document A/35/257, paragraph 116).

In answer to those in the United States who want to continue testing, it should be stressed that this is the one way that will ensure that the Soviet Union, which has carried out some six hundred nuclear tests in all as compared to about one thousand by the United States and is recognized generally as being behind the United States in nuclear weapon technology, will be able to catch up. If a CTB is agreed on and both sides stop all testing, the United States would lock in its advantage.

Ratification of these two treaties would not be regarded as a step toward the goal of a CTB. Most if not all of the nonnuclear countries—and not just the nonaligned ones—regard the two treaties as spurious and a mockery of a test ban. Since about 90 percent of all the tests have been below the level of 150 kilotons provided in each treaty, the establishment of that threshold is not considered by them to be a significant additional limitation on the 1963 Partial Test Ban Treaty. Instead ratification is seen as legitimizing continued testing both of warheads and of PNEs (peaceful nuclear explosions), which the three parties at the CTB negotiations had already agreed should be prohibited.

Moreover, judging from past experience with other partial treaties, if these two treaties are ratified and enter into force, the pressures for a CTB within the United States and other nuclear powers would probably erode. The Chinese and the French would also be encouraged to continue their testing.

Thus, the effect might well be that negotiations for a CTB would be abandoned or at least suspended, not just for three or four years but for a decade or more. There would be no assurance whatsoever that the CTB negotiations would be resumed in the foreseeable future or that any interim agreements could be achieved by scaling down either the number or the yield of future tests. The suggested approach of such interim agreements calls to mind Zeno's paradox in which the hare never quite catches up to the tortoise.

From the point of view of nonproliferation, it is almost universally acknowledged that a CTB is by far the best way to prevent the further spread of nuclear weapons. Certainly it would be more effective than any export regulations or safeguards on peaceful nuclear reactors and programs. In the absence of a CTB, the nonproliferation policy outlined by President Reagan on July 16, 1981, is only half a policy since it does not touch the more important aspect of halting the nuclear arms race.

No other measure of nuclear arms control has been so persistently demanded for so long by the nonnuclear states—both aligned and nonaligned—as a CTB. A total nuclear test ban is regarded by practically all nonnuclear states as the single most important, most feasible, and most easily attainable measure to halt the further proliferation of nuclear weapons by both the nuclear and the nonnuclear states. It is also regarded by them as a litmus test of the seriousness of the intentions of the superpowers to halt or control the nuclear arms race as they have committed themselves to do in the Nonproliferation Treaty. They reject the arguments of some U.S. scientists and military personnel that the United States must continue testing to develop better nuclear weapons.

At the 1980 conference to review the operation of the Nonproliferation Treaty, the nonnuclear nonaligned countries were ready to accept almost all the nonproliferation measures, which were later outlined by President Reagan on July 16, if the nuclear powers would agree to more diligent efforts to achieve a CTB and to a moratorium on further tests in the meantime. The Soviet Union was ready to agree, but not the United States, and the conference ended in failure.

Earlier this year several nonaligned nonnuclear states warned that, if the nuclear powers did not live up to their commitments under the Nonproliferation Treaty to halt the nuclear arms race and in particular to end nuclear tests, they would have to consider withdrawing from that treaty. The treaty permits a country to withdraw on three months' notice.

Instead of being a step forward toward a CTB, the entry into force of these treaties would be regarded by many of the nonnuclear countries, and in particular those that can be considered potential proliferators, as a step backward. They would quite likely regard it with either despair or cynicism. Some of them would also regard it as legitimizing testing and as an invitation to proliferation, especially for the carrying out of PNEs. It might even be considered by a few of them as providing the occasion or excuse to withdraw from the Nonproliferation Treaty.

If that should happen, the treaty could crumble, and the dam of nonproliferation could burst. We shall then have to worry not about preventing the proliferation of nuclear weapons, but rather about preventing their use.

The U.S. administration has abided by the two treaties since 1976 without ratifying them. It should continue to do so and also should agree to the early resumption of the CTB talks.   *(October 1981)*

5
Rethinking Arms Control

After strongly criticizing the SALT process in the late 1970s, Ronald Reagan and many officials in his administration later found themselves choosing to adhere to the strategic arms limits set by the SALT agreements. Those agreements in the long run turned out to be more durable than even their advocates might have expected. Nevertheless, when Ronald Reagan entered office in 1981, the SALT process and the elaborate, carefully negotiated restraints it embodied were widely believed to have come to an end. President Reagan proposed "deep reductions" as the new goal of strategic arms talks, but his negotiations with the Soviets, particularly after the initiation of the Strategic Defense Initiative, seemed to offer little hope of progress. With SALT apparently dead and no new arms control in sight, people more actively began to propose new ideas and rethink common assumptions about arms control and the prevention of nuclear war. Although reevaluations of arms control have and always should take place, they are especially significant in the Reagan years when a new consensus for post-Reagan arms control is needed and when interim or piecemeal measures might be the only kind of arms control possible.

From different perspectives, Richard Barnet and Christoph Bertram examine the most basic assumptions of arms control policy and offer some specific suggestions for progress. Herbert Scoville, Jr., offers a bold plan for an alternative path to effective arms control. The articles by Gary Hart and Richard Smoke and William L. Ury are primarily concerned with preventing a nuclear war caused by miscalculation or misunderstanding and with controlling nuclear crises.

James E. Goodby evaluates a new multilateral forum for the negotiation of risk reduction measures in Europe. Karl Pieragostini analyzes cooperative verification measures that go well beyond traditional national technical means of verification. Gerald M. Steinberg questions the process of formal arms negotiations and provides historical examples and several suggestions for informal restraints. Finally, Les AuCoin describes a military rationale for a nuclear weapons freeze. Taken together, the articles in this chapter offer a range of new or resurrected arms control ideas that appeared in the public policy debate during the Reagan years.

Arms Control for Real Security
Richard J. Barnet

Arms limitation is a means, not an end. The purpose of bilateral agreements or explicit unilateral arrangements to control arms is to create a political climate in which security can be enhanced. Hawks and doves seem to agree on one thing: the most important aspect of modern weapons today is the "perception" that they produce in adversaries and allies. Until nuclear stockpiles are reduced nearly to zero the physical elimination of nuclear weaponry does not guarantee the avoidance of catastrophic damage to the species and to the environment. The knowledge of weapons making would survive even radical disarmament. A downward adjustment of weapons levels would thus not in itself assure survival of the planet, much less freedom from anxiety for its inhabitants. One must not ask too much from disarmament.

However, what the nations of the world, especially the nuclear superpowers, say and do about weaponry will make the critical difference in world politics. There conduct determines whether the risk of confrontation or war by miscalculation grows or recedes, whether levels of international tension and personal anxiety rise or fall. Arms reductions are political messages no less than arms buildups.

Changing Perceptions

The critical function of a serious disarmament program today is to reflect and to dramatize changes in political perception. The commitment to a path of steady arms reduction, with verification increasing as arms levels drop, is a statement about sovereignty. Disarmament is a process of transferring trust from a primarily unilateral system relying largely on technology to a multilateral system based on building new political relationships. A serious disarmament program is a way of making two critical political statements (1) that there is no technological answer to security at any level of expenditure, and (2) that the security of any nation, no matter how powerful, depends upon the security of other nations.

Twenty years ago, it seemed that the two superpowers had embarked on a disarmament process with a clear goal and a clear strategy. The McCloy-Zorin joint statement committed the United States and the Soviet Union to a course leading to "general and complete disarmament." That document, like most general statements negotiated between adversaries, was a mixture of propaganda and serious thinking.

Today, the United States urgently needs to articulate a theory for arms limitation and an alternative vision of security in a disarmed world that will elicit broad public support. Until now, a lack of public understanding and support has rendered arms limitation politically vulnerable and has caused successive administrations to switch gears in arms negotiations, thereby destroying the political foundation of a stable relationship with the Soviet Union.

An alternative to war as a means of settling disputes is essential to long-term survival. This idea has seemed self-evident to practical people like John J. McCloy, Lord Mountbatten, Gen. Omar Bradley, and many others. Indeed, anyone who studies the long-term prospects of the existing state system cannot help but be pessimistic about basing security on the nation's ability to make war. Since the modern nation-state can no longer perform its two historic functions—neither defending the national territory in the classic sense nor providing a stable economy within national frontiers irrespective of developments in the world economy—it is evident that the nation-state must evolve into some other security arrangement or the global political order will eventually collapse in self-destructive anarchy.

Arms Control and Security

The primary purpose of arms control is to defuse the arms race so that political change can take place without risking the planet. How that change will turn out no one can say, but it is clear that neither U.S. political nor economic objectives can be achieved by the continuation of the arms race. Complete and general disarmament is an essential national goal because it recognizes the two critical realities of modern life: (1) that there can be no long-term security without the eventual elimination of nuclear stockpiles under a system of world order in which the threat of nuclear aggression is eliminated and (2) because of the threat of nuclear escalation war itself is a dangerous anachronism.

No arms control program can gain enduring political support unless it has a clear goal. This the Reagan administration lacks. It has been unable to offer a strategy that explains how huge increases in military spending can be translated into increased political options. New military capabilities will not substantially change the power relations of the superpowers because of the inherent political limits on using military power to achieve national objectives as presently defined. Thus a huge increment in conventional arms for Central America will not produce internal political change there of the sort that is defined by the administration as being in the national interest. The vulnerability of the U.S. energy system and the growing insecurity in the United States about access to natural resources will not be fundamentally affected by a large naval buildup. Similarly, the Soviet buildup is not translatable into either enhanced political or economic power.

The Freeze

Since arms are now primarily political statements, the process of arms limitation must be seen as an effort in political communication. A bilateral freeze on the production, testing, and deployment of nuclear weapon systems is a priority precisely because it can clarify intentions and change the messages that each side is sending to the other. The freeze is, of course, not a new proposal. It was discussed in the 1950s and proposed by President Johnson. It has been traditionally rejected by one side or another because it is perceived to perpetuate the strategic imbalance of the moment. Since there is no agreement between the United States and the Soviet Union, or indeed among the specialists within the United States, as to the "real" state of the military balance, there can never be an arms limitation agreement that depends upon achieving a future balance. A serious freeze agreement would constitute a political breakthrough because it would represent an official statement that the asymmetries in the military establishments of the two sides are far less significant than the shared risks of pursuing the especially dangerous next stage of the arms race. It would underscore a common understanding that the weapons about to be produced are more destabilizing than the ones already built, no matter who builds them.

The simple statement "enough is enough" can go a long way toward creating the political climate for significant arms limitation. A freeze can never be seen as an end in itself, for it can never be anything but temporary. The internal dynamics in the United States and the Soviet Union will press the arms competition in one direction or another. Any freeze will push either into a new arms buildup or into a process of arms reduction.

Nevertheless, a freeze, especially one with a specific time limitation, would provide breathing space for the superpowers to deal with serious options for improving the security of both sides. Such a move would be important for restoring Soviet confidence in the United States as a reliable negotiating partner, which would help create a favorable political climate in which to proceed rapidly beyond SALT. The SALT agreement could then be extended to include all other delivery systems beginning with the most destabilizing counterforce weapons on both sides.

The freeze will fail, however, unless it is negotiated rapidly. A quick agreement can be reached if each side convinces the other that it is serious. But if the freeze were sufficiently comprehensive, it would address the problem that so complicated the SALT negotiations. During the SALT II negotiations, technology proceeded at a fast pace and always threatened to render the negotiations obsolete. The freeze agreement ought to consist of a relatively simple set of bilateral undertakings that could be verified by national intelligence means, such as a mutual prohibition of further testing and deployment of missiles and new airplanes, with a series of additional measures to extend the agreement. Thus each side ought to take steps to reassure the other that in fact it was cutting back weapons production, fissionable material production, and other aspects of the nuclear arms race. Verification by national intelligence means could be achieved with a high degree of confidence if a production cutoff for *all* nuclear delivery vehicles could be agreed upon. But it is most unlikely that the two sides would agree to close down their production systems as a first-step measure. Therefore, partial production cutoffs should be undertaken not as legal obligations but as reciprocal unilateral measures to reinforce the basic agreement and to improve the climate for further agreements.

Nuclear Superiority

The test then of an arms control measure in the 1980s is whether it makes the right statement and creates the right perceptions. The freeze is an important starting point because it accepts the idea of parity. The real meaning of parity is that both superpowers, irrespective of numerical differences in weaponry or qualitative differences in their arsenals, can each do the same things with nuclear weapons, no more, no less. There is substantial evidence from the history of the U.S.-Soviet arms race that the overriding political purpose of the Soviet buildup is to prove this point. There is no way to resist acceptance of parity in this political sense except at the cost of an ever-escalating arms race. The freeze provides the opportunity to test the longer-term intentions of the Soviet Union without risk, for the near certainty of Soviet destruction in a U.S. retaliatory attack remains. The Soviet offer of a comprehensive freeze casts a welcome doubt on the assertions of administration spokesmen that the Soviet Union is striving for some sort of "superiority."

But parity must extend beyond the mere size of the nuclear arsenals and include the matter of deployment. At a time when the United States had a decisive qualitative and quantitative superiority in nuclear weapons it had a theoretical political advantage that it was unable or unwilling to use. The Soviet Union consolidated its military hold on Eastern Europe at a time when the United States had a monopoly on nuclear weapons. The United States did not intervene against the Soviets in the Berlin uprising (1953), the Hungarian revolution (1956), or the Czech invasion (1968), even though the Soviets lacked effective means of delivering a crippling nuclear attack on the United States. The conclusion one should draw from such a history is that nuclear superiority has always been a dubious political advantage because it cannot be translated into power during a crisis without communicating a specific threat, and that involves unacceptable moral and political costs.

The present ground rules governing the behavior of the superpowers are a vestige of an earlier day and reflect the era of U.S. nuclear superiority. A single standard of conduct applying to both sides is far more stable than the present deployment patterns for nuclear weapons, which do not rest on any legitimate principle and do not reflect the present power balance. The parity the Soviets seek should be reached by negotiation or else the issue will be decided by confrontation; nuclear weapons constitute a "security" system that neither the United States nor the Soviet Union nor the billions of people who make up the rest of the world can afford.

Redeployments

We ought therefore to seek restrictions on the deployment of nuclear weapons in new areas and initiate a process of withdrawal of nuclear weapons from so-called forward bases. The United States should begin the process with the unilateral withdrawal of nuclear warheads and supporting installations from Greece and Turkey, and from other areas peripheral to the Soviet Union where the threat and provocation to the Soviets is far greater than any contribution to U.S. or European security. It is all the more in the interest of the United States to undertake the process quickly since in many countries domestic opposition to foreign nuclear weapons on their soil is likely to increase. It should be a goal of U.S. policy that by the end of the decade the United States and the Soviet Union have no land-based nuclear weapons outside of their own territories, including battlefield or "tactical" nuclear munitions.

Such a process of nuclear redeployment would show a sensitivity to European concerns about being a launching pad for nuclear weapons that they do not control and about being "defended" by arms that will destroy them. U.S. forward-based nuclear weapons have lost whatever deterrent value they may have had in the past. These moves would strengthen relations between the United States and the nations of Europe.

A Message to Moscow

Perhaps the most important statement to be made by a freeze and by an orderly process of nuclear withdrawal would be that the United States no longer believes that it can fight and win a nuclear war. It is now clear that heightening the nuclear threat does not increase deterrence, although the Reagan administration has asserted the contrary. It has never been satisfactorily explained how it would increase the safety of Americans to create plausible dangers of a U.S. first strike in the minds of Soviet leaders. Escalating the cost of the arms race for the stated purpose of destabilizing Soviet society is a dubious strategy for making Americans safer. Such a strategy is not likely to make Americans *feel* safer either. As a consequence of dramatizing the nuclear threat to the Soviets, the United States will face a more dangerous Soviet Union, one that is prepared to sacrifice whatever is necessary to maintain the arms competition. The recent suggestion by Soviet officials that they will adopt a launch-on-warning strategy as an answer to the new U.S. buildup is a development that will make both nations more insecure.

It is in the interests of U.S. security to send clear messages to the Soviet Union. But the United States cannot design arms arrangements to do this unless it clarifies its own intentions for itself. The Reagan administration is sending Soviet leaders mixed signals; on the one hand it says that it favors agreement with the Soviets based on the necessity of coexistence. On the other, high officials, including the president at times, talk about hastening the demise of the Soviet system. One of the most effective arms controls measures that the United States could now take would be to cease all statements about desiring or anticipating an end to the Soviet system or any suggestion that that result is a legitimate objective of U.S. policy.

An Official Statement

The president of the United States should make as forthright a statement as the Soviet chairman has made about the disastrous consequences of initiating a nuclear attack. President Reagan should announce that the avoidance of nuclear war is the most fundamental security objective of the United States and that the pretense that the United States expects to win the war is more likely to precipitate the war than to avoid it. The president should welcome all such statements from Soviet leaders and seek to negotiate a clear, unequivocal, joint statement on a common perception of the nuclear reality. Military doctrine, training manuals, and speeches of generals could be continually tested against such a statement. A joint official statement about nuclear war would discourage irresponsible statements about nuclear "victory" and "survival" through absurd, provocative evacuation plans and would create a channel for providing mutual reassurance. U.S. experts on the Soviet Union would no longer have to carry on a sterile debate in U.S. journals about what the Soviets think. The statement would provide the framework for a review of unilateral measures, including changes in defense doctrine and training, to give it credibility.

European Security

The artificial separation between "strategic" arms limitations and "theater" negotiations should be ended. The U.S.-Soviet arms race is of critical concern to Europeans. The NATO alliance is based on a set of military presuppositions that are now obsolete, but close and cooperative relations between Western Europe and the United States are more important than ever. Genuine partnership between the United States and Europe in forging a common strategy for moving to an alternative security system through arms reduction is essential. The day is over when Europeans can be induced to give blind support to U.S. proposals and strategies as a test of loyalty. Only in the process of working out a new security relationship with the Soviet Union can the United States build a healthier relationship with Europe.

Nowhere is the communications function of arms control more important than in the matter of European defense. Troop reductions, nuclear-free zones, and the shift to a nonnuclear defense cannot make a Soviet attack impossible, but they can perform other important functions. First, a process of denuclearization evidenced by the elimination of battlefield nuclear weapons would signify the abandonment

230 • *The Race for Security*

of the increasingly incredible strategy of threatening to blow up Germany to save it. That threat is more frightening to the German people than to the Soviets and therefore actually undermines effective deterrence. The more Europe's defense depends on nuclear weapons, the more opportunities are open to the Soviet Union to play upon the legitimate fears of the people of Western Europe.

However, a so-called conventional defense, a replay of World War II in modern dress, would also destroy Europe. Moreover, the costs of a conventional buildup in the West capable of redressing numerical imbalances or opposing potential Soviet forces in size and quality would pose an unacceptable financial strain on European governments. (Given the reality that an attacker must concentrate a huge superiority in tanks and that battlefield density imposes limitations on the numbers of tanks that can actually be deployed at any one time, the present numerical imbalance in favor of the Soviet Union does not constitute the military threat that numbers alone would suggest.)

Defining Security

The security of the West is not enhanced by a military strategy that bankrupts and divides the alliance. Proposals for steady annual increases in the military budget in a time of economic crisis are weakening, not strengthening, the alliance. Indeed, the deterrence capability of the West will depend increasingly upon the economic and political health of European societies. No one rates a Soviet invasion as more than a hypothetical possibility. Most advocates of a European arms buildup claim that political pressure resulting from the supposed military imbalance is the real threat. But the strength of European nations depends far less upon having extra forces or extra hardware than upon the most basic foundation of security: the capacity to manage the economy and to govern effectively. A conventional arms buildup would adversely affect both.

The problem of European defense as presently defined is literally insoluble. There is a huge mental abyss that separates the world of the actual risk assessment and the world of day-to-day military planning designed to deal with hypothetical risks—that is, "worst case" contingencies. Just as the agreements between East and West Germany a decade ago put to rest the myth of reunification and greatly increased stability in Europe, new agreements are now needed that will put to rest the myth of the Soviet invasion by creating a military environment in which such an event appears increasingly implausible. The technical disagreements over the conventional military balance that hold up the mutual and balanced force reduction (MBFR) negotiations could be compromised within the context of the larger negotiating framework proposed here. A new version of the Rapacki Plan, a 1958 proposal to make central Europe a nuclear-free zone, that would include the thinning out of forces, confidence-building measures, and a process of significant reductions of national force levels would reduce capabilities for attack and thereby clarify intentions.

At the end of the process, the military environment on the continent would more accurately reflect actual political assessments: the East–West frontier would hardly be an undefended border like that between the United States and Canada, but it would no longer be in a state of permanent mobilization. Despite the interminable MBFR negotiations, the process does not have to be prolonged. The difficult technical issues become soluble when a political judgment has been made at the highest level that security requires a lower state of military readiness in central Europe. Conventional troop deployments should reflect the actual political sentiment. The democracies of Western Europe have the financial and human resources to match those of the Soviets in a conventional arms race. But the people of Europe do not have the heart for an arms race because they do not see what it will gain them. Were the United States and the nations of Western Europe to make the negotiations for a less threatening military environment in central Europe a top priority, the Soviets would be under considerable pressure to be forthcoming.

Conclusion

Changes of force levels and deployments would signify an end to the long obsession with a security problem that is both unreal and insoluble as now defined. These changes would also reflect the political reality that the United States and the European allies view other security problems—the deterioration of the world economy, North–South relations, the crisis of both liberal capitalism and social democracy—as far more serious security threats than the suppositious Soviet invasion. Individual countries could, if they so choose, take additional measures to deter a Soviet attack by arming the population and instructing them in Yugoslav-style resistance strategies. As the Yugoslav case suggests, the greatest deterrent to a Soviet attack is the projection of a will to resist. Loose and irresponsible talk about the Finlandization of Europe does nothing to enhance deterrence. It sends the same sort of messages to the Soviets as the erroneous statement that the Soviets have a "wide margin of superiority."

As long as the U.S. nuclear arsenal remains and the fate of Europe is seen as crucial to the world balance of power, the Soviets can never be sure that the United States would not strike the Soviet Union in the event of an attack on Europe. If a president decides to risk Armageddon it will not be because 300,000 U.S. troops are threatened or because of a nuclear weapon's already having been exploded on European soil, but because of a view, however, misguided, that national "survival" requires it. The task of arms control is to work our way out of this insane system under which security rests on deterrence and deterrence rests on the threats to end everyone's history, including our own.   *(June 1982)*

Arms without Control?
Christoph Bertram

Arms control is now suffering from three serious maladies: (1) the United States and the Soviet Union no longer seem to have the political will necessary for meaningful negotiations; (2) technology is fast outstripping the traditional instruments for limiting the arms competition and for verifying agreed limits; and (3) practically all the proposals presented in the current debate, while often intelligent or well-meaning or even both, offer highly inadequate directions for how to emerge from the present deadlock. My own proposal in these circumstances is twofold: to do everything to maintain what agreed restrictions on arms competition exist, and to proceed, unilaterally if necessary, toward a more rational concept and a more stable arsenal of nuclear weapons than we now have.

The Political Environment

Compared with the public rhetoric in Western political debates only a few months ago, it is amazing how routine and tired the call for arms control now seems. To some extent this is the product of emotional exhaustion, caused by the feverish controversy over NATO's nuclear modernization program in 1983. To some extent it follows from the realization that the world is not on the brink of nuclear disaster.

Moreover, the successful implementation of the first stages of NATO's nuclear program has had a decelerating effect on the attitudes of the two major powers. The Soviet Union, by demanding up to the last minute of Geneva negotiations a de jur recognition of its monopoly on land-based medium-range nuclear systems, has painted itself into a corner from which it will not emerge for a long time.

The United States, under the Reagan administration, seems content to leave the Soviets locked out of arms control. The United States would be wrong to offer eager concessions now. The administration, however, has not even been willing to offer the Communist leaders in the Kremlin, embattled as they are by economic squeezes and by the fear of being left behind in the technological race, any real indication of interest in a mutually acceptable agreement in the not too distant future. The Reagan administration has interpreted the firmness of most European governments over the NATO modernization program as further proof that one needs to be tough with the Soviets. It has dismissed the SALT II Treaty in a cavalier fashion (although it has observed some of its stipulations). It is, through its fascination with space-based antimissile defenses, signaling its disregard for the ABM Treaty. It is adamantly opposed to any restrictions on U.S. technological innovation, such as antisatellite warfare. Moreover, in all its proposals for strategic arms reductions, the Reagan administration has indicated that it seeks not a mere regulation of the nuclear arms race but a restructuring of Soviet strategic forces—an objective that is understandably both attractive to the West and unattractive, if not plainly unacceptable, to the Soviet Union. Whatever one may think of the intrinsic merits of current U.S. arms control proposals, they do not offer many incentives to a suspicious, diplomatically cornered, and politically uncertain Soviet Union. What is more, the administration makes few bones about the fact that this is precisely the message they want to convey to the Soviet leadership.

Although it is difficult to imagine that Moscow and Washington will never again sit down and negotiate in earnest over how to regulate the arms competition, this is likely to be a matter of years rather than months. It is true that a change in the White House would also produce a change in the official U.S. attitude toward a more constructive search for arms control possibilities. But—at this writing—such a change appears unlikely. It also remains uncertain whether the Soviet Union would be able (another succession crisis?) or willing (a bigger role for the military?) to respond constructively. Arms control, clearly, is not for today, only possibly for tomorrow.

The Technology Dynamics

Even if relations between the United States and the Soviet Union improve dramatically, arms control will have to contend with trends in military technology visible today that are likely to complicate the task of arms regulation and crisis prevention.

The first of these is the trend toward even shorter reaction times. The flight time of intercontinental missiles from launch to target is now about twenty minutes, that of intermediate ballistic missiles about ten minutes. The growing accuracy of delivery systems—toward a CEP (circular error probable) close to zero in the 1990s—means that reaction times, too, are being shortened drastically. If you want your missiles to survive an attack, you must fire them before they are destroyed by the attacker. This applies to nuclear as well as nonnuclear conflict. The main arms race today is less about numbers than about speed: who can hit, who can react more quickly.

Current speculations about a space-based antimissile system underline this race for speed. If you want to destroy an enemy missile from space before it has left the atmosphere and discharged its separate warheads on ballistic trajectories, you currently have no more than a few hundred seconds to identify, trace and destroy it. (The boost-phase could be reduced to forty seconds!) If you want to destroy incoming warheads from the ground, you have to deal with an attack that approaches its targets at the speed of 5 kilometers per second. The risk that computers, not human beings, will take the fateful decision of whether or not to launch a nuclear war will become real.

The second trend is toward the interchangeability of military systems, particularly of nuclear and nonnuclear weapons. It is true that this has always applied to dual-capable aircraft. But it is becoming significantly more pronounced. To compensate for the low accuracy of delivery systems, nuclear warheads were needed in the past to assure destruction of an enemy target. Now, precision-guided nonnuclear missiles and rockets have attained an accuracy rate that makes it possible for nonnuclear warheads to have the intended effect. However, the delivery systems of both nuclear and nonnuclear munitions look very much alike to the attacker, and they will be targeted not only against conventional but also against nuclear objectives. The U.S. modern cruise missile is a case in point: The same missile is envisaged both as a nuclear and as a nonnuclear carrier. General Bernard Rogers's plans to deal more effectively in Europe with the enemy's second-echelon forces are also based on ballistic delivery systems that, for the attacked, look very much like nuclear weapons before they explode. The Soviet Union is known to have concentrated increasingly on nonnuclear options to destroy the theater nuclear potential in Western Europe—again through missiles and aircraft that, before impact, look very similar to nuclear delivery systems. As a result, one of the few thresholds of warfare, the "firebreak" between nonnuclear and nuclear weapons, is rapidly turning into a fuzzy gray area. Will the defender take the risk of assuming that an attack which *could* be nuclear is only going to be conventional?

The third trend is toward dependence on highly sophisticated command, control, and communication in the conduct of strategic, theater, and local war. This raises a new and troublesome problem of vulnerability, much more serious than that of major weapon systems. While even missiles can hide behind the screen of mobility, major command centers are critically limited in their ability to evade attack. Redundancy may make up in part for this deficiency, but the basic dilemma persists: modern warfare is becoming increasingly dependent on the survival, in war, of highly vulnerable command and control.

The Proposals

The arms control of the future must seek to address these issues. However, most of the proposals debated today among governments, experts, and the media still refer more to the past than to the future. While they may have value in promoting agreement or in raising particular problems in the public debate, this limitation has to be kept in mind.

Most of the current proposals concern nuclear weapons. They range from incremental approaches such as merging the INF (intermediate-range nuclear forces) negotiations with the talks on strategic forces (START) and a build-down of nuclear arsenals through mutual agreement, to more radical suggestions such as that of a nuclear freeze or even regional denuclearization by the creation of nuclear-free zones. None of these proposals, I believe, can point the way to a more promising arms control future.

Linking INF and START is a popular idea for those who regard both strategic and long-range theater nuclear weapons as belonging to the same category. By the rules of geography, the advocates are likely to be situated in Moscow and, possibly, in Western Europe—but they are not in the United States.

Indeed, to link both types of negotiations would present the United States with a choice that the Western alliance has been determined in the past to avoid: that of a trade-off between strategic and theater nuclear forces that a joint ceiling for both would imply. It would invite the United States to decide whether the strategic deterrence of attacks against its homeland is more important than the strategic deterrence of attacks against Western Europe. Linking the negotiations would at best be awkward and potentially highly disruptive for the political cohesion of the West. In addition, the combination would not speed up the negotiations but protract them further.

The "build-down" proposal that is now supposedly integrated into the U.S. START position is an ingenious method for ensuring that weapons modernization not lead to ever-larger nuclear arsenals, and that weapon systems with many warheads be discouraged in favor of those with fewer warheads. Each new warhead installed would oblige the parties to eliminate, at different ratios, more than one warhead from their inventory.

As a proposal for START, however, it suffers from the deficiences of earlier negotiation positions presented by the Reagan administration. The Soviet Union rightly regards it as a means to impose on Soviet strategic forces a new and different structure. Because of the ratios favoring a shift away from land-based missiles to submarine-based missiles, the Soviet Union would have to pay an extraordinarily high price for its heavy reliance on land-based missiles. It is conceivable that the ratios might be revised to apply the same reduction factor across the board for all categories and thus become more negotiable for the Soviet Union. But the best the build-down would achieve even under those circumstances would be to correct one of the misguided developments of the past, namely, the multiplication of warheads on every missile.

The nuclear freeze, like all freezes, gambles on the future's being worse than the present. It freezes nuclear arsenals in their present, highly unsatisfactory configuration—a large, fixed vulnerable land-based weapons packed with nuclear warheads—and prevents any modernization, even modernization toward a more stable structure of nuclear forces. It is thus a desperate proposal and a profoundly apolitical one: Since things can only get worse, let us stick to what we have. There is no doubt that what we have is more than what we need, but also that it is badly configured and in need of reform if the mistakes of the past should not stay with us indefinitely. Moreover, a nuclear freeze, if it wants to prevent any qualitative change, is simply not verifiable; a fully verifiable nuclear freeze is simply a contradiction in terms.

Nuclear-free zones are, in the first and possibly only instance, a device not for arms control but for a change of political affiliation. A Nordic nuclear-free zone, limited to the Scandinavian countries, would have little military effect—unless it included the Soviet bases in Northern Europe as well, which is totally unrealistic to expect. Instead, it would loosen the political links between the Nordic countries that are members of the Western alliance and their partners in NATO. A nuclear-free corridor of 150 kilometers on both sides of the East–West divide, as proposed by the Palme Commission, would above all serve to crystallize German nostalgia for a neutral zone in the center of Europe. Its desired military effect would be much better served by unilateral withdrawal of short-range nuclear weapons from the Western arsenal than by protracted and complex negotiations between East and West.

Omitted from this critical appraisal are three nonnuclear negotiations: the Vienna talks on the reduction of conventional manpower in Europe, the Geneva negotiations on banning chemical warfare, and the Conference for Disarmament and Confidence-Building Measures in Europe, which is taking place in Stockholm.

All three have produced interesting approaches such as the notions, of confidence-building and of verification-by-challenge, and progress has been made through Soviet readiness to accept a measure of on-site inspection. However, even if one or all of them should succeed in the near future, the effect will be measured more in terms of political symbolism than by a significant control of arms. However valuable it would be to be able to demonstrate, for the first time since 1974, that East and West can agree on certain measures of military détente, this would remain peripheral to the major problem of regulating the nuclear competition.

The Priorities

The description of the state of East–West arms control presented here is not a cheerful one. The political will is absent for any major initiative, the dynamics of military technology threaten to reduce the political control over events in war, and the set of current proposals are either not promising or irrelevant to the new problems or both. What in these circumstances should be the Western priorities in arms control?

First, the United States should try to maintain the treaties and agreements that have been negotiated in the past. True, none of these agreements has been perfect. But each has been helpful. Even the much maligned SALT II treaty has served to provide a basis for holding the other side accountable. In fact, the United States, which refused to ratify the treaty, is now accusing the Soviet Union, which was willing to ratify, of having failed to observe some of its stipulations! The Antiballistic Missile Treaty of 1972 remains in force although both sides, in particular the United States, are displaying signs of restlessness. It provides the only available yardstick for constraining the search for active missile defenses.

But there is another, important reason why these agreements should not be dismissed by the West. International order will only develop through the respect of open covenants arrived at by both sides. It cannot build on broken contracts. Not even Soviet violations would justify an abrogation by the West unless these violations were of such magnitude as to deprive the whole agreement of any sense. This is not the case in any of the U.S. claims made recently against the Soviet Union.

Second, the West must rethink the weight that it gives to the verifiability of arms control agreements. The trend in Washington at the moment seems to be to make the ability to monitor compliance perfectly the supreme criterion for even entering into arms control negotiations; witness the recent reluctance to talk to the Soviets about controlling military competition in space. This is a questionable approach for two reasons. For one, it tends to discourage the search for a mutually acceptable verification regime before negotiations even begin. As the SALT II Treaty has shown, verification depends on the constraints agreed, and it would be disturbing if verifiability became the alibi for rejecting the search for such constraints in the first place. For another, there is the danger of confusing verification and the response to noncompliance. As the recent statements by the U.S. Defense Department on alleged Soviet violations have indicated, the problem has not been to identify violations so much as to decide how to respond if the explanation offered by the Soviets were deemed unsatisfactory. The real questions about verification are different: What degree of uncertainty is tolerable? And what response to noncompliance is warranted?

Third, it will be necessary to halt the trend toward shorter and shorter reaction time: arms control must seek to regain time for crisis management. This can be done through the negotiation of arms limitation, such as a regulation of military competition in space, agreements on lower warhead-ceilings per missile, even through an agreed increase in the number of missiles permitted to each side provided they carry no more than one warhead. It could also be done through the agreement of certain crisis procedures between East and West: a more reliable hotline, as proposed by the Reagan administration; nuclear risk reduction centers in Washington and Moscow, as suggested by a group of U.S. senators; and permanent communication through standing commissions between the major powers as well as in Europe.

But both these steps have to wait until the political climate between East and West has improved to make such bilateral or multilateral agreements possible. In the meantime, there is no reason why the West should not undertake unilaterally those steps that could lead to a more robust nuclear posture and that can be afforded in terms of security. Indeed, unilateral arms control is probably the most promising approach that is left. After all, arms are designed and deployed by unilateral decision. It is easier to decide oneself that one can do away with some weapon systems or do without some others than to negotiate about weapons limits with a military rival.

To reintroduce time into the military decision unilaterally can mean a number of things. It can mean strengthening conventional forces in Europe, capable of meeting but not conducting a surprise attack in order to weaken dependence on the early use of nuclear weapons. It can mean disposing of all but a few short-range delivery systems for nuclear weapons in Europe—regardless of whether the

Soviets follow suit. A U.S. decision to forgo the MX missile program of multiwarhead fixed ICBMs and to speed up instead the Midgetman project of one-warhead, mobile missiles would be a contribution to strategic stability even if the Soviets should persist in maintaining their present nuclear programs.

Would effective ballistic missile defense help to gain time? This is doubtful, for two reasons. First, no such system can be leakproof, and offensive weapons can still, at much lower cost, overcome the defenses that are conceivable even in the more distant future (although some protection for command and control centers could be desirable). Second, ballistic missile defenses, such as the currently much discussed space-based variety, depend themselves on such short reaction times that they do not gain time for the defender but increase the pressure for ever-faster and more automated responses.

Would a unilateral undertaking by the West not to use nuclear weapons first help to gain time? Probably not, because such a commitment is inherently incredible in the nuclear age. Nuclear weapons are weapons of last resort—and herein lies their deterrence value. Deterrence means precisely that you cannot be sure that the other side will not use nuclear weapons if pushed, and no formal undertaking will provide certainty to the contrary.

As these last two examples show, not every unilateral restraint helps to gain time. But there are those that do. A Western effort to increase the margin of time for political control, evaluation, and crisis communication would, I believe, be a major contribution to arms control in the 1980s and one that does not have to wait until East–West agreements become possible again. It would also contribute to rebuilding the much strained political consensus in the West over the reliance on nuclear weapons for security. One of the driving fears of the antinuclear movement, which also has affected many in Western societies who used to be uncritical toward nuclear weapons, is precisely that political control over nuclear decisions could be replaced by computer control, that the loss of time implied by modern technology leads to an abdication of politics in favor of automated programs. If we do nothing to halt the current trend, we risk not only losing the time we need to deal responsibly with international crisis and nuclear deterrence, but also the public support we need in order to maintain the credibility of deterrence itself.   *(October 1984)*

Reciprocal National Restraint: An Alternative Path
Herbert Scoville, Jr.

Every day the competition between the United States and the Soviet Union to develop and procure new nuclear weapons becomes more intense, and the risk increases that a nuclear conflict will break out either by accident or out of fear that the other nation will launch first. In addition to these growing dangers, new scientific analyses of the effects of nuclear war are reinforcing our very worst expectations of the extent of the disaster that a nuclear war can present to the future of humanity.

At the same time, the prospects for controlling these weapons and reducing the risk of their use are growing dimmer, and even existing restraints are in danger. The 1972 Antiballistic Missile Treaty, which has successfully improved U.S. security and provided the foundation for nuclear arms control, is in serious danger of being circumscribed or abrogated by missile defense programs in progress in the United States and the Soviet Union. The remaining limits on strategic offensive weapons embodied in the SALT I and II treaties are hanging by a thread, which may soon be cut by the Reagan administration, and the dialogue between government officials on both sides is venomous and cloaked in a mantle of public self-justification to serve narrow national and international political interests.

The leaders of the United States and the Soviet Union—and for that matter the leaders of most other countries around the world—are not acting as if they understood either the realities of nuclear war or the inadequacies of the policies they are following. None seems to recognize the urgency in dealing with the ever-increasing risks, and the steps taken today on both sides to procure new nuclear weapons will not easily be reversed five or ten years from now.

The resumption of the Geneva talks is a useful sign, but early results cannot be expected. If the nuclear arms race is to be halted, reliance can no longer be placed solely on negotiations and formal agreements. As valuable as formal agreements are, specific actions to reduce the risk of nuclear war should not await dotting all the *i*'s and crossing all the *t*'s of a negotiated and ratified treaty that satisfies the views of every extreme of the political spectrum. The danger we face is too urgent to wait for this to happen. Instead, the achievement of meaningful controls will require political leaders to make decisions that the people of the world want and deserve—to lead first by action and example.

The leaders of the United States and the Soviet Union should attack the arms race with a method that has been used effectively in the past toward the achievement of lasting arms control agreements—reciprocal national restraint (RNR). Independent national action to adopt a new nuclear policy or to discontinue a new weapon program would provide the basis for lasting arms control agreements and the reversal of the arms race. Such reciprocal national restraint would perhaps at first be relatively limited in scope, but once the process was underway, the cumulative effects could become very significant. I believe that a realistic model of such restraint can be applied to present strategic and arms control issues. Although current opportunities for this approach are encouraging, its success will require foresight and commitment.

Past Progress in Arms Control

Nuclear restraint has not been the hallmark of the superpowers' nuclear weapons policies in the past, and it is becoming less so every day. It is true that, since

Hiroshima and Nagasaki, all nations have refrained from using nuclear weapons in a conflict, and this critically important precedent should not be undervalued. But in every other aspect of nuclear policy, restraint has been wanting. History presents little evidence of a "substantially new manner of thinking" about atomic weapons that Albert Einstein warned was needed. Certainly, neither of the superpowers had demonstrated restraint as both have piled weapon on weapon and delivery system on delivery system. Both have developed plans for use of those weapons on each other's homeland, on the battlefields of Europe, the Middle East, and Asia, and on the seas around the world. These actions have provided a poor example to other nations that support nonproliferation and international nuclear constraint.

Significant international agreements to control and eliminate the threat of a nuclear conflict have been few and far between. The ABM Treaty of 1972 has been the most successful. It limits the development and deployment of ballistic missile defenses, including space-based systems. However, even this treaty, which President Reagan's Commission on Strategic Forces (the Scowcroft Commission) described as "one of the most successful arms control agreements," is in trouble. President Reagan's Strategic Defense Initiative, or "Star Wars" program, directly threatens the ABM Treaty. Although the Soviets have proposed nothing as grandiose as Star Wars, their missile defense programs also raise some treaty compliance questions.

The Limited Test Ban Treaty of 1963 was useful in halting nuclear explosions in the atmosphere, in outerspace, and under water, but it did not prevent underground testing, which both superpowers have pursued at a more rapid pace than ever before. The 1970 Nonproliferation Treaty was an important move toward international control of nuclear weapons, but unfortunately a number of important nonnuclear nations have refused to become parties. Furthermore, the United States and the Soviet Union have not lived up to their commitment in that treaty to negotiate seriously to limit their nuclear programs. As a consequence, the NPT is coming under fire from nonnuclear nations, undermining the upcoming NPT Review Conference in the fall of 1985.

The extended length of the negotiations process between the United States and the Soviet Union is a serious problem. SALT I, which included both the ABM Treaty and the Interim Agreement on Offensive Weapons, took two and a half years to negotiate. Even with this groundwork, SALT II took seven years to negotiate and still has not been ratified.

Meanwhile, new weapon developments have been moving forward without any restrictions and have outpaced the negotiations to control them. First came MIRVs and later, very accurate guidance systems that threaten command and control centers and the land-based missile leg of deterrent. Next came air-, land-, and sea-based cruise missiles, which present extraordinarily difficult verification problems. Weaponization of space is moving ahead much faster than efforts for outer space arms control. It is clear that present approach to arms control cannot keep up with this pace.

Bargaining Chips

Arguments are frequently made that new developments in military technology can provide bargaining chips and inducements to get the other side to negotiate seriously. Even if a weapon program has little or no military value or even degrades security by increasing nuclear instability and the risk of war, that program is often promoted in the name of arms control. In fact, often the lesser the military value of a weapon, the more vigorously is the bargaining chip rationale argued.

The MX missile is a perfect example. Each MX will have ten accurate warheads capable of destroying Soviet ICBMs in their silos and other important strategic targets in the Soviet Union. The missiles will be based in vulnerable fixed silos, an impractical basing mode for retaliatory weapons. For these reasons the MX can only be seen by the Soviets as a system that threatens their nuclear forces through a first strike. And for these reasons, the mere existence of this weapon, with its inherent vulnerability and its offensive capability, could encourage the United States to use it, or the Soviet Union to launch its own missiles, in a future crisis. Faced with this danger, both the United States and the Soviet Union would be better off without this destabilizing weapon. Nevertheless, the MX is being used for negotiating leverage. Although official U.S. policy states that the MX is not a bargaining chip, administration officials and members of Congress have repeatedly claimed that the missiles are needed to show U.S. resolve and obtain leverage at the negotiating table in Geneva. The idea that more arms will lead to more arms control, particularly with regard to the MX, is a poor rationale for a new weapon and a losing strategy for arms control.

Another bargaining chip example is the U.S. decision in 1969 to deploy the Safeguard ABM. Henry Kissinger took a revisionist view of history when he wrote on September 23, 1984, in the *Washington Post*, "President Nixon finally submitted a plan for an American ABM to Congress in 1969. After Congress went along with the President, the Soviets opened up the very negotiations they had rejected two years earlier." Although the Soviets had resisted Secretary of Defense Robert McNamara's overtures at Glassboro in 1967 and elsewhere, they did agree to start negotiations on ABMs in June 1968, more than a year before President Nixon sought the Safeguard program and the Senate approved it by a fifty to forty-nine vote.

The Soviet Union will never agree to any arms limitation that would leave it in a position of military inferiority, either real or only apparent. The Soviets are politically sensitive about their superpower status and will do everything to promote the perception of equality with the United States. Although they will not always build forces symmetrical to those of the United States, they will insist on the appearance of overall strategic parity. They will not allow the United States to have an obvious lead in such technological developments as MIRVs, ABMs, cruise missiles, or future space weapons. Promoting weapons as arms control bargaining chips is like playing a dangerous game of Russian roulette, with world survival at stake.

How Reciprocal National Restraint Works

Alternatives to the bargaining chip theory do exist. The idea of reciprocal national restraint is just the opposite of the bargaining chip theory because it takes the initiative to discontinue rather than proceed with a weapon program. As long as both sides are buying new weapons that threaten each other, the arms race will continue unabated, rendering arms control negotiations ineffective. Negotiating limits on an ongoing weapon program is extraordinarily difficult because the negotiators must always attempt to capture a moving target. Conversely, reciprocal national restraint, or even national restraint by one of the parties, would help to corral a weapon program, thus providing the impetus for the parties to reach a meaningful agreement. The initiative to stop a weapon program would better place the United States in a position to negotiate a formal agreement.

RNRs can be successfully implemented if several guidelines are followed. Decisions and pronouncements on national restraint should be made by the president, thereby demonstrating that the act of restraint is a national policy. An action of restraint backed by presidential authority would ensure the policy's most effective application, although congressional restraint, such as withholding funds for a weapon program, could also be effective.

Even though every effort should be made to obtain reciprocation to an action of restraint, the initial move should not always be dependent on a response. Suspended procurement of new weapons can be in the United States' interest regardless of how the Soviets may respond. The cancellation of the MX missile, a dangerously destabilizing weapon, is a good example. Although reciprocation is not the most important aspect of a national restraint policy, the action would have to be two-sided over time. No country can make unilateral move after unilateral move. Eventually, some response must come from the other side.

Reciprocation should be applied on a very broad basis rather than requiring precise symmetry in actions of restraint. Because the security goals of the two nations are not identical, the respective military forces enlisted to satisfy these goals are necessarily different. Furthermore, the political factors affecting military decisions in the two countries are distinctively clear. For example, the Soviets concentrate heavily on land-based missiles whereas the United States emphasizes its outstanding sea power.

This asymmetrical approach can produce domestic political difficulties. An important factor impeding the ratification of the SALT II Treaty was the provision that allowed the Soviet Union to keep existing large ICBMs while denying them to the United States. Despite the fact that this provision was negotiated at Vladivostock by President Ford and Henry Kissinger as a trade-off against an agreement permitting the United States and NATO to retain all so-called forward-based systems, domestic political arguments against ratification of the treaty were based upon the perception that such inequality was unacceptable. National leaders must confront this perception factor when applying national restraint, though they must also understand that precise symmetry cannot be a criterion if this approach is to succeed.

An effective policy of reciprocal national restraint does not necessarily have to lead to a formal arms control agreement. Our objective is not to have arms control agreements; it is to make nuclear war less likely. Nevertheless, reciprocal national restraint should not mean that more formal commitments should be forgone. In fact, such restraint can be seen as a valuable first step in facilitating the eventual achievement and ratification of arms control treaties. No longer will arms programs be barreling ahead while negotiators are securing all the details that must be sought in a formal treaty.

A number of cases demonstrate the success of the national restraint approach. At the initiative of President Eisenhower the United States and the Soviet Union agreed in the fall of 1958 to suspend further nuclear tests for one year. A year later President Eisenhower announced that the United States would no longer be bound by this moratorium, but the United States did not recommence testing without prior announcement. In August 1961, after the French began testing, the Soviet Union began an extensive test program and the United States soon followed suit. Although this preliminary attempt at reciprocal national restraint was not an immediate success, it helped set the stage for the Limited Test Ban Treaty of 1963.

In June 1963 at American University, President Kennedy announced that the United States would stop atmospheric nuclear testing provided the Soviet Union exercised similar restraint. President Kennedy said, "Such a declaration is no substitute for a formal binding treaty, but I hope it will help us achieve one." In a few months this simple show of restraint became a multinational agreement, the Limited Test Ban Treaty, that has subsequently been joined by most of the world. This example demonstrates how national restraint provided the momentum to achieve a formal agreement that has, in my view, been a very important factor in preventing the spread of nuclear weapons to other nations.

The Limited Test Ban Treaty is not the only successful example of this technique. In 1969 President Nixon made the national decision that the United States would no longer carry out any programs to develop, test, or procure offensive biological or toxin weapons. This decision was not made just to promote arms control; the United States simply did not find this type of warfare to be in its security interest. This initiative was followed within two years with the successful negotiation of the Biological Weapons Convention, by which more than one hundred nations have agreed to discontinue offensive biological warfare programs.

Specific Application of RNR

The subject that has generated the most public attention in the last fifteen years is offensive strategic weapons. We have now had SALT I, SALT II, START, and negotiations on intermediate-range nuclear forces. Little real, lasting progress has been made in controlling offensive strategic weapons. Ongoing weapons programs, such as the U.S. MX and the Trident II and the Soviet SS-24 and SS-25 missiles, have a strong momentum that has continued on through the inevitably long negotiations, and the prospect of strategic defenses will only encourage more offensive weapon developments.

A national decision could be made tomorrow that henceforth the United States would not test any MIRVed ballistic missiles. MIRVed ballistic missiles, especially new types with more advanced characteristics and better guidance systems that threaten the retaliatory capability of the other side, are the most destabilizing of nuclear weapons. The United States could make a decision to halt the testing of all such missiles, old and new, provided the Soviet Union responded in kind. A MIRV test ban would effectively halt the deployment of the MX missile and the further development of the U.S. Trident II, as well as any future Soviet counterpart. It would stop improvements in the U.S. Minuteman III and the deployed Soviet SS-17, SS-18, and SS-19 ICBMs, and the new ten-warhead SS-24.

A MIRV test ban would promote some other weapon systems, such as the single-warhead Midgetman and the Soviet SS-25. Midgetman enthusiasts might support such a move because less threatening single-warhead missiles would be emphasized over the dangerous MIRV. As preferable as single-warhead systems might be, the missile test ban could go one step further. Once both countries had stopped MIRV testing, a ban might be extended to the testing of all long-range ballistic missiles.

A total missile ban would be easier to verify than a partial ban. As an illustration, suppose that the mayor of New York City had a choice of either enforcing a total ban on cars parking in the street (garages would provide all legal space) or allowing all cars built before 1985 to park in the street. If the second choice were made, the mayor would have to create a major enforcement process that could be too cumbersome. A total ban, however, would be much easier to enforce. Likewise, if some missile tests were allowed there would be trouble distinguishing whether a given test was of a new missile or was a repeat of an old one. Currently, arguments of this nature exist with the Soviet Union over whether its SS-25 is a new missile or an acceptable modification of the old SS-13. If all ballistic missile tests were banned, the verification process would be more manageable. This is the kind of initiative that may propel the whole strategic arms control movement forward.

A comprehensive test ban is another example of where the United States could take national action of restraint. Negotiators who were involved in the comprehensive test ban negotiations in 1978 have stated that, if there had been a political decision to do so, the United States could have reached an agreement within six months. Halting U.S. and Soviet tests would be a very important move toward the establishment of a favorable climate for slowing the proliferation of nuclear weapons to additional nations. Although it calls for a total change in the policy of the Reagan administration, a decision to stop testing has been made in the past and could be made again.

Since the primary objective of arms control is to reduce the risk that nuclear weapons might actually be used, a program of reciprocal national restraint might provide the basis for the eventual declared policy of no-first-use. No-first-use states that nuclear weapons will not be used unless a possible aggressor uses them first. Such a declared policy would reduce the threat of a first strike and the likelihood that nuclear weapons would be used in a battlefield situation. Moreover, a no-first-use policy would help to improve present U.S.-Soviet relations.

What practical action, then, could be taken in the direction of a no-first-use policy? First, U.S. policymakers should remember that the Soviet Union has already stated that it would not be the first to use nuclear weapons. Although this may only be a political statement, it is on record. This presents the United States with options to reciprocate in practical fashion.

One practical step could involve so-called battlefield nuclear weapons. U.S. military commanders are already concerned about the exposed condition of these weapons near the East–West border in Europe. They fear that their positions would be rapidly overrun, forcing a "use them or lose them" situation. In the event of such a conflict, the president would be under strong pressure to release the weapons promptly, thus starting a nuclear conflict that would be impossible to control. The United States might make a national decision to withdraw such battlefield weapons to reduce the threat of escalation into a general nuclear war. This action of reciprocal national restraint could be a concrete step toward a no-first-use policy or toward establishing a nonnuclear zone.

Another option that would facilitate movement toward no-first-use would be to give up the idea that the United States must deploy the so-called neutron bombs (enhanced radiation weapons), designed to make it more credible that the United States would use nuclear weapons in the event of a nuclear conflict in Europe. The security argument in favor of the neutron bomb is that it could be used effectively against tanks with less collateral damage and would therefore deter the Soviets from conventional attack in Europe. The neutron bomb is an overrated antitank weapon because if it does not destroy the tank, an irradiated tank crew might not die for several days, an unsatisfactory battlefield situation. More important, the NATO allies want no part of this weapon, so the administration has produced and stored them in the United States in the hope that some day the nation can deploy them in Europe. The United States could therefore without any loss of security announce that it was giving up the neutron bomb program to demonstrate its interest in reducing the risk of early first use of nuclear weapons and to encourage the Soviet Union also to take concrete steps to demonstrate their commitment to a no-first-use policy.

Finally, one cannot address strategic arms control without addressing the problems of ballistic missile defenses, particularly President Reagan's Star Wars proposal. This program, which was launched by President Reagan's speech of March 1983, created a wholly new impetus to the arms race. If the Star Wars program proceeds, there is no question that arms control as we hope for it in the future will only be a dream of the past. Clearly, if ABM defenses move forward on either side an arms race in both offensive and defensive weapons will be set off. Antiballistic missile systems and weapons for space warfare are overriding problems that we have to circumscribe if nuclear arms are to be controlled.

Fortunately, the ABM Treaty of 1972 is still in existence. It bans nationwide defenses and the testing and deployment of space-based and mobile antiballistic systems. Thus the initial task is to exercise national restraint on programs that would undermine this treaty. Both the United States and the Soviet Union must adopt such a stance. Actions such as construction of the Soviet Krasnoyarsk radar and the U.S. Pave Paws radars, which appear to violate the treaty, must be avoided. If questionable events are observed, they should be promptly and frankly dealt with in the Standing Consultative Commission and every effort made to resolve the problem in a manner that preserves the basic objectives of the treaty.

Antiballistic missile programs must not establish schedules for future treaty violations. Public announcements that the United States will disregard the treaty, or simply amend it to serve the nation's desires, can only hasten its demise and nullify any attempts to control nuclear weapons. Blind infatuation with space as a military theater cannot be allowed to destroy the basic fabrication of U.S. security. Reciprocal national restraint is essential, and it is none too soon for the leaders of both countries to reconfirm in parallel announcements their intention of maintaining and fortifying the ABM Treaty and refraining from actions that undermine it.

Another program closely related to Star Wars is the development of antisatellite systems, those that destroy space vehicles. The United States is much more dependent than the Soviet Union on satellites, both for military and civil uses. Furthermore, satellites are the United States' main window into the Soviet Union. They are vital to U.S. national security. An arms race to develop means of shooting down satellites in space is clearly not to the advantage of the United States. Therefore, every effort should be made to achieve an ASAT ban. Such negotiations are already complicated by verification problems. If either side continues its antisatellite testing program, ASAT systems will be increasingly difficult to control. This is an excellent opportunity for national restraint.

In this case the Soviet Union was first to the punch. Since 1982 the Soviets have not conducted any tests of antisatellite systems, and they have stated that they have done this to promote negotiations. Thus, they have set an example of national restraint. The United States should reciprocate now given the tremendous gain resulting from controls on ASAT systems. Any risks in this action are minor compared with the risks of accelerating the arms race. It is encouraging that Congress has already taken an active role in trying to restrain the ASAT competition.

Weapon programs need not be the only object of reciprocal national restraint. Restraint must also be demonstrated in the political relations between the United States and the Soviet Union. Confrontational rhetoric must stop, and arms control negotiations should not be allowed to become a public forum for self-justification and satisfaction of narrow domestic purposes. The present frosty climate must be altered, because if poor relations continue, the two sides will find it more difficult to recognize that their strongest common interest is to avoid nuclear war. By building upon that common interest, new developments will improve the climate for the discussion of all issues, thus establishing an atmosphere suitable to confront the particular problems of controlling specific weapons.

Nuclear weapons cannot remain a political tool for domination in the international arena. The suicidal hope that the procurement of more new weapons will force the other side out of the arms race must be abandoned. None of the specific proposals mentioned here has much chance of achieving success unless there is mutual understanding of the catastrophic nature of nuclear war and the political will to take significant steps toward control.

Reciprocal national restraint can be an important step toward "a substantially new manner of thinking" that Einstein warned was needed. The public must understand that national restraint is not a policy that sells U.S. security down the river, but rather is a policy that increases that security. It is a safer policy than procuring more weapons that make nuclear war more likely. Reciprocal national restraint is our best hope for progress in the years ahead.   *(June 1985)*

Arms Control: Toward a Redefinition
Gary Hart

The Reemergence of Arms Control

To a degree that few in this country anticipated even a few years ago, the control of nuclear weapons has reemerged as one of the most urgent issues of our time. At first glance, the American public's turnabout on this issue seems little short of breathtaking. As recently as the 1980 presidential campaign, a large segment of the U.S. electorate seemed to view arms control and its central achievement, the SALT II Treaty, as direct causes of the decline in U.S. military power and international political will. The SALT process, it was alleged, had permitted the Soviet Union first to match and then to surpass the United States in virtually all categories of nuclear weaponry.

Today, by contrast, we are witnessing an unprecedented outpouring of concern about an accelerating arms race and the possibility of nuclear war. Demonstrations, local referenda, and "teach-ins" nationwide testify that the demand for arms control—and against arbitrary increases in nuclear weapons—is alive and well. Moreover, it is articulate, broadly based, and increasingly well-organized.

The reemergence of arms control as a central issue on the national agenda is the result of several distinct though related developments. The first development was President Carter's decision to withdraw the SALT II Treaty from Senate consideration in the wake of the Soviet invasion of Afghanistan in December 1979. This decision effectively halted the twenty-year U.S.-Soviet effort to limit strategic nuclear weapons. At first, the interruption in negotiations caused little domestic anxiety. It was perceived as a kind of prolonged recess, during which U.S. leaders could evaluate failures, reassess objectives and reformulate strategy. However, when the new Reagan administration failed to identify the pursuit of arms control as an important policy objective, the American public began to grow uneasy. The administration believed—incorrectly as it turned out—that the lack of visible constituency for SALT in the United States indicated a more general distrust of and disregard for arms control. In part because of this assumption, President Reagan offered no arms control policy during the first eighteen months in office.

Second, some senior administration officials indicated the belief that it was possible to wage and survive a "limited" nuclear war through a combination of "surgical" nuclear strikes, improved command, control, and communications and active civil defense measures. To the public, the administration's rhetoric signaled the replacement of the traditional U.S. doctrine of nuclear deterrence with an ill-defined strategy for "fighting and winning" a nuclear war.

Third, the administration proposed a significant expansion of U.S. strategic nuclear forces to counter perceived Soviet superiority. The Department of Defense requested and received funding to begin production of the B-1B bomber and the MX missile, to accelerate the procurement of Trident ballistic missile submarines, to speed up development of the Trident II submarine-launched ballistic missile, and to purchase large numbers of sea-launched cruise missiles for deployment on nuclear attack submarines. The administration anticipates an increase of six thousand to eight thousand strategic nuclear warheads by 1990.

These three developments have had a powerful and visible impact on the public consciousness. Increasingly and from many quarters the administration has been urged to define its position on arms control and to reconsider its stated policies on defense. The dominant theme of these expressions has been that the government should enter into immediate negotiations with the Soviet Union to end the nuclear arms race and to prevent the outbreak of nuclear war. Regrettably, little support has been generated for either the ratification or the renegotiation of the existing SALT II agreement, which contains a number of important provisions to limit delivery systems and warheads, as well as valuable qualitative constraints.

Resumption of the Debate in Congress

In the United States Congress, concern over the administration's arms control and nuclear weapons policies has crystallized into two major proposals. The first is the "freeze" resolution. It urges the United States and the Soviet Union to negotiate a complete halt to the further testing, production, and deployment of nuclear weapons. The second proposal advocates the attainment of strategic "equality" with the Soviet Union, to be followed by the imposition of a bilateral freeze, and then by negotiated reductions. Several other senators have urged the resumption of super-power negotiations to limit strategic arms.

As the tide of public and congressional concern rises, the administration is seeking to regain the initiative on arms control by signaling its interest in negotiations. On May 9, 1982, President Reagan advanced a set of strategic arms control proposals and indicated his willingness to negotiate with the Soviets. In his remarks the president outlined a two-stage plan; the first stage would seek to reduce warhead totals by a third, and the second phase would concentrate on deep reductions in missile throwweight.

The Primacy of Numbers

Although significant differences separate the freeze resolution from the approach favored by the administration, both share an important basic assumption: that limiting the number of weapons can, by itself, reduce the likelihood of war. In this, they are part of a long tradition in arms control, dating back to the Versailles treaty of 1919 (which restricted the size of the German army) and the Washington Naval Conference of 1922 (which limited the number of capital ships of the major maritime powers). Even the Interim Agreement on Strategic Offensive Forces, part of the 1972 SALT agreements, sought to enhance the security of the two superpowers simply by restricting the numbers of strategic nuclear delivery vehicles.

The historical record of such attempts has been less than encouraging. Traditionally, weapons ceilings have done little more than confirm an existing state of affairs. In none of the examples cited here did the signatories go on to negotiate substantial reductions in the number of controlled weapons. (In two of the three cases, the Versailles treaty and the Washington Naval Conference, the agreements actually broke down within a few years of their signing.) More often than not, the effect of quantitative arms control has been to rechannel the arms race into areas not covered by the agreement in question. Of perhaps greater significance, simple constraints on numbers offer no guarantee that weapons themselves will not be *used*.

The special urgency we associate with the control of nuclear weapons is directly related to their enormous destructive potential. Nuclear war is more than a continuation of war by other means; it is an entirely new form of conflict for which we have no frame of reference. Its potential consequences are beyond our ability to comprehend. It is this simple yet all-important reality of the nuclear age that compels us to make a quantum leap beyond the modest objective of numerical limits on weapons systems.

Prevention: A New Approach to Arms Control

We must fundamentally change the way we define the objectives of arms control. The United States and the Soviet Union must resume the strategic dialogue interrupted in 1979. While we cannot abandon the goal of deep, across-the-board reductions, we must refocus the negotiations specifically on measures to achieve stability and *prevent the use of nuclear weapons*. Preventing the use of the central organizing principle for future arms control talks. It is the clearest definition of the problem we face and it is consistent with the requirements for a strong national defense.

Talks focused on preventing the use of nuclear weapons should have four initial objectives:

First, new measures are needed to prevent the possibility of a nuclear exchange through accident or miscalculation. As the size of the U.S. and Soviet nuclear arsenals has grown, so too has the requisite number of personnel and the sophistication of the equipment necessary to manage them. Inevitably, these developments have increased the possibility that human or mechanical error could trigger a nuclear exchange. In 1980 Sen. Barry Goldwater and I led a Senate Armed Services Committee investigation into the continuing serious problems with the computers of the North American Air Defense Command (NORAD); during one eighteen-month period, NORAD experienced 151 false alarms—one of which lasted a full six minutes, or one-fifth the time it would take an ICBM-launched warhead to reach its target in the United States.

As disturbing as the problems with U.S. systems are, it is even more troubling to contemplate the Soviet systems. No one in the United States knows with any degree of confidence how reliable Soviet personnel and computers are. This ignorance only underscores the importance of taking joint and immediate steps to reduce the likelihood of starting a nuclear war by mistake. Talks on prevention should seek to:

1. Update the 1963 "Hot Line Agreement" to ensure instant, continuous, and secure communications between the two heads of government during a crisis

2. Update and extend the 1971 U.S.-Soviet agreement on accidental nuclear war to provide accurate and reliable notification of any accidental launch

3. Establish a jointly staffed crisis control facility in which personnel from the United States and the Soviet Union would monitor all nuclear weapons-related activities, including missile tests launches

Second, we must improve verification capabilities on both sides. Without adequate verification, arms control agreements are transitory and meaningless. Yet current constraints on verification hamper bold advances in arms control agreements. For example, constraints on seismic detection undermine prospects for a ban on testing of nuclear weapons. And the inability to distinguish nuclear-armed cruise missiles from those without nuclear warheads constrains efforts to limit these missiles.

To enable comprehensive, durable advances in arms control—and to remove a convenient smoke screen for opponents of all arms agreements—the United States should challenge the Soviets to join in a Manhattan Project on verification. This project could unite our scientific and diplomatic communities to make breakthroughs in the means of guaranteeing treaty compliance. Scientists from both nations could pursue technological improvements in the means of verification, while diplomatic personnel could develop confidence-building measures, such as a joint code of conduct for accidents or crises in space. As the first Manhattan Project made the United States the pioneer in nuclear arms, a Manhattan Project for verification could make the United States the pioneer in nuclear arms control.

Third, we must prevent the use of nuclear weapons by third parties, including "new" nuclear weapons states and terrorists. Six countries have the demonstrated capability to produce nuclear weapons; as many as twenty countries could possess such weapons by the end of the decade. As the supply of nuclear experts, technologies, and materials continues to grow, so does the possibility that nuclear weapons might "trickle down" to terrorists and other extranational groups.

The United States and the Soviet Union cannot solve the problems of international nuclear proliferation bilaterally. The two countries, however, can undertake new initiatives to strengthen both the 1968 Nonproliferation Treaty and the safeguards of the International Atomic Energy Agency.

Under the IAEA inspection system, it is virtually impossible for authorities to detect the diversion or misuse of nuclear materials. Inspections consist primarily of audits of inventory records and are announced well in advance. Inspectors must be approved prior to the visit, and they are forbidden to look for clandestine nuclear activities. For these reasons, careful consideration should be given to a revised IAEA inspection system that would permit more thorough and extensive monitoring with fewer constraints.

Stronger U.S.-Soviet leadership will be required to invigorate the existing nonproliferation regime and to convince nonnuclear weapons states to forgo acquisition. Ultimately, the only truly effective way to prevent the spread of nuclear weapons is to enhance the security of those nonnuclear countries that feel especially vulnerable to international aggression and to reduce the incidence of interstate violence. In this, the two superpowers bear a special responsibility and must take a more determined lead.

Fourth, we must reduce the vulnerability of both sides' nuclear retaliatory forces to preemptive attack. The increasing technical sophistication of nuclear weapons systems has undermined the stability of the nuclear balance of terror. In recent years, the two superpowers have acquired impressive counterforce and countersilo capabilities that increase the temptation to strike first in a crisis.

The secure capacity to respond to an adversary's nuclear first strike is the very foundation of mutual deterrence. The United States and the Soviet Union should agree on enforceable steps to stabilize the strategic balance of forces. Continuation of the 1972 Antiballistic Missile Treaty would be an important first step. Special consideration should be given as well to limitations on nuclear weapons systems and defense-related technologies that are particularly destabilizing in their effects. For example, the two countries should consider a gradual and verifiable reduction in the number of highly accurate MIRVed ICBMs. These missile systems pose a formidable threat to the retaliatory forces of the other side and should be replaced with fewer, survivable, single-warhead missiles. Constraints are also needed on anti-satellite weapons. If deployed, antisatellite weapons could disrupt vital command, control, and communications facilities. Limitations on strategic antisubmarine warfare activities might also be considered. In all cases, U.S.-Soviet arms control efforts should be directed toward enhancing the survivability of each side's second-strike forces.

Finally, we must continue to seek meaningful reductions in the overall numbers of nuclear warheads and their delivery systems—strategic, theater, and tactical. Most arms control analysts recognize that a smaller force of reliable, survivable weapons systems, tightly controlled, would constitute the best deterrent for both countries. The numerical limits and qualitative constraints contained in the SALT II Treaty represent an excellent starting point for any future negotiations. The treaty itself, properly amended, should be reported out of the Senate Foreign Relations Committee and submitted to the full Senate for ratification without additional delay.

On February 24, 1982, I introduced Senate Resolution 323 urging the immediate resumption of U.S.-Soviet negotiations, with special emphasis on preventing the use of nuclear weapons. These STOP talks—for Strategic Talks on Prevention—would go beyond the traditional concept of arms reductions. Implicit in STOP is the recognition that limiting the numbers of nuclear weapons, while important, is not the single objective for arms control. Only a concerted effort to prevent the use of nuclear weapons—by accident, miscalculation or design—can save us from the holocaust of nuclear war.   *(May 1982, updated May 1985)*

Beyond the Hot Line: Controlling Nuclear Crises
Richard Smoke
William L. Ury

Deterrence, the bedrock concept of contemporary theorizing about strategy and arms control, aims at preventing any intentional nuclear war. Precisely because of the success of mutual deterrence, many analysts have come to believe that the danger of a deliberate nuclear war is quite small. The greatest danger now is that war might start in some way that neither side intended, through miscalculation or accident.

One worrisome possibility is that, should either side adopt a launch-on-warning posture, a false alarm could trigger a massive attack. At least equally worrisome is the possibility that in some intense crisis, decision makers could lose control of rapidly moving events, which could quickly escalate into a nuclear exchange that no one originally intended. The sequence of events and decisions by which the Sarajevo crisis of 1914 rapidly escalated into World War I is often cited as a loose but sobering analogy.

Just how serious is this danger now? In September 1982, the Arms Control and Disarmament Agency asked us to examine past crises, especially U.S.-Soviet ones, and propose better ways of controlling any future ones. This research became a major program of the Nuclear Negotiation Project at Harvard Law School. A final report, entitled "Beyond the Hotline: Controlling a Nuclear Crisis," was submitted in March 1984.

We concluded that the risks of inadvertent clash, already significant, may be growing. A number of actual and potential trouble spots where U.S. and Soviet interests conflict continue to pose hazards of dangerous escalation. In spite of the enhancement of the hot line, no one can have high confidence that East–West crises like the one that erupted in the midst of the 1973 Middle East war will always be contained. New dangers are joining the traditional ones. Nuclear capabilities seem likely to proliferate, and one or more weapons may fall into the hands of terrorists interested in acting either as blackmailers or possibly as *agents provocateurs*.

Crises seem endemic to the contemporary international system, and typically impose on decision-making processes four demands that are hard to cope with simultaneously: high stakes, short decision time, high uncertainty, and few feasible, perceived options. Under these conditions it is all too easy for leaders simply to react to events and to fail to take initiatives that could control escalation.

Our report discusses a number of proposals intended to help them:

1. A *joint crisis control center* at which U.S. and Soviet specialists would work side by side to help defuse crises would be valuable for the delicate tasks of interpreting and authenticating information, and of reconciling divergent information on the two sides. Staff officers who already knew each other and had experience working together could resolve communication difficulties that might otherwise be serious. To be effective, the center should have twin locations in Washington and Moscow, linked by instant teleconferencing.

In advance of any crisis, this joint, professional working group could anticipate and study those types of possible crises, such as those involving technical breakdowns and accidents, in which the two sides may have strong shared and few conflicting interests.

2. The center staff might also be able to help develop *standard crisis procedures*, which at higher levels the two sides might agree upon, both to facilitate crisis resolution and to head crises off ahead of time. For instance, both sides now use informal cues to indicate in a crisis that they are keeping their "hands off their holsters." These cues could be enlarged and made more reliable. The successful Incidents at Sea Agreement, which created procedures for preventing an isolated naval incident

from escalating, might become a model for similar agreements regarding military air traffic, accidental intrusions across boundaries, and other situations.

3. Washington and Moscow (or any two potential adversaries) might agree in advance on a *crisis consultation period* in the event certain specified contingencies occur. In the case of the superpowers, an unlikely but exceedingly dangerous possibility is the single nuclear detonation on either's territory, the purpose and perhaps even the origin of which is not immediately clear. Agreements currently in force require the superpowers to "notify" each other if such an event is imminent, and to "consult" over any imminent risk of war. A feasible next step is to define a period during which no hostile action will be taken, assuming only one or a small number of detonations occur. Although such a period would be underenforceable, top leaders on both sides would have strong incentives to observe it and even to seize upon it as a means of preventing otherwise uncontrollable escalation.

4. *Enhanced roles for third parties* could be a valuable step toward controlling regional crises in which almost any action by East or West might be freighted with too much significance. The useful international mediation and peacekeeping that takes place today could be taken to its logical next step, perhaps under United Nations auspices. An international mediation service could be created with senior, globally respected figures who could help mediate conflicts before they become crises. There might also be constituted a Rapid Deployment Peacekeeping Force made up of soldiers from many countries and able to arrive quickly in a trouble spot to separate antagonists *before* fighting begins or is renewed. Greater use should also be made of regional congresses, which can bring together adversarial and mediating nations and groups in search of a resolution, or at least a containment, of a local crisis.

5. *Regular cabinet-level talks* could be held between the U.S. and Soviet defense and foreign affairs officials. These talks could help create and then oversee the crisis control center, the agreed procedures, and perhaps other elements of this crisis control system. Such talks could become a permanent, ongoing part of the U.S.-Soviet relationship, insulated from its political vagaries by the fact that they would be focused on the one strong common interest—avoiding any inadvertent war. Cabinet level talks would also give important decision makers on both sides a chance to know each other personally, something often desired but lacking in past crises.

6. Finally, a *Presidential crisis control briefing* could help prepare every new president and his main advisors during the preinaugural period. Any president will likely make a real, hands-on nuclear crisis decision only once, if ever. Yet this decision would be the most important decision he would ever make. Some practice is necessary. The accumulated wisdom and experience of past crises and some personal "experience" gained through vivid simulations could help a new president appreciate the difficulties of keeping an intense crisis under control.

None of these proposals should be oversold. Unless handled with considerable care, many of them could raise certain problems, including disinformation at critical moments, intelligence leaks, added bureaucracy, and foreign perceptions of U.S.-Soviet condominium. In each case, the possible pitfalls demand careful assessment.

At the same time, such measures to control crises have the advantages of dealing directly with what many agree is the greatest danger, the risk of a war no one intended. They have a "neutral," nonpolitical quality that may make agreements possible even in the current East–West climate. And measures to control crises, unlike those to reduce the levels of arms, do not run much risk of invoking fears of inferiority on either side. For all these reasons, crisis control offers one of the promising opportunities today to reduce the risk of nuclear war. The eighty-two to zero vote in the Senate suggests that taking strong new steps to control crises is an idea whose time has come.

Recent events indicate steadily growing interest among Congress, government officials, and the public in crisis control. A jointly staffed crisis control center has been a familiar concept for many years among specialists. It received a powerful impetus in 1982 when Sen. Sam Nunn and the late Sen. Henry Jackson, joined by Sen. John Warner, began to advocate it both publicly and privately. President Reagan proposed new confidence-building measures (CBMs) in speeches in June and November 1982. The U.S. and NATO later tabled additional CBMs at the Stockholm Conference on Disarmament in Europe talks (CDE) which convened in January 1984.

On April 11, 1983, Secretary Caspar Weinberger released a report recommending several new crisis control measures. These included a joint military communications link between the Pentagon and Soviet military headquarters, the installation by both sides of direct, high-speed communications links from each capital to its own embassy in the other capital, and the enhancement of the hot line to add a high-speed facsimile capability. The last suggestion met with a favorable response from the Soviet Union. Working groups met in Moscow and Washington in late 1983 and early 1984. Formal agreement was announced on July 17. This represents the only arms control agreement successfully concluded between the superpowers in the last several years.

On June 15, 1984, a resolution (S.R. 329) was brought before the Senate. It commended the Reagan administration for taking useful steps toward crisis control and went on to urge the president to open negotiations with the Soviets aimed at creating a jointly staffed crisis control center. The unanimous passage of the resolution by a vote of eighty-two to zero highlights the opportunities that exist today to take strong steps to control crises. *(October 1984)*

The Stockholm Conference: Negotiations on Reducing the Risk of War
James E. Goodby

It takes an acronym to popularize arms control talks: witness "SALT," "START," or even the unpronounceable "MBFR." A conference whose initials are

"COCASBMADIE" has little chance of coming easily to one's thoughts and still less to the headline writer's attention. Thus, for the past year and a half a major conference addressing the problem of how to reduce the risk of war in Europe has gone almost unnoticed by the U.S. press, despite the fact that it may produce the first East–West arms control agreement since 1979.

The proper and immediately forgettable name of the Stockholm Conference is the Conference on Confidence- and Security-Building Measures and Disarmament in Europe. The task of the conference is to negotiate cooperative measures that would enhance confidence and security in Europe. The historical and political roots of the conference lie in the Helsinki Final Act, the tenth anniversary of which was commemorated in July of this year. The confidence-building measures put into effect by the Final Act call for notifying the other parties twenty-one days in advance any military maneuvers that exceed 25,000 troops and for inviting observers to such maneuvers. The measures are voluntary, contain no real means of verification, exclude nearly all of the European Soviet Union, and include only the largest military exercises. The concern behind these agreements is that a lack of "timely information" about military operations in Europe could give rise to suspicion and possibly to reactions that would lead to an escalating military crisis. Although even these simple arrangements have not been implemented as well as the Western nations had hoped—no U.S. observers have been invited to a Warsaw Pact exercise since 1979—they have established the norms of *expected behavior* on which the negotiators in Stockholm are trying to construct a more far-reaching system of cooperative security arrangements.

The negotiations in Stockholm are a test of whether NATO, the Warsaw Pact, and the European neutrals can put in place agreed procedures that will make their military operations more predictable and less prone to misinterpretation. They seek also to put in place procedures that could be used to head off a military crisis developing from miscalculation or simply because of an inability to clarify an ambiguous and worrisome military operation. In essence, the objectives are the same as those of more traditional arms control negotiations: to enhance stability, to make the threat or use of force less likely, and to improve the prospects for a future marked by more civil, humane behavior among nations.

There is a fundamental distinction to be made of course between the Stockholm negotiations and those of Geneva and most other postwar arms control negotiations. The latter aim at *arms reduction*. The Stockholm Conference aims at *risk reduction*. Perhaps because arms reduction is not a direct objective of the Stockholm talks, arms control experts have tended to think of risk reduction as not central to present-day security needs and therefore not worthy of the intense interest and the lobbying efforts given to those more traditional negotiations, particularly nuclear arms reduction.

This is a mistaken attitude. Even accepting the risk-reduction measures may deal with nebulous, ill-defined problems—ignorance, misjudgments, and chance—anything to reduce the possibility of an unintended war is worth pursuing. Nearly everyone's scenario for the outbreak of nuclear war begins with some lower-level, conventional conflict, itself possibly the result of miscalculation, which escalates beyond the capacity of governments to control.

Europe has a higher concentration of military force than any other continent in the world. It will remain, for a long time to come, the front line of contending political and social systems. Sudden unexplained military operations in such a place, especially in times of tension, could be the beginning of a conflagration. The Stockholm Conference was constituted to deal with this problem, and for this reason alone it deserves the attention of the American public.

Confidence-building measures, or, as I prefer to call them, risk-reduction measures, can offer an important second track for arms control, one that complementing traditional kinds of arms control, could increase international stability and lower the risk of war. They can be defined as cooperative military arrangements between states intended to increase understanding about the intentions behind the military practices of those states. The ultimate objective of confidence-building measures is to increase stability by reducing occasions for misunderstanding, miscalculations, or misinterpretations about military activities, occasions that could create tensions and, if not clarified, escalate into crises or open conflict.

While arms reduction agreements seek to increase long-term stability by regulating types and levels of forces over an extended period of time, confidence-building measures seek to increase short-term stability during periods of intense and possibly turbulent international confrontation. This is the risk-reduction side of the coin. On the other side of the coin, however, such measures should strengthen stability during "normal" times as well; they should prevent crises before they arise, not just defuse them once they start. In this lies the confidence-building nature of these measures. Johan Jørgen Holst of the Norwegian Institute of International Affairs suggests, "We should look at confidence-building measures as management instruments designed to reduce pressures from arms on the process of politics during peacetime and on decision-making in crisis and war."

Although the multilateral agreement in the Helsinki Final Act is often considered the genesis of confidence-building measures, the most effective measures have in fact been bilateral agreements between the United States and the Soviet Union. The 1963 hot line agreement is perhaps the best known of these. This arrangement is relatively simple: a dedicated teletype link between Washington and Moscow. The purpose is to maintain a reliable channel for communication between the political leaders of the two countries to assist them in avoiding misunderstandings and in defusing potentially dangerous incidents or developments. The hot line has proved its utility, for example, during the 1973 Middle East war. It is now being upgraded by the addition of high-speed facsimile capabilities.

The U.S.-Soviet Accidents Measures Agreement of 1971 contains, inter alia, the very important provision that the parties will notify each other immediately in the event of an accidental, unauthorized or unexplained incident involving possible detonation of a nuclear weapon. This agreement was elaborated upon further in June of this year when the United States and the Soviet Union signed an understanding in which they agreed to consult, using the hot line, in case of the threatened or actual use of a nuclear weapon by a third party.

A provision of the SALT II agreement requires advance notification of all multiple ICBM launches or of single ICBM launches planned to extend beyond the national territory of the launching site. In the START negotiations, the United States proposed to expand this measure to require notification of all ICBM and SLBM launches.

The 1972 Incidents at Sea Agreement defines a whole set of "rules of the road": norms of behavior for U.S. and Soviet naval units operating in proximity to each other on the high seas. The agreement has led to a marked decrease in potentially dangerous naval encounters between the two countries.

In addition to these agreements, the United States is actively studying other confidence-building measures, such as the nuclear risk reduction centers that have been proposed by Senators Sam Nunn and John Warner. President Reagan made specific proposals for other measures in his speech to the United Nations in September, 1984, and in his speech to the European Parliament in Strasbourg on May 8. Proposals for confidence-building measures are also on the table in the nuclear negotiations in Geneva.

Compared with U.S.-Soviet bilateral measures directed at very specific situations, the confidence-building measures of the Helsinki Final Act are relatively general in their stated objectives. The Helsinki measures are intended to eliminate "the causes of tensions which may exist among [states]," "strengthen confidence among them," and reduce "the dangers of armed conflict and of misunderstanding or miscalculation of military activities which could give rise to apprehension, particularly in a situation where the participating states lack clear and timely information about the nature of such activities." There is an obvious disconnection between the requirements of the Helsinki measures, which are very modest, and their stated objectives, which are broad, even sweeping. Thus the measures serve mainly as political gestures reflecting the state of East–West relations rather than as militarily significant instruments designed to affect that relationship.

After ten years of experience, the weakness of the Helsinki confidence-building measures is evident. Although notification has been given for more than one hundred military maneuvers involving more than 2 million troops, one can hardly say that tensions in Europe have been eliminated or that confidence has been strengthened among the states of East and West. The basic requirements of the Final Act measures are too limited to provide the participating states with a substantially improved understanding of military activity in the region and thus are too limited to affect the behavior of the military organizations involved or the governments behind them. In some instances, the existence of these confidence-building measures has actually contributed to increased tensions when one side has suspected the other of failing to provide notification for a maneuver that crossed the 25,000-troop threshold, as happened in 1981 when the Soviet Union mounted, without proper notification, the major exercise called Zapad 81 on its border with Poland at the time the Solidarity Free Trade Union was at the peak of its influence.

In spite of these weaknesses, the Helsinki confidence-building measures have been important in political terms. They have legitimized the concept that openness and cooperation among states, even on sensitive security issues, is a desirable and potentially effective way to improve relations and maintain peace. The measures have created certain minimal standards of expected behavior. After Helsinki, the question is no longer whether such ambitious confidence-building measures are desirable, but whether they can be made effective.

In order to improve and expand the Helsinki-type measures, the United States and its NATO allies have proposed in Stockholm a set of six mutually reinforcing confidence-building measures that call for:

1. An exchange of information about the structure of forces on the continent
2. An exchange of annual forecasts of military exercises planned for the coming year
3. A more detailed notification of specific exercises forty-five days in advance
4. Mandatory invitation of observers to all notifiable activities
5. Verification and compliance
6. Development of improved means of communication

The thirty-five participants in the Stockholm Conference are poised on the edge of negotiations that will begin very soon to provide solid evidence as to whether the conference will be successful. During the first several months of the talks the Western nations held very little in common with the Soviet Union, although the NATO countries and the neutral and nonaligned countries shared the view almost from the beginning that the conference should try to build on the notification and observation regime established by the Helsinki Final Act. The Romanian delegation also introduced a paper that supported the idea of developing the Helsinki confidence-building measures.

The Soviets spent a great deal of time in the early days of the conference attacking the Pershing II and cruise missile deployments in Western Europe and arguing that only "large-scale political proposals" were capable of dealing with the threat to peace that had arisen on the continent of Europe. Their proposals called for the non-first-use of nuclear weapons, support for nuclear-free zones, a chemical weapons ban in Europe, and a freeze and reduction in military budgets. None of these proposals attracted any support from any quarter. Two other Soviet proposals, however, did find some resonance in Stockholm. One was a proposal for an agreement not to use force or the threat of force; the other provided for improvements, only vaguely specified, in the notification and observation provisions of the Final Act. President Reagan's offer of June 4, 1984, to discuss the Soviet proposal on non-use of force in exchange for Soviet agreement to concrete confidence-building measures (CBMs) foreshadowed the kind of outcome now being seriously pursued in Stockholm.

In the spring of 1985 the NATO countries tabled a comprehensive, ready-to-sign set of proposals; during the summer of 1985 the Warsaw Treaty countries introduced working papers and offered clarifications of their thinking regarding notification and observation of military activities, and further developed their thinking on a non-use of force treaty. The neutrals have been working intensively on an elaboration of their analogous proposals and probably will table the results of their work sometime in the fall.

For the first time in the conference, the issues separating the two sides can now be defined in relatively narrow terms:

1. The Western allies believe that the threshold for notification of military exercises should be both lowered and made more verifiable. This would be accomplished by providing for ratification of military operations by units rather than by manpower level, and specifically by requiring notification whenever an army division departs from its garrison. The Soviets hold that a numerical threshold is an equitable and meaningful measure of reckoning military capability and that smaller-scale military activities are of no interest in terms of surprise attack.

2. The Soviets want to preserve the Final Act's definitions of military operations (that is, *movements* and *maneuvers*). The Western allies argue that one all-embracing definition—*out of garrison activity*—would enhance verifiability.

3. The NATO countries believe that confidence building requires notification and the right of observation by all participants of land-force operations down to low levels in order to establish patterns of normal behavior. The Soviets hold that the parties should only provide notification for a few large-scale activities that could be seen as a threat to peace, and observers only from selected countries might be invited to military exercises on some unspecified basis.

4. The Soviets want to include air and naval operations, whether or not these are part of land-force activities, on the theory that such operations are capable of sudden surprise strikes. The NATO allies maintain that combined arms activities are the real harbingers of the threat or use of force, that independent air activities would require massive verification measures, and that information on activities off the coast of Europe, in accordance with the agreed terms of reference for Stockholm, would be made available under NATO proposals if such activities were functionally a part of notifiable land-force operations.

5. The NATO allies believe that on-site inspection may be needed in exceptional cases, while the Soviets maintain that "national technical means," augmented by "consultation," should be adequate.

6. The NATO allies want an annual exchange of information on the structure and location of land forces and land-based air forces to help evaluate the significance of military operations. The Soviets denounce such an exchange as "espionage" and offer to provide very limited information in connection with notification of military operations.

7. The Soviets want to impose a ceiling of 40,000 men on any land-force exercise on the theory that this would inhibit surprise attack. The NATO allies are

prepared to consider constraints on military operations (they regard their proposal for an annual forecast of military activities as having a constraining effect). However, they believe that a constraint proposal applying with equal impact on the two alliances is not yet on the horizon because of the many asymmetries between NATO and Warsaw Pact forces.

Although this partial list of issues demonstrates deep philosophical differences between East and West, and some involve serious questions of principle, there is presently no reason to think that these differences cannot be resolved.

Whether Stockholm succeeds or not, the need for effective confidence-building measures is evident. Whatever the success of other kinds of arms control in reducing the size of today's arsenals, the world will have to live with large numbers of potentially devastating weapons for a very long time to come. Thus, it is incumbent upon our governments to do everything possible to ensure that those weapons are never used. That is the potential role of confidence-building measures in the arms control spectrum: to erect barriers against the use of force, to establish practical arrangements for avoiding situations that, for whatever reason, could lead to confrontation, conflict, and the war nobody wants.

The immediate result of enacting a confidence-building regime, such as the one proposed by the Western allies, would be to make the European military situation more predictable and stable. It would not obviate the need for strong defense capabilities, and it would not reduce the military potential of either side. But it would reduce the element of uncertainty surrounding military activities. It would reduce the risk that a country caught off guard by a sudden unexplained military operation might react, or overreact, in a way that could start a chain of events leading to war. This regime would make military behavior more predictable, giving planners and decision makers time to calculate their response, and lower the risk of miscalculation, misinterpretation, and mistake. These risks are increased by pressures of time and the need to make decisions with insufficient information.

Such a confidence-building system would not guarantee peace. No agreement in itself will prevent war. But if a confidence-building system were in place, any country, by breaking the announced pattern, would be sounding an alarm, warning others that a threat to the security of Europe might be in the offing and permitting steps to be taken to cope with the situation. This early, clear warning of a potential threat could be especially important for the democracies, which need time for potential decisions required to initiate a military response to a threat.

In addition, an effective confidence-building system would help prevent or at least raise considerably the political costs of suddenly mounting a military activity in response to an unexpected political development in Europe. Short of conditions threatening actual war between East and West, this regime would be particularly effective in restricting the possibilities of threatening or using force for political intimidation.

If enacted, a set of confidence-building measures such as those proposed by the Western allies would contribute to a more secure Europe. It would make the risk of confrontation and conflict less likely. Perhaps equally important, in the long run, it could provide a solid foundation for even broader, more significant forms of military cooperation. Eventually, such a system and its successors could lead to easing some of the sharper edges of confrontation in the East–West relationship, little by little replacing confrontation with cooperation. *(September 1985)*

Cooperative Verification
Karl Pieragostini

Anyone listening to the increasingly loud debate over verifying arms control agreements might easily gain the impression that the United States must either rely solely on "national technical means" (NTM) or get the Soviets to agree to highly intrusive forms of on-site inspection (OSI). In fact, U.S. experience in negotiating with the Soviet Union shows that there is a wide spectrum of cooperative actions useful to verification. Precedents have been established for measures to increase the effectiveness of NTM, to provide for limited but important forms of OSI, to allow the emplacement of so-called black box sensors, and to foster resolution of treaty-related problems.

Aiding NTM

During the negotiation of SALT II, agreement was reached on important measures to aid NTM. These included pledges to refrain from hindering the collection of treaty-related information by either interfering directly with NTM sensors or by using deception to conceal relevant information. Additionally, the two sides worked out definitions, counting rules, and special earmarking design features to assist the counting and evaluating of weapons by NTM.

In SALT and other negotiations, U.S. and Soviet officials have also established the precedent of a periodic exchange of information related to a treaty. Such an exchange of data, and its periodic updating, can assist NTM in two ways: by enhancing the technical capabilities of NTM, and by providing a given baseline from which NTM can operate.

The Threshold Test Ban Treaty, for example, includes agreement to exchange data on geographic boundaries and geological characteristics of designated test sites. The treaty also calls on the parties to share data from a certain number of tests to allow the calibration of seismic equipment. Both sets of data would improve the capabilities of seismic monitoring. Unfortunately, because the United States has not ratified the treaty, this exchange of data has not occurred.

Another important aid to NTM involves the notification of events, both before and after they occur. The SALT II Treaty stipulated that prompt notification had to be given of the first and last test launches of the one new ICBM allowed. The Peaceful Nuclear Explosions Treaty requires postevent confirmation of the actual time of the explosion and the data derived from it.

Advance notification allows the monitoring side to prepare and position its sensors to test certain activities. It can also be used by one side to advise the other that it is introducing a new system that is of a type not covered by the treaty but that could possibly be mistaken for one that is. The more advanced information one side gets of the other's actions, the less likely it is that intentions will be misread.

Postevent information provides a useful check on the data collected by NTM. Finally, the United States and the Soviet Union have agreed on collateral constraints to ease the verification burden on NTM. Collateral constraints are restrictions designed to provide additional hurdles for the prospective cheater.

SALT II sought to prohibit either side from maintaining or acquiring a rapid reload capability for its ICBMs. To do this it banned the development, testing, and deployment of systems for rapid reload. It also, however, as collateral constraints, prohibited the storage of more than one missile at a site and banned the provision of storage facilities for more than one missile per site.

In future negotiations, aids to national technical means would be useful in verifying more ambitious arms control agreements, such as the freeze. Collateral constraints would be especially important.

The freeze relies heavily on mutually reinforcing restraints to prevent the introduction of any new nuclear weapon systems. To beat this overall prohibition a cheater would have to beat the individual prohibition on fissile material production, and those on the testing, production, and deployment of warheads, delivery vehicles, and, in most cases, launch platforms.

Collateral constraints could also be useful in verifying a freeze on the deployment of ground-launched cruise missiles by placing restrictions on their main-base storage facilities. The same sort of constraint could be used for warheads, with a ban being placed on the building of new storage depots or the enlarging of existing ones.

On-site Inspection

On-site inspection is a much more intrusive form of monitoring than is the use of NTM, or even NTM aided by the cooperative measures outlined above. It involves the actual presence of foreign nationals in or near sensitive military related facilities. OSI can be thought of as coming in four basic varieties: general, selective, control posts, and progressive.

General. General OSI is the most sweeping. It would allow unrestricted access at any time by one side to those facilities and weapons systems of the other constrained by a treaty. It is therefore the least likely to be negotiated in the near future.

That is not to say that it would be impossible to negotiate. The Antarctic Treaty, to which the United States and the Soviet Union are parties, bans any military activity on that continent. To ensure compliance, it provides that inspectors designated by signatories to the treaty will be allowed access at any time to any and all areas of Antarctica, including all stations, installations, and equipment, and ships and aircraft at discharge or embarkation points. Inspection provisions in the Outer Space Treaty are similar, but less sweeping. The treaty prohibits nuclear weapons from being placed in orbit or on any celestial body. It also prohibits any other form of military activity on celestial bodies. To ensure compliance, all installations on the moon or other celestial bodies are open to inspections, but objects in earth orbit (for example, satellites and space stations) are not. Additionally, unlike the Antarctic Treaty, the inspections are on the basis of reciprocity, with advanced notice required. Nevertheless, both treaties establish the precedent of general on-site inspection.

It was possible to agree on such intrusive OSI primarily because of the nature of the agreements. Both are preclusive treaties, in that they prohibit a certain type of future activity rather than put constraints on current practices.

Selective. Selective OSI places greater restrictions on the activities of inspectors: it could restrict their number, when they may visit, where they may go, what they may inspect, what equipment they may use, with whom they may speak, what they may ask, and so forth.

The United States has proposed selective on-site inspection on several occasions. In working papers and proposals submitted to the U.N. disarmament committee in the mid-1960s, the United States called for a cutoff of fissionable material production, to be monitored by selective on-site inspection. The United States raised the issue of selective on-site inspection in discussions with the Soviets on a proposed ban on MIRVs. There have also been numerous proposals and working papers submitted to the United Nations by the U.S. government and others concerning on-site inspection to confirm the nonproduction of chemical weapons and the destruction of their stockpiles.

The U.S.-Soviet Peaceful Nuclear Explosions Treaty has detailed provisions for selective on-site inspection. For group explosions with a planned aggregate yield over 150 kilotons designated personnel from the monitoring side are allowed prior access to the site to inspect it and install monitoring equipment. These inspectors would be present to confirm that the explosion is in fact for peaceful purposes, and to verify that no single explosion exceeds 150 kilotons in yield. The treaty, however, has not been ratified by the United States and is, therefore, not formally in effect.

Central to the Nonproliferation Treaty's safeguards program are selective on-site inspections by personnel of the International Atomic Energy Agency. The program is designed to deter the diversion of nuclear material from peaceful to weapons purposes and is based on a comparison between information provided by the inspected country and that gained through independent inspections by these IAEA personnel.

They are allowed to examine records; make independent measurements; check the host country's measurement and control equipment; observe measurement, sampling, and calibration activities, and request duplicate or additional samples and measurements. The inspectors do not, however, have unrestricted freedom of action. They are accompanied by state representatives, cannot operate any equipment, and do not have unlimited access to site facilities.

The safeguards program has established important precedents. An international body has been given responsibility for the verification of a multilateral treaty, a move away from reliance simply on NTM supplemented by bilateral cooperation. While the NPT requires that only nonnuclear weapons state signatories be subject to safeguards, the United States unilaterally offered to submit some of its nuclear facilities to safeguards to lessen criticism that the treaty was discriminatory. This began in 1981. The British and French also agreed to allow the safeguarding of some of their facilities. At the June 1982 U.N. Second Special Session on Disarmament, the Soviet foreign minister followed suit and expressed the Soviet Union's readiness to place several nuclear power plants and research reactors under IAEA control, and negotiations with the IAEA will begin in May or June 1983. Both the United States and the Soviet Union have, therefore, agreed in principle to selective on-site inspection by an international agency.

Selective OSI need not rely on a predetermined set of rules and procedures. Inspections need not be obligatory and regularly scheduled. In 1966 the Swedish delegation to the United Nations suggested a voluntary control procedure described as "verification by challenge." It is based on the notion that "it is easier to prove your own innocence than somebody else's guilt." Under the scheme, when one party suspects another of infringing a treaty provision, this suspicion is made known, and the accused party is expected to provide sufficient information to allay the other's suspicions, including, if needed, an invitation to on-site inspection. During the negotiations on a comprehensive test ban, the United States and the Soviet Union agreed to the use of verification by challenge.

Control Posts. The use of control posts is similar to selective OSI in that the freedom available to inspectors is limited. It differs in that the inspectors from one country are permanently stationed on the soil of another. Inspectors could be stationed at crucial junctures in the transportation network, such as airfields and railway stations, to monitor militarily significant traffic. Inspectors could also be assigned to important weapons facilities, such as production plants, where they would be given enough access to ensure that the prohibited activity was not underway, but not so much that the military secrets were put in jeopardy.

Both the United States and the Soviet Union have proposed such control posts during negotiations on mutual force reductions in Europe. A U.S. draft treaty submitted in July 1982 provides for manned entry and exit monitoring points for the observation of troop movements required by the treaty. The Soviets, in February of 1982, had tabled a draft that also called for monitoring posts.

Progressive. Progressive on-site inspection is an attempt to meet objections to both general and selective OSI. Some argue that general OSI is too sweeping and intrusive ever to be accepted by any state. Others complain that selective OSI is so restricted in practice that it is ineffective. Progressive OSI attempts to match, at the outset, the level of inspection with both the level of arms control involved and the degree of mutual confidence present. It thereby satisfies advocates of selective OSI. It also, however, aims to build confidence by gradually increasing the scope of inspections, thereby satisfying those who want more than selective OSI.

The scope of inspections can be increased progressively by type of facility, intensity of inspection, or geographic area. In the first case, only certain types of facilities would be covered initially, perhaps the least sensitive militarily, and once confidence in the process increased, other types of facilities would be included. For example, it would probably be easier to agree on inspections of facilities closed by a treaty, than to agree on inspections of facilities whose output is only limited, as these latter facilities may be involved in other sensitive operations not restricted by the treaty. As mutual confidence in the procedures increased, however, these other facilities could gradually be incorporated into the inspection process. In other instances, the facilities and sites to be inspected could be fixed, but the number and freedom of access of inspectors could gradually be increased. Finally, the geographic area open to inspection could slowly be enlarged. In these ways, selective OSI could incrementally move toward general OSI, but only as fast as the confidence of the parties allowed.

Black Boxes

As noted at the outset of this article it is sometimes mistakenly assumed that there are only two forms of technical monitoring: nonintrusive, remote sensing from satellites and other such platforms; and instrusive, on-site inspections by foreign nationals. The current U.S. administration withdrew from negotiations on a comprehensive test ban and refused to endorse two treaties limiting the yields of current underground tests because national technical means were considered insufficient for verification. On-site inspections were said to be necessary. There is, however, a third way, which has the accuracy of on-site inspection without the same degree of intrusiveness.

The use of on-site, tamperproof remotely monitorable devices, often referred to as black boxes, has already been agreed to in principle by the United States and the Soviet Union. In 1978 at the trilateral CTB negotiations, after much internal discussion, the Soviets agreed to a U.S. proposal that each party accept ten seismic stations on its territory for the duration of the treaty. The United States agreed that these stations, referred to as national seismic stations (NSS), would be owned and manned by the host country, although they would have high-quality instrumentation and special devices to ensure that the data from them could not be falsified.

The data would be transferred to the monitoring nation by satellite relay. Unfortunately, the agreement subsequently ran into problems over the number and location of stations on British territory.

The U.S. Arms Control and Disarmament Agency and the IAEA have been testing a monitoring system that applies the same general principle to the verification of nonproliferation. It is called remote continuous verification.

Discussion Forums

Finally, the U.S.-Soviet experience has shown how very useful a discussion forum can be in the proper functioning of treaties. The SALT process has produced the Standing Consultative Commission, in which U.S. and Soviet delegates sit down to discuss treaty matters. Other treaty negotiations have provided for similar forums. A 1980 report to the United Nations by parties to the CTB negotiations noted that the United States, the Soviet Union, and Great Britain agreed that there would be "provision in the treaty for direct consultations, and for the exchange of inquiries and responses among treaty parties in order to resolve questions that may arise concerning treaty compliance." The Peaceful Nuclear Explosions Treaty requires that the United States and the Soviet Union "establish promptly a Joint Consultative Commission" to consider compliance and other treaty related issues. Such a forum provides a means for establishing the procedures needed to implement treaty provisions. Additionally, unforseen circumstances can be discussed, and the treaty could even be amended. Most importantly, a forum provides the opportunity for complaints to be aired and resolved.

In sum, the failure to reach agreement on intrusive on-site inspection does *not* mean that progress on arms control is impossible. Much has been accomplished in the way of cooperation between the United States and the Soviet Union on verification. The cooperative measures noted here are on the table waiting to be picked up and used in other treaties. There is, of course, room for improvement, but precedents have been set and a degree of momentum generated. The danger is that these gains will be eroded if the United States does not ratify agreements that were painstakingly negotiated and if it continues to use "verification" as an excuse for not going forward with arms control.   *(June 1983)*

Informal Arms Control: Restraint without Ceremony
Gerald M. Steinberg

For the past thirty years, arms control has generally been pursued through formal negotiations in the United Nations, the multi-nation disarmament conferences, and, in the case of the test ban and SALT, special forums. In each case, delegations were appointed, proposals were carefully prepared and exchanged directly, and a formal document was sought.

The results of these efforts are meager, and while there are many systemic reasons for this failure, the formal process is partly to blame. Arms control is a process of negotiation and mutual accommodation, and is characterized by the exchange of proposals in which each state tries to gain maximum concessions from opponents while attempting to minimize its own.

This fundamental element of negotiations leads to inflexibility and slow processes. In formal exchanges of proposals, each side is reluctant to make concessions prematurely and clings to particular positions as long as possible. Even if concessions are substantively acceptable, they may be resisted for fear that the country's bargaining reputation will be damaged, and, in the future, opponents will await concessions rather than offer their own.

This process can be illustrated in the Comprehensive Test Ban Treaty, in which the United States agreed, after great debates, to a maximum of seven inspections per year. The Soviet Union would only accept three. While the substantive difference was trivial, neither side would revise its position, and the negotiations failed.

Bureaucratic Obstacles

The requirement for precise written proposals and the lengthy process of internal political negotiation they entail also contributes to the slow pace of formal arms control negotiations. Decision-making processes involve many conflicting interests, are time consuming, and lead to inflexibility. In a contest between groups, the various sides seek to gain support for their perspectives and often overstate their cases. As a result, any attempt to change positions is very difficult, requiring the "unselling" of a previous position and the reselling of a new one. Positions become inflexible and concessions are less likely. For example, during the Eisenhower administration's consideration of test ban proposals, the conflicts between the Department of Defense, the Atomic Energy Commission, the Joint Chiefs of Staff, and at the end, the Presidents' Scientific Advisory Committee (PSAC), and the requirement for consensus resulted in an essentially static U.S. position. While the evidence is not clear, one can assume that some form of internal negotiations in the Soviet Union also lead to a slow Soviet response time.

In the area of arms control and weapons development, in which the pace of technological innovation leaves little time for control, these factors are of great importance. Slow decision making allows for the development of new weapons, often rendering negotiations moot.

Furthermore, the internal negotiation that marks formal negotiations itself undermines the goals of arms control. During the Limited Test Ban negotiations, President Kennedy accepted increased underground testing and expanded deployment of nuclear weapons to gain the support of the Joint Chiefs of Staff (JCS). During SALT I, the Trident SLBM was accelerated in exchange for JCS support. The ratification effort for the SALT II Treaty led the Carter administration to support the MX. In other words, the costs of gaining internal consensus for restraints are counterproductive.

Informal Alternatives

In the wake of these process-related obstacles to successful formal arms control negotiations, informal alternatives involving mutual restraints without the explicit negotiation of a treaty have been suggested. In the absence of a formal set of negotiations, the inherent obstacles to speedy and successful outcomes discussed earlier could be avoided. Formal conferences would be eliminated, along with the tedious exchange of proposals and responses. Instead, each side would adopt a series of unilateral restraints that would be contingent on the acceptance of reciprocal restraints on the other side.

It is clear that informal processes have the potential for failure. There are always incentives to "play to the galleries" by announcing unilateral proposals designed to embarrass the other side. In the past, both the United States and the Soviet Union have indulged in this behavior. In 1958, the Soviet Union declared a nuclear test moratorium after an extensive test series. When the United States continued to test, the Soviet Union enjoyed a propaganda victory. Similar highly visible declarations of "restraint" in the areas of theater nuclear forces or a nuclear freeze may lead to similar outcomes.

In addition, an informal negotiating process that involves the clear articulation of positions may not eliminate those elements that cause delay and inflexibility. An explicit proposal, whether officially presented by representatives across a table, or announced unilaterally in a press conference or speech, is still likely to involve interested government agencies. No administration is likely to declare publicly a halt in deployments without first gaining the support of the JCS, DOD, Congress, and so forth. Thus, the need for consensus among disparate actors and interests would still exist.

Lowering Visibility

By lowering the profile of negotiations and eliminating the highly visible declarations of intent and contingency, the probability of reaching successful informal arms control can be increased. Without such explicit declarations, the role of propaganda as well as the continuing impact of slow and inflexible bureaucratic decision making can be limited. Instead, proposals can be communicated informally, either explicitly between representatives of both sides, or implicitly, through actions and behavior that indicate intentions.

Informal communication of proposals and responses would diminish or eliminate many of the obstacles inherent in the formal process. Such negotiating processes also facilitate the use of "trial balloons," since proposals can be most readily floated with minimum risk when they receive no publicity. Concessions can then be announced simultaneously with a quid pro quo from the other side.

Decision making would be centralized more readily than in formal talks. No single bureaucratic actor could control or block concessions. Informal bargaining could take place via indirect bargaining, allowing for a higher rate of concessions. Specific restraints could be chosen by a small centralized group, as when the Harriman mission's work finally led to the Limited Test Ban Treaty in 1963.

The possibilities for success are illustrated in the informal limitations that developed in the area of military space systems such as orbital bombs, reconnaissance satellites, and antisatellites. Despite the military disutility of orbital bombs, the U.S. military opposed a ban on them. Avoiding formal negotiations, the United States pursued limitations via unilateral statements and informal discussions. The initial "agreement" in 1963 took the form of parallel but unilateral declarations and a U.N. resolution. It was only in 1967 that these pledges were codified in a formal treaty.

Similarly, during this period, the Soviet Union threatened to develop antisatellites to block U.S. reconnaissance satellites. As a deterrent, the United States began its own antisatellite effort. In the mid-1960s, however, a centralized decision-making process in this area resulted in a change in U.S. policy. An effort was begun to gain acceptance of reconnaissance satellites through a series of indirect signals and statements. This effort succeeded, and reconnaissance satellites were tacitly accepted while the development of orbital antisatellites was slowed.

In these examples, common interests were realized through an informal process. In the United States, decision making was centralized, and bureaucratic actors were excluded. Formal negotiation via specially appointed representatives was eschewed, and a formal treaty was not sought. While one can point to particular aspects of these cases that contributed to success, it is clear that the outcomes stand in contrast to those in the formalized arms control processes. The obstacles that are inherent in formal processes did not play a significant role in these negotiations.

Of course, these examples are not sufficient to demonstrate that informal processes should be adopted in all arms control negotiations. The cases are unusual and quite distinct from the familiar attempts to limit the development and deployment of weapons. In addition, there are potential disadvantages to informal arms control processes and agreements. For example, such agreements are likely to be relatively imprecise, compared to formal written treaties. This imprecision may lead to disputes over the boundaries of the restraints. Given the conflict over this issue that has occurred in the case of the formal SALT I and ABM treaties, such ambiguity would not serve the interests of arms control. There is, however, reason to believe that in cases in which boundaries are sharply defined, informal restraints would lead to fewer disputes. Without precise terms upon which chronic opponents of arms control can seize, restraints that are essentially observed would not become the subject of political disputes.

Formal treaties may also be seen as longer lived and less subject to unilateral abrogation in times of conflict or changing technology. However, the validity of this assertion is also uncertain. International agreements, whether formal or informal, are only honored as long as the parties see it in their interests to do so. While a formal document may serve as a stronger "firebreak," informal agreements may generally be as durable as treaties.

Finally, it could be argued that by excluding key domestic actors, such as the military from decision making, restraints will not be tenable. The evidence from the cases here, however, contradicts this assertion. The ability of these actors to undermine the objectives of the president and the cabinet is severely reduced by an informal process. In the absence of a ratification, the congressional platform usually used by these interests is less available. Former Secretary of Defense Robert McNamara was able to cancel many military space programs despite the opposition of the Air Force, the JCS, and members of Congress, whereas a formal treaty restraining these systems might not have been ratified.

In summary, it would appear that the utility of formal arms control negotiations is limited and that in some cases, informal processes and agreements are more likely to lead to mutual restraint. Thus, instead of rejoicing over the resumption of formal negotiations, the arms control community should recognize the inherent limitations of processes that are addressed to the political, and not military, theater. In their place, the utility of informal negotiations should be considered.   *(June 1982)*

What Good Is a Freeze? Nailing Shut the "Window of Vulnerability"
Les AuCoin

It is astonishing that, as nuclear weapons budgets continue to grow and the security created by these weapons continues to shrink, the nuclear freeze is widely regarded as more of a political movement than as serious arms control.

Because its proponents have not sufficiently emphasized the national security advantages of the freeze, the debate has focused on the secondary issue of verifiability. While the verifiability of the key elements of the freeze is clear, this does not in itself make the freeze any good. After all, a treaty could be at the same time verifiable and disastrous.

In fact, a bilateral freeze is both verifiable and immensely beneficial. It is the most promising deterrence-augmenting device available to the United States today—far better than any proposed weapon. In particular, the freeze will do more for intercontinental ballistic missile survivability than any currently proposed weapon or arms control initiative.

ICBMs as Has-beens

Since the early 1970s, there has been considerable debate over how well U.S. ICBMs could survive a massive surprise Soviet attack. Could such an attack be coordinated? Would their missiles, under wartime conditions, keep their theoretical accuracy? Some experts, including Kosta Tsipis of M.I.T., argue that more than half of U.S. ICBMs could survive such an attack. Others, primarily weapons advocates and opponents of arms control, argue that as few as one-fifth would survive.

In this discussion, let us assume the predictions of the pessimists are right, and U.S. ICBMs are highly vulnerable. As we will see, even under its opponents' assumptions, the case for the freeze is overwhelming.

To whatever extent ICBM vulnerability exists, it is largely due to the monumental increase in Soviet ICBM accuracy over the past decade and a half. In 1968, a typical Soviet ICBM warhead would miss its target by more than a mile. Today, that miss distance is down to about one-eighth of a mile, rendering destruction of a U.S. silo by a single Soviet ICBM warhead more probable than not. The problem has been made more severe by the advent of Soviet MIRV technology, which permits the Soviets to target two warheads against each U.S. silo, compounding the attack's effect. (Even more than two attacking warheads per silo are available, but because of nuclear fratricide they cannot be used quickly enough to be effective. The radiation, blast, and dust from the first nuclear warhead exploding over a specific target will tend to destroy or disable any warheads following closely behind. While there is a small "window" of time through which a precisely scheduled second warhead could avoid destruction by its predecessor, it is impossible even in theory to fit a third warhead through this window. The third warhead would have to wait many minutes or hours for the dust to settle. But before the dust settled, the victim's ICBMs could safely escape.)

Deterrence can of course continue without ICBM survivability. U.S. bombers and submarine-launched ballistic missiles are highly effective. But the more varied a deterrent can be made, the more secure it will be against unexpected countermeasures. ICBM survivability is worth keeping.

This desire for a multiarmed deterrent has been uppermost in the minds of U.S. strategic planners; various new weapons and arms control solutions have been offered to prevent the loss of the ICBM deterrent.

The ostensible rationale behind the MX and Midgetman ICBM programs is to increase the survivability of U.S. ICBM warheads after a Soviet first strike. More than thirty basing modes, including the Carter administration's racetrack and the Reagan administration's Dense Pack, have been studied by the U.S. Air Force and by various presidential commissions. None of these has reached full-scale development; all have been found, in one way or another, to be unworkable. The MX, thus, is slated for deployment in old—and presumably vulnerable—Minuteman silos. If Midgetman somehow avoids cancellation, it too will probably use silo basing for lack of an alternative. (Semihard mobile basing for the Midgetman is also being considered, but its technical and cost risks would be high. It certainly would be more expensive than silo basing, and the U.S. Air Force will prefer to spend the funds elsewhere. Moreover, while its survivability could be good against an ICBM attack, which gives the transporter thirty minutes to run away from the targeted point, semihard mobile basing would not survive well against a depressed-trajectory attack, which would give less than five minutes warning. There would be insufficient time for the mobile system to exercise its mobility.)

President Reagan's START plan was aimed, in rhetoric although not in substance, at reducing ICBM vulnerability. The arms control package developed in 1982 by my colleague Albert Gore (D–Tenn.) sought the same goal. And SALT II, if combined with a multiple-point ICBM basing system, would also have increased ICBM survivability. But START has progressed little beyond the propaganda stage, the Gore plan has been watered down into a nearly meaningless adjunct to START, and SALT II is in limbo.

As a result of this failure to find either a military or an arms control solution, the ability of Soviet ICBMs to carry out a first-strike attack against U.S. ICBMs has been advancing rapidly, while the ability of U.S. ICBMs to survive has not.

Hardening and the Freeze

Four major factors determine the probability that an ICBM silo will survive an incoming ballistic warhead: Increasing the hardness (strength) of the silo increases the probability that the silo will survive; conversely, increasing the explosive power, reliability, or accuracy of the attacking warhead decreases survivability.

Over the past fifteen years, U.S. silo hardness has more than tripled, from approximately 600 pounds per square inch (psi) blast overpressure resistance to the present 2,000 psi. The United States has also doubled its number of ICBM warheads from 1,054 to about 2,140 by replacing single-warhead Minuteman I missiles with triple-warhead MIRV Minuteman IIIs. At the same time, the explosive power of the typical Soviet ICBM warhead has dropped from one megaton to about one-half megaton.

Nevertheless, advances in Soviet missile accuracy have more than made up for U.S. silo hardening. Far fewer U.S. ICBMs would survive an attack today than in 1968. Hardening U.S. silos has not been entirely wasted—even more would succumb had the United States not done it. Still, hardening and MIRVing obviously have not saved as many U.S. ICBM warheads as would be desirable. And the worst is yet to come. If Soviet accuracy continues to improve, U.S. ICBM survivability will continue to decline, reaching near zero even as silos are further hardened.

The limits of silo hardening are not clear. Reports in the trade press suggest that present Soviet silos are hardened to approximately 6,000 psi. Small-scale Defense Nuclear Agency tests suggest that superhardness in the tens of thousands of psi may be possible, although applicability of these studies to full-size structures is controversial.

There has been speculation on the possibility of what might be called "ultrahard" silos: nearly indestructible devices hundreds of thousands of psi hard. Administration spokesmen have suggested that these would render Soviet accuracy irrelevant.

In theory, this is correct. But in practice, it is like building a barrel that can survive a plunge over Niagara Falls. What matters is not the barrel but the person inside. A missile sufficiently powerful and accurate to create such overpressure will also place the silo in the explosion's crater. If a silo is itself bounced into the air and left lying on the bottom of the crater, it will not matter if the silo structure is intact. Ths missile will not fire. Even if the silo is only under the rim of the crater, the missile will be unable to fire up through the many feet of dirt piled up at the rim. Recent press reports indicate that such accuracy is clearly achievable; and if this hypothetical indestructible object meets the attacker's irresistible force, the attacker will win.

The United States has been losing the hardness/accuracy race and will continue to lose unless it redefines the rules. But the nuclear freeze is an amazingly effective way to change the rules of the race, loading them in favor of survivability and deterrence.

Hardness can be useful, *provided it is combined with a weapons freeze*. The freeze affects nuclear warheads and delivery vehicles but not basing systems or launch platforms. In particular, it places no restrictions on silo hardening.

Had Soviet accuracy been frozen fifteen years ago, the United States would not even face the appearance of vulnerability today. We cannot, of course, turn back the clock. But if the United States can hold Soviet accuracy close to today's level, ICBM vulnerability can be contained and even reversed. The nuclear freeze does that, and more. By limiting accuracy but at the same time allowing hardening to proceed, the freeze enables hardness to win the race.

Freeze Dynamics

Conventional wisdom holds that research and development cannot be closely monitored, and that technological advances are therefore difficult to control by negotiated agreement. Perhaps. But because flight testing of ballistic missiles can be verified with very high confidence, the *application* of accuracy-related technology can thereby be controlled.

The key to the freeze is its complete ban on ballistic missile flight testing. This will confine to military insignificance any future increases in Soviet accuracy.

Missiles are complex devices. Without flight tests it is impossible to know exactly how one component will interact with another. Computer analysis and captive testing are useful, but they cannot simulate the acceleration, vibration, temperature changes, and other phenomena of real flight. Anyone inclined to believe that a new missile technology can be reliably deployed without flight testing should consider that five new ballistic missiles—the Soviet SS-X-24, SS-X-25, and SS-NX-20, and the U.S. MX and Pershing II—saw their first test in this decade, and four of the five first tests failed.

If flight testing were prohibited, national leaders on both sides would know the first rehearsal would count as the final performance. Soviet planners fully understand that installing a new guidance upgrade and having it fail in the midst of a first strike would, as the saying goes, spoil their whole day.

Under the freeze, a Soviet missile designer would have this choice: He could stick with his present force, which is adequate for deterrence and retaliation but not good enough for a comprehensive countersilo first strike. Alternatively, he could install new, theoretically better but untested guidance systems, software, reentry materials—and risk catastrophic failure. Neither course leads to a high-confidence first strike. This is precisely the predicament in which we should seek to place the Soviets. The freeze would do it.

Improving Accuracy

That a zero-test environment will mean absolutely unvarying missile performance forever is unlikely. A completely static freeze is not realistic, but neither is it necessary.

Small incremental accuracy improvements can be made without testing. The gravitational and geodesic irregularity of the earth, for example, is a moderate contributor to ballistic missile inaccuracy; its further measurement by satellite would continue in the absence of ballistic missile flight tests.

Some missile components could also be clandestinely tested in military or civilian space vehicles. But this would be of limited utility, because the trajectory and reentry characteristics of ballistic missiles are distinct from those of orbiting space flights. These distinctions could and should be further widened by treaty provisions prohibiting space flights that appear to overlap key ballistic missile characteristics.

The cost and inconvenience thereby imposed on the space programs of both sides could be substantial. But we can pay the cost from the savings generated by the freeze itself, and we can live with the inconvenience. Prevention of a nuclear first strike must have higher priority than any space program.

"Rusting"

Running contrary to the possibility of improved accuracy under zero-test is another, more powerful consequence of the freeze that will, in time, lower both Soviet accuracy and reliability.

Because tests of existing ballistic missiles as well as new types would be prohibited under a freeze, problems in component aging and design would inevitably arise. Some component aging problems can be detected and the components replaced. But high-confidence fixes, especially of design problems, will be impossible without flight testing. Other defects will be undetectable and unknown in the no-test freeze environment.

Loss of confidence in untested weapons will affect both sides. But unlike the relatively undemanding deterrence mission, a disabling counterforce first strike requires very high accuracy and reliability. The best way to shift the nuclear balance away from first strike and toward deterrence is to force both sides to let the weapons sit untested. A possibly "rusty" missile is not an attractive first-strike weapon.

The Freeze Advantage

An example of the protection the freeze gives to ICBM survivability is shown in tables 5–1 and 5–2, and in figure 5–1. (These tables use standard calculation methods and, in consideration of probable fratricidal effects, assume that the attack is limited to two warheads per silo.)

Table 5–1 shows the number of reliable warheads surviving in the mid-1990s if the United States follows the current administration's modernization program, including START and Build-down, which allow 2,500 ICBM warheads for each side. While President Reagan has requested only 100 MX missiles, it is no secret that the U.S. Air Force desires many more. Let us assume a fully modernized deployment of 175 MX missiles with ten warheads each, plus 750 single-warhead Midgetmen. The Soviet Union is assumed to build an identical force to comform to START and Build-down. The table considers two conditions, both well within the reach of Soviet technology by the mid-1990s: Under the first condition Soviet ICBMs are assumed to be qualitatively similar to the U.S. MX, which

Table 5–1
U.S. Reliable ICBM Warheads Surviving with Modernization (Mid-1990s)

U.S. Silo Hardness	MX-quality Attack	Satellite-guided Attack
2,000 psi (present U.S.)	10	< 10
6,000 psi (present Soviet)	40	< 10
10,000 psi	100	< 10
20,000 psi	260	< 10

Source: Office of Congressman Les AuCoin.

Table 5–2
U.S. Reliable ICBM Warheads Surviving with a Freeze (Mid-1990s)

U.S. Silo Hardness	Worst Case (10% Soviet Accuracy Gain)	Static Freeze (No Change from 1984)	Rusting Missiles (1% Annual Accuracy and Reliability Loss for 20 years)
2,000 psi (present U.S.)	330	440	660
6,000 psi (present Soviet)	780	910	1,020
10,000 psi	940	1,130	1,160
20,000 psi	1,210	1,370	1,310

Source: Office of Congressman Les AuCoin.

the administration plans to deploy in 1987. Under the second condition, ICBMs on both sides are assumed to add precision satellite guidance.

Table 5–1 demonstrates that, even with full ICBM modernization and substantial silo hardening, very few U.S. ICBM warheads would survive a Soviet first strike. The benefit of silo hardening quickly melts away in the face of advancing Soviet accuracy. In the absence of a freeze, the U.S. ICBM deterrent will be gone.

Table 5–2 shows how U.S. ICBMs would survive a Soviet first strike under a nuclear freeze. It considers three different conditions: The first condition is a worst case in which, even though Soviet missile testing is frozen, the Soviets manage to forestall any weapon degradation and instead increase their accuracy by 10 percent. The second condition is one of no change from present Soviet missile capability. The third condition assumes that, as a result of "rusting" under zero-test, missile accuracy and reliability drop 1 percent per year for twenty years on both sides.

Since some modernization and some "rusting" are probably inevitable, the net effect of the freeze presumably would lie somewhere between the two examples. But even the worst freeze case in table 5–2 is better than the best nonfreeze case in table 5–1. Moreover, if U.S. silos were hardened to match Soviet hardness levels of 6,000 psi, the worst freeze case would give the United States at least three times as many surviving ICBM warheads as the best nonfreeze case.

Zero-Test Essential

While some commentators have suggested that a freeze should permit a limited number of ballistic missile tests, this would be a serious mistake. Even if superhardness is achievable, the strategic success of the freeze requires that flight tests of existing as well as new-type ballistic missiles be prohibited. If the United States permits the Soviets to flight-test their SS-18s and SS-19s, there will be no verifiable

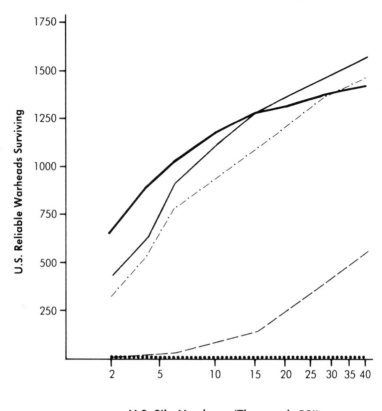

U.S. Silo Hardness (Thousands PSI)

With a Freeze	With modernization
——— rusting missiles	— — — — — MX-quality attack
——— static freeze	••••••••••••• Satellite-guided attack
—·—·—·—·— worst case freeze	

Source: Office of Congressman Les AuCoin.
Note: Figure 5–1 summarizes the effects of hardening silos against a theoretical Soviet ICBM counterforce attack in the mid-1990s. The harder U.S. silos are built, the greater number of U.S. missiles can survive to retaliate. A nuclear freeze, which would include a prohibition on missile flight testing, would stall Soviet gains in missile accuracy. Any of the three freeze conditions described by AuCoin would ensure far better U.S. ICBM survivability than President Reagan's modernization and arms control program.

Figure 5–1. Summary of Conterforce Attacks: U.S. Reliable Warheads Surviving with a Freeze and Modernization (Mid-1990s)

way to prevent progressively better accuracy from putting U.S. ICBMs into the disastrous, nonsurvivable, nonfreeze conditions shown in table 5–1. Although the present Soviet SS-18s and SS-19s carry a reliability handicap because of their liquid fuel, if their accuracy is unconstrained they can become nearly as effective first-strike devices as any new-type ICBM.

Moreover, the psychological significance of zero-test may even exceed its technological significance. The longer the time since the last flight, the more reluctant any national leader will be to roll the dice and risk his nation's survival on the proposition that his disabling first strike will be successful.

The freeze is a high-confidence plan for ICBM survivability without incurring the cost of a single new missile. It will be effective not only against attack by ICBMs but against the even more dangerous eventuality of attack by accurate submarine-launched ballistic missiles, which could strike with significantly less warning.

In addition, the freeze will prevent testing and deployment of Soviet depressed-trajectory ballistic missiles, which could reach even inland airbases too quickly for U.S. strategic bombers to escape. It will prevent testing and deployment of new weapons systems that are difficult to monitor. Deep cuts in the world's nuclear arsenals will thus be much easier to make. Finally, because the freeze will reduce first-strike potential and increase survivability on both sides, it is as much in the interest of the Soviet Union as of the United States. It will enhance stability and reduce the chance of nuclear annihilation for all concerned.

It is incumbent upon freeze opponents to show an alternative that offers equal or greater security at equal or lower cost.   *(September 1984)*

Appendix:
Strategic Nuclear Forces of the
United States and the Soviet Union

Total Launchers	U.S.	U.S.S.R.
ICBMs	1,014	1,398
SLBMs	640	944[a]
Bombers	268	150[a]
	1,922	2,492

Total Warheads[b]	U.S.	U.S.S.R.
On ICBMs	2,114	6,420
On SLBMs	5,632	3,120
On Bombers	3,484	760
	11,230	10,300

Recent U.S. Changes:

Five B-1B bombers assumed to be carrying 8 SRAMs and/or gravity bombs each are now operational. Five B-52G squadrons (98) are now fully equipped with ALCMs. Each aircraft carries 12 ALCMs on external hangers. Twenty-one B-52H aircraft have been converted to carry ALCMs, with the entire force to be completed by 1989. B-52H will eventually carry 12 wing-mounted ALCMs and 8 additional weapons in their bomb bays. Seven Trident submarines have joined the fleet, and the eighth began sea trials on May 28, 1986. (Excluded are about 150–200 nuclear long-range SLCMs which are now operational on about 25 attack subs and surface ships.[b]) The ten-warhead Peacekeeper ICBM is in flight testing and will become operational in late 1986. Retirement of Titan II missiles continues at the rate of about one per month.

Recent Soviet Changes:

Forty Bear-H bombers with AS-15 ALCMs are now operational. Fifteen Bison bombers have been dismantled as Bear-Hs are deployed. The status of the remaining 30 Bisons is in dispute.[a] Seventy-two mobile SS-25s are now deployed at eight bases, and 72 SS-11 launchers have been dismantled in compensation. The 10-warhead SS-X-24 may be deployed in rail-mobile launchers in late 1986 with silo deployments to follow. Two Delta IV submarines have begun sea trials, and a third has been launched. They each carry 16 SS-NX-23 SLBMs, which are still being flight tested. The TU-160 Blackjack bomber is not expected to become operational until 1988 or 1989. The fourteenth Yankee-class sub was removed from service as the fourth Typhoon entered sea trials.

[a]Soviet SLBM totals do not include 39 non-SALT-accountable SS-N-5 missiles on Golf-II submarines. Soviet bomber totals exclude 30 MYA-4 Bison bombers, which are under dispute. The U.S. believes that they remain SALT-accountable; the Soviets claim that they have been converted to refueling tankers and should not be counted.

[b]Weapons totals apply SALT II counting rules, whereby all missiles are assumed to carry the maximum number of weapons released during testing, except for the 288 U.S. C-3 SLBMs, which have been tested with 14 MIRVs but which are deployed with 10 warheads or less. Warhead numbers do *not* include U.S. and Soviet long-range SLCMs or weapons aboard U.S. FB-111 and Soviet Backfire aircraft. Actual U.S. bomber loadings and bomber weapon inventories may differ from those appearing in this chart, because of assumptions used in calculating these figures.

U.S. ICBMs	Launchers	Warheads	Soviet ICBMs	Launchers	Warheads
Titan II	14 × 1	14	SS-11	448 × 1	448
Minuteman II	450 × 1	450	SS-13	60 × 1	60
Minuteman III	550 × 3	1,650	SS-17	150 × 4	600
	1,014	2,114	SS-18	308 × 10	3,080
			SS-19	360 × 6	2,160
			SS-25	72 × 1	72
				1,398	6,420

U.S. SLBMs	Launchers	Warheads	Soviet SLBMs	Launchers	Warheads
C-3	256 × 10	2,560	SS-N-6	304 × 1	304
C-4	384 × 8	3,072	SS-N-8	292 × 1	292
	640	5,632	SS-N-17	12 × 1	12
			SS-N-18	224 × 7	1,568
			SS-N-20	80 × 9	720
			SS-NX-23	32 × 7	224
				944	3,120

U.S. Bombers	Launchers	Warheads	Soviet Bombers	Launchers	Warheads
B-52G (ALCM)	98 × 12	1,176	Bear-H (ALCM)	40 × 8	320
B-52G (Pen.)	69 × 14	966	Bear	110 × 4	440
B-52H (ALCM)	21 × 12	252		150	760
B-52H (Pen.)	75 × 14	1,050			
B-1B (Pen.)	5 × 8	40			
	268	3,484			

Breakdown of U.S. Forces:

ICBM levels assume 14 Titan II, 450 Minuteman II and 1,650 (550 × 3 MIRV) Minuteman III warheads. *SLBM levels* assume 28 Poseidon submarines (16 with 16 C-3 missiles carrying 10 warheads per missile and 12 with 16 C-4 missiles each with 8 warheads) and 8 Trident submarines, each with 24 C-4 missiles carrying 8 warheads per missile. *Bomber levels* include 263 B-52 and 5 B-1B bombers in the active inventory. Bomber loadings assume 3,484 weapons (1,428 ALCMs and spaces for 2,056 bombs and SRAMs). Excluded are 62 FB-111 aircraft under the Strategic Air Command and about 250 B-52s in storage at Davis Montham airbase and on display. FB-111s reportedly carry 2 SRAMs and 4 bombs (360 total).

Breakdown of Soviet Forces:

ICBM and SLBM warhead levels assume full MIRVing of SS-17s, SS-18s, SS-19s, SS-N-18s, SS-N-20s, and SS-N-23s, although actual loadings are probably less. *SLBM levels* include 20 Yankee, 38 Delta and 4 Typhoon-class nuclear missile carrying submarines. Three of the Typhoons are operational and one has begun sea trials. The SS-NX-21 long-range SLCM reportedly will be deployed later this year.[c] *Bomber levels* include 150 TU-95 Bear bombers. The average force loading is assumed to be 4 weapons per aircraft, either bombs or air-to-surface missiles, except for 40 Bear-H bombers, which are assumed to carry up to 8 AS-15 ALCMs. Excluded are 30 MYA-4 Bison bombers[c] and 270 TU-26 Backfire aircraft, 145 of which are assigned to Soviet Air Armies and 125 to Soviet Naval Aviation. (Each Backfire in the Air Armies is assumed to carry 2 bombs or 2 air-to-surface missiles, for a total of 260 weapons.)

[c]Twelve SS-N-8s are on 1 Hotel-III and 1 Golf-III missile submarine.

Chart prepared by Arms Control Association staff, May 29, 1986. Derived from data supplied by the Department of Defense, Joint Chiefs of Staff, and the Arms Control and Disarmament Agency.

Index

About the Contributors

Les AuCoin is a congressman from Oregon. He serves on the House Appropriations Subcommittee on Defense.

John C. Baker is a Ph.D. candidate in the Department of Political Science at Columbia University and is a coauthor of *Soviet Strategic Forces: Requirements and Responses* (1982).

Desmond Ball is the head of the Strategic and Defense Studies Center at the Australian University in Canberra, Australia. He is a coauthor of *Strategic Nuclear Targeting* (1986).

Richard J. Barnet is a senior fellow of the Institute for Policy Studies, which he helped found in 1963. During the Kennedy administration he was an official of the State Department, the Arms Control and Disarmament Agency, and a consultant to the Department of Defense.

Christoph Bertram is the political editor of the West German weekly *Die Zeit*. Until 1982 he was the director of the International Institute for Strategic Studies in London.

Richard K. Betts is a senior fellow at the Brookings Institution and contributing author to *Nonproliferation and U.S. Foreign Policy*, edited by Joseph A. Yager (1980).

Barry M. Blechman is the president of Defense Forecasts, Inc., a research and analysis firm in Washington, D.C. He served as assistant director of the U.S. Arms Control and Disarmament Agency from 1977 to 1979.

McGeorge Bundy is a professor of history at New York University. He served as special assistant for national security affairs to Presidents Kennedy and Johnson.

Albert Carnesale is a professor of public policy and academic dean at Harvard University's John F. Kennedy School of Government. He served on the U.S. delegation to SALT I. He is a coauthor of *Hawks, Doves and Owls: An Agenda for Avoiding Nuclear War* (1985).

Peter Clausen is senior arms analyst for the Union of Concerned Scientists. He was a nonproliferation policy specialist in the U.S. Department of Energy from 1978 to 1981 and following that was a fellow at the Woodrow Wilson International Center for Scholars until 1983.

Sidney D. Drell is director of the Stanford Linear Accelerator Center and co-director of the Center for International Security and Arms Control. He is coauthor with Philip Farley and David Holloway of *The Reagan Strategic Defense Initiative: A Technical, Political, and Arms Control Assessment* (1984).

Lewis A. Dunn was the chief U.S. coordinator for the Nuclear Nonproliferation Treaty Review Conference of 1985 and is assistant director for Nuclear and Weapons Control of the U.S. Arms Control and Disarmament Agency.

William Epstein is a senior special fellow at the United Nations Institute for Training and Research. He was for many years the senior official in charge of disarmament at the United Nations.

Philip J. Farley is senior research associate at the Center for International Security and Arms Control at Stanford University. He is coauthor along with Sidney Drell and David Holloway of *The Reagan Strategic Defense Initiative: A Technical, Political, and Arms Control Assessment* (1984).

James E. Goodby is former head of the U.S. delegation to the conference on Confidence- and Security-building Measures and Disarmament in Europe. He wrote this article while on leave from the State Department as a research professor at the Institute for the Study of Diplomacy at Georgetown University.

Albert Gore, Jr., is a Democratic senator from Tennessee and a member of the Senate's Arms Control Observers Group.

Robert C. Gray is associate professor and chairman of the Department of Government at Franklin and Marshall College. In 1979–80 he was an international affairs fellow of the Council on Foreign Relations, serving as a policy analyst in the Office of the Secretary of Defense.

G. Allen Greb is a research historian in the Program in Science, Technology, and Public Affairs at the University of California, San Diego, and assistant director of the Institute on Global Conflict and Cooperation. He is currently working with Herbert York on a three-year research project on the Strategic Defense Initiative.

Gary Hart, a Democratic senator from Colorado, serves on the Senate Armed Services Committee where he is the ranking minority member on the Strategic and Theater Forces Subcommittee. He served as congressional adviser to the SALT II negotiations in 1977 and to the U.N. Special Session on Disarmament in 1978.

Marie M. Hoguet is the former program coordinator of the National Security in the Nuclear Age project. She is the former education coordinator of the Arms Control Association.

David Holloway is a senior research associate at Stanford University's Center for International Security and Arms Control. He is a coauthor of *The Reagan Strategic Defense Initiative: A Technical, Political, and Arms Control Assessment* (1984), along with Sidney Drell and Philip Farley.

Rodney W. Jones is a former senior fellow and the director of Nuclear Policy at Georgetown University's Center for Strategic and International Studies. He edited a book entitled *Small Nuclear Forces and U.S. Security Policy* (1984).

Spurgeon M. Keeny, Jr., is the president and executive director of the Arms Control Association and a former deputy director of the U.S. Arms Control and Disarmament Agency.

Edward M. Kennedy is a Democratic senator from Massachusetts and a member of the Senate Armed Services Committee.

Richard T. Kennedy is ambassador-at-large and U.S. representative to the International Atomic Energy Agency. He also serves as special adviser to the secretary of state on nonproliferation policy and nuclear energy affairs and coordinates U.S. nonproliferation efforts. He previously served as under secretary of state for management and as commissioner of the Nuclear Regulatory Commission.

George A. Keyworth II is a former science adviser to the president and director of the Office of Science and Technology Policy. He previously headed the laser fusion research and the experimental physics division at Los Alamos Scientific Laboratory, which he joined in 1968.

Michael Krepon is a senior associate at the Carnegie Endowment for International Peace where he works on verification and compliance issues. He is the author of *Strategic Stalemate: Nuclear Weapons and Arms Control in American Politics* (1985).

Thomas K. Longstreth is a legislative assistant for arms control to Senator Edward Kennedy and a former Arms Control Association associate director for research and analysis. He is coauthor of *The Impact of U.S. and Soviet Ballistic Missile Defense Programs on the ABM Treaty* (1985).

Jack Mendelsohn is the deputy director of the Arms Control Association. He is a former senior Foreign Service officer who was a member of the U.S. SALT II and START delegations.

Robert S. Norris is a senior research associate with the Natural Resources Defense Council in Washington, D.C.

Karl Pieragostini is a member of the political science department at the University of Vermont. He has also been an analyst at the Institute for Defense and Disarmament Studies.

John B. Pike is a staff assistant for space policy at the Federation of American Scientists. He is coauthor of *The Impact of U.S. and Soviet Ballistic Missile Defense Programs on the ABM Treaty* (1985).

John B. Rhinelander, the legal advisor to the U.S. SALT I delegation, is a partner of Shaw, Pittman, Potts & Trowbridge in private law practice in Washington, D.C.

Jonathan Rich is a former staff assistant for arms control at the Federation of American Scientists and is a former research assistant at the Arms Control Association.

Herbert Scoville, Jr., is the former assistant director for Scientific Intelligence at the Central Intelligence Agency. He served as assistant director for science and technology at the Arms Control and Disarmament Agency. Dr. Scoville is a former president of the Arms Control Association and author of *MX: Prescription for Disaster* (1981).

Marshall D. Shulman is director of the W. Averell Harriman Institute for Advanced Study of the Soviet Union at Columbia University and former Soviet affairs special adviser to the secretary of state during the Carter administration.

Leon V. Sigal teaches government at Wesleyan University and is the author of *Nuclear Forces in Europe* (1984). He is an editor and coauthor of *Alliance Security: NATO and the No-First-Use Question* (1983).

Walter B. Slocombe is former deputy under secretary for defense for policy planning, 1979–81, and director of the Department of Defense SALT Task Force. He is currently a partner of Caplin & Drysdale, Chartered.

Gerard C. Smith is chairman of the Arms Control Association. He was the chief U.S. delegate to SALT I and director of the Arms Control and Disarmament Agency. He is the author of *Doubletalk: The Story of SALT I* (1980).

Richard Smoke is professor of political science and research director of the Center for Foreign Policy Development at Brown University. His most recent book is *National Security and the Nuclear Dilemma* (1984).

Leonard S. Spector is the author of *Nuclear Proliferation Today* (1984) and *New Nuclear Nations* (1985), annual reports prepared under the auspices of the Carnegie Endowment for International Peace. He has been active in the nonproliferation field for many years, working at the Nuclear Regulatory Commission and on the Senate Energy and Nuclear Proliferation Subcommittee, where he served as chief counsel from 1978 to 1980.

Paul B. Stares is a research associate in the Foreign Studies Program of the Brookings Institution. He is the author of *The Militarization of Space: U.S. Policy 1945–1984* (1985). He is coeditor of *The Exploitation of Space: Policy Trends in the Military and Commercial Uses of Outer Space* (1985).

Gerald M. Steinberg is a post-doctoral fellow at the M.I.T. Center for International Studies.

Strobe Talbott is the Washington bureau chief for *Time* magazine and is *Time*'s long-time diplomatic correspondent. He is the author of *Deadly Gambits: The Reagan Administration and the Stalemate in Nuclear Arms Control* (1984).

Ronald L. Tammen is chief of staff to Sen. William Proxmire (D–Wis.). He is a former CIA weapons analyst and author of *MIRV and the Arms Race* (1973).

William L. Ury is director of the Nuclear Negotiation Project at Harvard Law School. He is coauthor of *Getting to Yes: Negotiating Agreements without Giving In* (1981) and coauthor of *Beyond the Hotline* (1985).

Joel S. Wit is an analyst in the Office of Strategic Force Analysis, Bureau of Intelligence and Research, Department of State. He wrote his article while working as a consultant in Washington, D.C.

About the Editor

Robert Travis Scott is the associate director for publications at the Arms Control Association and editor of *Arms Control Today*, the A.C.A.'s monthly news journal.